You are cordially invited to the

BEST CHOICES

IN

LOS ANGELES

Published in the U.S.A.

Best Choice Series:
Best Choices in the Rural North Willamette Valley
Best Choices on the Oregon Coast
Best Choices off Oregon's Interstates
Best Choices in Central and Eastern Oregon
Best Choices in Portland and the North Willamette Valley
Best Choices In Northern California/Bay Area Edition
Best Choices in Northern California
Best Choices in Western Washington
Best Choices in Orange County
Best Choices in Arizona
Best Choices in Colorado
Best Choices in San Diego
Best Choices in Sacramento
Best Choices in San Francisco
Best Choices in the Tampa Bay Area
Best Choices in Central and Southeast Texas
Best Choices in the Seattle-Tacoma Area
Best Choices in Eastern Washington
Best Choices in New Mexico
Best Choices in Alaska
Best Choices in Idaho
Best Choices in British Columbia
Best Choices off Oregon's Interstate 5

Future releases:
Best Choices along the California Coast
Best Choices in Oregon
Best Choices in Western Pennsylvania
Best Choices in Central Florida
Best Choices in Utah
Best Choices in St. Louis
Best Choices in Atlanta
Best Choices in Maryland and Delaware
Best Choices in Miami and the Keys

For additional copies, write or call:
Gable & Gray, The Book Publishers
PO Box 880
Medford, Oregon 97501-0063
In Oregon: 1-800-622-7753
Outside Oregon: 1-800-522-7753

Managing Editor	Jane Crawford Picknell
Author	Myles Montgomery
Editor	Robin Speake
Associate Editors	Debra Grande
	James Kelly
	Joseph R. Kiefer II
Assistant Editors	John M. Cunningham
	G. Reneé Getreu
	Lorene A. Huey
Editoral Assistant	Thomas J. Reeder
Writing Director	Gary S. Corwin
Writers	Carrie Beets
	Geraldine Baldassare
	Susan Brown
	Elizabeth A. Buell
	Patrick C. Claflin
	Barbara Ferguson
	Joseph G. Follansbee
	William D. Hagle
	Maury Hill
	Merritt Scott Miller
	Michael E. Oliver
	Betty Pennington
	Debra Sherwood Rudloff
	Roy Scarbrough
	Sky
	Thomas Yates
Illustrations	John C. Benson Jr.
	Ted Barr
	Jan Forrest
Cover Design	Laura Kay
Cover Photo	Greater Los Angeles Visitors and Convention Bureau
Maps & Computer Graphics	IMPAC Publications
	Scott McKay
Publisher's Agents	Patty Mitchell,

Lawrence Holmes, Marya Knudsen, Ken Kravitz,
Betty Lewis, Jeni Martinez, Rocky Martinez, Carolyn Nathan,
Bonnie Robinson, Diane Saher, Fern Shaw, Greg Stock

Library of Congress Catalog Card Number: 88-82272
ISBN: 0-944729-51-7   First Edition 1988

FOREWORD

Welcome to *Best Choices in Los Angeles.* I invite you to join me in the adventure of discovering the best attractions, restaurants, beaches, museums, events and businesses L.A. has to offer. The stories, maps and business reviews within this complete guide have been designed for several reasons: for shopping and dining tips, as an itinerary planner, and as an informational guide to let you know more about the area you're visiting.

My life has been filled with challenging excursions in almost every state within our richly diverse nation and beyond. Each area offers something special that sets it apart from the others. For example, the Oregon Coast is one of the most beautiful coastlines I have ever seen, Colorado offers the splendor of the Rocky Mountains, while Los Angeles has its inviting climate and diverse lifestyles. Seattle's Space Needle caps the city's picturesque skyline and the famous hydroplane races provide entertainment for all. My adventures have taken me on a cruise past the White Cliffs of Dover, I have walked through the markets of Bangkok, marveled at the grand castles of Germany and ridden a burro along the country roads of Mexico. My feet love to travel, my eyes love to see the world and my mind loves to remember all of those places as I pass my discoveries on to others.

But enough about me! You purchased this guide to explore the *Best Choices in Los Angeles.* Without further ado, here's how to use this book:

Each section begins with an introduction to a region in Los Angeles County highlighting major freeways, population, attractions, local events and history which will provide you with enlightened opportunities and ideas for exploration. Towns and areas are listed alphabetically in the Table of Contents. In the text, each business is listed alphabetically within its corresponding category. This guide's description of the businesses and services will give you an idea of the "Best Choices" you may look forward to as you encounter them on your travels. To find specific catagories, businesses, as well as area features, turn to the index in the back of the book.

We may not have found every "Best Choice" in Los Angeles County, and would love to hear about it when you encounter a "Best Choice" that merits mention and is not included in this book. If your contribution is interviewed and selected for the next edition, Gable & Gray will happily ship you any one *Best Choice* book you desire as a

"Thank you." Simply select the book from the list of already published editions at the front of this guide and mention your preference in your letter. If you would like to order other books, please call Gable & Gray at (800) 522-7753.

The editors and writers who have contributed their creative vitality to the compilation of this guide trust you will find it a valuable addition to your travels.

Join me now as we visit the *Best Choices in Los Angeles.*

MYLES MONTGOMERY

TABLE OF CONTENTS

LOS ANGELES COUNTY

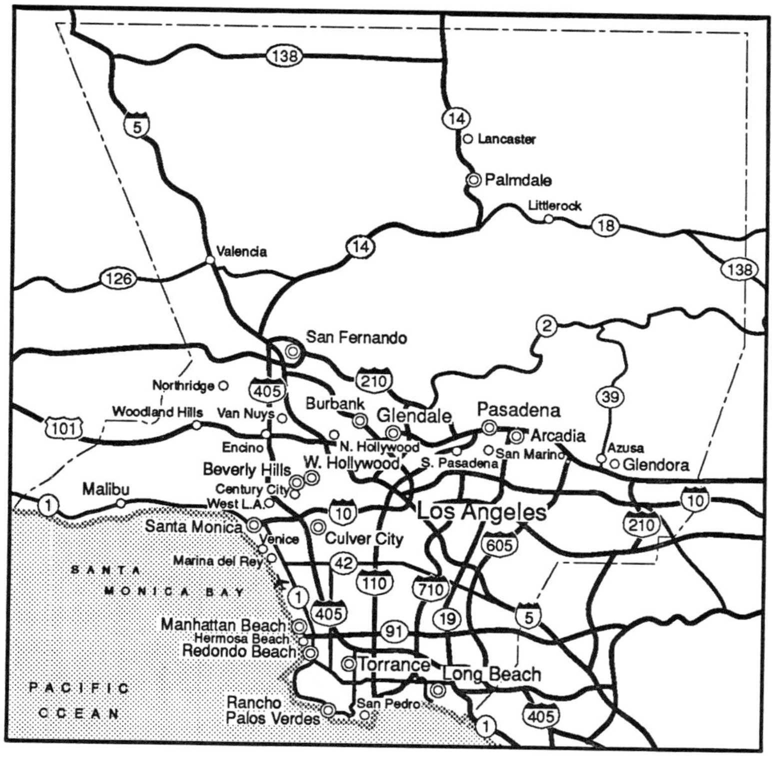

GREATER LOS ANGELES

There's no place like Los Angeles; everyone agrees, whether it's the copy writer for a chamber of commerce brochure, or a gag writer for the Tonight Show. But, there is little agreement over what L.A. is or is not.

Some see the region as fast paced, while others envision laid back folks spending their days sipping piña coladas and lounging around swimming pools. There are also notions about Southern California being the "conservative" home of Ronald Reagan and Richard Nixon. And, just as common, are people's impressions of L.A. as the birthplace of strange religious cults.

Thumb through a visitor's guide to Los Angeles and you will see stunning photographs of white sand beaches, yacht harbors bathed in a rose colored sunset, gladiator like football players hustling to the scrimmage line, as well as darkened auditoriums, opulent dining rooms, and views of mighty skyscrapers and snowcapped mountains. As any visitor to this land will happily discover, these images are not tricks of photography, but familiar sights in Los Angeles.

Los Angeles is one of the most maligned cities in the nation. Comedians force us to acknowledge the eye stinging smog, aggravating traffic tie ups, and problems that just about any big city has to live with. Johnny Carson can remark that "The only live culture in Los Angeles is in a yogurt shop," and be sure to raise a belly laugh from his sidekick.

We laugh because we have heard of jarring L.A. images such as the Tudor mansion with Byzantine columns, or the drive-in church where the faithful don't have to leave their cars. Los Angeles County may be the only place on earth an elegant British ocean liner has become a floating hotel and tourist attraction. The region may never live down Frank Lloyd Wright's famous remark about the nation having been tilted on edge, causing all loose debris to tumble into the L.A. basin.

The truth is that Los Angeles has one of the highest concentrations of creative talent of any place on earth. Local boosters call L.A. the entertainment capital of the world, and can support that claim simply by pointing to show business related endeavors. Once you step into the region's art galleries, concert halls or live theaters, you will find world class entertainment.

Los Angeles' influence on style and fashion is undeniable. Because the city's post World War II growth was primarily a move by mid-western families taking advantage of the climate and other geographical amenities, the city had long held a reputation for being something of a middle America mecca with its rows of conventional tract homes. This conventionality has served as a backdrop to the region's tendency to spawn the offbeat and bizarre.

Even in the 1950s Los Angeles was known as a birthplace of new fads, strange cults or unusual religious and social movements. When the rest of the country maintained subdued standards of dress, Los Angelenos grew accustomed to seeing folks on the street sporting more colorful, if not more peculiar fashions. Men dared to go out hatless and women stockingless. Summer outfits were worn in winter, and vice versa. Today, as then, housewives go to market with furs thrown over blue jeans and Hawaiian shirts. A seasoned Angeleno doesn't even bother to bat an eye when someone with blue hair and a nose ring walks by.

If this is not your first time in L.A., but it has been some years since you have visited, expect to see some changes. During the past decade greater Los Angeles has undergone economic, social and political changes greater than any other major United States city. Travelers to Los Angeles County are also treated to one of the most diverse and dramatic displays of natural features within a single region on earth. Within this metropolis you'll find fertile valleys, rugged mountains, broad flatlands and miles of sandy beaches.

Los Angeles' warm climate is one of the most pleasant on the planet. The physical contrasts are so great you can experience the

Riviera, Alps and Sahara Desert all in L.A. County. And the region's people are as varied as its topography.

In spite of the post war boom that attracted midwestern families to the region, L.A. today is one of the most racially and ethnically diverse centers of population in the United States. At last count no less than eighty-six languages were spoken in Los Angeles public schools. Because the majority of Los Angeles citizens claim non-European ancestry, the city can be considered the nation's first major third world city. It has the largest Mexican population outside of Mexico, the largest Chinese population this side of China, and the same can be said for the Koreans, Filipinos and Vietnamese who live in L.A.

When one tries to imagine this city, no single image stands out. Paris has its tower, London its Big Ben, San Francisco its bridge; but Los Angeles has no single focus. Instead, L.A.'s identity is found in a kaleidoscope of images; from the glass skyscrapers in the downtown financial district to the East L.A. *barrio*, to the lavish estates of Bel Air and Beverly Hills, to the row after row of bungalows in the San Fernando Valley.

It would be a mistake to imagine the Los Angeles metropolitan area as a single entity. The twelve million people who live within an hour's drive of downtown L.A., live and work in a complex system of residential and business communities. Most cities contain a central core; Los Angeles, however, is better described as about twenty urban village cores, each with its own business, retail, housing and entertainment centers. This can be confusing for the uninitiated.

You'll find separated independent towns completely surrounded by the city of Los Angeles, and many communities that maintain a separate identity, yet are technically part of the 451 square mile city. When planning a visit, it's best to think in terms of what might lie in each region; whether it's the downtown region with its civic center and high rise buildings, the elite hillside estates or coastal communities of the Westside, the beaches of the South Bay Region or the vast residential tracts of the San Fernando Valley.

Less than a quarter of the county's population lives within the L.A. city limits. Los Angeles County measures some seventy-five miles from north to south and about seventy miles east to west, covering more than 4,000 square miles. About half of the land is mountainous. The northern part of the county is comprised of desert and mountains, while the southern portion lies on a broad plain sloping gently from the mountains to the ocean. Most of the city is spread out on this plain, with the city's downtown district lying at mid-point between the mountains and the sea.

The San Gabriel Mountains rise, less than forty miles from the sea, to heights of 8,000 to 10,000 feet. These mountains and the other surrounding mountain ranges are something of a mixed blessing. Although they offer a wealth of recreational opportunities and spectacular home sites, they are partially responsible for Los Angeles' notorious smog build up. They maintain a barrier against which dirty air becomes trapped in the L.A. basin as the fumes from millions of cars and trucks continues to pour into the atmosphere. Because the encircling mountains contain relatively few passes, the highways leading in and out of the region must traverse high mountain canyons, or skirt the coast just above the high tide line. Within the basin the freeway network is massive.

The county's coastline forms two wide bays. The northern two thirds of the coastline consists of the broad Santa Monica Bay and contains the communities of Santa Monica, Venice, Redondo Beach and Palos Verdes. On the south coast, the coastline makes another jog to form San Pedro Bay, which faces south and contains San Pedro, with its shipping operations, and the city of Long Beach. Beaches are strung out along this coastline and nearly all are open to the public.

In addition to beaches, the bays hold several marinas. Thousands of small pleasure craft crowd into no less than seven manmade marinas where a life style dominated by the ocean reigns. Foremost among these marinas is Marina del Rey. Dredged out in the 1950s and 1960s, Marina del Rey is heralded as the largest marina in the United States with nearly 6,000 boat slips. It is surrounded by a lively complex of condominiums, apartments, restaurants and shops.

If the Los Angeles life style is laid back, it is laid back in appearance only. In spite of an air of informality, this is a center of big business, high finance and high tech. Los Angeles rivals New York in attracting highly ambitious people. The demand for housing is so large that many newcomers are tearing down fashionable properties valued in the millions to build lavish 10,000 square foot structures in their place.

People change jobs more often in Los Angeles than just about anywhere else. What's more, there are more self employed people in the Los Angeles region than in any other American city. Among the ranks of the self employed are writers, attorneys, real estate agents, designers and computer specialists. Many have opted to work at home and avoid the freeway traffic jams. When telecommuting becomes the norm for the rest of the nation, Los Angeles is likely to be the model.

If the economies of all the nation's were ranked according to gross national product, most could not match the $250 billion in goods and services produced in the Los Angeles metropolitan area. The nations of Australia, India, Spain and Switzerland would all fall below L.A.'s level of production. Retail sales in this area of twelve million people surpasses sales within the New York City region with its eighteen million people. And, because of the diversity of the L.A. area economy, it is very nearly recession proof. The major players in the economy are aerospace, entertainment, finance, manufacturing, government services, health care, insurance, international trade, oil production, real estate development and tourism.

The television and movie industries play one of the most visible roles in the economy, but in terms of its direct economic impact and the number of people employed, it is overshadowed by less glamorous enterprises. Nevertheless, some 75,000 people in L.A. County are directly or indirectly employed in the entertainment industry. This includes everyone from the caterers who serve lunch to film crews, to hairdressers and carpenters to your favorite film star.

Finance is becoming increasingly important in Los Angeles. For years San Francisco was the West Coast financial center. No more. In 1986 Los Angeles surpassed Chicago in bank deposits. Although it continues to hold a second place position behind New York, L.A.'s growth rate in financial activity is catching up with the Big Apple as major international banks choose Los Angeles as the place they prefer to do business.

Although one would not associate L.A. with the smokestack industries of big manufacturing centers back east, manufacturing does have a high profile in the economy. More than one out of every five jobs in Los Angeles County relates to manufacturing. Aviation and aerospace has been a major contributor to the manufacturing sector of the economy for several decades, making it the largest aerospace center in the world. Lockheed, Northrop, Rockwell and TRW all maintain important design and manufacturing operations in the area. The concentration of high tech operations surpasses that of the San Francisco Bay Area's Silicon Valley.

Detroit may lead the nation in the production of automobiles, but eight of the nine Japanese auto companies maintain their United States headquarters in the L.A. metropolitan area. Each of the big three U.S. auto makers operate design centers in the Los Angeles region.

The volume of foreign trade in Los Angeles is nearly thirty percent more than the San Francisco and Seattle ports combined. Much of this volume is owed to spectacular growth in recent years. In 1970 L.A. showed $5 billion in trade volume, which jumped to nearly $64 billion by the mid-1980s. That has been good news for job seekers. International trade has generated some 300,000 local jobs, not just on the docks, but also in related activities such as law, finance, advertising and public relations.

It is hard to believe this powerful and popular corner of the world was originally a Native American village built around a peaceful water source.

When the first Spanish explorers came to the Los Angeles basin, it was already home to 5,000 to 10,000 Indians. Along the banks of what was the only year round stream in the region was a village called *Yang-Na*. Just one day after Gaspar de Portola's expedition arrived in the village, Father Juan Crespi renamed it *Nuestra Senora la Reina de los Angeles* or "Our Lady Queen of the Angels." Although the priest went quickly to work to convert the Indians, his efforts would center around the new mission he and local natives built several miles to the east.

The first Spanish settlement would not be established until 1781 along the stream that would be called the Los Angeles River. The Spanish government was anxious to settle the region so food could be produced to supply the garrisons defending Spain's claim to California. The plan was to recruit twenty-four families who would be given land, an allowance of ten pesos a month and all the livestock and farming equipment they would need to get started. It was a splendid deal, but the country was remote and, despite the rigorous recruitment effort in the Mexican states of Sonora and Sineloa, only about a dozen near destitute families agreed to make the move to the site that would one day be one of the world's greatest cities.

During the first forty years of its existence, the little agricultural village did well for itself. By 1790 the initial population of forty-four settlers had grown to 140. By 1820 a town of single story adobe structures housed some 600 residents. The town further prospered after the Mexican Revolution of 1822 when restrictions against outside trade were eased. By the time of the 1836 census, the sleepy agricultural village had diversified, offering its residents a wide variety of services. There were no less than sixteen merchants, seven shoemakers, three hatters, two doctors, six tailors and thirteen prostitutes.

Mexican rule ended in 1848. It was not long before the town of 1,700 had its first English speaking school and Protestant Church. The gold rush in Northern California brought new prosperity to the town as ranchers and farmers discovered they could fetch good prices for their livestock and produce.

With connections to markets 400 miles to the north, the town was no longer an isolated community. Ships landing at San Pedro harbor replaced ox carts, and stage lines to San Francisco and Santa Fe made long distance travel easier. By the late 1860s the population of Los Angeles was around 5,000 and the region continued to grow steadily thereafter.

With railroad connections becoming available in 1876 to San Francisco and to the east in 1885, there was little to hold back development of the region. Prosperity brought thousands of visitors, initiating Los Angeles' first tourist trade. The agricultural age created a large number of settlements and towns, thus creating the beginning of the region's characteristic sprawl.

The decentralized communities continued as the region became urbanized, and maintained a high degree of economic independence. Over time, however, nearly all the agricultural land would be built over, thus creating the dense and sprawling metropolis we see today. The Los Angeles River, along whose banks the first Spanish settlement began, is now a wide concrete *barranca*. Dry most of the year, the riverway now serves as a place to train bus drivers.

LIFE IN THE FAST LANE

DRIVING IN L.A.

by Roy Scarbrough

There's no denying the L.A. freeway system is confusing to those who have not learned to find their way around, and that can take some time when you consider the area is served by no less than thirty freeways, eight of which radiate from the downtown loop.

It would be a lot easier if the freeways were laid out on a simple north-south/east-west basis, like other many metropolitan areas. But, L.A.'s sprawl and scattered communities required an amorphous transportation network to serve the many destinations.

Los Angeles was the first city to become big after the age of the automobile. Because weather conditions where just right for year round use of the horseless carriage, it became the ideal form of transportation for the independent traveler. By the early 1920s Los Angeles had the highest automobile ownership rate in the world, about one car for every three people.

By 1923 the number of people who commuted to work by car was rapidly catching up with those who rode the old streetcar. It was estimated that some 650,000 people entered downtown every day by automobile. And plans were already underway to designate major traffic streets on which cross traffic access would be limited.

Los Angeles completed its first freeway in 1940. It ran from Arroyo Seco to Pasadena and it had been in the planning stages since about 1920. It was modeled after Connecticut's Merrit Parkway, the Pennsylvania Turnpike and the German autobahn. With all of the fanfare of the Pasadena New Year's celebration then in progress, Governor Olson dedicated a six mile segment of what he called the "west's first freeway."

It was soon discovered that future freeways would have to have lanes less narrow and curves less sharp. Today's freeways are a far cry from the first one. But so are the demands the region places upon it. Drivers experienced with the system try to avoid peak traffic times. When the traffic is light, it does move fast.

For the visitor, it can be quite an experience to try to keep a sharp eye on traffic and, at the same time, navigate the system. By most standards, L.A. drivers tailgate. If you're cruising at seventy miles an hour, don't expect the driver behind you to maintain the customary seven car length distance that every Driver's Ed textbook recommends. And if you're poking along at sixty-five miles an hour, the driver behind you may be so close that you can admire his dental work.

The best way to handle driving Los Angeles' roads is to get a good local map of the L.A. region. Decide which freeways you'll need to use to reach your destination; determine how far the exits and interchanges are from each other and watch the signs. Try to get in the proper lane one or two miles ahead of time. You can't count on someone going out of their way to let you cross four lanes of traffic as you approach your exit.

Nearly all of the major freeways are named for destinations. It simplifies things when all you have to remember is to take the Pasadena Freeway to get to Pasadena or the Santa Monica Freeway to head out to Santa Monica. These freeways are also designated by customary numbers, which makes them easier to find on the map.

Here is a run down of the major freeway arteries:

- **I-405**, usually called the **San Diego Freeway** runs generally north and south. It passes through the San Fernando Valley, past Beverly Hills on its way toward Long Beach and San Diego.

- **I-10**, also called the **Santa Monica Freeway,** offers drivers an east-west route that interchanges with the San Diego Freeway in Santa Monica. As this route heads east, with passes through inland communities before it becomes the San Bernardino Freeway, it is a good freeway to take when you're trying to get somewhere between Santa Monica and downtown L.A.

- **I-5**, the state's most important north-south artery enters L.A. County at its extreme north inland corner. Called the **Golden State Freeway,** I-5 passes through the San Fernando Valley. Where it hits I-10, the 1-5 adopts a new name: the **Santa Ana Freeway.**

- The **Glendale Freeway** is another north to south freeway offering access to the Glendale and Pasadena area.

- The **Foothill Freeway,** also known as **State Highway 2,** runs east and west and heads up into the Angeles National Forest from Pasadena.

- The **Ventura Freeway, State Highway 34,** offers east-west access and passes through the San Fernando Valley and heads out to **Pasadena Highway 101,** also called the **Hollywood Freeway,** which first runs north to south through Hollywood, but then changes directions, running west toward Pasadena where it will merge with the Ventura Freeway.

The Hollywood Freeway makes good connections with beach bound freeways and it will take you to the San Fernando Valley.

- **Old Highway 1,** or the **Pacific Coast Highway** hugs the spectacular coastline, passing through picturesque beach communities.

DOWNTOWN

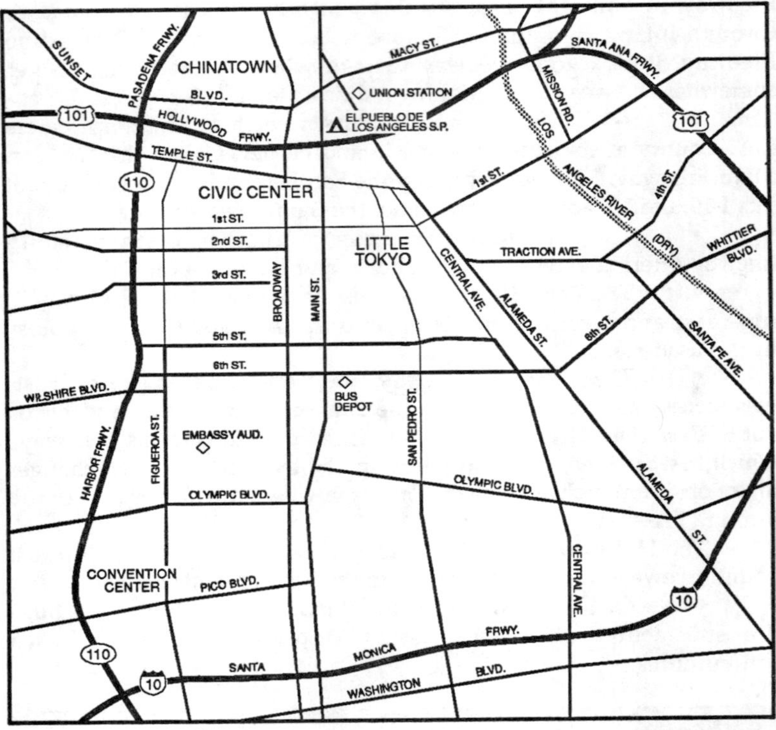

For years Los Angeles was famous for being a city that seemed to have no downtown. What Gertrude Stein said of Oakland, many would say of downtown Los Angeles: "There is no there, there." But you'll put away these notions as soon as you see the gleaming steel and glass skyscrapers rising out of the center of the city.

As a recent press release from the Los Angeles Visitors and Convention Bureau proclaims, you can "Say goodbye to L.A.'s cultural wasteland." Gone are the days when a city art museum would stash a Picasso or Jackson Pollock painting in the back room in favor of less "controversial" work.

Close inspection of the busy streets will reveal a vibrant shopping area, a frantic financial district, an active civic center, colorful ethnic neighborhoods, world class cultural institutions, elegant hotels, fine restaurants and fashionable shops.

Los Angeles' shopping district is the biggest city shopping district west of Chicago. The civic center is the largest concentration of government buildings outside of Washington D.C. In addition, you'll find a colorful wholesale flower market and the charm of Chinatown and Little Tokyo.

No longer is downtown Los Angeles the laughing stock of sophisticated big cities. It is clear something of a renaissance is being enjoyed downtown, as an upscale center for business and entertainment is developing. Although Los Angeles' attractions are generally spread far and wide, downtown offers visitors one of the few opportunities in the region to explore a wide variety of sights, sounds and experiences on foot.

Park your car and hoof it. You'll find everything within a few blocks of each other. The downtown district falls between First Street on the north, Olympic Boulevard to the south, with Alameda and Figueroa defining its east and west boundaries. Consider avoiding driving altogether by taking the bus downtown. Once there, you can hop aboard a DASH mini bus that will take you all through the area. With a pocket full of change you can get on and off whenever you're inclined.

A walking tour conducted by the Los Angeles Conservancy is another way to get your bearings in the downtown area. A trip up to the observation area on the twenty-seventh floor of City Hall, or the Westin Bonaventure Hotel's revolving rooftop lounge will also orient you to your surroundings.

The best time to get a big city feeling is during the week when downtown is bustling with activity and thousands go in and out of the high rising office towers and fine department stores. On weekends many of these businesses are closed, but there will be more than enough to see downtown.

To fully appreciate just how remarkable the downtown's turnabout has been, one needs only to reflect back as recently as the 1960s. Most of the buildings were old, and little had been done to dress up the town since the 1930s, in spite of the rapid regional growth.

For the first thirty years of the twentieth century, downtown L.A. did enjoy what many call its "classic" or "golden" era. Streetcars rattled through along the boulevard and fashionable shoppers and theatergoers strolled the street. Several large department stores conducted lavish fashion shows every spring and fall.

Early on, the city imposed a 150 foot height limit on buildings; as an earthquake safety measure and to please the influx of mid-western families who preferred their new city not remind them of Chicago and New York. With the post-World War II boom, the downtown section could no longer accommodate all of the business without high rise office buildings.

As a result, the city began to spread to outlying communities. Major department stores and other retailers followed their customers to the suburbs. As the region entered into a thirty year period of decentralization, the downtown area experienced a thirty year period of minimum growth.

In 1957 the city repealed its height limit, but it would not be until the late 1960s that the era of renewed construction would begin. It began in 1968 when the Union Bank built its forty-two story skyscraper between 4th and 5th streets. Not to be outdone, the Crocker Bank raised its five sided high rise edifice at Sixth and Grand Streets. That same year, the Atlantic Richfield Company would erect twin fifty-two story towers to occupy an entire block between Flowers and Figueroa. Underneath would be a plaza containing two underground shopping malls that continue to be one of the favorite regional shopping spots. In 1973 First Interstate Bank moved into a new sixty-two story building, the tallest building west of Chicago.

One of the most impressive of these buildings is frequently a downtown visitor's first stop. Located at the base of the two black granite towers of the Atlantic Richfield and Bank of America Buildings is the Greater Los Angeles Visitors and Convention Bureau's Visitor Information Center. You find it at Level B at 515 South Figueroa Street. There maps and brochures containing information on local sights are offered. Tickets to a television game show are also a possible find at the Information Center.

Just across the street from Arco Plaza is the gleaming Westin Bonaventure Hotel. Its five mirrored glass towers resemble stacks of new silver dollars. Inside a futuristic atmosphere, six levels of shops and restaurants connected by a labyrinth of walkways and9 twisting staircases greet you. Pedestrian sky bridges connect the hotel with several other impressive buildings, including the World Trade Center, the Union Bank and the Bunker Hill Towers. One of the more elegant downtown buildings is the L.A. Hilton Hotel and towers, which in recent years completed a major renovation.

In contrast to the new L.A. with its towering monuments of glass and granite is the sixty year old Central Public Library at 5th and

Grand Avenue. Fire ravaged the building in 1986 and reconstruction was still underway in 1988, but one can still appreciate the combination of Roman, Egyptian and Spanish architecture in this 260,000 square foot structure. The repairs and restoration, including restoration of the many beautiful murals, is scheduled to be completed by 1991.

If high culture is what you're looking for, you'll find plenty of it downtown with its fine theaters, concert halls and museums. Just north of the City Center at 1st Street and Grand Avenue is the Los Angeles Music Center, home of the renown Joffrey Ballet. The Academy Awards ceremony is held there. Also within the Music Center, is the Dorothy Chandler Pavilion where you can attend a Broadway show or a performance by the Los Angeles Philharmonic.

More music and dance performances are available at the Center's Mark Taper Forum and the Ahmanson Theater. The Embassy Theatre on Grand Avenue and 8th Street frequently hosts performances of concert music. In addition to classical, chamber and operatic performances, the 1,600 seat theater, on occasion, hosts jazz ensembles. Escorted tours of the facility are available.

Another product of downtown's cultural renaissance is the performing arts center: The Los Angeles Theatre Center at Spring and 5th Streets. The complex boasts four theaters, restaurants, a bar and free parking. Expect to see performances from some of the nation's leading playwrights, as well as the works of emerging dramatists.

ATTRACTIONS

• Too much of a good thing is sometimes overwhelming. Fortunately **Pershing Square** offers a respite from the steel and glass. This patch of greenery right downtown is a good place to kick back amid palms and flowers as street vendors hawk their wares. Noontime concerts are a regular feature of the square.

• An insider's glimpse of the busy world of finance is close at hand at the **Pacific Stock Exchange** on Beaudry near Figueroa Street. A public viewing area has been set aside so visitors can watch the stock traders scramble to execute buy and sell orders from around the globe. The morning hours beginning at 7:00 a.m. offer the liveliest trading activity.

• Another type of commodity trading takes place at the **Grand Central Market**. You'll find all manner of fruits, vegetables, candies, meats and seafood being bought and sold from scores of stalls piled with everything from rare spices to pig heads. No plastic wrap here; this is traditional non-supermarket produce shopping. Located between 3rd and 4th Streets, the Grand Central Market is a lively place where much of the business is conducted in Spanish.

• If you find your way to the west side of downtown, you're likely to pass the **Wholesale Flower Market** on Wall Street. Although most of the serious buying and selling between growers and wholesalers is done in the early morning hours, it remains a colorful place to visit throughout the day.

• For the fashion conscious, a trip to the **garment district** should not be missed. You'll find no shortage of material to spend money on, but your dollars can go a little further with the discounted designer wear available at several of the shops.

• It seems only fitting that glittery downtown L.A. would contain one of the largest jewelry centers in the world. The **St. Vincent Jewelry Center** located at the historic **Vincent Square** on Hill Street is home to more than 200 jewelry retailers. There you'll find an incredible variety of old and precious gems and jewelry pieces.

• The area just east of downtown contains a remnant of Los Angeles' Spanish and Mexican heritage. **Olvera Street** is one of the oldest streets in Los Angeles. In the 1930s Olvera Street was a kind of alley, or dilapidated dirt road that was turned into a colorful Mexican market place.

The cobblestone street is lined with shops and stalls where visitors have for decades shopped for souvenirs and Mexican handicrafts that range from inexpensive to extravagant. You can watch candles being hand dipped, or a blacksmith at work. A glassblower will shape molten glass into delicate objects. Musicians stroll the streets filling your ears with South of the Border sounds.

• Not far away, along the northern section of Hill and Broadway is **Chinatown** where you'll find many good and moderately priced Chinese restaurants.

Unless you are the person who has everything, you might be tempted by the quaint **wishing well**. Skill counts, because your penny will have to land in a bowl or large spoon held by one of the happy looking figures perched on the well.

Follow your nose to the wonderful aroma of a nearby bakery and watch a machine make fortune cookies. Evenings are a special delight as lantern covered lights brighten the main mall in Chinatown.

• For the most authentic Chinese atmosphere, head southeast to **North Spring Street**, where you'll find traditional Chinese markets, herb shops and restaurants.

• Another microcosm of culture in downtown Los Angeles is **Little Tokyo**, which is bordered by 1st, Main and 3rd Streets and Central Avenue. Arrive early, before most of the tourists, and you'll see the Japanese shopkeepers start their day by washing windows. Little Tokyo is a cohesive and active district of Japanese businesses and restaurants. As is the custom in Japan, restaurants display plastic replicas of their food in their windows.

• The **New Otani Hotel and Garden** has a beautiful and soothing Japanese rooftop garden five floors above the ground.

• Within the **Japanese Village Plaza** are fish ponds, stone walkways, elegant shops and fine restaurants.

• The **San Antonio Winery**, at 6737 Lamar Street, was founded in 1917, making it the oldest winery in Los Angeles still in operation. Visitors can take a self guided tour through the original winery buildings, constructed from boxcar sidings, where huge aging vats are stored. A small museum maintains a display of wine making artifacts. In addition to wine tasting, a sandwich shop and delicatessen are on the grounds and visitors can sit among barrels of aging wine. For information, call (213) 223-1401.

• The **Los Angeles Children's Museum**, 310 North Main Street, is a place where children can touch, feel and probe the world around them. Kids can enter a TV studio and give a weather report, or walk into a hospital emergency room to play doctor or nurse. The museum even contains a street exhibit full of buses, cars and motorcycles. Other exhibits give children opportunities to build and design objects. For information, call (213) 687-8800.

• To experience what it is like at a big city newspaper, take the **Los Angeles Times Tour.** The one hour tour takes you through the newsroom, page composing section, distribution area and past the massive presses which are almost always whirling away at breakneck speed. In the lobby headlines and news stories of some of the most important historical events of the twentieth century are displayed. You'll find the newspaper's building at Second and Spring Street. The tour is available on weekdays; no reservations are required. For information, call (213) 972-5000.

- The **Museum of Contemporary Art**, sometimes called MOCA, is one of the shining examples of the L.A. cultural renaissance. The design of the building itself is a work of contemporary art. Nearly 100,000 square feet arranged on seven different floor levels include galleries, a sculpture court, auditorium, bookstore and library. The museum is located at 250 South Grand Avenue at California Plaza. For information call (213) 621-2766.

- The **Temporary Contemporary Museum** at 124 North Central Avenue is on the cutting edge of contemporary art. The facility was first opened as a temporary exhibit hall for the Museum of Contemporary Art, but it has become a permanent adjunct to MOCA. The 55,000 square foot museum, with its informal loft like exhibition space is located in Little Tokyo. For information, call (213) MOCA.

- For a display of really "turned on" art, check out the **Museum of Neon Art** on Traction Avenue, two blocks east of Alameda Boulevard. This is a one of a kind museum featuring an electric and eclectic display of neon lit and kinetic art. Call (213) 382-6622.

- More than 130 years of Wells Fargo Bank and western history is on display at the **Wells Fargo History Museum** in the towering Wells Fargo building at 333 South Grand Street. You'll find five major exhibit areas, as well as slide and video presentations. It's open weekdays.

- **Los Angeles Theatre Center**, 514 South Spring Street, features performing arts in four theaters. For information, call (213) 627-6500, ext. 267.

- The **Los Angeles Music Center**, 135 Grand Avenue, is a three theater complex that includes the **Dorothy Chandler Pavilion, Mark Taper Forum** and **Ahmanson Theatre.** Call (213) 972-7483 for information.

- Some of old L.A.'s Mexican buildings have been preserved at the **El Pueblo De Los Angeles State Historic Park.** Located on Alameda Boulevard, the park is just east of the downtown section. A free tour begins at the visitor center inside the **Sepulveda House.** Among the sites is the **Avila Adobe**, the city's oldest building, which was built in 1818. For information, call (213) 628-1274.

• Los Angeles is paradise for those interested in sports. Spectator activities such as tennis, ice hockey and professional basketball is played at **The Forum** in Inglewood. This Roman-inspired sports and entertainment arena is the home of the L.A. Lakers. Parking is about four dollars. For more information call (213) 673-1300

• Baseball fans will want to visit **Dodger Stadium** at 1000 Elysian Park Avenue, just north of the Civic Center. This is a baseball and special events stadium, seating 56,000. The Dodger baseball season is from April through October. For information call (213) 224-1400.

• For an inexpensive walking tour of the downtown area, call the **Los Angeles Conservancy,** (213) 623-CITY.

ACCOMMODATIONS

BEVERLY PLAZA HOTEL
8384 West 3rd Street
Los Angeles, CA 90048
Tel.   (213) 658-6600
       (800) 33-HOTEL CA
       (800) 62-HOTEL US
Visa, MasterCard and AMEX are accepted.

So, your travel plans are taking you to the west side of Los Angeles near Beverly Hills, Hollywood or maybe La Cienega. If you want to treat yourself right, visit the Beverly Plaza Hotel. It is conveniently located to both business and shopping in the Westside and offers an intimate, charming elegance in hotel accommodations.

The Beverly Plaza Hotel is a recently built hotel featuring 100 guest rooms. All rooms have well stocked mini bars, hair dryers and telephones in the bathrooms. Amenities include daily valet service, thick terry cloth bathrobes for your use and turn down service. There are two floors of guest rooms exclusively for non-smoking patrons. The hotel offers personalized and friendly service. There is a concierge available to help with car rentals, tour tickets, dinner reservations and anything else that you might need assistance with. They provide complimentary transportation within a five mile radius. There is a full health club with sauna, Jacuzzi and swimming pool. The Beverly Plaza

Hotel has the space, capacity and staff available to host small to medium sized meetings and full banquet facilities.

In addition to their personalized hotel service, they boast Rembrandt's Restaurant, known for its "avant garde American cuisine" and full bar service. You'll remember a meal at Rembrandt's with pleasure. For a personal touch in the big city, check in at the Beverly Plaza Hotel.

THE BILTMORE
506 South Grand Avenue
Los Angeles, CA 90071
Tel.   (213) 624-1011
         (800) 421-0156 US
         (800) 252-0175 CA
         (213) 612-1545 FAX
Visa, MasterCard, AMEX and Discover are accepted.

This beautiful, historic landmark hotel has recently undergone a $40 million restoration. All public space, meeting rooms and sleeping accommodations have been meticulously restored to their original 1920s splendor and all mechanical systems have been replaced or updated to 1980s convenience.

Each of the hotel's 700 sleeping accommodations, including suites, have been thoughtfully and luxuriously reappointed to meet the needs of today's traveler. As a part of the restoration, the hotel has added a special amenity package called The Gold Program. This package includes a variety of unique amenities, including butlers. It is designed for the corporate executive, business or leisure traveler. The Biltmore's sixteen banquet and meeting rooms are among the most opulent in the city. When not being used for conventions and events, many of the meeting rooms become sets for television series, motion pictures and TV specials.

Formal dining is enjoyed at the Biltmore's famous Bernard's dining room which features award winning cuisine and service. For less formal dining, the Court Cafe offers contemporary American cuisine in a warm and relaxed atmosphere. The ornate Galley Bar is one of downtown Los Angeles' choicest watering holes. The elegant 100 year old billiard table beyond the bar adds to the clubby atmosphere. The Grand Avenue Bar swings nightly with all star jazz entertainment and cools down in the afternoon with a gourmet cold buffet. The Biltmore's services and amenities are manifold.

Recognized as an historic landmark,The Biltmore has hosted presidents, kings and Hollywood royalty since it opened in 1923. The Biltmore remains at the center of the revitalization of Los Angeles serving travelers, convention groups, business people and the community.

HYATT REGENCY LOS ANGELES
711 South Hope Street
Los Angeles, CA 90017
Tel.   (213) 683-1234
        (800)-228-9000

The Hyatt Regency is twenty-four stories of bold sophistication. In keeping with the vibrant contemporary pace of Los Angeles, guests have easy access to the financial district, entertainment and shopping. 487 spacious rooms and suites are available and each accommodation has a built in safe, where for a small fee, valuables can be stored. Complimentary safety deposit boxes are also available at the front desk. Fax and Telex communications are easily arranged as is foreign currency exchange.

Guests familiar with the Gold Passport will find special floors designated for their use. These frequent Hyatt visitors will be treated to complimentary coffee, tea and newspapers each morning as well as all the other services reserved for holders of these cards. For luxurious comfort and lavish pampering, choose the twenty-third and twenty-fourth floor rooms of the Regency Club. This quiet sanctum is accessed by private key. These elite floors sport a private Jacuzzi available by appointment and a two story lounge. Each morning a complimentary continental breakfast is served as well as hors d'oeuvres each evening at the honor bar.

The pastel decor is the mood setter of the Pavon, serving elegant nouvelle cuisine specialties. The more casual atmosphere of the Sun Porch is open for dining all day. For breathtaking, rooftop dining, try the revolving Angels Flight restaurant. Angels Flight specializes in artfully prepared French and Continental meals as well as a spectacular view. Guests gather at the Lobby Bar for relaxation and nightly upbeat, live entertainment. For keeping the body fit and the mind alert, the Health Club offers free weights, computerized life cycles and weight stations which can be adjusted to individual heights and strengths. After the workout, relax and enjoy the sun on the outside terrace which accesses the redwood deck and Jacuzzi.

Guests are encouraged to take advantage of the services of the hotel concierge for assistance in arranging transportation or tours to immediate entertainment offered by the L.A. Convention Center, Memorial Coliseum, Dodger Stadium, the Music Center and the Museum of Contemporary Art. The Hyatt Regency is ideally located for quick freeway access to Santa Monica Beach and Disneyland. Whether for business or pleasure, experience the vibrance and vitality of Los Angeles through a stay at the Hyatt Regency.

MA MAISON SOFITEL
8555 Beverly Boulevard
Los Angeles, CA 90048
Tel. (213) 278-5444
All major credit cards are accepted.

For the luxury of a fine commercial European hotel in the heart of Los Angeles, enter the doors of the Ma Maison Sofitel. The hotel is adjacent to the Ma Maison Restaurant and is managed by Accor, one of the largest hotel companies in the world. The combination represents their ability to provide the highest level of European service and experience.

The Sofitel is centrally located near Beverly Hills, restaurant row and the Pacific Design Center. Its 311 rooms and thirteen suites feature country French decor. The nine foot high ceilinged rooms are filled with country pine furniture. The French know how to live. Each room contains many extras, here are just a few: over nite valet service and a message voice telephone system which records messages. Hotel amenities include a health club, swimming pool, and concierge service. For a country like atmosphere, enjoy afternoon tea and a continental breakfast. For meals you have two choices: La Cajole for California casual or Ma Maison for fine dining.

For a taste of France at prices you can afford, try the Ma Maison Sofitel. The hotel has special facilities for business people including nine up to date meeting and banquet rooms that vary widely in their facilities. Whether you're on a holiday, business trip, or family reunion you'll love being treated like a madame or monsieur, California style.

THE NEW OTANI HOTEL & GARDEN LOS ANGELES
120 South Los Angeles Street
Los Angeles, CA 90012
Tel.   (213) 629-1200
        (800) 252-0197 CA
        (800) 421-8795 US and Canada
Visa, MasterCard, AMEX and Diners Club are accepted.

Imagine a hotel staff that speaks nineteen languages. That's what you'll find at the New Otani Hotel. You'll discover the best of the Japanese culture in the hotel's elegant accommodations, fine dining establishments, and other unexpected amenities.

The building stands next door to Weller Court, a mini Rodeo Drive that offers some of the finest shopping in the Los Angeles area. All of the guest rooms feature individual door chimes, security scopes and black-out drapes. Guests may store their favorite beverage in the room's refrigerator and enjoy a late night movie on color television. Choose a unique two room Japanese style suite that combines a deluxe Western style parlor with a large, elevated tatami room. These rooms are the only ones of their kind in Southern California. Another one of a kind feature is the glorious half acre garden, patterned after the famous ten acre New Otani Gardens in Tokyo. Designed at a cost of $500,000, the garden offers visitors rare red rocks from Sado Island, Japan, and 100 species of eye pleasing vegetation. You'll especially enjoy the brilliantly colored flowers and the winding walkways, inspired by the Zen tradition. It's not surprising that engaged couples frequently say their vows there.

Guests will also enjoy the choice of three restaurants, including A Thousand Cranes, well known for its superb Japanese cuisine. You'll also appreciate the loving care of the masseuses, who offer European massages and Shiatsu fingertip massage. While you relax in the Japanese baths as an honored guest at the New Otani Hotel, you'll discover the full flavor of Japanese hospitality.

PARK SUNSET HOTEL
8462 Sunset Boulevard
Los Angeles, CA 90069
Tel.   (213) 654-6470
         (800) 821-3660 Reservations US and Canada
All major credit cards are accepted.

The convenient location near some of Hollywood's most famous attractions makes the Park Sunset Hotel a top choice for accommodations. Its warm, cozy atmosphere also makes it perfect for families.

Recently refurbished, the hotel features eighty-four all new guest rooms, including one bedroom suites with fully equipped kitchens. You'll find direct dial phones with message indicator lights, a must for business people. All rooms have remote control cable television, air conditioning and an AM/FM radio. If you enjoy the sun, relax in the heated pool and on the sun deck. Women will enjoy the full service beauty salon and skin care center. Business people should take note of the excellent meeting facilities, plus they'll find the fine restaurant a pleasant setting for a business dinner or luncheon. For a late night snack, the room service is hard to beat. Before you take your well deserved rest in the king size bed, spend a moment enjoying the panoramic view of Los Angeles from your room's window. You might be inspired to visit the world famous Comedy Store which is only a block away.

Many other interesting attractions are only a short drive or walk away, including Century City, downtown Los Angeles, Hollywood, the Marina area and Disneyland. Magic Mountain, Knott's Berry farm and Universal Studio are also nearby. For convenience, the Park Sunset Hotel is certainly a "Best Choice."

THE SHERATON GRANDE
333 South Figueroa Street
Los Angeles, CA 90071
Tel.   (213) 617-1133
         (800) 325-3535
Visa, MasterCard, AMEX and Diners Club are accepted.

Service is the true measure of a world class hotel. The Sheraton Grande certainly has service as well as luxury accommodations in the glittering heart of Los Angeles. This Four Star hotel is located near the

Los Angeles Convention Center, adjacent to the Pacific Stock Exchange and at the hub of freeways that take you to Southern California attractions such as Disneyland, Universal Studios, Beverly Hills and Rodeo Drive.

A butler is present on each floor of The Sheraton Grande. Every detail of the guest's comfort is attended to. The butler will shine shoes, press clothes, waken you in the morning with complimentary coffee and a newspaper of your choice. Anything the butler can't do another staff person can. There is the Clef d'or concierge staff to arrange complimentary use of nearby tennis and health club facilities, to inform you of local attractions, make arrangements for theater tickets and provide rental car service. There is even an overnight valet and laundry service. Room service will serve you a snack, meal or miniature banquet in your quarters any hour of the day or night.

The Sheraton Grande pampers guests with the rich beauty of its decor and its AAA personal service. The Sheraton Grande is unrivaled in every level of luxury with spacious, impeccably appointed guest rooms, exquisite dining experiences, sparkling entertainment and on site conference facilities.

SHERATON PLAZA LA REINA HOTEL
6101 West Century Boulevard
Los Angeles, CA 90045
Tel. (213) 642-1111
Major credit cards are accepted.

To experience the ultimate in luxury hotels, you must visit the Sheraton Plaza La Reina. Located at the Los Angeles airport, the Sheraton Plaza La Reina offers excellent accommodations, hospitality and special services that will make your trip to Los Angeles memorable.

The hotel features 807 luxurious guest rooms. They boast an elegant, ultramodern business center with a variety of meeting room sizes and a full audio-visual center. With three hotel restaurants and two lounges, the Sheraton Plaza La Reina offers a wide choice of cuisine and dining ambiance. Whether your preference is intimate elegance or lively after dinner music and dancing, the Sheraton Plaza La Reina has wonderful food and congenial service. Standard guest amenities include such services as complimentary shuttle bus service to and from your airlines, twenty-four hour room service, twenty-four hour clothes pressing service, laundry facilities, an exercise room, heated swimming pool and spa, hair salons for both men and women, foreign currency exchange and a multilingual concierge.

The Sheraton Plaza La Reina Hotel is centrally located to visitor attractions such as Disneyland, Knott's Berry Farm South, Beverly Hills, Century City, Universal Studio Tours, the Hollywood Bowl and many more. Whether your needs are accommodations for one person or a large business group, you will find the Sheraton Plaza La Reina has the room and service to fill your every requirement. For an pleasurable stay in Los Angeles, try the Sheraton Plaza La Reina.

ST. JAMES'S CLUB
8358 Sunset Boulevard
Los Angeles, CA 90069
Tel. (213) 654-7100
All major credit cards are accepted.

World class hospitality is found all over the world, but one group of private membership hotels stands out as the best of the best. Only the St. James's Club of Los Angeles, along with counterparts in Paris, London and Antigua, can make this claim.

The newest of the St. James's Clubs, the Los Angeles version is located in the venerated Sunset Tower on Sunset Boulevard. The Tower was completed in 1931 and was once the home of stars such as Errol Flynn, Carole Landis, Marilyn Monroe, John Wayne and others. But in the 1950s and 1960s, the Tower fell into disrepair, and was eventually slated for demolition. Due to its magnificent art deco architectural features and its prominence in Hollywood history, the building was placed on the National Register of Historic Places. In 1984, competition yachtsman Peter de Savary and the St. James's Club purchased the building and spent $40 million on a restoration and reconstruction program. The exterior was totally stripped and now features a pale gray color with silver highlights. Designer and project director David Becker also commissioned furnishings from Italy, which represent a revival of art deco museum pieces.

Accommodations include two penthouse suites, two townhouse suites, thirty executive one bedroom suites, and forty deluxe rooms. At the time of this printing deluxe double bedrooms were available from $180, suites from $280 to $375 and penthouses and townhouses from $595 to $1000. The St. James's Club of Los Angeles offers private or corporate memberships.

Temporary residential membership is also open to those wishing to take advantage of the Club's accommodation on a daily basis and is subject to availability. A membership charge of $8.00 per day, as of this printing, is added to the guest's bill. This category of membership is only available to those requiring room reservations and provides full access to the Club and all its facilities for the duration of the guest's stay.

The club also offers a heated outdoor swimming pool, a fully equipped health center and sauna, and other classic amenities.

Guests in the Members Dining Room are provided with a magnificent view of the city below, while seated beneath art deco skylights. The restaurant features a blend of contemporary French and California styles. The discretion and privacy of the St. James's Club will make your decision for membership one of the "Best Choices" of your life.

SUNSET MARQUIS HOTEL AND VILLAS
1200 North Alta Loma Road
Los Angeles, CA 90069
Tel. (213) 657-1333
All major credit cards are accepted.

Nestled in the hills of West Hollywood, this hotel and villa complex offers a true reflection of the Southern California life style. Elegance, beauty and a casualness pervades the premises.

The Sunset Marquis features 120 guest rooms and twelve private villas. The hotel and villas overlook four acres of landscaped grounds. The Sunset Marquis offers a full array of complimentary amenities with room service breakfast orders, suites with kitchens, and patios or balconies in all accommodations. Many items such as irons, hair dryers, clock radios and typewriters are available on request. The hotel provides full maid service both morning and night.

The villas are tastefully decorated in contemporary Mediterranean style. They include sunken living rooms, wood burning fireplaces, high beam ceilings and hardwood floors. They are furnished with baby grand pianos and brass canopy beds as well as having cedar lined closets, oversized baths with bidets and Jacuzzi tubs. You can even have the luxury of a butler. You will enjoy the unique elegant atmosphere at the Sunset Marquis.

WESTIN BONAVENTURE
404 South Figueroa Street
Los Angeles, CA 90071
Tel.   (213) 624-1000
          (800) 228-3000
Visa, MasterCard, AMEX and Discover are accepted.

Situated in the heart of dynamic downtown Los Angeles and acknowledged as a masterpiece of contemporary hotel design, The Westin Bonaventure's soaring cluster of five towers houses a city within a city.

The amenities offered by the Westin Bonaventure include thirteen restaurants, five lounges, over thirty retail shops, a garden deck, outdoor heated swimming pool, live entertainment, free cable television and in-room movies, concierge service, express check out, non-smoking rooms, travel agency and car rental services, twenty-four hour room service, evening maid service upon request, fitness facility privileges and in-room wall vaults. All 1,474 guest rooms located on the tenth to thirty-second floors have spectacular floor to ceiling views. The sixty-six suites in eight categories accommodate groups from ten to 150 people for hospitality.

The Westin Bonaventure is the largest downtown convention hotel with twenty-four meeting rooms, all recently renovated. The hotel sports two ballrooms, The California and the Catalina, an exhibition hall and six food and beverage outlets which include Beaudry's, Top of Five, Sidewalk Cafe, Lobby Court, Bonavista Lounge and the Flower Street Bar. The Westin Bonaventure has its own shopping gallery with over thirty retail outlets. Also, guests are within minutes of downtown Los Angeles' garment and jewelry districts as well as several major shopping centers.

The Westin Bonaventure offers every possible comfort and modern technological service. The hotel is owned by the Los Angeles Bonaventure Company and managed by Westin Hotels and Resorts.

ANTIQUE SHOP

LAVENDER AND LACE
656 North Larchmont Boulevard
Los Angeles, CA 90004
Tel. (213) 856-4846
Hrs: Tue. - Fri.   10:30 a.m. - 6:30 p.m.
         Saturday   10:00 a.m. - 5:00 p.m.
Visa, MasterCard and AMEX are accepted.

You can recapture the romantic wistfulness of the Victorian era when you visit Lavender and Lace in Los Angeles. This fine shop features vintage linens, laces and Victorian clothing.

Owner J.J. Jenkins has loved collecting handmade treasures from a bygone era, and she's picked out her favorites to display for you. You'll love browsing through the English white clothing, and trying on the Victorian petticoats and bodices. You'll find Victorian christening gowns and costume jewelry. To add a unique, decorative touch to your house, ask about the beautiful antique and reproduction lamps, frames, hatboxes and other gifts. But hurry, J.J. says that as soon as they come in, they're snapped up.

Picture your bed graced with some of the luxury bedcovers, shams, quilts and bed pillows. Pick one of the store's antique pine furniture pieces from England or an authentic piece of wicker furniture.

Enjoy a complimentary cup of tea whilst you browse through a selection of illustrated books on English country estates, cottages and inns. For years, Lavender and Lace has provided authentic Victorian clothing and antiques to interior designers, studio set decorators and magazine stylists. Visit Lavender and Lace on your next trip to Los Angeles.

APPAREL

AMERICAN RAG COMPAGNIE
150 South La Brea Avenue
Los Angeles, CA 90036
Tel. (213) 935-3154
Hrs: Mon. - Sat.   10:30 a.m. - 10:30 p.m.
          Sunday   12:00 noon - 7:00 p.m.
Visa, MasterCard and AMEX are accepted.
Also,
1355 Bush Street
San Francisco, CA 94109
Tel. (415) 474-5200

Shopping for world class garments in a world class store at down home prices is only part of the fun at American Rag Compagnie. The guest book at this contemporary store reads like a who's who in global fashion.

These elite know where to find the wide range of quality and style demanded by a varied crowd, from fashionable street people to the international "understated set." The world fashion press has also noted American Rag Compagnie's style and abilities. *Elle, Harper's Bazaar, Women's Wear Daily* and many other magazines have featured the store in their European, Asian and American editions. American Rag's articles are housed in a 10,000 square foot building at the heart of the new trendy La Brea area. High raftered ceilings and "motel script" blue neon atop the store's facade persuade clothes conscious visitors to come inside and browse. Jewelry, hats and sunglasses are just some of the many, many types of accessories sold. The special black and white section features formal wear. The store also has a 60's dream section, an American young designers area and a Glamor section featuring clothes from the 40s and 50s. American Rag Compagnie carries thousands of used clothing items including "European Endless" reconditioned classic clothing such as riding pants and Tyrolean jackets.

Whether buying new or fully reconditioned used clothing, this store is a fun shopping experience, with prices everyone can afford.

Perhaps this is why *W* magazine chose American Rag as the only "in" retail store on their recent list of "what's in and out" in California.

AVEDON, 8620 Melrose Avenue, Los Angeles, CA. Tel. (213) 659-9606. In this sophisticated shop you'll find elegant European styled clothes for men and women.

BARBARA WILLIAM CRAVATS
150 South Fairfax
Los Angeles, CA 90036
Tel. (213) 933-0600
Hrs: Winter   Mon. - Sat.   9:00 a.m. - 6:30 p.m.
       Summer   Mon. - Sat.   9:00 a.m. - 7:00 p.m.
                    Sunday   10:00 a.m. - 5:00 p.m.
Visa, MasterCard, AMEX and Discover are accepted.

Fashion today for men is no less demanding and critical than it was in the days of Beau Brummel, who set the tone for all English dandies. It is not always easy to know what is considered fashionable. Barbara William Cravats has been a haberdashery for three decades and has a reputation for the finest quality and service in men's fashion. Customers come back year after year, generation upon generation.

Having grown up in a family of haberdashers, owner Barbara Williams developed a unique flair in combining just the right neckwear with whatever suit or shirt one may have in mind to create the appropriate impression or appearance. This same attention is found in all lines of quality merchandise carried at Barbara William Cravats. Within her shop, which is reminiscent of haberdashery shops of the 1920s, tucked away inside antique wardrobes, is a selection of magnificent fashions for men. Barbara Williams Cravats lines include Countess Mara shirts, sport and golf shirts recognized the world over, jump suits patterned after World War II Air Force fatigues, and sweaters and cardigans made from the world's finest wools. You will also find Christian Dior socks, sleeveless slipover vests, camel and cashmere scarves, and of course, an exclusive line of neckwear— everything to make your wardrobe complete.

Located on the main walkway of the shop area at the Farmers Market, Barbara Williams Cravats is your "Best Choice" in men's fashions. It is "Why the 'regulars' have been coming back and bringing their sons with them for the last three decades."

BARTEL-CHAPTER IV
203 North Larchmont Boulevard
Los Angeles, CA 90004
Tel. (213) 462-5310
Hrs: Mon. - Sat.   10:00 a.m. - 5:00 p.m.
Visa and MasterCard are accepted.

Bartel-Chapter IV is brimming with racks of marvelously matched outfits for children from sizes infant through fourteen. Owners Lyla and Bill Bartel have collected classic lines of children's clothes from casual sportswear to fancy cotillion dresses.

Over the years, Bill and Lyla have built a reputation of displaying distinctive lines of children's clothing and their trademark is a special look of classic quality. Labels show such names as Sylvia Whyte, famous for girl's and boy's dressy velvets as well as sporty cottons to suit the seasons. The Grande Dame of children's wear, Florence Eiseman, matches fine imported fabrics and intricate appliques to create a classical line. Absorba is a French cotton line for babies which features layettes, sportswear, knits and woven garments. Soft, luxurious, one hundred percent French cottons for boys and girls are made by Ozona. The Bartels carry a large selection of Oshkosh overalls and sportswear. Lyla and Bill are known for their creative mixing of colors and fibers, such as matching tailored jackets with velvet or flannel pants. For dressing up, Bartel-Chapter IV carries a wonderful line of pretty party dresses and matching accessories.

Imported toys from Brio, wooden tops from Sweden, cheerful stuffed animals and Ambi toys from Holland are also featured at Bartel-Chapter IV. Whatever your choice from Bartel-Chapter IV, you can have it wrapped in their famous bright red boxes with the gold imprint. Or, they will send your purchase anywhere in the United States via UPS. Choose an outfit for your own child or give someone a very special gift of distinctive quality clothing from Bartel-Chapter IV.

BUY BABY BUNTING
6256 Wilshire Boulevard
Los Angeles, CA 90048
Tel. (213) 935-KIDS
Hrs:　Mon. - Thu.　10:00 a.m. - 6:00 p.m.
　　　Friday　　　10:00 a.m. - 3:00 p.m.
　　　Saturday　　Closed
　　　Sunday　　　11:00 a.m. - 5:00 p.m.
Visa, MasterCard and Discover are accepted.

Yaffa and Paul Stark are the parents of four children and have eight grandchildren, so their business is a natural. They also love Los Angeles and said recently, "when we saw this store location, it was love at first sight."

This is just the place for parents looking for clothes for their preemies, newborn, toddlers and youngsters. It is also stocked with toys and gifts for friends looking for something for a shower, and for proud grandparents shopping for that something special. Sizes range from preemie to fourteen for girls and seven for boys. Lines include Finger Paints clothing with Lurex, for girls, who can also complement their ensembles with pretty Poppy Cosmetics; wash off nail polish, strawberry mousse hand cream, sweet lilac body lotion and scented hair clips. This store is also the only children's shop in Los Angeles to carry the Comfort Line of products, which includes Comfort Float for baths and the Comfort Tote Bag, a lightweight hospital proven carrier to provide orthopedic support for your baby's head and spine. The Middleton Dolls are a very popular item that are so intricately detailed that it's hard to remember they aren't real. All toys are educational, non-toxic and conform to California's state health and safety regulations. Among them you'll find an entire range of stuffed toys by Country Critters and Applause. There's an equally impressive assortment of Baby Mockasin by Nowa-Li of Sweden. Yaffa and Paul try to carry American made goods in both natural fabrics and mixtures. These include such standard lines as Health-tex, Carter's, Spencer's, Oshkosh and Buster Brown, as well as a selection of shoes, sizes 0 through ten.

If you have children of your own, know friends who do, or are in any way involved with youngsters, you'll do yourself a great favor by stopping by this establishment. Customer satisfaction is of paramount importance at Buy Baby Bunting.

CARAVAN
7710 Melrose Avenue
Los Angeles, CA 90046
Tel. (213) 651-0718
Hrs: Mon. - Thu.   11:00 a.m. - 8:00 p.m.
          Fri. - Sat.   11:00 a.m. - 9:00 p.m.
          Sunday   12:00 noon - 6:30 p.m.
Visa, MasterCard and AMEX are accepted.

In Los Angeles, you will find wonderful leather clothing and accessories at Caravan. An interesting atmosphere of oriental mystique and California casual greets you as you walk into this comfortable store and stroll among the displays arranged on bleached hardwood floors, where you'll notice fine leather clothing in pink, mint green and bright jewel like colors.

Co-owner Moshe Aelyon is a graduate of fashion merchandising and an expert in leather design. He will be happy to assist you in coordinating the perfect leather outfit including unusual and finely tooled handbags and belts. Wallets from Italy and Turkey, extraordinary leather jackets, two piece ensembles, hand embroidered tops and coordinated skirts and tops decorated by hand with jewels are also offered at Caravan.

Caravan extends special services such as alterations and you may special order. The owners of Caravan have been involved in the wholesale leather industry for over three years and will guide you to a leather outfit well within your means. Caravan's dedication to personal service and the highest quality and workmanship of their merchandise make this a "Best Choice" in the Los Angeles area.

DESIGNER LABELS FOR LESS
860 South Los Angeles Street
Los Angeles, CA 90014
Tel. (213) 627-3059
Hrs: Mon. - Sat.   9:30 a.m. - 5:30 p.m.
         Sunday   11:00 a.m. - 5:30 p.m.
Visa and MasterCard are accepted.
Also,

Ellay Designers Outlet
1905 South Figueroa
Los Angeles, CA 90007
Tel. (213) 746-2347

17555 Ventura Boulevard
Encino, CA 91316
Tel. (818) 907-7382

22844 Hawthorne Boulevard
Torrance, CA 90505
Tel. (213) 375-7100

Agoura
29370 Roadside Drive
Agoura Hills, CA 91301
Tel. (818) 991-2378

1801 Dyer Road
Santa Ana, CA 92705
Tel. (714) 261-6678

The Cooper Building
860 South Los Angeles
Los Angeles, CA 90015
Tel. (213) 627-3059

2245 South Sepulveda Boulevard
West Los Angeles, CA 90064
Tel. (213) 479-7892

Whether it's your principles or your checkbook that keeps you from paying outrageous prices for clothing, there's no need to worry about it any more. A few years ago Diane Murray and Eve Nober decided to open a women's clothing store that sells first class merchandise at prices affordable to the working woman. The idea took off, and they are now anticipating opening their ninth outlet in the Los Angeles area.

The two women live up to their motto "Designer Labels For Less." Each of their eight stores has rooms filled with racks of bold, refreshing, exciting, new designer fashions, as well as traditional and classic designs at low, low prices. Every item is always fifty to ninety percent less than the retail price of "regular" clothing stores. After you pick out that just right evening dress, without walking out the door you can find the shoes, hat, belt and gloves to go with it. You'll find convenience and quality at prices you can afford. They also carry casual wear including a large line of denim and sportswear. Their eight convenient locations are open seven days a week; a perfect schedule for the working woman.

Luckily, Diane and Eve had the foresight and sensitivity to create the type of store where everyone feels welcome. Now you don't have to be in the upper income tax bracket to dress well. Designer Labels For Less takes the stress off of your pocketbook and allows you to shop, relax, and enjoy.

TRADITIONALLY SUITED
WOMEN'S WEAR FOR BUSINESS AND PLEASURE
735 South Figueroa
Seventh Market Place at Citicorp Plaza
Los Angeles, CA 90017
Tel.   (213) 624-5777
Hrs: Mon. - Fri.   8:00 a.m. - 7:00 p.m.
          Saturday   10:00 a.m. - 6:00 p.m.
Visa, MasterCard, AMEX and Diners Club are accepted.

This elegant shop, with its burgundy mahogany, brass trim, pink and black marble, oriental accents and fresh flowers, is the creation of owner Linda Menar. Linda, who has a background in business, management consulting and data processing, was frustrated by not being able to find the right clothes for business. After extensive market research, she opened her shop, which is based on the concept of beautiful business dressing for the way women work.

The clothes offered at Traditionally Suited are custom selected for the store. You won't find department store merchandise here, but you will find beautiful suits that are elegant in color, style and texture and dresses that reflect a conservative, yet individual style. All the accompanying accessories you need are here, too. You'll find a wealth of clothes to take you from the office to the theater.

Traditionally Suited offers excellence in selection and service and many extras that shoppers will appreciate. Free tailoring and alterations are offered on anything sold. The helpful, knowledgeable staff will assist in wardrobe planning and make in-home and in-office calls for the executive woman too busy to shop. Making sure that their customers are totally satisfied and happy is of paramount importance to Traditionally Suited. For the best in quality, service and perfect clothes for business, this is the place to shop in Los Angeles.

ART GALLERIES

BURNETT MILLER GALLERY
964 North La Brea Avenue
Los Angeles, CA 90038
Tel. (213) 874-4757
Hrs: Tue. - Sat.   10:00 a.m. - 5:30 p.m.
Credit cards are not accepted.

If you're open to art that challenges and intrigues one's senses then you probably already understand that art can be anything that makes us see ordinary things anew. In that case, the Burnett Miller Gallery is your kind of place.

The Burnett Miller Gallery specializes in the international, the contemporary and the avant-garde. Representing these qualities are the works of Antony Gormley, a contemporary sculptor from England whose work speaks of his emotional involvement in the world around him. Ulay and Marina Abrmovic are two artists who work together in combining elements of form and performance. You might see works that take advantage of the immediacy of Polaroid photography. Past exhibits, for example by Charles Ray, have included a box filled with ten gallons of Pepto-Bismol, framed glass panes filled with ink, wires that protrude and retract randomly from the gallery wall and a section of the concrete wall that obliterates its own texture by whirling at 3,500 rpm.

Compared to other galleries, this one time Max Factor lipstick factory from the 1930s will seem sparse. The exposed steel girders and concrete floors create a feeling of spaciousness, rawness and magnitude. Miller, who is a former curator of the prestigious La Jolla Museum of Contemporary Art, is selective and you will find only a few important pieces on display at one time. But if you're in search of the missing link between minimalism, kinetic sculpture and process art, look no further than the Burnett Miller Gallery.

CLASSIC ARTFORMS
9009 Beverly Boulevard
Los Angeles, CA 90048
Tel. (213) 273-6306
Hrs: Mon. - Fri.   9:30 a.m.-5:30 p.m.
         Also by appointment.
Visa and MasterCard are accepted.

This gallery breaks the traditional mold of stuffy galleries by being fun and alive. The beauty of its own decor is incredible and owner/frame craftsman, Robert J. Bentley, adds to the exciting ambiance by being helpful and charming.

Opened in 1976, this gallery and framing shop offers a wide variety of art selections and framing choices. The gallery offers lithos, fine prints, engravings, accessories, sculpture, graphics, custom framing and watercolors along with unique and unusual gifts for anyone on your list. Classic Artforms also carries contemporary paintings by a variety of artists, both known and unknown. The gallery itself is very light and spacious, with an enormously varied collection of modern to traditional art. There is a dramatic collection of all media of sculpture in brass, bronze, marble and alabaster. And for collectors who love the unusual, Classic Artforms has a large display featured in the front windows.

Robert J. Bentley lectures to art classes across Southern California and is a very interesting and learned man. He offers many framing specialties such as wood, metal, metal leaf, acrylic, white wash, gold leaf and museum and conservation framing. His shop also has complete fabric matting capabilities. Robert will also track down certain pieces of art for you and will help if you are interested in making investments in art. This lovely gallery is filled with a wide variety of media from which you can choose gifts or pieces with which to decorate your own home. This gallery of art thriving with enthusiasm and beauty is your "Best Choice" for galleries in L.A.

FRANCINE ELLMAN GALLERY
671 North La Cienega Boulevard
Los Angeles, CA 90069
Tel. (213) 652-7879
Hrs: Tue. - Sat.   10:00 a.m.-5:00 p.m.
       Also by appointment.
Visa and MasterCard are accepted.

The Francine Ellman Gallery, an innovative gallery on the cutting edge of the Los Angeles art scene, is known for exhibiting American contemporary painting and sculpture by artists with established records of accomplishment.

Francine Ellman, who has been involved with the Los Angeles art scene for nearly twenty years, is best known for her ability to seek out new, exciting and provocative works from talented artists and exposing them to the ever expanding Los Angeles art community.

Set back from La Cienega Boulevard in a quiet and shady courtyard, the Francine Ellman Gallery is outstanding in a neighborhood well known for its fine art galleries. The gallery space occupies a former "artist's loft" which has been extensively renovated. Leaving important architectural detailing exposed, such as the open beamed ceiling which tops the walls reaching over twenty feet in height, Francine Ellman enjoys the ability to comfortably exhibit works of various dimensions and scale.

Francine does not necessarily address the popular trends in the art market of today, but chooses to expose the talents of artists whose work will stand the test of time as a result of its innovation and creative importance.

The gallery format is such that exhibitions change on a continuous basis with each show lasting approximately one month. Some of the artists represented by the Francine Ellman Gallery are Meg Freeman, a contemporary realist painter whose witty compositions juxtapose people in unlikely interior spaces, creating a commentary on the underlying insanity of life; Jim Sajovic whose focus is women and their perception by society, and Ken Matsumoto, whose sculpture of steel, glass and concrete poetically recreates natural harmonic forms.

For a fresh look into the variety and innovations of today's art world, visit the Francine Ellman Gallery. You'll find it a place full of changing exhibits, always provocative and exciting.

JACK RUTBERG FINE ARTS
Modern and Contemporary Painting,
Drawing, Prints and Sculpture
357 North La Brea Avenue
Los Angeles, CA 90036
Tel. (213) 938-5222
Hrs: Tue. - Fri.   11:00 a.m. - 6:00 p.m.
       Saturday   11:00 a.m. - 5:00 p.m.
       Or by special appointment.

Fine art should be viewed in a place as fine as Jack Rutberg Fine Arts in Los Angeles. This top of the line gallery features the best in modern and contemporary painting, drawing, prints and sculpture and represents some of the most sought after names in the art world.

Located on La Brea Avenue, Jack Rutberg Fine Arts is in a renovated building that dates back to the 1930s. Visitors will find a 5,600 square foot gallery with small viewing rooms off the main gallery. Other work is displayed in another enormous light-filled gallery to the rear. The upstairs rooms display works of modern and contemporary artists. Artists include Burkhardt, Baron, Hundertwasser, Brauer, Glauder, Graham, Weisberg and Falkenstein. This gallery is a main resource for many important dealers. National and international museums often call on Jack Rutberg Fine Arts for an addition to their collections. Serious novice art collectors will receive a fine education in what's what and who's who in the current art world when they visit this gallery. You'll also discover important European and American works from the late nineteenth century to the present. Impressionist and Early Moderns are two of the specialties at Jack Rutberg Fine Arts.

Fine prints—Picasso, Renoir, Matisse and Chagall—are also available. If you wish a private look at the best of the best, ask for a special appointment, although appointments are not required.

JERRY SOLOMON ENTERPRISES, INC.
960 North La Brea Avenue
Los Angeles, CA 90038
Tel. (213) 851-7241
Hrs: Mon. - Fri.   8:30 a.m. - 5:30 p.m.
Visa and MasterCard are accepted.

Jerry Solomon Enterprises, Inc.'s custom picture framing business is devoted to their clientele, which extends throughout the United States and into Asia and Europe. Their quality workmanship, service and variety in products is what makes their framing service one of the best in the country. Specializing in different and unusual frames, the clientele consists of collectors, museums and upscale interior designers. With the ample facilities of 60,000 square feet and fifty-five employees, almost any task can be accomplished. Carvers actually work on the premises and the shop will also do antique furniture and antique frame restorations.

One reason for his popularity is that Jerry Solomon is one of the few people in the country who will work with twenty-two carat gold leaf. Solomon is involved in carving and gold leafing the exquisitely beautiful doors and ceiling pieces for the owner's private apartment in the Trump Building in New York City. Besides also doing pedestals and sculpture bases, Solomon and the other artisans are carving the prototypes of furniture for hotels across the country. A vast selection of moldings, both handcarved and machine made, are close at hand, as are the materials that are used to do the custom picture matting and framing. Solomon offers all different types of finished lacquer including white gold, antique and distressed.

To house all of this incredible artwork and creating, plus a restoration department for paintings, requires a six story building. Walking through the different floors of artisans molding, matting, gilding and refinishing is an experience never to be forgotten. The smells of lacquer, paint and the sight of artists with masks, firing and cutting the metal and wood frames is a definite must when you are in Los Angeles.

M GALLERY
8649 Sunset Boulevard
Los Angeles, CA 90069
Tel. (213) 652-4964
Hrs: Mon. - Sat.   10:00 a.m. - 9:00 p.m.
          Sunday   12:00 noon - 6:00 p.m.
Visa, MasterCard and AMEX are accepted.

Jewelry can often transcend the fine line between art and fashion. In the eighteenth century the French Comte d'Artois owned a set of diamond buttons, each of which had a miniature clock encased inside it. Representing a commitment to raise jewelry to the level of art, M Gallery features unique creations by innovative leaders in the field of Wearable Art.

Inspired by a very creative jewelry store in New York City, Kathleen Archer and Michael Dawkins decided to open a shop dedicated to jewelry as both an art form and a fashion statement. Pieces by Robert Lee Morris, Katherine Post, Patricia Von Musslin, Stephen Dweck and other artists have been assembled in a gallery like setting. Necklets, armbands, earrings, bracelets and rings fashioned in brass, sterling silver and gold plate are displayed in a manner that enhances each piece and highlights the talents of each individual artist. Exotic pieces in ivory and ebony enhance the sheen of the skin, shadow the collar and add a gleam to the ear.

Artists who violate traditional form and explode conventional boundaries are constantly advancing jewelry to the level of fine art. Galleries such as the M Gallery transcend the mediocre and present jewelry as a wearable form of fine art.

MANY HORSES GALLERY
740 North La Cienega Boulevard
Los Angeles, CA 90069
Tel.   (213) 659-0802
          (213) 659-0737
Hrs: Mon. - Sat.   9:00 a.m. - 5:00 p.m.
          Also open by appointment.
Visa and MasterCard are accepted.

Many Horses Gallery shows one of Los Angeles' better collections of contemporary Southwestern art. The quality art shown has become a resource within the bustling Los Angeles interior design trade. The gallery also caters to the design trade and the collector.

Works by R.C. Gorman, John Nieto, Glen La Fontaine and Ben Wright are featured. Owner Roy LoBianco has represented R.C. Gorman from Gorman's beginning works to his most recent pieces. LoBianco shows Gorman's original prints and selected pastels, oils and woodblocks. Many Horses Gallery highlights fine South Western pottery, Kachina dolls, all mediums of fine art prints, original paintings, bronze, alabaster and ceramic sculptures, weavings, baskets, large drums and masks. Expert packing and shipping are a special service offered by LoBianco.

Both private collectors and professional interior designers will find outstanding Southwestern art at Many Horses Gallery.

RICHARD/BENNETT GALLERY
332 1/2 North La Brea Avenue
Los Angeles, CA 90036
Tel. (213) 931-4933
Hrs: Tue. - Sat.   11:00 a.m. - 5:00 p.m.
        Or by appointment.
Visa and MasterCard are accepted.

It's not unusual to find prominent contemporary art collectors at the Richard/Bennett Gallery. The gallery contains some of the most important current works and styles in contemporary art. Located in one of the oldest historical buildings on La Brea Avenue, the 1930s vintage space has been completely converted and renovated to display painting and sculpture.

The Richard/Bennett Gallery is interested in exploratory forms of art including those which seek out paths to new artistic frontiers. Owners Richard Heller and Bennett Roberts strive to keep clients informed of the progression of the artists whose work they've exhibited. The gallery presents the work of Noel Canfield, a sculptor in steel, and Bruce Fuller, who works in stone; Norton Wisdom, "the godfather of L.A.'s underground art scene." Other artists include Cameron Shaw, Craig Roper, Robert Catalusci, Anselm Kiefer, Sigmar Polke, Francesco Clemente and Julian Schnabel. Many artists discovered at Richard/Bennet Gallery have triumphed in major museum exhibitions around the world. The gallery enjoys assisting curatorial efforts with museums and private institutions in Los Angeles and abroad.

Viewers at Richard/Bennett find themselves surrounded by unusual sculpture and paintings including enormous figures, bizarre, yet beautiful shapes and distinctive colors. Whether you're a top collector, a novice collector or a lover of beautiful objects, you'll find what you're looking for at Richard/Bennett Gallery.

SAXON-LEE GALLERY
7525 Beverly Boulevard
Los Angeles, CA 90036
Tel. (213) 933-5282
Hrs. Tue. - Sat.   10:00 a.m. - 5:30 p.m.
      Also open by appointment.

The spacious and warm gallery surroundings of the Saxon-Lee Gallery exhibit the very finest in contemporary paintings, sculpture, drawings, ceramics and art furniture. Featured are younger, mid-career and well known established artists. Co-owners Dan Saxon and Candace Lee have an excellent reputation with collectors from all areas of the country. They have impeccable taste in the selection of abstract, figurative and representational art.

In addition to their spirited main gallery exhibitions that change monthly, one can also walk through their large Atrium gallery where Mr. Saxon and Ms. Lee are seated. Adjacent to the Atrium is their outdoor sculpture court. Also, one can see a wide variety of art in their private viewing room, upstairs loft space and back storage areas. In the evening, the main gallery is transformed into a one hundred seat theater for performances, lectures and musical events.

The current list of artists featured at Saxon-Lee Gallery are known by all who collect fine art. From the east coast are: Red Grooms, Judy Rifka, Mac Adams, Heide Fasnacht, Georgia Marsh, Michelle Stuart, Dan Rizzie and Ed Rainey. From the west coast are: Peter Shire, Gronk, Kenneth Capps, Michael Gregory, Rose-Lynn Fisher, Raul Guerrero, Betye Saar, Ilene Segalove, Luis Serrano and Robert Walker. Many of these artists show works of museum quality and exhibit in museums internationally.

The gallery is open twelve months a year, with much of the art priced for moderate budgets. Ample free parking is provided in the gallery's own parking lot adjacent to the building.

SPACE
6015 Santa Monica Boulevard
Los Angeles, CA 90038
Tel. (213) 461-8166
Hrs: Tue. - Sat.   11:00 a.m. - 5:00 p.m.
      Also open by appointment.

Under the directorship of Edward Den Lau, this spacious, second floor gallery is now in its thirteenth year at the same Hollywood location, not far from the Los Angeles Municipal Art Gallery in Barnsdall Park.

SPACE represents mid-career and emerging artists, and includes on its roster more non-figurative sculptors than any other Los Angeles gallery. Their artists live in Japan, Europe, California and other U.S. states, with an emphasis on California artists.

Stylistically, there is no common denominator. What unites SPACE's artists is a strong commitment to materials and process, and a consistently high level of craftsmanship. Their works encompass all mediums, and gallery visitors are offered a good sampling. In addition to the current exhibits, works by other gallery artists are on display in specially designated areas, such as the "open storeroom" or the lounge.

SPACE artists have shown in museums nationally and overseas, and are well represented in public and private collections all over the world. There is a strong individual bent to this gallery. It is epitomized by the diverse sensibilities of its artists. To some of them, the term "idiosyncratic" could be applied.

The following are among the painters and sculptors represented: Masami Teraoka, Norman Lundin, Seiji Kunishima, Ann Page, Bella Feldman, Pepo Pichler, Kazuo Kadonaga, Doug Young, Bob Alderette, Robert D. Anderson, Tom Eric Stanton, Minoru Ohira, Robert Glover, Judith Foosaner, Wes Christensen, John Rose, Roberta Eisenberg, Samuel Lemly and Norman Schwab.

YESTERYEAR, LTD.
8684 Melrose Avenue
Los Angeles, CA 90069
Tel. (213) 659-5080
Hrs: Mon. - Fri.   9:30 a.m. - 5:30 p.m.
         Saturday   10:00 a.m. - 4:00 p.m. December only.
Visa and MasterCard are accepted.

You'll easily recognize this bright shop by its arched window painted in pink and green. Once inside Yesteryear, Ltd., you'll marvel at the vastness of the collection of fine old prints and antique accessories ranging from the inexpensive to the extravagant. It has been a decorator's source for unique artwork for more than fifteen years.

You'll find unusual one of a kind items from all over the United States and Europe. Discover old art prints in all sizes and themes including botanical, hunting, children's subjects, animals and architecture. Yesteryear's black and white engravings are expertly hand colored by the staff.

Yesteryear's distinctively framed prints, matted exclusively in fabrics such as silks, tweeds, prints, plaids, are found all over the world in private residences, restaurants and hotels.

In addition to custom framing their own prints, Yesteryear will gladly frame your cherished artwork, photographs, needlepoints and other items. The gallery specializes in unique shadow box framing of your pieces, or select from the hundreds of antiques such as corkscrews, combs, laces, kitchen utensils, men's articles and other baubles in stock.

Yesteryear takes pride in personalized service. Explain your decorating problem as exactly as possible and they can almost guarantee an inspired solution. They also offer conservation framing and will arrange shipping anywhere in the world.

BAKERIES

FRANCES BAKERY AND COFFEE
404 East 2nd Street
Los Angeles, CA 90012
Tel. (213) 680-4899
Hrs: Mon. - Sat.   8:00 a.m. - 7:00 p.m.
       Sunday   9:00 a.m. - 6:00 p.m.
Credit cards are not accepted.

The plain storefront stuck amongst fifteen other shops in the mini-mall does little to prepare you for the wonders waiting inside the Frances Bakery.

The interior was designed to perpetuate the sensation of being amongst ornately decorated cakes. The human faces, scroll work and detailed moldings are rendered in palpable relief. Instead of being white, part of the relief has been blushed in colors of light pink, lavender and green. Overhead is a magnificent and ornate crystal chandelier. In addition to coffee and pastries, customers may purchase fine porcelain cups, saucers, plates and figurines as well as an assortment of teas.

Frances Bakery has begun wholesaling its products to one of the most quality conscious airlines in Brazil. Try the pastries, browse amongst the fine china, decoratively displayed, or just take in the mouth watering aromas.

SWEET LADY JANE
8360 Melrose Avenue
Los Angeles, CA 90069
Tel. (213) 653-7145
Hrs: Mon. - Thu.   8:30 a.m.-7:00 p.m.
       Fri. - Sat.   8:30 a.m.-11:30 p.m.
Visa and MasterCard are accepted.

For delicacies with flavor that is beyond belief and a charming English setting, Sweet Lady Jane is the place to go. This combination bakery and tea room offers the finest of American and European desserts in a quaint atmosphere that gives glory to the ornate beauty of furniture from the past. Centrally located near the junction of Melrose Avenue and Orlando, Sweet Lady Jane is decorated in the style of authentic English tea rooms. The English Bob Cratchett lights, Holophane glass lighting and beveled glass mirrors are set off by high ceilings complete with stained glass skylights. Mirrored cases, only seen in places such as Harrods of London, mirror the delectable pastries and cakes displayed in beautiful wood cases. Without a doubt, Sweet Lady Jane is an experience in quality.

This quality extends to the items offered on the menu, too. Made from only the freshest ingredients, some favorites are exquisitely delicious dark chocolate walnut brownies, white chocolate brownies and a wonderful selection of authentic European breads, such as crusty French bread and European style whole wheat bread. Creamy cheesecakes range in style from white chocolate to Oreo cookie and are delicious treats for anyone. Deluxe fruit tarts are a big hit as they use only fresh fruits such as strawberries, raspberries, plums and peaches. If chocolate is your fancy, you're in luck. Sweet Lady Jane has everything from imported Swiss chocolate desserts and a super dense decadent cake to white and dark chocolate layered Mousseline Desserts decorated with white and dark chocolate curls.

This charming bakery and tea room uses only the purest ingredients, even the Danishes are made from pure butter and homemade custard cream or fruit fillings. Traditional desserts like Napoleans are made with the finest custard and fresh fruit. For those who have a plainer taste in pastry, there is a delicious selection of real butter sponge cakes layered with lemon or mousse filling. Sweet Lady Jane is the only place in Los Angeles that makes English Wedding cakes. Made with real fruit cakes that are covered with Marzipan and royal icing, these are just one of the many special occasion cakes that can be made to order by the talented decorators at Sweet Lady Jane, your "Best Choice" for the Los Angeles area.

BED & BREAKFAST INNS

SALISBURY HOUSE
2273 West 20th Street
Los Angeles, CA 90018
Tel. (213) 737-7817
Visa, MasterCard and AMEX are accepted.

Los Angeles offers several different types of accommodations to choose from, ranging from Five Star hotels to roadside motels. If you want a change of pace, make reservations at the Salisbury House bed and breakfast in the West Adams district of Los Angeles.

This *craftsman* style home built in 1909 exemplifies the first original residential architectural design to come out of Southern California. Unlike its more formal Victorian predecessors, the Salisbury House features spacious rooms in an earthy, informal setting. All of the rooms feature authentic period antiques and decor. There are five rooms, including the Rose and Green rooms that offer queen size beds. The Rose and Green rooms share a bath. You may choose the Blue Room, which features a queen size bed, a private bath and a romantic bay window seat. The Sun Room offers a full size bed in one room, while an adjoining sitting room sleeps two in twin trundle beds. The Sun Room also has a private bath. For true turn of the century luxury, ask for the Attic Room; 600 square feet on the third floor featuring a king size bed and private bath with claw foot tub. You'll want to enjoy the Salisbury House breakfast, served in the formal dining room, buffet style. Enjoy classic American treats such as waffles, sausage, honey bran muffins and fresh fruit cobblers.

Centrally located, Salisbury House is near freeways that will take you in all directions in a short time. You are close to Beverly Hills and the L.A. County Museum in one direction and can easily be in downtown Los Angeles in the other. Innkeepers Alice and Si Torvend want you to enjoy the comfort of a fine home on your visit to Los Angeles. Salisbury House is a perfect change of pace.

TERRACE MANOR
1353 Alvarado Terrace
Los Angeles, CA 90006
Tel. (213) 381-1478
Visa, MasterCard and AMEX are accepted.

One of the first bed and breakfast inns in Los Angeles, Terrace Manor is a registered National Historic Landmark. The house features a collection of leaded and Art Nouveau stained glass windows of rare beauty. Premium woods such as tiger oak and mahogany are used throughout the house on paneling, doors, fireplaces, beams and a massive staircase. The house is filled with antiques and art that owners Sandy and Shirley Spillman have collected over the years.

Each of the five bedrooms in this restored Victorian home has a private bath and a theme decor such as the Wicker Room, charmingly done in white wicker, or the Collector's Room containing Victorian novelties such as a wonderful perfume bottle collection. In the morning you'll enjoy an outstanding gourmet breakfast featuring Eggs Florentine with sausages, Eggs Benedict, Peach Crepe, Fritatta, omelettes or quiche with fresh coffee or tea. Coffee or complimentary wine and a light repast are available in the late afternoons at an informal social hour in the parlor or the library.

Terrace Manor not only offers superior accommodations, but is also conveniently located in downtown Los Angeles near the business district, Convention Center, Chinatown, Olvera Street and the University of Southern California. Terrace Manor's relaxing, peaceful atmosphere, excellent breakfasts, guest passes to Hollywood's famed Magic Castle and its highly rated recommendation by AAA Auto Club make it a "Best Choice."

 # CANDLE SHOP

CANDLES BY DREW
150 South Fairfax
Farmer's Market
Los Angeles, CA 90036
Tel. (213) 935-2380
Hrs: Mon. - Sat.   9:00 a.m. - 6:30 p.m.
          Sunday   10:00 a.m. - 5:00 p.m.
Visa and MasterCard are accepted.

The old saying, "put a candle in the window for me" has been taken to heart by Candles by Drew. This enchanting shop specializes in candles from around the world. It's not hard to locate Candles by Drew in famous Farmer's Market. Follow the sweet scent of bayberry, strawberry, vanilla and honey to the Village section of the market.

Exotic candles in fantasy shapes and materials exhibit the quality of an age old craft. The most popular candles are the ivory, solid beeswax. The bees know how to make wax which is heat resistant and long lasting. Honeycomb candles will not bend in hot weather and give a maximum amount of burning time. The candles come in a rainbow of colors. There are twisted candles and sculpted candles in animal or fantasy shapes.

Candles by Drew also carries a splendid selection of candle holders and accessories fashioned in glass, brass and crystal. Hurricane lamps, some of which date back twenty years, are also carried. Candles by Drew will ship anywhere in the United States. Brighten up your home with a candle from Candles by Drew.

CANDY STORE

U.S. CHOCOLATE, INC.
7322 Melrose Avenue
Los Angeles, CA 90046
Tel. (213) 931-2829
Hrs: Mon. - Sat.   11:00 a.m. - 7:00 p.m.
          Sunday   12:00 noon - 6:00 p.m.
Credit cards are not accepted.

Consider for a moment a fresh strawberry dipped in rich dark chocolate or a cluster of grapes and cashews bonding in a sensuous union with thick milky white chocolate. Do these images tantalize your taste buds? Then go directly to U.S. Chocolate, Inc.

U.S. Chocolate, Inc. is a rare find. It is a place brimming full of unusual chocolate and candy items. The smell of fresh chocolate is overwhelming. It is difficult to restrain oneself so close to so many chocolate delights. Will power wilts in the face of Amaretto, Cognac, Apricot Brandy or Strawberry and Cream filled chocolates. Multi colored chocolate rosebuds on long stems are just the ticket for a special occasion gift. The store's shelves hold candies that older people say they haven't seen for years. There is a line of Gummi products such as Gummi Cherries, Gummi Peaches and Gummi Coke Bottles. The colorful display of Jelly Beans invites the hand to play. Here too you can find the classic Jaw Breakers and other *nonpareils*. U.S. Chocolate, Inc. offers a large selection of molds so you can have any piece of chocolate made specifically for the special person in your life.

U.S. Chocolate, Inc. offers the largest and finest selection of chocolates and specialty candies in Los Angeles. After one visit to U.S. Chocolate, Inc. you'll dream of truffles and sugar plums dancing in your head.

CAR RENTALS

BUDGET RENT A CAR, THE LUXURY LINE
300 South La Cienega Boulevard
Los Angeles, CA 90048
Tel.   (213) 659-3473
        (800) 826-7805
Hrs: Mon. - Sun. 7:30 a.m. - 11:40 p.m.
Visa, MasterCard, AMEX, Diners Club and Budget Corporate
Cards are accepted.

"Have we got a number for you," say Marc and Rhoda Fogel of Budget Rent a Car, The Luxury Line. And, indeed they do. Every type of car, from compacts to Cadillacs, Rabbits to Rolls, are ready to roll for you.

The Luxury Line specializes in the world's finest automobiles, combined with gracious personalized service. The Fogel's goal is to make your rental experience as effortless and enjoyable as possible. The Luxury Line exclusive personalized service includes free airport pick up and drop off, delivery of the car of your choice to your home, office or hotel, and limousine service. The entire selection of cars is available by the day, week or month. The cars are perfectly maintained, late model, low mileage automobiles equipped with automatic transmission, air conditioning, power steering and stereo sound systems. Cellular car phones are available in most of the cars.

From a Jeep Wrangler to a Jaguar XJS Convertible, the Fogels have a car to suit your needs. And, they have convenient, no hassle service to match. Pick a number from Budget Rent A Car, The Luxury Line.

COLLECTIBLES

TIFFANY CREATIONS
6333 West 3rd Street
Los Angeles, CA 90036
Tel. (213) 931-8894
Hrs: Winter   Mon. - Sat.   9:00 a.m. - 6:30 p.m.
                  Sunday   10:00 a.m. - 5:00 p.m.
      Summer   Mon. - Sat.   9:00 a.m. - 7:00 p.m.
                  Sunday   10:00 a.m. - 6:00 p.m.
Visa, MasterCard, AMEX and JCB are accepted.

"The unusual is the usual at Tiffany Creations." Waterfalls splash, musical carousels turn, whimsical delights fill the eye and heart with joy for young and old.

Located on 3rd Street at Fairfax Street in the heart of world famous Farmer's Market (opposite gate #2), Tiffany Creations is a Pandora's Box of mythical, Victorian and magical creations of wondrous imagination. Tiffany Creations displays a grandiose collection of figures in pewter by Michael Richer and others. They also boast the largest selection of David Winter's cottages, pubs and castles in Southern California. Annette Petersen's Wee Forest Folk tiny mouse collection are great for every holiday and occasion. Tom Clark's gnomes and wood spirits from the Cairn Studio are known to bring good luck, wealth and happiness to the home which harbors them.

"You'll love discovering Tiffany Creations", for Christmas the year round. Tree toppers, magnets and bread dough ornaments made exclusively for the store are unique and look like fine porcelain. Local artist Pamela creates many one of a kind masterpieces. Hand sculpted dogs and cats by Pence curl themselves into soap dishes, business card holders, planters and every other conceivable shape and use. Don't miss a trip through Tiffany Creations' magical world of pewter, gifts and collectibles.

COSMETICS

VANITY INC., MAKE-UP STUDIO
714 North La Cienega Boulevard
Los Angeles, CA 90069
Tel. (213) 659-7011
Hrs: Mon. - Sat.   11:00 a.m. - 6:00 p.m.
          Appointments anytime.
Visa, MasterCard and AMEX are accepted.

The application of make-up is a true art, but often the myriad of products and techniques available can be baffling. Faced with this problem, many of the world's most beautiful faces go to Los Angeles' first make-up studio: Vanity Make-up Studio.

Service is this establishment's middle name. Women, and in the last few years, men, discover a variety of ways to apply the latest products. You may also test the best ways to combine the products to produce a personal look. Walk-in customers select the mini-makeover, featuring a seasonal update of colors within a fifteen minute make-up application. The natural glamor make-up application is a forty-five minute application, by appointment. This service is excellent for street wear or events such as weddings. Customers sometimes request studio make-up for photography sessions or video and film production. Vanity Make-up Studio also offers lessons, from two hour intensive individual lessons, to group classes over a five week period. Those interested in a career in make-up can take the professional make-up artist classes. You'll enjoy all these services in a bright and airy studio. The natural light helps you select the best colors and tones to match your skin.

Everything in this shop caters to the senses, from the vanilla scented Italian talc to the Tahitian perfumes. All products are selected for their purity and quality. Hollywood stars and jet setters have made Vanity Make-up Studio a "Best Choice."

 # FISHING TACKLE

LORDS OF THE FLY
12227 Wilshire Boulevard
Los Angeles, CA 90025
Tel. (213) 820-7546
Hrs: Tue. - Sat.   10:00 a.m. - 6:00 p.m.
Visa, MasterCard and AMEX are accepted.

Whether you are a once a year fisherman or a weekend diehard, sleuthing out new flies or the perfect lures for that special fishing spot can be time consuming and disheartening. Lords of the Fly offers an affable solution to the tackle dilemma.

This fly fishing pro shop is owned and run by three dedicated fly fishermen. They feature brand name fly fishing gear such as Fenwick, Hardy Brothers, Columbia, Danner, Pflueger, Metz, Orvis and many more. They offer everything imaginable in rods, reels, flies, all related tackle, clothing, boots and waders. They also provide custom rods and flies, rod repair services and rentals. They give classes in casting and tying. The shop specializes in exotic tackle, cane rods, collector reels and fly fishing schools and guides. They lead expeditions and float trips. Yearly fishing expeditions include such places as Canada and the Florida Keys. One can obtain personalized fly fishing instruction through the store at the Arcularius Ranch at Mammoth Lakes, California. Whether you are a novice angler or a veteran seeking to hone your skills, they can accommodate your needs.

If you are looking for that special spoon, wiggler or plug or want to start from scratch and completely revamp your fishing gear, you will find Lords of the Fly a complete fly fishing supply shop. For that perfect lure or piece of tackle you have been looking for, try Lords of the Fly.

FROZEN YOGURT

THE CULTURED CLASS
8719 Santa Monica Boulevard
Los Angeles, CA 90069
Tel. (213) 657-8350
Hrs: Sun. - Thu.   11:00 a.m. - 11:00 p.m.
       Fri. - Sat.   11:00 a.m. - 12:00 midnight
Credit cards are not accepted.

Come in and become a part of the cultured class. Whether you sit on the outdoor patio and watch the rich and famous savor their yogurt or simply have it to go, The Cultured Class, rated Four Stars by *Los Angeles Magazine*, is the gourmet's frozen yogurt.

Imagine 240 ways to develop a connoisseur's palate: A rotating selection of 160 flavors and eighty toppings creates infinite possibilities for enjoying this healthful dessert. And with their specialty pies and shakes, you can take it a step further.

One thing for sure, you'll never be bored at The Cultured Class. It is open seven days a week and offers take out. No credit cards please.

FURNITURE STORES

CONTEMPO WESTWOOD CENTER
Westwood Village
10886 Le Conte Avenue
Los Angeles, CA 90024
Tel.   (231) 208-4107
        (213) 208-5454 Westwood Playhouse
Hrs: Mon. - Sat.   10:00 a.m. - 7:00 p.m.
       Sunday   12:00 noon - 5:00 p.m.

Not often are commercial ventures combined with historical preservation and the arts. It is even rarer still when such mixtures are as successfully enduring as is Contempo Westwood Center. The building was erected as a Masonic Temple in 1929. In 1973, Contempo Westwood Furniture moved in and started a thoughtful process of restoration and conversion that has led to the blending of a furniture store, a gift store, a restaurant and a five hundred seat theater. The complex is now named Contempo Westwood Center.

The furniture area is an artful showcase for the finest in Scandinavian furnishings. Taking advantage of the original building, the main floor is both a display area and the foyer to the theater. One browses among leather chairs, dining tables, wall systems and other fine furnishings. A second floor holds more accessories for the home, including rugs and lighting systems. Contempo Westwood Center also holds a gift gallery, stocked with a broad selection of crystal, jewelry, crafts and clothing. Scandinavian, Navajo, Mexican and other cultures are represented. After a day of shopping or before a show, the stone courtyard is a perfect place to relax and enjoy the offerings of Stratton's Restaurant. Theatrical presentations featured at Westwood Playhouse vary from professional musicals and drama to one person shows by the likes of Ian McKellan and Ella Fitzgerald.

The delightful combination of elements that comprise Contempo Westwood Center are European in style and attitude. There is a warmth and compelling sense of harmony that sets the entire venture apart from the norm.

COUTURIER GALLERY, 166 North La Brea Avenue, Los Angeles, CA. Tel. (213) 933-5557. Couturier Gallery specializes in the American arts and crafts period of furniture, ceramics and lighting.

UMBRELLO
8607 Melrose Avenue
Los Angeles, CA 90060
Tel. (213) 655-6447
Hrs: Mon. - Fri.   9:00 a.m. - 5:30 p.m.
          Sat. - Sun.   10:00 a.m. - 6:00 p.m.
Visa, MasterCard, AMEX and Diners Club are accepted.

When De Wayne Youts opened Umbrello here in 1977, the Southwest look in interior design was just an extension of his own past. Little did he know that it would become the biggest trend to hit the interior design world in the eighties.

"I came about this honestly," he explains, recalling his own childhood on the open range. With stores in Santa Fe, New Mexico and New York City, he observes, with more than a bit of wonder, "You know, I've been doing this for so long that if anyone comes to town with anything remotely in this style, someone sends them here." Umbrello is, in effect, a museum of the old and new. Guatemalan rugs, linens and pillows, cowhide chairs, fetish dolls, old spurs and chaps, pottery cow skull hangings, Southwest paintings, masks from Mexico, mirrors with antler frames, drums from Taos, colorful lacquer gourds, beaded and silver jewelry, cactus clocks, pine framed beds, antique trasteros, paintings by Russell Hamilton, rawhide ropes, Spanish Colonial pieces, country ranch and farm furniture from New Mexico, Texas, the Rio Grande Valley, Arizona and California handwoven Navajo and Zapotec Indian rugs and a marvelous line of handwoven placemats and napkins. Several lines of pottery and dinnerware fill this converted private home with more Southwest authentica than you'll find anywhere.

Whether you're an architect with a large complex to design, a professional looking to upstyle your office, or simply someone who appreciates the Southwestern ambiance, you need look no further. At Umbrello you've found it.

GIFT SHOPS

FANTASIES COME TRUE, 7408 Melrose Avenue, Los Angeles, CA. Tel. (213) 655-2636. This adorable shop is stocked with one hundred percent Disney merchandise from 1930 to the present. There is a lot of original art work from the Disney Classics and memorabilia in all media.

HOLLYWOOD NEON
7456 Melrose Avenue
Los Angeles, CA 90046
Tel. (213) 852-9611
Hrs: Mon. - Sat.   11:00 a.m. - 6:00 p.m.
Credit cards are not accepted.

When people think of Hollywood, they often think of names up in lights or seeing the city of Los Angeles at night for the first time. Many of those bright lights come from Hollywood Neon.

Located on busy Melrose Avenue, Hollywood Neon began as the L.A. Cactus Company in 1977. Slowly, it evolved into a business creating and selling neon signs. Today, Linda Toliver and Lee Sankowich awe customers with their intricate, colorful designs using simple gases excited by electricity. Don't be put off by the store's interior; it's deliberately painted black and gray to show off neon's glorious colors. You'll find designs ranging from bizarre and outrageous to traditional. You may spend some time examining the neon collages, desk top neon ornaments, personalized neon clocks or enjoy a reproduction of antique neon work. A neon art deco sign works perfectly for hard to decorate space. If you can't find a design that's just right for you, Linda and her assistant Tim Ottman will work with you to create a design only you own. You'll find neon art in just about any shape and size. It's Hollywood Neon's specialty.

Hollywood Neon has become a mecca for Hollywoodlanders who seek the unique and creative. Visit Hollywood Neon, and take home one of the bright lights of Hollywood.

LOVE GIFTS
8541 Melrose Avenue
Los Angeles, CA 90069
Tel. (213) 273-1261
Hrs: Mon. - Sat.   10:00 a.m. - 5:30 p.m.
Visa, MasterCard and Corporate Accounts are accepted.

There are certain events in life that call for special remembrance. From birthdays to anniversaries, from a "job well done" to a love rekindled, these are the times that are made memorable by a surprise from Love Gifts.

The spirits of romance and imagination pervade the products and services of this enchanting shop. The mother/daughter partnership of Gloria Cornelius McCary and Lea Sandoval has taken the motto "Gifts are our business" and infused it with a personal style and adventure. They offer a complete shopping service that allows one to handle gift selection by telephone. But the real treat is entering the building and feasting on the aromas and visual delights that fill its country French interior. From pottery and fine silver to gourmet food items, the line of products allows you to personalize a gift with style. Among the many quality labels available are Floris of London, Palacek Baskets and Furniture, Beatrix Potter Collectibles and Paper White Linens. An enjoyable way to take advantage of the wonderful array is to choose from the various "Theme Baskets." Better still, let the atmosphere of the shop inspire you to create your own special combination of gifts.

When the occasion calls for something unique for someone special, call or visit Gloria or Lea. Let them help you generate the warmth that comes from giving something from the heart.

THE MARGARET CAVIGGA QUILT COLLECTION, 8648 Melrose Avenue, Los Angeles, CA. Tel. (213) 659-3020. This shop boasts over 400 hand quilted antique and new quilts, circa 1805 through the present, with sizes ranging from crib through king.

NORDIC COUNTRY
150 South Fairfax #21
Farmer's Market
Los Angeles, CA 90036
Tel. (213) 857-0027
Hrs: Summer
       Mon. - Sat.   9:00 a.m. - 7:00 p.m.
       Sunday   10:00 a.m. - 6:00 p.m.
       Winter
       Mon. - Sat.   9:00 a.m. - 6:30 p.m.
       Sunday   10:00 a.m. - 5:00 p.m.
Visa, MasterCard, AMEX and Discover are accepted.

If you wanted, anywhere else, what this establishment has to offer, you'd be doing your shopping in Reyjavik, Stockholm, Copenhagen or Helsinki. A delightful prospect, granted, but not always practical. Nordic Country can't transport you to Scandinavia, but it can sure make you think you're there.

This Farmer's Market gift shop carries a tremendous and absolutely impressive selection of gifts from the region. Especially popular are the carvings of trolls, those supernatural creatures of Scandinavian folklore. Explains co-owner Ingrid Thomson, "I grew up with trolls. My mother always told me that if I did not behave, the trolls would raise me. I was scared, especially of the trolls I grew up with. The Swedish ogres are mean and nasty. The Norwegian trolls are nicer and good luck." They are also startlingly exquisite pieces of art, and certainly in keeping with the emporium's total concept. It's here that you'll find Swedish crystal, Royal Copenhagen porcelain, famous Mats Jonasson full lead crystal renditions of animal life, Norwegian solid black crystal cats, lilac crystal animals, birds and paperweights from Sweden, and that rare pink elephant that is always hard to find. The list goes on to include high quality Swedish ceramic candelabras, Rokokko-Tinn pewter servers, Baltic amber jewelry from Denmark, Norwegian and Danish jewelry, and typical Norwegian old fashioned wedding brooches. Norwegian knitted sweaters of 100% wool are an especially popular item, both for their craftsmanship and their renowned durability.

In an area teeming with import/export business, Nordic Country is in a class by itself. One is definitely safe in assuming that there is none like it in the entire Southern California area.

OGGETTI, Century City Shopping Center, Los Angeles, CA. Tel. (213) 277-0889. This shop features handmade and decorated fine Florentine paper and accessories from Italy. You'll also find gift boxes, calendars and frames.

OPERA SHOP OF LOS ANGELES
8384 Beverly Boulevard
Los Angeles, CA 90048
Tel. (213) 658-5811
Hrs: Mon. - Fri.   10:00 a.m. - 9:00 p.m.
       Saturday   10:00 a.m. - 6:00 p.m.
Visa and MasterCard are accepted.

The house lights dim. The orchestra is tapped to silence by the Concert Master's baton. Great crimson curtains rise to reveal the singers, and the orchestra soars into music. Opera magic has begun. Keeping the magic of opera curling through our imaginations is the happy task of Ray Crenna and Larry Rappaport in their Opera Shop of Los Angeles.

As rich as a stage setting for the most lavish opera, the fascinating store contains a wondrous array of gift treasures, all with a musical motif. The Opera Shop carries a full line of classical video cassettes and compact disks of opera, ballet and music, a superb line of rare musical theme books, a special collection of jewelry in ivory, silver and gold, an extraordinary collection of bronze, porcelain and papier mâché masks. Gorgeously dressed, wigged and powdered dolls made in the images of opera characters smile and curtsy from the shelves. Exquisite silk scarves and rare Polish opera posters, imported figurines and music boxes vie for center stage. Bear lovers will be delighted with the opera theme bears. Lace Carmen fans from Spain shade impish faces of jester heads, and handmade puppets are ready to perform your favorite scenes. And, of course there are opera glasses.

Of special note are the gift baskets created around an operatic motif, where you may choose from Russian, German, French or Italian. Your basket will be filled with gourmet food items and selected video tapes of composers and operas from the chosen country. All gifts from the Opera Shop can be beautifully wrapped with paper and ribbon reflecting a musical composition. A trip to the Opera Shop of Los Angeles will bring cheers of Bravo! and Encore!

PAPER SHOP
150-5 South Fairfax Avenue
Los Angeles, CA 90036
Tel. (213) 935-4938
Hrs: Mon. - Sat.   9:00 a.m. - 6:30 p.m.
          Sunday   10:00 a.m. - 5:00 p.m.
Visa and MasterCard are accepted.

You'll find this charming little shop by its stained glass windows overlooking the Farmers Market and you'll be delighted at the availability of parking, somewhat of a definite premium in Los Angeles.

Walk in and you'll find an establishment filled with party goods from all over the world. A full party line includes paper flowers, napkins, place settings and a plethora of decorations. The Victorian masks from England are magic as well as both rare and unique. The stationery department is one of the most complete in Southern

California and what you can't find, you can order. This shop prints its own napkins, stationery and memo pads to exact customer specifications. They fill the helium balloons they sell and make many colored bouquets for special occasions. They also carry over 100 patterns of paper guest towels and a variety of invitations for all occasions. There's a big selection of paper and fabric ribbons in many colors and widths, from flat to super shiny; multi-colored wrapping paper and gold and silver ribbon from Europe. The garlands of multi-colored paper from China and Denmark are a particular favorite and for those who enjoy stickers, there are rolls and rolls of them. The many hued cellophane food containers have been approved by the FDA and customers from all over the country are still ordering the calendars and guest books they purchased when they dropped by during a vacation or family visit to the area.

Whatever the season, holiday or special occasion, if you want variety and uniqueness, you'll stop here before going anywhere else. And then, of course, you won't need to go anywhere else.

PEACE AND PLENTY
7320 Melrose Avenue
Los Angeles, CA 90046
Tel. (213) 937-3339
Hrs: Mon. - Sat.   11:00 a.m.- 6:00 p.m.
      Open Sundays during Christmas.
Visa, MasterCard and AMEX are accepted.

As a child you may have heard stories from your grandparents about the thick eiderdown quilts that they used to have on their beds, and about the quilting parties their mothers used to have and all the bright cloth swatches they used to make the beautiful patterns. This Early American art is filled with spirit and love, and it shows in everything made then. Peace and Plenty is an old English political slogan and Sabra, the owner, chose it because it is something everyone wishes for, and it reflects the spirit of American folk art which is bountifully available in this charming shop.

Peace and Plenty, located in the busy section of Melrose Avenue, is alive and active with many people and shops around. The front of the store is bright and cheerful with full glass windows. Inside, high ceilings with white painted rafters give the shop an open, gallery like feeling. Quilts hang on the walls and on simple geometric stands, while wall units display the vast array of pottery and other gift items.

There are so many fabulous old quilts for you to choose from, it will make you feel as if you are at a country farmers market in early America. The antique quilts on display were made anywhere from 1850 through 1940, and are mostly from the Midwest and Pennsylvania. At any given time there are at least one hundred of these quilts. For those who want to learn about the history of quilting, a marvellous selection of books on the subject are on hand. These books cannot be found anywhere else in Los Angeles.

Peace and Plenty also carries a line of contemporary crib quilts for children that are washable and easy to take care of. Peace and Plenty has also acquired a reputation for having a very unusual selection of greeting cards. These cards render to times past and will make anyone smile with their warmth. Handpainted folk pottery from America, Italy and Portugal is also available. Papier mâché hand painted animal figurines, hand painted pottery cottages and mugs, old fashioned rag mats, pot holders and pillows—these are just a few of the handmade and collectible items that your great grandmother used to make, and are now sold at Peace and Plenty. As a gift for a dear friend, or for your own home, anything from this store will create a feeling of love, warmth and times past.

GOURMET FOOD

CAVIAR AND FINE FOODS, INC.
6610 Melrose Avenue
Los Angeles, CA 90038
Tel.   (213) 937-6800
           Ask for Betsy.
Hrs: Mon. - Fri.   8:30 a.m. - 4:30 p.m.
Credit cards are not accepted.

The finest Iranian or Russian Malossol caviar from the Caspian Sea, Beluga, Golden Osetra and Sevruga caviars; the words roll off the tongue with ease and delight as do the beautiful, savory sturgeon eggs themselves. These extraordinary caviars and other palate stimulating treats are offered at Caviar and Fine Foods, Inc. in Los Angeles.

Caviar and Fine Foods has been the leading importer and distributor of fine foods on the West Coast for the last thirty- five years. When you visit the shop on Melrose Avenue you will discover sliced or whole London Smoked Scotch Salmon, Norwegian, Canadian, and domestic varieties of smoked salmon. Imported *foie gras* of all types, fifteen varieties of fresh paté, smoked eel, trout, sturgeon and mussels are all available. You will find appropriate accompaniments such as cornichons, biscotts, croissant or cracottes. Take home some of the world's first class Malossol caviars whether it be Beluga, Golden Osetra or Sevruga. Indulge in hedonistic joy, because it is low in calories and an extremely healthy snack.

You are invited to call or write Caviar and Fine Foods for a price list and other information concerning their products. They will ship anywhere. When you call just ask for Betsy. The expert service, knowledge of the finest foods and an outstanding reputation make this a "Best Choice" in Los Angeles.

JEWELRY STORES

LOLITA'S, 10250 Santa Monica Boulevard, Los Angeles, CA. Tel. (213) 277-7148. When looking for glittering jewelry, fine sculptured gold and silver necklaces, bracelets and rings, visit this "Best Choice."

SCULPTURE TO WEAR
8441 Melrose Avenue
Los Angeles, CA 90069
Tel. (213) 651-2205
Hrs: Mon. - Sat. 11:00 a.m. - 6:00 p.m.
Visa, MasterCard and AMEX are accepted.

Many think of art as something to hang on a wall or put on a pedestal. At Sculpture to Wear, art is something worn around a neck, a wrist or on an ear. This gallery offers the finest in art jewelry.

With its high profile location on Melrose Avenue, Sculpture to Wear fits in perfectly with the nearby galleries. Artists that show particular innovation, creativity and skill are selected from all over the country. Many of the artists are recognized masters in their field, and have been acknowledged by top national and international critics. Their pieces are one of a kind or of a very limited edition. Though the gallery has been open only a year, many pieces displayed have already become collector's items. The gallery presents four or five exhibitions per year, including 1987's *The Singular Brooch*. This show featured contemporary interpretations of a form used since ancient times. Individual artists are also shown, including Samuel Shaw. His spirited jewelry was inspired by the music of jazz artists of the late 1950s. 1988 saw an exhibition of Enid Kaplan's colorful works, entitled *Resonant Aliens*. You'll enjoy all of the shows in a small intimate gallery dedicated to displaying sculpture designed to decorate the human form.

If you have a chance to try on some of the pieces, allow owner Jan Ehrenworth to tell you the story behind them, and you'll discover a whole new world of art to wear.

KALEIDOSCOPES

KALEIDO
Antiquarius Center
8840 Beverly Boulevard
Los Angeles, CA 90048
Tel. (213) 276-6844
Hrs: Mon. - Sat.   11:00 a.m. - 6:00 p.m.
Visa, MasterCard and AMEX are accepted.

Through your eyes, colors and shapes come alive, beautifully creating images that capture your imagination. A kaleidoscope is a work of art—one that can change into a thousand other works of art with a twist of your hand. At Kaleido you will find the finest contemporary kaleidoscopes by today's most innovative and talented artists. Each piece is beautifully designed; some look like the telescopes of medieval astronomers or the scepters of troll kings. Every kaleidoscope is sure to provide a very special form of beauty and enjoyment year after year.

Kaleido, located in the east corner of the Antiquarius Center, is the first store in the United States to sell nothing but kaleidoscopes. The surroundings lend a relaxed feeling to your shopping and ample valet and street parking is available. Kaleido is an intimate shop with large windows filled with the most amazing assortment of kaleidoscopes. Kaleido carries the best collection of kaleidoscopes at retail prices available in the United States. Every possible variation on the basic kaleidoscope design is fashioned by today's most original artists from around the world, is sold at Kaleido. Special and rare items, such as a tiny one inch long kaleidoscope, ones with semi-precious stones inside and one shaped like a biplane can also be found here.

There are two main groups of kaleidoscopes; hand held ones that come with a rack or holder, and parlor ones, which stand by themselves and look like elegant telescopes. Some of the parlor scopes are aimed at spinning trays of flowers or picture wheels that turn to achieve their wondrously exquisite effects. Most kaleidoscopes are made of wood or brass and decorated with jewels or stained glass. Prices range from three dollars for a little cardboard model, to $3100 for a unique quarter scale model of the world's largest kaleidoscope. Kaleido has the atmosphere of a fine gallery, but visitors are invited to pick up and explore the magic of kaleidoscopes. Gazing at the myriad reflections of shards of colored light and crystal snowflakes as the end pieces turn is a fascinating and mesmerizing experience. A whole new world can be opened up to you through the kaleidoscopes at Kaleido.

NEW AGE PRODUCTS

MINERALE
8380 Melrose Avenue Suite 100
Los Angeles, CA 90069
Tel. (213) 655-9865
Hrs: Mon. - Sat.   12:00 noon - 7:00 p.m.
         Sunday   12:00 noon - 5:00 p.m.
Visa and MasterCard are accepted.

"Los Angeles' finest Crystal Shop," is what *Los Angeles Magazine* calls Minerale. Offering the largest variety of fine crystal jewelry in Los Angeles, it is well known for its decorator pieces of large clusters of crystals that are often used by interior decorators, and are also appropriate for your personal decorating tastes in the home.

Clear paned glass windows give a spacious and open look to this beautiful gallery, located on the corner of Orlando and Melrose Avenues. Exquisite in itself, this gallery presents the most unusual pieces of polished and natural crystals found anywhere. The crystals come from Brazil, Korea, Italy, the United States, India, Madagascar and Mexico. If you need to learn about crystals before buying, there is a wide variety of books on crystals and the knowledgeable owner and his assistant will gladly help you with any need that you may have. They also carry all types of minerals, pyramids in crystal and agate and rose quartz. Other minerals include selenite, with white shaded and unusual formations; halite, with a pinkish tint; calcite, a cluster of cream tinted crystal; smoky quartz; druzy quartz; okenite, a moon surfaced quartz with balls of fluff like material; celestite; halite; sulfer crystals; and fluorite, which is dark purple and shaped almost like Italian hilltop villages because of the many layers of minerals. Handmade pieces that have been carved and set on rosewood stands are also available as are specialty items such as beautifully fashioned Chinese figurines and perfect spheres in glass, clear quartz, rose quartz, amethyst, green fluorite, obsidian and calcite. There is a large glass case filled with lovely silver jewelry inlaid with semi-precious jewels. Some favorites are topaz, rose quartz and silver arm bands set with unusual shaped pieces of amethyst, pyrite and other semi-precious stones.

This fun gallery will astound you with the unique and magical shapes of the crystal clusters. Every size, shape, color, and aura is in this gallery. They also carry a large tourmaline collection, in a wide variety of colors that stretches the imagination. Everywhere you look in this gallery, all that the eye can see is beauty. This gallery is a must for serious crystal collectors.

NIGHTCLUB

THE COMEDY STORE
8433 Sunset Boulevard
Los Angeles, CA 90069
Tel.   (213) 656-6225
          (213) 650-6268
Hrs: Mon. - Sun.   8:00 p.m. - 2:00 a.m.
Visa, MasterCard and AMEX are accepted.

The Comedy Store is a laughing matter. It's really more than a joke, it is one long string of giggles, guffaws and belly laughs. That's exactly what owner Mitzi Shore had in mind when she took over the old Ciro's nightclub and turned it into a showcase of comedy talent.

Some of the best comedy talent in the United States has passed through The Comedy Store's doors. Comedians such as Whoopi Goldberg, Roseanne Barr, Robin Williams, David Letterman, Howie Mandel and Garry Shandling got their start on The Comedy Store stage. Shore's idea behind the club is to offer a continuous comedy show. The Comedy Store houses three showrooms: The Mainroom, which seats 450; The Original Room, which seats 250; and the intimate Belly Room, for women comediennes only. The Comedy Store's interior color scheme is red, black and white. Shore has lined the walls with special wallpaper decorated with caricatures of famous comedians. Dazzling neon sculptures flash in the main lobby. Signatures of all the comedians who have worked at The Comedy Store are scribbled on the exterior walls.

The Comedy Store has three other locations beyond the original West Hollywood location. You can enjoy seeing the future stars of comedy perform in Las Vegas, Universal City and La Jolla. Call (213) 656-6225 or 650-6268 for complete information on schedules of shows. According to Mitzi Shore, "You ain't seen nothing yet!"

RESTAURANTS

ABACUS
11701 Wilshire Boulevard
Los Angeles, CA 90025
Tel. (213) 207-4875

Hrs:	Lunch	Mon. - Sat.	11:30 a.m. - 3:00 p.m.
	Dinner	Sun. - Thu.	5:00 p.m. - 10:00 p.m.
		Fri. - Sat.	5:00 p.m. - 11:00 p.m.

Visa, MasterCard, AMEX, and Diners Club are accepted.

Abacus, one of the best Chinese restaurants in Los Angeles, is best known for its excellent authentic Chinese and seafood cuisine, its elegant ambiance, and the personalized service to its patrons. Owners, Richard Fong, Sue Tsao and Anne Wu, insist on the best of everything for their customers, from the absolute freshness of the seafood used in their creations to the beautiful surrounding decor, featuring a sophisticated palette of salmon, rose, and mint green. The entry foyer's smooth onyx marble hints at the elegance to come. A fresh rose sits atop each white linen topped table, framed by the black chairs that have been lacquered to a beautiful sheen. Chinese antiques from the owner's personal collections, and Sue and Anne's Oriental artwork complete the tranquil setting.

The diner may select from such Chinese dishes as Beggar's Chicken, which is baked in clay and stuffed with rice, lotus seed, and crunchy chestnuts or Peking Duck, which requires advance notice of thirty minutes or more, in addition to other delicacies. However, the tempting glimpses of live shrimp, squid, lobster, abalone, scallops, and various shellfish in the crystal tanks may entice you to choose one of chef Li-Kang Yen's seafood creations. His background in Western, Taiwanese, and Cantonese styles of food preparation has garnered him a considerable reputation, especially for his Hunan and Szechuan dishes.

Abacus offers such special services as: occasional cooking classes, preparation of virtually any Mandarin dish with proper notice, a take-out and delivery service, private banquet rooms and dessert selections including a spectacular ice mold for groups of six or more that is illuminated from within and filled with seasonal fruits such as kiwi, strawberries, apples, oranges and melons. If desired, it can be embellished with ice cream. Its masterful presentation further enhances the quiet grace found throughout Abacus.

BERNARD'S
506 South Grand Avenue
Los Angeles, CA 90071
Tel. (213) 612-1580
Hrs: Lunch   Mon. - Fri.   11:30 a.m. - 2:00 p.m.
       Dinner   Mon. - Thu.   6:00 p.m. - 10:00 p.m.
                    Fri. - Sat.   6:00 p.m. - 10:30 p.m.
All major credit cards are accepted.

With respect for the culinary masters while maintaining a flair for the new, executive chef Roger Pigozzi artfully supervises an average of 200 meals per day at Bernard's, The Biltmore Hotel's award winning restaurant. The combination of classic French cuisine with the best of Regional and American, baroque architectural designs, and the melodic sounds of a concert harpist in the background contribute to a relaxing, memorable dining experience.

Fine meals are served against a setting of antique oak and hand decorated heavy beamed ceilings. You can begin luncheon,

Villeroy and Boch china, with an appetizer: Carppacio of Smoked Scottish Salmon, Westcott Bay Oysters, or hot Fettuccine topped with Beluga Caviar. Favorite entrees include Fresh Poached Salmon, Seafood Pot a Feu in a light Bouillabaisse, or Tenderloin of Pork with a mustard and pear sauce. The consistency and quality of food extends naturally to the dinner menu. Enjoy dining in the sunken central dining area at a table of blue linen dramatically illuminated by pin-spot lights. Indulge in an appetizer of fresh escargot with caviar served in a pastry shell, before an entree of daily fresh fish, Grilled Medallions of Veal with Artichoke Fettuccine, or Breast of Chicken stuffed with Chicken Mousse. Top the meal off with an exquisite dessert of Baked Pears and Pistachio Cream or Genoise Cake Veronique with white grapes marinated in wine with a cream and liquor sauce.

It's time you treated yourself to the best in fine dining at The Biltmore's Bernard's where you'll find the best in service, the best in cuisine, for the best customers.

BORDER GRILL, 7407 1/2 Melrose Avenue, Los Angeles, CA. Tel. (213) 658-7495. The Border Grill features food like you would find in Mexico City and the Yucatan, served in a contemporary setting. Try the fresh Corn Tamales and soft Crab Tacos.

CAFE MAMBO
707 Heliotrope Drive
Los Angeles, CA 90029
Tel. (213) 663-5800
Hrs: Wed. - Mon.   8:00 a.m. - 11:00 p.m.
All major credit cards are accepted.

On the outside, it looks like a mint green Pee Wee's Playhouse and inside, its sunshiny walls, well manicured plants and familiar art work conspire with a small but distinctive Caribbean style California nouvelle to make Cafe Mambo as chic as the Cha Cha Cha, the ten star eatery from which it spun off.

Consider the "best breakfast," an omelette of summer squash, red and green bell peppers, zucchini and red onion. The morning diner might also want to sample Huevos Chorizos, scrambled eggs with chorizo, pico de gallo and refried black beans All egg dishes come with potatoes and toast. For lunch, there is the traditional grilled hamburger with fresh lettuce, tomato, red onion, and a choice of avocado, bacon, mozzarella, cheddar or Swiss. All sandwiches also come with a choice of fries, red cabbage slaw or eggplant. The dinner menu was launched toward the end of last year and includes swordfish, salmon, prime rib, chicken, duck, soft shell crab, pork chops and pizza.

It's small, with seating for forty-five, so you'll definitely want to call for reservations. It's also usually crowded, so if you like the company of the rich and famous while you dine, you'll want to sample Cafe Mambo, one of L.A.'s newest and hippest cafe restaurants.

CATHERINE - A CHAMPAGNE BISTRO
143 North La Brea Avenue
Los Angeles, CA 90036
Tel. (213) 930-2230
Hrs: Tue. - Thu.   6:00 p.m. - 12:00 midnight
       Fri. - Sat.   6:00 p.m. - 2:00 a.m.
       Sunday Brunch   11:00 a.m. - 3:00 a.m.
All major credit cards are accepted.

The best restaurants in the world combine a sensuality of decor with food that would put any gourmet into gastronomic heaven. Such places are rare, making them treasures when discovered. Such is Catherine-A Champagne Bistro in Los Angeles. Destined to become one of the great *clubs prive'es* of California, Catherine features decor that would delight any eighteenth century French king, and food that even the most finicky gastronome will savor.

Look for the large glass window surrounded by twinkling lights and walk upstairs to the Salon, a French Regency style gathering room, where Los Angeles artists come to share a drink, a meal, and conversation. Relax in Louis XV furniture imported from Italy and enjoy the neo-classic paneling which graces the walls. Muted colors illuminated by the softest candlelight accent the wonderful meals. Catherine is an ideal spot for a romantic interlude. You may begin your meal with Seafood Griddle Cakes with Creole Remoulade and Baked Oysters with Roasted Garlic and Herbs. As an entree you may try the oak grilled Duck Breast with Cabernet Sauce, served with berries and sliced vegetables. The perfect finish to your meal may be Champagne Sorbet with fresh berries and a light Hazelnut Mocha Torte.

Afterwards, relax with a glass of champagne. Owner Catherine Domont has made her dream come true at Catherine-A Champagne Bistro.

CENTRAL PARK CAFE
11604 San Vicente Boulevard
Los Angeles, CA 90049
Tel. (213) 826-6686
Hrs: Lunch
     Mon. - Fri.   11:30 a.m. - 3:00 p.m.
     Dinner
     Mon. - Sun. 5:00 p.m. - 11:00 p.m.
     Bar
     Mon. - Sun. 5:00 p.m. - 2:00 a.m.
Visa, MasterCard, AMEX and Diners Club are accepted.

Sally Gilbert took over the Central Park Cafe two years ago and with the help of chef Sarah Weintraub's talented creations, it has thrived ever since. Customers actually ask to be called when warm Scallop Salad or Hungarian Mushroom Soup is on the day's menu.

The homemade soups, pasta, and pastries are all made from the freshest ingredients daily. Over twenty-five variations of chicken salad are rotated as one of the day's special luncheon selections. Regular customers recommend Spicy Chicken with corn tortillas, marinated onions and black beans, or Grilled Salmon with tomato caper Beurre Blanc. For dessert, the ultimate chocolate creation, Queen Mum Cake with raspberry sauce competes with another favorite, Bread Pudding topped with nutmeg butter sauce.

The old charm of this establishment feels like New York City with its exposed brick walls, posters of New York's Central Park, hardwood floors and tables draped with beige cloths. There is a magnificent mahogany bar that serves twenty imported beers by the bottle, in addition to twenty fine wines by the glass.

Nostalgia laced jazz and classical music fill the restaurant and reflect the owner's belief that dining should be a relaxing and comfortable experience in a neighborly atmosphere. She also believes in having fun, and provides a daily trivia question on a big blackboard as a friendly invitation to test your wits. If you come up with the answer, you win a free glass of house wine.

CHAMPAGNE

10506 (Little) Santa Monica Boulevard
Los Angeles, CA 90025
Tel. (213) 470-8446
Hrs: Lunch   Tue. - Fri.   11:30 a.m. - 2:30 p.m.
      Dinner   Tue. - Sun.   6:00 p.m. - 10:30 p.m.
Visa, MasterCard, AMEX and Diners Club are accepted.

Three superlative menus in one welcome the diner to Champagne, a formal restaurant featuring California French cuisine. Although in operation for only a year, this fine establishment has already earned a reputation as one of the best in Los Angeles.

The first section of the menu is entitled Contemporary, and reflects Southern California's sunny and beautiful lifestyle. At the same time, selections are executed to the disciplined standards of fine French cuisine. Examples from this menu include Three layered Crayfish and Eggplant Cake, with onions, red bell peppers, and black olives in a crayfish sauce; and Crispy Norwegian Salmon, cast iron fried with leaf spinach, braised endive and black peppercorn sauce. The menu's second section, Spa Cuisine, is an extension of the Contemporary cuisine with less sodium and calories. The Spa Cuisine features Roasted Eggplant Soup with red bell peppers and basil confetti. It's rated at 150 calories. Champagne's most popular menu section is Rustic cuisine. Items on this menu include Grilled Marinated Quail Salad and a Country Cassoulet of white beans, lamb sausage, pork loin, duck confit and bacon.

You may enjoy all these exquisite culinary treats in an elegant yet comfortable surrounding with a gracious and helpful staff in attendance. The setting of high backed tapestry chairs and dark green plush carpet complements the creative cuisine of Champagne.

CHIANTI CUCINA

7383 Melrose Avenue
Los Angeles, CA 90046
Tel. (213) 653-8333
Hrs: Mon. - Sat.   11:30 a.m. - 11:30 p.m.
      Sunday   6:00 p.m. - 11:30 p.m.
All major credit cards are accepted.

Imagine a restaurant so popular that it spawns another. Now put the two of them next to each other and you have Chianti Cucina.

Chianti, the original establishment, was opened in 1938 and is a landmark for many entertainment industry leaders. While both restaurants serve the same authentic Northern Italian cuisine, each offers a unique dining experience.

With its murals, candles and romantic atmosphere, Chianti is Old World charm at its finest. The dining experience is enhanced by a staff of well schooled waiters and a kitchen that believes in fresh foods. The large menu is filled with classic fare and house specials such as Fettuccine Alfredo and Tortelloni d'anatra ai fiori di zucca, pasta filled with duck and covered with zucchini blossom sauce. The other half of this restaurant duet is a bit more casual. At Cucina, one can enjoy watching the chefs prepare meals in the open kitchen, where delectable aromas will tease your palate. When the doors open, Cucina fills with diners, and it stays that way all evening. The excellent food and exciting clientele generate energy that turns eating into a memorable event. The menu changes daily and epitomizes the attitude of "a few things done very well."

Whether you fancy a romantic Old World experience, with pampering waiters and soft lights, or a more casual, up-tempo dining experience, Chianti Cucina offers the best of both worlds. Since this is a very popular spot, reservations are a must.

CITRUS
6730 Melrose Avenue
Los Angeles, CA 90038
Tel. (213) 857-0034
Hrs: Lunch   Mon. - Sat.   12:00 noon - 3:00 p.m.
         Dinner   Mon. - Sat.   6:30 p.m. - 11:00 p.m.
Visa, MasterCard and AMEX are accepted.

Innovative, provocative, superlative, and refreshing are fitting descriptions of a dining experience at Citrus. Located at the corner of Citrus and Melrose Avenue, Citrus is the genius of chef and owner Michel Richard. Already distinguished in the Los Angeles area for his premier talent as a *pâtissier*, he now lends his creative flair to the appetizing temptations offered exclusively at Citrus.

Dine in either the outdoor patio under white canvas umbrella canopies or inside in the spacious well lighted contemporary dining room. Observe the chefs at work under the supervision of Michel Richard while they create culinary delights designed to please all of the senses as well as the appetite. Entrees are a work of art in addition to being unequivocally delicious. Adventurous diners will enjoy the full spectrum of appetizers and entrees available at Citrus. Luncheon and dinner menus consist of such unusual creations as Crab Cole Slaw, made with sweet Blue Crab meat; Veal Tenderloin with horseradish sauce and potato garlic puree; and Santa Barbara Shrimp, with a ragout of white beans and lobster broth topped with crunchy brioche crumbs. Entrees change on a daily basis as Michel continues to add dazzling new choices to his selection. Caramel Napoleon with homemade liquorice ice cream is only one of the luxurious desserts featured.

Rated as one of the "Best New Restaurants of 1987" by both *U.S.A. Today* and *Esquire,* Citrus will delight you in many ways. Frequented by such famous personalities as Joan Collins, Robin Williams, and Mel Gibson, Citrus is one of the hottest restaurants that California and the Los Angeles area has to offer. For an unforgettable dining experience, make the "Best Choice," make it Citrus.

CITY
180 South La Brea Avenue
Los Angeles, CA 90036
Tel. (213) 938-2155
Hrs: Mon. - Sat.   11:45 a.m. - 11:45 p.m.
          Sunday   5:00 p.m. - 11:00 p.m.
Visa, MasterCard and AMEX are accepted.

Los Angeles Times restaurant reviewer, Ruth Reichl, writes of City, "a small cafe grows up and goes to town!" City is a success story of two very talented chefs, Mary Sue Milliken and Susan Feniger. They are two of L.A.'s most exciting and innovative chefs, respected by their peers and revered by their clientele. Together they have created more than a restaurant.

When they cook and serve their eclectic menu in their startling new restaurant it can only be described as a "happening." You may enjoy such dishes as Roasted Sweet Pepper or Poona Pancake as an appetizer; Roast Black Cod with horseradish and lime or Marinated Tandoori Steak. Desserts are a City specialty. Dazzle your palate with an old fashioned Bread Pudding; Black Velvet, a rich chocolate torte with crumbled almonds and scotch; or Lemon Hazelnut Meringue.

While other chefs attempt to put a personalized stamp on their food, Milliken and Feniger are almost radical in their traditionalism. They almost make a religion of studying other culture's food; they travel to a country, learn about its food and return home to prepare it in a most straightforward manner, as close to original methods as possible.

City has an excellent wine list (in the top ten in the city), a selection of fine cognac and a full bar. City To Go is a daily take out service and includes most of their regular menu dishes including fine desserts.

DAR MAGHREB
7651 Sunset Boulevard
Los Angeles, CA 90046
Tel. (213) 876-7651
Hrs: Mon. - Fri.   6:00 p.m. - 11:00 p.m.
         Saturday   5:30 p.m. - 11:00 p.m.
         Sunday   5:30 p.m. - 10:30 p.m.
Visa and MasterCard are accepted.

The lure and romance of Morocco, the thrill and excitement of Ali Baba and his forty thieves and the exotic mystery of provocative belly dancers can be yours in addition to an irreproachable evening of dining pleasure at Dar Maghreb. Dar Maghreb has recreated the splendor of the Alhambra of Granada, which includes the spectacular Moorish columns lining the patio as well as the decorative floors of serpentine and Carrara marble.

Feast in either of the Berber rooms, resplendent in warm tones of brown, orange, beige and gold. Recline among pillows and cushions while being served on huge round brass trays on low wrought iron bases. Or choose one of the Rabat Rooms, decorated in rich blues and golds. From the rugs to the fixtures, the utensils to the staff's costumes, everything is authentically Moroccan. Meals begin with either a spicy lentil soup or an appetizing salad of cooked and raw vegetables which may include zucchini, eggplant, green peppers, tomatoes and cucumber with coriander, cumin, olive oil and parsley and then followed by *b'stila*—a dish of chicken, almonds, eggs and spices wrapped in exceptional thin pastry, served hot and sprinkled with powdered sugar and cinnamon. Your main meal consists of a variety of meat dishes which may include lamb, pigeon, chicken, quail, shrimp, rabbit or beef, each delightfully prepared.

Enjoy the exotic splendor of Moroccan architecture, feast upon a banquet fit for royalty, and enjoy the atmosphere and the many diversified customs of the Moroccan culture at Dar Maghreb—Your little bit of Morocco, located on Sunset Boulevard.

FRAGRANT VEGETABLE RESTAURANT
11859 Wilshire Boulevard
Los Angeles, CA 90025
Tel. (213) 312-1442
Hrs: Sun. - Thu.   11:30 a.m. - 10:00 p.m.
         Fri. - Sat.   11:30 a.m. - 11:00 p.m.
Visa, MasterCard and AMEX are accepted.
Also,
108-110 North Garfield
Monterey Park, CA 91754
Tel. (818) 280-4215

The tradition of vegetarianism in Chinese culture is rooted in the religious customs and beliefs of Buddhist monks. Over time, they became experts in the culinary skill of preparing vegetables in an endless assortment of entrees, both for themselves and for the ever demanding tastes of their emperors. At the Fragrant Vegetable Restaurant, owners S. T. Cheung and Julie Hau continue this tradition and add to it their own special creations.

Starting with the basic ingredients of bean curd and wheat gluten, the chef prepares dishes that only resemble shrimp, chicken, pork and beef. To this is added a variety of sea and land vegetables and the end result is a culinary delight for the most discerning tastes. Entrees include such impressive choices as Buddha's Cushions, layers of bean curd wrapped around mushrooms and other vegetables with spinach, black moss and black mushrooms, or Peking Ribs created from deep fried pecans, green peppers and pineapple chunks in sweet and sour sauce. Vegetarian Dim Sum is also offered. Many dishes are served with hand sculptured vegetables, adding an extra delight to already heightened senses.

Man may not live by bread alone, but rather by vegetables after one visit to the Fragrant Vegetable Restaurant. Exotic, adventuresome and savory are only a few of the words that will describe your dining pleasure.

HOP LI
526 Alpine Street
Los Angeles, CA 90032
Tel. (213) 680-3939
Hrs: Mon. - Sun.   11:30 a.m. - 10:00 p.m.
Visa and MasterCard are accepted.

The floating restaurants of Aberdeen in Hong Kong serve dishes made from recipes centuries old. These venerable establishments have no fixed location and can only be reached by aquatic taxis. The inconvenience is immaterial because the food is unlike any to be found anywhere.

It was a dream of Hop Li owner Albert Eng to create foods reminiscent of that found in those premier floating restaurants. Offering an astounding assortment of Chinese meals, Hop Li comes as close as any restaurant ever will to that dream. Crab or oyster in ginger and green onions, twice cooked scallops, fat succulent shrimp so tender you can eat the shell and all, make up only the tip of this culinary iceberg. Shark's Fin Soup, Minced Squab with Bamboo Shoots and Lettuce, Sea Cucumber and Black Mushrooms with Duck Feet, steamed flounder served atop its batter cloaked and deep fried skeleton which is not only edible but incredible is still only the tip of the iceberg. A smooth, quite thick but not overly starchy black bean sauce bursting with fresh garlic is used on many of the dishes, and it will delight you.

Warm moist towels are presented after the meal as are fresh orange slices to refresh the palate. Food to go, banquet menus and special menu changes every month add to the appeal of this versatile restaurant. All the Hop Li restaurant lacks is the Hong Kong harbor as a backdrop.

HOT WINGS CAFE
7011 Melrose Avenue
Los Angeles, CA 90027
Tel. (213) 930-1233
Hrs: Mon. - Thu.   11:00 a.m. -12:00 midnight
       Fri. - Sat.   11:00 a.m. - 2:00 a.m.
       Sunday   5:00 p.m. - 12:00 midnight

East Coast delicacies such as Buffalo Chicken Wings, New York style skyscraper deli sandwiches, homemade soups and desserts are served in this high tech, spacious eatery located one half block east of La Brea, on Melrose Avenue. Hot Wings Cafe is a great place to go for a summer supper, midnight snack or to pick up a picnic lunch.

Hot Wings Cafe is always filled with people talking and munching on one of the many tasty treats prepared daily. It will be hard to decide which East Coast city you'll want to munch into! Choose the Hartford Grinder, Philly Cheese Steak, New York deli, or Boston fish and chips. Traditional burgers, Reuben and French dip sandwiches are available as well as fresh tuna, poultry and seafood salads. The specialty of the house is the Buffalo Style Chicken Wings, deep fried to a golden brown without batter; mild, hot and extra hot, accompanied by crispy celery sticks and homemade blue cheese dressing. An interesting selection of California wines and imported and domestic beers are available. Non-alcoholic beverages include assorted herbal teas, Espresso, Cappuccino and Cafe au lait. You'll be glad you saved room for dessert when you indulge in a bowl of rice pudding or Italian Gelato.

All the food is fresh, homemade, with a taste of the East Coast in every bite. The reasonable prices make this one of L.A.'s best bargains. They also do catering and will deliver large orders. For all the excitement of L.A., stroll down famous Melrose Avenue to fun and trendy Hot Wings Cafe.

IL PANINO, 250 South Grand Avenue, Los Angeles, CA. Tel. (213) 617-1844. This cafe is located in the Museum of Contemporary Art. Serving authentic Italian sandwiches on fresh crusty bread, antipasto, salads and soups, dining becomes a cultural experience.

THE IVY
113 North Robertson Boulevard
Los Angeles, CA 90048
Tel. (213) 274-8303
Hrs: Lunch   Mon. - Sat.   11:30 a.m. - 3:30 p.m.
         Dinner   Mon. - Sat.   6:00 p.m. - 11:00 p.m.
Visa, MasterCard, AMEX and Diners Club are accepted.

Friendly, casual service, attention to detail and simple, delicious food have made The Ivy a real find. This cozy restaurant, housed in an early California farmhouse, has been in business since 1980. The Ivy's great reputation with local diners and visitors alike is well deserved.

The decor is unpretentious and charming, creating the perfect atmosphere for fresh California cooking by Chef/Owner Richard Irving. The two inside dining rooms are decorated with eighteenth and nineteenth century American antiques and Navajo rugs. In addition, there is a rose garden and a front porch for outside dining. The menu offers a variety of appetizers, including fresh Corn Chowder, Louisiana Crabcakes, an unbeatable Caesar salad, the lettuce is grown in Irving's garden, fresh soft-shell crabs and spicy Santa Fe Chili. Dinner entrees feature homemade pasta, mesquite grilled meats and fresh fish. Popular choices include fresh barbecued Tuna, Black Pepper Shrimp, Abalone or Meat Loaf with whipped potatoes. Offerings from the Mesquite Grill include Lime Chicken, fresh Salmon or Swordfish, Louisiana Shrimp and Cajun Prime Rib.

The wine list is extensive and fairly priced. And the special Ivy drinks are made the old fashioned way—using only the freshest ingredients—no bar mixes here. All The Ivy's delicious desserts are baked on the premises daily as is the homemade bread. Coffee served in an oversized chocolate cup, available for sale next door at Indigo Seas, is ground fresh daily and brewed to order. 1920s and '30s dance band music fills the air and helps to make your dining experience at this "Best Choice" restaurant complete.

L'ERMITAGE
730 North La Cienega Boulevard
Los Angeles, CA 90069
Tel. (213) 652-5840
Hrs: Mon. - Fri.   6:30 p.m. - 10:00 p.m.
          Saturday   6:00 p.m. - 10:00 p.m.
Visa, MasterCard, AMEX and Diners Club are accepted.

People who know Los Angeles know the City of the Angels attracts the best of everything; the best clothes, the best cars, the best lifestyles. Los Angeles also sports some of the best restaurants, and L'Ermitage tops the list.

Credit the late restauranteur Jean Bertranou with bringing the finest of haute cuisine to Los Angeles in 1975 and creating L'Ermitage. And, credit present owners Dora and Jean-Pierre Fourcade with adding recent touches that bring an air of understated elegance to L'Ermitage. You'll relax by the woodburning fireplace in the front room and enjoy a cocktail on the patio by the fountain. Each of the professional staff members will serve you as if you were the only customer in the house. Order gourmet dishes from the menu featuring a French based, modern cuisine. For an appetizer, request the fresh salmon smoked right at L'Ermitage and served either sliced with capers or as Salmon Tartare. As an entree you might choose Fillet of St. Pierre, stuffed with fish mousse, served with potato scales and herbed butter. Try the Saddle of Rabbit filled with spinach and sweet garlic. Be sure to select one of their excellent wines to complement your meal.

The L'Ermitage chef, Michel Blanchet, never disappoints and continues to prove he is one of the great chefs of the day. You know Los Angeles attracts the best, and at L'Ermitage, you'll experience the best.

L'ORANGERIE
903 North La Cienega Boulevard
Los Angeles, CA 90069
Tel. (213) 652-9770
Hrs: Mon. - Sun. 6:30 p.m. - 11:00 p.m.
Visa, MasterCard and AMEX are accepted.

Many restaurants in Los Angeles have succumbed to the appeal of the mesquite grills or faddish notions about food, but not l'Orangerie. If you want classic French cuisine in an atmosphere of the elegant eighteenth century France, you must visit this extraordinary establishment.

Upon entering l'Orangerie, your heart and palate are prepared for a glorious eating experience. You'll be seated in a building guaranteed to remind you of the architecture at Versailles, with high, arched French windows. Sculptured orange trees and clipped hedges create the tone of a formal French garden. Relax amid fresh flowers and the music of Mozart as your waiter takes your order. Owners Gerard and Virginie Ferry offer cuisine that was chosen the number one favorite in the 1987 *ZAGAT L.A. Restaurant Survey*. For an appetizer, sample the home smoked salmon or a salad with poached eggs and hot bacon bits. Check the daily special for an entree, or choose the farm raised Squab with Foie Gras. Try the Filet of Lamb Tenderloin served with meat juices and blue cheese. For dessert, ask for the Chocolate Coffee Cake with espresso sauce.

From the fragrance of the delicious cuisine to the light and airy atmosphere of the decor, l'Orangerie is one of the finest restaurants in the Los Angeles area.

L.A. TRATTORIA
8022 West 3rd Street
Los Angeles, CA 90048
Tel. (213) 658-7607
Hrs: Lunch   Tue. - Fri.   11:30 a.m. - 2:30 p.m.
      Dinner   Tue. - Fri.   5:30 p.m. - 10:30 p.m.
                 Sat. - Sun.   5:30 p.m. - 12:00 midnight
Visa, MasterCard, AMEX and Discover are accepted.

At L.A. Trattoria you'll experience everything an authentic trattoria is expected to be. An ambiance of quiet charm and simplicity prevails to create a haven for casual dining away from the hustle and bustle of everyday life. Subdued lighting, large mirrors appointed throughout the room and tables draped in white linen accord the perfect setting for the focal point of your dining experience.

L.A. Trattoria specializes in cuisine that is predominantly from Northern and Southern Italy. Marvelous Antipasti selections include Cassuloa di Melenzane alla Parmigiana, an eggplant parmigiana in a casserola; or Vongole e Cozze all Luciana, clams and mussels in a light tomato sauce. Fettuccine al Sugo d'Agnello, fettuccine in lamb sauce and Galletto allo Spiedo, broiled chicken in a lamb sauce are other house favorites. Specialties of the day include additional entrees, pastas and appetizers. Champagne, wine and beer are available to complement your entree. To top off your dining pleasure relax with a cup of espresso or cappuccino. Catering and banquet arrangements can be facilitated at L.A. Trattoria with the same Italian flair and excellence.

L.A. Trattoria has become a popular eatery for the young and artistic elite of Los Angeles. Rome, Naples and Florence have nothing up on L.A. Trattoria when it comes to zesty Italian cuisine!

LA BRUSCHETTA
1621 Westwood Boulevard
Los Angeles, CA 90024
Tel. (213) 477-1052
Hrs: Lunch
      Mon. - Fri.   12:00 noon - 2:00 p.m.
      Dinner
      Mon. - Sat.   6:00 p.m. - 10:30 p.m.
Visa, MasterCard, AMEX and Diners Club are accepted.

For an elegant experience in dining combined with classic Italian cuisine with contemporary overtones, try La Bruschetta. The food is magnificently created by a true Italian, Chef Pasqualato. One of the most highly respected Italian chefs in Los Angeles, his thirty years of experience bestow perfection upon his creations.

This attractive restaurant, tastefully decorated in hunter green carpeting, white table linens with green underlays, simple cane chairs, hexagonal white on white china and floor to ceiling wine racks, is complete with ficus tree and flowers on each table. Contemporary art on loan from the Landau Gallery decorates the walls and is rotated monthly.

Chef Pasqualato, a master with fresh fish and seafood, creates mouthwatering masterpieces with dishes like Gamberi Al Prosciutto E Brandy, shrimp wrapped with prosciutto ham in brandy sauce; and Spigola Al Cartoccio Con Gamberi E Limone Verde, a striped bass in papillote made with shrimp and lime. There are numerous daily appetizers, pasta and fresh fish specials and fresh seasonal game is available daily. The Antipasti lunch includes six items that change each day and which can be served as appetizers or a complete lunch. Other specialties include Mille Foglie Ri Carcioli E Crema, a puff pastry with baby artichokes and cream sauce; Nodino Di Vitello Ai Funghi E Fontina, veal T-bone with wild mushroom sauce and fontina cheese; and Pollo Alla Diavola, chicken complemented with a mustard rosemary sauce.

To accompany the perfect Italian meal, co-owner Edoardo Bucci, a highly respected wine expert, will help you choose from an extensive selection of wines from Italy and California. For those with discriminating tastes, this selection includes rare Italian wines seldom found in America. La Bruschetta is a stylish Italian restaurant without pretense, but with friendly, attentive and professional Italian service. This is a place that you know will be around for a long time.

LA CAJOLE
8555 Beverly Boulevard
Los Angeles, CA 90048
Tel. (213) 655-1991
Hrs: Mon. - Sun.   6:30 a.m. - 2:00 a.m.
Visa, MasterCard, AMEX and Diners Club are accepted.

Located in the heart of Los Angeles, La Cajole offers a variety of specialty foods with European, Asian and Mexican influences. Combining California casual with the excellence of European service, this contemporary restaurant has been patterned after the famous Paris brasserie La Coupole.

"Brasserie" comes from the French word *brasser*, which means "to brew." It now refers to unpretentious restaurants where the focus is on good food, beer and drinks; they often become popular gathering places. The French brasserie La Coupole received notoriety after it allowed emerging French artists to paint their creative works on columns within the restaurant in return for food. These budding artists included Picasso, Matisse and Cezanne. In the La Coupole tradition, La Cajole has recreated the style of these painters on the many columns that adorn the restaurant's interior. The eclectic menu is only surpassed by the contagious spirit and fun of this brasserie, making it the ideal gathering place for L.A.'s spontaneous diners.

La Cajole is conveniently located in the Ma Maison Sofitel. Invite your friends to join you for a wonderful evening at this "Best Choice" for casual dining in the Los Angeles area.

LA GROTTE, 529 East Seaside Way, Los Angeles, CA. Tel. (213) 437-2119. A quaint French provincial decor is your setting for delightful Continental cuisine with a French flair. They're open for lunch and dinner.

LA PASTERIA
7212 Melrose Avenue
Los Angeles, CA 90046
Tel. (213) 934-7259
Hrs: Lunch   Mon. - Fri.   12:00 noon - 2:30 p.m.
      Dinner   Mon. - Sat.   6:00 p.m. - 11:30 p.m.
Visa, MasterCard and AMEX are accepted.

If you are looking for one of those lovely trattorias which abound in the South of France and Italy then a visit to La Pasteria will be the best choice you can make. Here in this relaxed country style setting, a blend of terra cotta and cornflower blue with white patio style furniture, you can choose to sit in the front courtyard overlooking Melrose Avenue or the patio at the rear which is the most inviting and most highly sought after. There, among plants and colorful flowers on balmy California evenings, you can sit under the rollback roof beneath the stars and enjoy hearty Italian cooking with a special French accent.

On being seated you are served a delicious appetizer called Panzanella, a pungent concoction of chopped tomatoes, basil, onions and fried croutons along with a basket of fresh steamed clams "in season." Then onto some of the finest freshly made pasta dishes you will taste on the West Coast. The Angel Hair Pasta with tomato sauce and fresh basil, Fusilli with broccoli, mushrooms, garlic and red pepper, or the Tagliatelli Capo Collo, peas, mushrooms, cream and cognac are all delicious. La Pasteria also presents a calorie counter menu so you can enjoy fine Italian cuisine for as little as 300 calories.

There is a choice selection of grilled poultry and fresh fish and, of course, the delicious desserts. Gilles Szumacher, the former manager of the Moustache Cafe is always on hand to greet you. It is due to his efforts of providing a friendly and relaxed atmosphere that clientele return again and again to enjoy the food and setting of La Pasteria.

LA SALSA
11075 West Pico Boulevard
Los Angeles, CA 90064
Tel. (213) 479-0919
Hrs: 7:00 a.m. - 12:00 midnight

La Salsa is one of the fastest growing Mexican restaurant chains in Southern California and that alone says something. If it wasn't good, it wouldn't be popular.

Owner Howard Kabrins eight years ago wanted cuisine which would reflect not only the Mexican countryside, but the cities and towns as well. The chefs who cook there are known as taqueros, and one of their traditional specialties is *Antonjitos Mexicans* which means "little cravings." You will also find a complete meal consisting of soft tacos, and two corn tortillas with chicken, skirt steak or pork. All meat is marinated in lime juice, garlic, and pepper, then charbroiled.

They're open almost all day and can be found in Prince Ranch Farmers Market, Fashion Island, Newport Beach; North County Fair, Escondido; Horton Plaza, San Diego; Little Santa Monica Boulevard, Beverly Hills; Roscoe and Sepulveda, Van Nuys; and Kinross Avenue, in Westwood Village. Look for another fine restaurant to open soon in Montebello and in Malibu. So for Mexican food that has become a legend from San Diego to Van Nuys, it's **La Salsa.**

LE CHARDONNAY
8284 Melrose Avenue
Los Angeles, CA 90046
Tel. (213) 655-8880
Hrs: Lunch   Mon. - Fri.   12:00 noon - 2:00 p.m.
          Dinner   Mon. - Thu.   6:00 p.m. - 10:00 p.m.
                            Fri. - Sat.   6:00 p.m. - 10:30 p.m.
All major credit cards are accepted.

When you're in the mood for a meal at an authentic French bistro you could catch the next flight to Paris or drop in to L.A.'s own Le Chardonnay. This classic French bistro offers a dining experience you'll not soon forget.

Modeled after a bistro in Paris, Vagenende on the Boulevard St. Germain, Le Chardonnay captures the ambiance of la belle epoque Paris in French art nouveau style with distinctive carved wood molding, gleaming brass and rich, dark wood paneling, and like any good Paris bistro, there is an abundance of mirrors and glass throughout the restaurant. The menu is a singular combination of French bistro and California Nouvelle. The extensive appetizer menu includes delicious steamed New Zealand mussels with Dijon mustard, white wine, shallots and chives, and a savory ravioli stuffed with Sonoma goat cheese and herbs with sage sauce. For an entree the chef recommends the Medallions of Venison sauteed with black peppercorns and served with celery root fritters and Armagnac pepper sauce, or Grilled Dover Sole with Italian parsley butter sauce and tomato. There are also classic bistro dishes such as roast chicken on the spit with pommes frites, bouillabaisse with rouille and garlic croutons, veal kidneys and sauerkraut with smoked fish. For dessert the Profiterolles with warm chocolate sauce and the white and dark chocolate mousse cake with black currant coulis come highly recommended. There is a large wine list which includes forty-five different California Chardonnays.

A beautifully romantic, turn of the century bistro, you'll feel like you have been transported to Paris the moment you walk through the door. The food, the service and the atmosphere of Le Chardonnay combine to create a dining experience you'll want to relive again and again.

LE DOME RESTAURANT
8720 Sunset Boulevard
Los Angeles, CA 90069
Tel.　(213) 659-691
　　　(213) 659-6918
Hrs:　Lunch　　　Mon. - Fri.　12:00 noon - 6:00 p.m.
　　　Dinner　　　Mon. - Sat.　6:00 p.m. - 12:00 midnight
Visa, MasterCard and AMEX are accepted.
Reservations are necessary.

Much of Le Dome Restaurant's clientele hails from the recording industry and other bastions of the performing arts. They visit Le Dome for the best cuisine this side of Paris. Owners Michel Yhuelo and Eddie Kerkhoff have put together a menu that's eighty percent French, twenty percent continental and 100 percent delectable.

You may take lunch or dinner in an atmosphere of elegant chic while people watching in the huge lounge or power lunching in the dining room. Begin your meal with an appetizer of Veal Tortellini with red bell pepper, basil and Madeira sauce; a fresh fish soup served with *rouille,* garlic croutons and Gruyere or an Escarole Salad with bacon and poached egg. An old fashioned lamb stew with carrots, turnips and pearl onions, Osso Bucco "Le Dome" style served with mixed rotelli or the fresh fish of the day steamed, poached or grilled are a few of the entree selections. Luscious desserts such as *creme brulee,* Chocolate Mousse served in an almond shell or a cheese plate are the perfect finish to a fine repast. The wine list features eighty percent French and twenty percent California wines.

Le Dome accommodates private parties of up to sixty people and provides valet parking. Be aware that this is the place to visit dressed to the nines; jackets are required for gentlemen and reservations are necessary. The original cuisine, excellent service and sophisticated atmosphere make Le Dome a "Best Choice" in Los Angeles.

LEW MITCHELL'S ORIENT EXPRESS
5400 Wilshire Boulevard Near La Brea
Los Angeles, CA 90036
Tel. (213) 935-6000
Hrs: Lunch   Mon. - Fri.   11:30 a.m. - 2:30 p.m.
         Dinner   Mon. - Sat.   5:30 p.m. - 10:00 p.m.
All major credit cards are accepted.

With seven years of top awards behind them, including being named *Restaurateur of the Year,* Lew and Louise Mitchell provide outstanding service in a truly beautiful and sophisticated setting. Original art and nautical artifacts adorn the four art deco dining rooms. Rich oriental carpets grace the floors and good use is made of mirrors.

Lew Mitchell's Orient Express, the only Four Star Chinese restaurant in Los Angeles, serves the finest Mandarin and Szechuan cuisine. The lunch menu offers a variety of imaginative dishes such as Beijing Beef Salad, Roast Duck on Rye and Singapore Omelettes. This is one of *the* places for power lunching in Los Angeles. Lew Mitchell's Orient Express provides the facilities for sales meetings. Fried Scallops with Szechuan Peppers, Hot Chili Shrimp in Lettuce Cup, a sizzling plate of Java Beef with Zucchini or spicy Bon Bon Chi, consisting of torn chicken, cucumber, *agar agar,* sesame bean paste and hot chili are just a few of the outstanding dishes served at dinner.

MSG is not used. Be sure to ask for the wine list; Lew Mitchell's has a Three Star wine cellar.

After dinner, in the lounge you may dance to the music of Alan Ascher on the piano. Reservations are suggested for this "Best Choice" in Los Angeles. Visit Lew Mitchell's Orient Express and "indulge in your choice of Mandarin or Szechuan style Chinese dishes meticulously prepared and served in an atmosphere of understated sophistication."

LOCANDA VENETA, 8638 West 3rd Street, Los Angeles, CA. Tel. (213) 274-1893. Here in "the countryside of Veneta," you can eat Northern Italian cuisine in Los Angeles. The simple, country style food is always freshly made and delicious.

MA MAISON
8555 Beverly Boulevard
Los Angeles, CA 90048
Tel. (213) 278-5444
Hrs: Mon. - Sat.   11:30 a.m. - 2:30 p.m.
                     5:30 p.m. - Closing
Visa, MasterCard, AMEX and Diners Club are accepted.
Reservations are recommended.

Patrick Terrail is once again the charismatic host to L.A.'s rich and famous. The creator of the original Ma Maison restaurant has joined with Accor Corporation to offer innovative French and Californian cuisine in the same distinctive manner as the original legendary restaurant that dominated the Los Angeles culinary scene for over a decade.

In a French Country Inn setting, Ma Maison offers artistic food presentations as pleasing to the eye as they are to the palete. They fit perfectly within the California lifestyle so easily enjoyed in the Atrium setting. The cuisine changes daily to take advantage of the great diversity available at the California markets. Enjoy many of the original Ma Maison recipes that still prevail, such as the Ma Maison Chicken Salad.

This superb restaurant is centrally located adjacent to the Ma Maison Sofitel in the center of Los Angeles. Make reservations today and enjoy this "Best Choice" in Los Angeles fine dining.

MANDARIN COVE, 8500 Beverly Boulevard, Los Angeles, CA Tel. (213) 652-3742. Located at the top of the Beverly Center, in this restaurant you'll find large display cases of fresh fish and lobsters and authentic Mandarin dishes.

MEL AND ROSE'S
7313 Melrose Avenue
Los Angeles, CA 90046
Tel. (213) 930-0256
Hrs: Sun. - Thu.   8:00 a.m. - 1:00 a.m.
          Fri. - Sat.   open late.
Visa and MasterCard on purchases over ten dollars are accepted.

Rose Cohen was serving her famous cinnamon apple cobbler at the Newport News Canteen in 1944 when her soon to be husband Mel was a mess cook aboard the *U.S.S. New Jersey. I'll be Seeing You* wafted from the canteen's loudspeaker as Mel took a bite of Rose's cobbler. Mel looked into Rose's eyes and said the three little words that changed their lives, "this is delicious." When they married, Rose catered her own reception and Mel vowed to someday open a restaurant so the whole world could share Rose's cinnamon apple cobbler.

Today Mel and Rose's on Melrose street is a roaring success. It's always crowded with people from all walks of life: rock stars, the rich, the poor, the famous and the infamous. Rose's cinnamon apple cobbler has expanded into a three page menu which includes several Rose and Mel recipe combinations. Listed as "L.A.'s favorite" is Mel's Bombardier Chili, allegedly containing ten bottles of dark beer in each batch. Mel claims, there are eight bottles in the chili and two in the cook! Mel's Worldly Burgers and Melts are also popular. Choose a Bootcamp burger or a Champs Elysee Burger, Rose's romantic favorite.

Shaped like an old fashioned diner, long and narrow with counter seats on swivels, Mel and Rose's is the place to people watch and enjoy a good old fashioned 1940's style meal.

MILLE GRAZIE RISTORANTE, 7699 Melrose Avenue, Los Angeles, CA. Tel. (213) 653-2739. Mille Grazie is a unique ristorante featuring fish, pasta and specialties from Naples.

MIRIWA DIEM SUM AND SEAFOOD RESTAURANT
747 North Broadway
Los Angeles, CA 90012
Tel. (213) 687-3088
Hrs: Lunch   Mon. - Sun.   9:00 a.m. - 3:00 p.m.
          Dinner   Mon. - Sun.   5:00 p.m. - 9:30 p.m.
Visa, MasterCard, AMEX and Diners Club are accepted.

Miriwa Diem Sum and Seafood Restaurant is an elegant and unexpected dining adventure. The Miriwa is exciting from the surprising entrance to the excellent Cantonese cuisine. An amazing eighteen foot waterfall greets you at Miriwa's entrance. As you ascend by elevator or stairs to the next landing, you are transported into another world. Fabulous imported Chinese decor will surround you. Rich marble is everywhere. Bubbling cool water aquariums full of live seafood accentuate the unusual. Background music is contemporary Chinese.

Lunch hour diners will be treated to the Cantonese treat of *diem sum*. More than 100 different Diem Sum items are served to guests from rolling carts. The cocktail lounge features exotic island drinks such as Lost Cargo and Rickshaw. The dinner menu is true Cantonese with entrees such as Scallops with Black Bean Sauce, Minced Squab with Lettuce, Sizzling Steak and Sweet and Sour Fish. "Clay Pot" specialties tempt the adventurous diner with Brisket of Beef with White Radish in Clay Pot or Bean Cake with Eight Precious in Clay Pot. Finish your meal with a dessert of Sweet Chilled Lychee or Sweet Bird's Nest Broth.

Miriwa, meaning beautiful and elegant, truly lives up to its name. Miriwa has been delighting visitors and residents of Los Angeles for over ten years. Try exciting dining at Miriwa Diem Sum and Seafood Restaurant next time you visit Chinatown.

PACIFIC DINING CAR, 1310 West 6th Street, Los Angeles, CA. Tel. (213) 483-6000. For close to fifty years this great steak house has been providing downtown Los Angeles with classic grilled meats, excellent wines and sumptuous private dining car decor and service.

THE PANDA INN RESTAURANT
10800 West Pico Boulevard (197)
Los Angeles, CA 90064
Tel. (213) 470-7790
Hrs: Mon. - Sun.   11:30 a.m. - 10:30 p.m.
Visa, MasterCard and AMEX are accepted.
Also,

3488 East Foothill Boulevard	102 Santa Monica Place
Pasadena, CA 91107	Santa Monica, CA 90401
Tel. (213) 681-2700	Tel. (213) 393-6447

111 East Wilson Avenue
Glendale, CA 91206
Tel. (818) 502-1234

Here is Mandarin and Szechuan Chinese cuisine at its most delectable. Its relaxing decor with tasteful displays, a helpful staff and consistent quality ensure a fine dining experience, time after time.

The comprehensive menu is traditional and yet innovative with many items unique to The Panda Inn. Traditional dishes such as Shrimp in Garlic Sauce, Spicy Chicken with Peanuts or Chicken Salad are brought to new heights with refined sauces. The unique Panda Beef with its tangy tangerine sauce, and the crisp Sweet and Pungent Shrimp which literally melts in your mouth, are the new taste sensations.

The Panda Inn also offers a complete catering service, plenty of free parking and, with four restaurants serving the greater Los Angeles area, it is also among the most convenient and certainly the most popular restaurants. That's the Panda Inn, where tradition lingers and the food is sublime.

PASTA ETCETERA
8650 Sunset Boulevard
Los Angeles, CA 90069
Tel. (213) 854-0094
Hrs: Mon. - Sat.   9:00 a.m. - 10:00 p.m.
Visa, MasterCard and AMEX are accepted.

Opened eight years ago as Pasta Pasta Pasta, Pasta Etcetera was the first to cater to the "food to go" crowd, providing some of the best pasta dishes in Southern California. When the demand grew for the store's multitude of pasta delicacies, owner Jon Gould decided to open a restaurant. His was the first outside dining restaurant on Sunset Boulevard and the first to offer gourmet take-out service. Customers proclaimed his establishment first class.

One glance at Pasta Etcetera's take-out menu and you'll see why. Try the Ravioli, the Pasta Primavera, the Pasta Romano or the Caprino, spinach linguini, Montrachet goat cheese and *enoke* mushrooms served in a garlic olive oil dressing. You may sample the unusual and delicious Szechuan Tortellini, veal filled tortellini in Szechuan sauce, and pasta is not all, ask for the Polo Agrodolce, sauteed chicken breast pieces, roasted red peppers, capers and olives in a slightly sweet and sour dressing, or the Corn Battered Red Snapper in a fresh salsa. If you want to create your own meal, order sauces such as Bolognese, Pesto or Ragu to take home in a pint container.

If you like, Pasta Etcetera will cater your business breakfast, lunch, tea or dinner needs. Their catering services range from full service party planning to delivery of any of their forty dishes on beautifully decorated disposable platters. Pasta Etcetera also offers fabulous gift baskets and outdoor dining. Californians love a first, and Pasta Etcetera tops the list.

PATOUT'S
2260 Westwood Boulevard
Los Angeles, CA 90064
Tel. (213) 475-7100
Hrs: Lunch   Mon. - Fri.   11:30 a.m. - 2:30 p.m.
      Dinner   Mon. - Thu.   6:00 p.m. - 10:00 p.m.
                    Fri. - Sat.   6:00 p.m. - 11:00 p.m.
      Sunday Brunch   11:30 a.m. - 2:30 p.m.
Visa, MasterCard, AMEX and Diners Club are accepted.

If you enjoy Cajun food and can't break away for a quick trip to Louisiana, or if you're from Louisiana and are homesick for some down home cooking, then Patout's is the place for you. The Patouts are a family of authentic Cajun chefs from New Iberia, Louisiana. They have all won gold medals and Best of Show awards at Louisiana culinary shows for their original creations.

They serve delectable cuisine in a restaurant with a marked Southern atmosphere right down to the Spanish moss hanging over the front of the building. They begin with a lush harvest of fresh local seafood and create such delicacies as Oysters Gigi, which are stuffed oysters, chicken and sausage gumbo. The lunch and dinner menus change daily. Lunchtime offers five to six appetizers, three salads and seven entrees to choose from. Dinners include their special signature dishes.

Don't forget dessert. No one can tickle a sweet tooth like a southern cook. There are all sorts of tempting pleasures like sweet potato-pecan pie, Key Lime pie and bread pudding with a whiskey caramel sauce. For a totally unique dining experience from beginning to end, Patout's will offer you a delectable odyssey.

PERINO'S
4101 Wilshire Boulevard
Los Angeles, CA 90010
Tel. (213) 487-0000
Hrs: Lunch   Mon. - Fri.   12:00 noon - 2:30 p.m.
        Dinner   Mon. - Fri.   6:00 p.m. - 10:00 p.m.
                        Saturday   6:00 p.m. - 11:00 p.m.
All major credit cards are accepted.

Live chamber music in the dining room sets the overall tone of Perino's and reflects its love of tradition and standing as a landmark in the Hollywood community. But the jazz in the Oakroom Bar at Perino's signals its new desire to attract young clients.

Perino's has been a Wilshire Boulevard fixture since 1932. Taking note of its success, the restaurant moved to its present location in 1950. The premises include a large entrance hall, a piano bar called the Oakroom Bar, a dining room, and two banquet rooms. The dining areas are excellent for an intimate evening with loved ones. Perino's cuisine rates among the top for tastiness and value, which is proved by the steady stream of celebrities who have frequented the restaurant. The banquet manager, a thirty year veteran, recalls when Frank Sinatra, Charlton Heston, George Burns, Vincent Price, and Groucho Marx used to come by. Bing Crosby and his family came to Perino's for Christmas dinner. When the present management took over the restaurant in 1986, they kept the classic dishes of Perino's, but made the menu primarily Northern Italian. All ingredients are imported, and all selections, except bread, are made on the premises. Some of the favorite selections include Crespelle alla Florentina, crepes stuffed with ricotta cheese, spinach and béchemal and topped with meat sauce. Another favorite is Rondelle di Radicchio, ravioli filled with radicchio lettuce in mascarpone sauce.

In the near future, Perino's plans to expand on the live piano music during dining hours and may feature a singer and a band that will appeal to contemporary musical tastes. Both the past and the present make Perino's a must on anyone's gourmet itinerary.

PINAFINI
8612 Beverly Boulevard
Los Angeles, CA 90048
Tel. (213) 854-3039
Hrs: Mon. - Sat.   11:20 a.m. - 2:00 a.m.
      Sunday   5:30 p.m. - 2:00 a.m.
Visa, MasterCard and AMEX are accepted.

Don't be surprised if you recognize this restaurant as one featured on your favorite TV show. Situated in the heart of Los Angeles on the ground floor of the Beverly Center, Pinafini has become a hot spot for television and location productions. The prevailing style is high-tech; expanses of white walls and white tiles accented in pink and blue neon, the center bar towards the front of the restaurant and large glass paned windows create an ambiance similar to a New York loft.

Menu selections are predominantly Northern Italian. Begin your dining experience with an appetizer of Mozzarella Fritti, mozzarella cheese crisply fried with marinated sauce; or Insalata Coi Salpicon Padovon, a mixed salad of radicchio, lettuce, tomato and cucumber served with the house dressing. The leading entree inspirations include Cappelini all Checca, angel hair with fresh tomato, basil and garlic; and Rafioleti Coi Zucchini, ravioli stuffed with ricotta cheese and spinach, sauteed with a creamy zucchini sauce. Another favorite is Polastro Con Salsa Di Funghi, grilled breast of chicken marinated with aromatic herbs. Each entree is complemented with a delicious pocket of freshly baked herb bread. A wonderful selection of champagnes, Italian and California wines are available.

Pinafini is becoming "the happening place" for the "in crowd" in Los Angeles. This is an ideal locale for Cappuccino in the late afternoon, happy hour and an evening of scintillating dining and entertainment.

PRIMI
10543 West Pico Boulevard
Los Angeles, CA 90064
Tel. (213) 475-9335
Hrs: Lunch   Mon. - Sat.   11:30 a.m. - 2:30 p.m.
          Dinner   Mon. - Sat.   5:30 p.m. - 11:30 p.m.
                            Sunday   5:00 p.m. - 11:30 p.m.
Visa, MasterCard, AMEX and Diners Club are accepted.

Novice gourmets willing to try unusual foods but at the same time unsure of some of the strange ingredients, often want to sample a little bit of this or a little bit of that. Diners in this frame of mind might like to stop in at a restaurant called Primi, short for *primi piatti*, or "first plates."

First timers will find the menu at Primi suited just for them. As they wait for service, they can get a taste of the restaurant's sleek Italian design, with its clean lines and high ceilings. Perhaps you'll sit in the enclosed patio suitable for dining in all weather conditions. When your waiter arrives, ask him for a dish of cold antipasti featuring Green Calamari Stuffed with Shrimps and Basil, and served with salsa. Or sample Minced, Marinated Duckling wrapped in spinach with vinaigrette. Salad lovers might like the Warm Chicken Salad with fresh greens topped with a Gorgonzola Cheese Sauce. Those interested in trying pasta might like Fettuccine Carbonara with Pancetta, eggs and asparagus. Or sample the Gnocchi with a Ragu of Lamb. Primi features an extensive menu of Risotti; Risotto Verde with Green Vegetables, Risotto with Quails in a sauce of cream and butter, and Risotto with Radicchio and Gorgonzola, to name just a few.

For dessert, pick from among warm Pear Tarts with Grand Marnier sauce, or Tirami Su, lady fingers in chocolate, Amaretto and Zabaglione. After trying all these favorites at Primi, the novice gourmet will soon become an expert on Italian food.

RACERS CAFE
359 North La Cienega Boulevard
Los Angeles, CA 90048
Tel: (213) 652-8896
Hrs: Mon. - Sat.   11:00 a.m. - 10:00 p.m.
Some credit cards are accepted.

Some people are content to merely keep up with the vogue in eating trends while others are on the leading edge of creating them. Racers Cafe has created an eclectic selection of natural, vegetarian cuisine that will delight even the most discerning of palates.

Racers Cafe features a blend of Italian and Mexican flavors in their vegetarian dishes. The adventurous will be delighted with the multitude of combination platters. Naturally blended with herbs and spices, each has its own exotic taste. A sampling includes Ocean Blend, imported jackfruit mixed with bell peppers, seaweed, and lemon juice; King Chi Blossom, a melange of imported banana blossoms, mixed bell peppers, celery and lemon juice; and Vita Green, a medley of spinach, cabbage, chard, fresh mint and green onions mixed with avocado. Mexican vegetarian entrees include a variety of enchiladas, tacos, flautas and tostadas. Natural fruit pies are beyond definition, but among the best are blackberry peach, mango blueberry, and Indian banana raspberry. No sugars, salts or preservatives are used in the preparations of any of the selections.

For a refreshing change from traditional fare, come to Racers Cafe. Located on the busy shopping street of La Cienega, a large glass paned front provides for exciting and entertaining "people watching." Light and airy, appointed in pinks, blues and grays, with sculptured art form tables, the ambiance is one of California sophistication. Dining at Racers Cafe is a "Best Choice" for both the body and the soul.

REX IL RESTORANTE
617 South Olive
Los Angeles, CA 90014
Tel. (213) 627-2300
Hrs: Lunch   Mon. - Fri.   12:00 noon - 2:00 p.m.
       Dinner   Mon. - Sat.   7:00 p.m. - 10:00 p.m.
Visa, MasterCard, AMEX and Diners Club are accepted.

Not even in Italy can you find Italian food like this served in such an elegant atmosphere. Owner Mauro Vincenti went all out when he combined the culinary expertise of chef Vito Gnazzo with the one of a kind location of this unique dining establishment.

Rex is located in one of the most extraordinary thirties art deco buildings in Los Angeles, the newly refurbished Oviatt Building. You can picture the likes of Bogart and Bacall having a smoke against the backdrop of Lalique glass, massive thirty foot pillars and finely veneered walls. The restaurant is named after a famous Italian luxury liner; the interior reflects the image of luxury liners of the 1930s. The exciting menu features the cuisine of *nuova cucina* or new Italian cooking. The emphasis is on fresh ingredients, elegantly yet simply prepared. Featured appetizers such as pheasant salad or Arlecchino Tagliolini, white, green, red and yellow pasta tossed in butter and sage, or Ravioli stuffed with game can be enjoyed with one of the fine Italian, French or California wines. Favorite entrees include baby salmon in shrimp sauce, fricassee of fish, filet of lamb tenderloin sliced and napped with red wine and lamb stock sauce and fennel au gratin and other finely prepared choices. After dinner, save room for an exquisite dessert of pistachio pie or soft Gianduja ice cream. Your choice of superb cognacs, vintage ports dating back to 1945, or grappa can be sipped while enjoying a live jazz band. Dance the night away on the exquisite black marble dance floor.

I'll bet even Al Capone and Elliott Ness could find cause for celebration if they met in the congenial atmosphere of Rex. Tell your pisanos about the most unique Italian restaurant in town, the best since they left the old country.

ROSALIE'S AT 385
385 North La Cienega Boulevard
Los Angeles, CA 90048
Tel. (213) 657-3850
Hrs: Lunch
        Mon. - Sun. 11:30 a.m. - 2:30 p.m.
        Dinner
        Mon. - Thu. 6:00 p.m. - 10:30 p.m.
        Fri. - Sat.   6:00 p.m. - 11:30 p.m.
        Sunday   5:30 p.m. - 10:30 p.m.
All major credit cards are accepted.

When deciding where to dine, you usually are forced to pick a cuisine, not a restaurant. Fortunately, you have been saved from such choices by Rosalie's at 385. This superb restaurant serves

Southwestern, French, Southern American and Italian dishes. The appealing and interesting food is savory, and dining in the comfortable, airy restaurant is quite a pleasant experience. The service is informal and the black turtleneck clad servers offer professional and attentive service. Large tables are spaced comfortably apart, making conversation in normal tones possible.

Rosalie's at 385 was opened in 1987 by the owners of the well known Rosalie's in San Francisco. Spurred on by the success in San Francisco, they opened this restaurant with the goal of offering something for everyone in a relaxed and attractive setting. The high sloping ceilings, salmon colored decor and Japanese pieces of art accentuate this spacious restaurant. With inside seating for 200 and a patio that seats seventy, you rarely have to wait too long for a table. Rosalie's also offers a banquet room for private parties.

If you are in for a quick luncheon, the creamy Asparagus Soup will satisfy the need to eat quickly, but with style and taste. Or if salads are more your style, the Caesar salad is exquisite. Start your dinner with appetizers such as the Crab Capellini Balls with jicama and yellow peppers, or Prawn Tamale with cilantro oregano butter. Among the many entrees to choose from, a few favorites are the Grilled Rabbit wrapped in pancetta with prickly pear and orange glaze served with grilled fennel; the Filet of Beef with grilled vegetables in red wine sauce; and Fresh Corncakes with shredded chicken, salsa, creme fraiche and a fried banana. If you're still hungry, a fresh fruit crisp with cream or a chocolate indiscretion will finish any meal with zing. To accompany Rosalie's delicious menu is an extensive and varied wine list that is discriminating enough for anyone's taste.

The piano bar, which is open Tuesday through Saturday, offers a great place to entertain or to be entertained. Rosalie's is a great place for a party, celebration, or meeting of any kind. Rosalie's at 385 is a very interesting and chic place to eat. The ambiance, decor and service abounds with style and the food is delicious. Rosalie's at 385 is a must visit for anyone visiting L.A.

SARNO'S CAFFÉ DELL'OPERA
1714 North Vermont
Los Angeles, CA 90027
Tel. (213) 662-3403
Hrs: Sun. - Thu.   11:00 a.m. - 11:00 p.m.
       Fri. - Sat.   11:00 a.m. - 1:00 a.m.
Visa, MasterCard and AMEX are accepted.

Situated in the heart of L.A.'s studio district, you'll find the fun, the music and the exquisite food of old Italy at Sarno's Caffé Dell'Opera. Sarno's is a happy, fun filled family restaurant where the film industry's famous drop in from time to time to enjoy the superb food and high spirited entertainment.

The music and laughter of the opera are to be found every night at this Los Angeles landmark. Typically Italian, the atmosphere is very informal with lots of noise and cheer. People come from far and near to join in the singing and merriment, but that is not the only reason people return to Sarno's again and again; the food is outstanding. From Pizza alla Napoletana to the complete Italian Dinners, everything on the menu is made with tender loving care. For your dining enjoyment, the chef recommends the Chicken alla Cacciatora or the Mozzarella in Carozza. Both are favorites of the local studio people. For a change of pace, try one of Sarno's fantastic Pasta al Dente dinners such as Broccoletti al Pesto, Rigatoni or Mostaccioli, all made with fresh sweet butter, imported olive oil, fresh eggs and milk. Be sure to ask to see the wine list. It features some of the best Italian wine to be found west of Naples.

From the lovely stained glass windows depicting great moments in opera to the fast, courteous service, everything at Sarno's Caffé Dell'Opera is designed to please and delight the customers. Stop in, sample their fine food and unrivaled entertainment, and who knows, you might just catch a glimpse of the stars.

SEVENTH STREET BISTRO
815 West 7th Street
Los Angeles, CA 90017
Tel. (213) 627-1242
Hrs: Lunch   Mon. - Fri.   11:30 a.m. - 2:00 p.m.
         Dinner   Mon. - Fri.   6:00 p.m. - 10:00 p.m.
         Dinner   Sat. - Sun.   5:30 p.m. - 10:00 p.m.
Visa, MasterCard, AMEX and Diners Club are accepted.

Seventh Street Bistro, a lively and elegant restaurant in downtown Los Angeles, owes its historic framework and ambiance to a bank. The Bank of America occupied the ground floor of the Fine Arts Building from 1931 on. During renovation of the building portions of the bank's elaborate decor were woven into the design for the bistro. The result is a rich and sophisticated architectural setting for a successful and celebrated restaurant.

A young French Chef, Laurent Quenioux, is the greater part of Seventh Street Bistro's success. Chef Quenioux turns out finely crafted works of art that disappear in minutes, but require years of practice to make. Quenioux draws on his knowledge of the classic repertory in interesting ways. He sometimes brings back forgotten dishes such as Lobster a l'Americaine or Cassoulet. The latter becomes lighter and more appealing to Southern Californian tastes by cooking all the ingredients separately rather than together. Often, Quenioux uses little used ingredients that were once taken for granted.

The Chef creates a new menu weekly and a few dishes change daily. The diner may notice that there are fifteen desserts and only ten entrees. Quenioux, who graduated in pastry at Maxim's loves *pastillage*, the art of architectural confectionery. His sweets are works of art. Consider a puff pastry filled with warm, cinnamon spiced apples or a raspberry studded lemon custard with a sparkling orange sauce or a silky chocolate and hazelnut terrine in a pool of mocha sauce. Seventh Street Bistro is a strikingly handsome restaurant with wildly delicious food.

SIAM ORCHID
8500 Beverly Boulevard, Top Floor
Los Angeles, CA 90048
Tel. (213) 652-6000
Hrs: Mon. - Sun. 11:30 a.m. - 10:00 p.m.
       Buffet   Mon. - Sun. 11:30 a.m. - 3:30 p.m.
Visa, MasterCard and AMEX are accepted.

In 1982, well known financier, Sasima Srivikorn perceived a scarcity of restaurants which catered to Thai cuisine in the Los Angeles area. As a resident of Bangkok, she decided to fulfill that need by establishing a restaurant which would serve native Thai cuisine in a world class atmosphere. Supervising every step of the construction, Siam Orchid is the result of her creative vision.

One hundred and forty Thai lanterns provide sparkle to an already charged atmosphere, and eight hand painted teak panels depicting the various Thai holidays, rituals, and ceremonies grace the walls of Siam Orchid. Over seventy-five menu selections are available for your dining pleasure, which includes Tom Yum Goong, a seafood dish with lime soup, sprinkled with Thai herbs; or Gam Poo Pad Prink, a crab claw fried with chili and black bean sauce. Curry dishes include such selections as Panang Nua, a beef dried curry; or Gang Garee Gai made of chicken curry served with cucumber dip; and a variety of chicken, beef, pork and seafood entrees await your pleasure.

Seated in either Western or Asian style and surrounded by the splendors of Thailand, you will love discovering the rich and varied flavors that await you at Siam Orchid. Located at the Los Angeles Beverly Center, it has become one of the premier restaurants in the Los Angeles area and caters to travelers from across the country and around the world.

SOFI, 8030 1/2 West 3rd Street, Los Angeles, CA. Tel. (213) 651-0346. Sofi offers authentic home style Greek cuisine in a classic setting. At Sofi's you don't have to be a gyro to order one.

STEPPS RESTAURANT
Wells Fargo Center
350 South Hope Street
Los Angeles, CA 90017
Tel. (213) 626-0900
Hrs: Lunch
          Mon. - Fri.   11:00 a.m. - 3:00 p.m.
          Saturday   11:00 a.m. - 4:00 p.m.
          Appetizers in the bar
          Mon. - Fri.   3:00 p.m. - 5:00 p.m.
          Dinner
          Mon. - Fri.   5:00 p.m. - 10:30 p.m.
          Saturday   4:00 p.m. - 10:30 p.m.
          Sunday   4:00 p.m. - 9:30 p.m.
          Bar open until 11:30 p.m.
Visa, MasterCard and AMEX are accepted.

At Stepps Restaurant in the Wells Fargo Center you can try beers chosen by world beer authority Michael Jackson while enjoying the contemporary atmosphere, fresh seafood, premium meats and homemade pasta.

Los Angelenos come from all over the L.A. area to sample starters such as Fresh Oysters on the Half Shell, which are shucked to order, and peruse the extensive beer and wine lists. Diners should consult the day's Fresh List to see what region the day's oysters came from. Other appetizers include Coconut Beer Shrimp with Cajun Marmalade. Seafood dishes include fresh King or Silver salmon available throughout the year. Meat is especially good at Stepps, as the beef is Certified Nebraska Select and is custom inspected for marbling and tenderness. Only Mexican mesquite charcoal is used for grilling. Meat dishes include Grilled Lamb with a fresh herb crust. Stepps menu offers tasty desserts, including fresh Lemon Mousse and Chocolate Truffle Pie.

Stepps is also available for private parties, offers catering and box lunch programs, valet parking and has a shuttle that runs to and from the Music Center. When visiting the downtown Los Angeles area and such sights as the Museum of Contemporary Art, the Music Center or the Los Angeles Theatre Center, visit this "Best Choice."

TAIX FRENCH RESTAURANT
1911 Sunset Boulevard
Los Angeles, CA 90026
Tel. (213) 484-1265
Hrs: Mon. - Sat.   11:00 a.m. - 10:00 p.m.
          Sunday   11:00 a.m. - 9:00 p.m.
Visa, MasterCard and AMEX are accepted.

Taix French Restaurant recently celebrated sixty years and three generations of exquisite French *cuisine provençale*. It is known for its authentic country French food, generous portions, and daily specials at moderate prices.

The luncheon menu features an assortment of fresh fish, beef dishes and pasta, as well as chef specials. Complete dinners are served with a choice of soup and salad, vegetable and potato, and sherbet. An array of á la carte items for the lighter eater or to accent your meal include Escargots, Pâte, Hearts of Palm and salads. For a fine French country meal enjoy a choice of a variety of fish and seafood as well as meat dishes: Shepard's Pie, Short Ribs Provencale and New York Cut Steak. A different specialty entree is featured every day of the week. Wednesday's highlight is Vol au Vent. It would be well worth the visit just to sample their wines from their famous, resonably priced cellar.

The tradition of serving fine French fare continues with either regular or banquet dining. Be sure to ask the catering or banquet managers about holding larger parties for twenty to 180, or for special events.

THE TAM O'SHANTER INN
2980 Los Feliz Boulevard
Los Angeles, CA 90039
Tel.   (213) 664-0228
          (213) 664-4024
Hrs: Lunch   Mon. - Fri.   11:00 a.m. - 3:00 p.m.
          Dinner   Mon. - Thu.   5:00 p.m. - 10:00 p.m.
                              Fri. - Sat.   5:00 p.m. - 11:00 p.m.
                              Sunday   4:00 p.m. - 10:00 p.m.
Visa, MasterCard, AMEX and Diners Club are accepted.

If you enjoy the charm of the Scotch, The Tam O'Shanter Inn is the place for you. This fine old family style pub has been at the same location longer than any restaurant in Los Angeles and under the same management for sixty-five years. People keep coming back for the fine food, drink, and good cheer.

If you take a walk past The Tam O'Shanter Inn, the cozy atmosphere of the four fireplaces and friendly faces will beckon you to enter. Once inside, you won't want to leave. The cuisine is classic American and English. The specialty of the house is four different cuts of prime rib served with a whipped horseradish sauce. You'll think you're in England when you taste the likes of the Toad in the Hole, a dish of Yorkshire pudding filled with filet mignon, onion, bell pepper and burgundy brown sauce. Other favorites include Spit Roasted Duckling, five daily specials, and for you fish lovers, Fishmonger Salad with crab, scallops and Bay shrimp. Save room for dessert; choose from daily special souffles, including Chocolate Grand Mariner, trifle, bread pudding and more. Bass ale and Watneys ale are on tap, served with hand carved sandwiches of roast and corned beef, Chef Ivan's chili, beer spiced shrimp, potato skins and more. Sunday brunch is offered with free flowing champagne and a wide variety of heavenly English food such as corncakes and Glendale sausage and Yorkshire pancakes. Other features include a lively bar, with a piano bar and entertainment nightly.

With so much to offer, you're going to have to stop by and find out just how much fun you can have at this Scotch style pub. You can schedule a private party or join in on the one that's already in progress.

TOP OF FIVE
404 South Figueroa Street
Los Angeles, CA 90071
Tel. (213) 612-4743

Hrs:	Lunch	Mon. - Fri.	11:30 a.m. - 2:30 p.m.
	Dinner	Mon. - Thu.	6:00 p.m. - 10:30 p.m.
		Fri. - Sat.	6:00 p.m. - 11:30 p.m.
		Sunday	6:00 p.m. - 11:00 p.m.
	Brunch	Sunday	10:30 a.m. - 2:00 p.m.

Visa, MasterCard, AMEX and Discover are accepted.

Located on top of one of the five spectacular Westin Bonaventure glass towers, the Top of Five is famous for its dramatic 360 degree view of Los Angeles. Top of Five makes the most of its spectacular setting with Bonavista, a revolving cocktail lounge located one flight below Top of Five's dining room. One complete turn every hour treats guests to panoramic views of the city below.

Specialty cocktails and complimentary hors d'oeuvres are featured in the lounge. The restaurant itself serves fresh American cuisine for lunch Monday through Friday, and brunch on Sunday. Dinner and cocktails are served seven days a week. Best lunch items include Spinach Fettuccine with Goat Cheese and Vegetables, Linguini, Shrimp, Mushrooms and Feta Cheese, Baked Halibut with Juniper Berry Sauce. Outstanding dinner items include mesquite grilled Silver Salmon with Dill Butter and Broiled Tiger Prawns stuffed with pine nuts and seasoned bread crumbs. Fresh strawberries marinated in Kirsch with chilled sabayon and served in a goblet with cherry schnapps in the bottom make a delicious ending to a meal in the sky.

Enjoy the glittering lights of Los Angeles thirty-five stories above the city while dining at Top of Five, one of L.A.'s most celebrated view restaurants.

VIOLET'S RESTAURANT
1712 Colorado Boulevard Eagle Rock
Los Angeles, CA 90041
Tel. (213) 255-4562
Hrs: Sun., Wed., Thu.   5:00 p.m. - 10:30 p.m.
      Fri. - Sat.   5:00 p.m. - 12:00 midnight
All major credit cards are accepted.

Violet's, an award winning restaurant in Eagle Rock offers uncommonly good Russian and Armenian fare in a comfortable and romantic atmosphere. This establishment reflects the exotic background of owner Violet Pashinian. Of Armenian and Russian heritage, she was born in Shanghai, lived in Brazil and was raised in Glendale and Hollywood in a restauranteuring family.

The elegant, intimate ambiance sets the stage for many of the house specialties. You may begin your meal with caviar and champagne or Siberian Pelimeny; a deep fried ground beef ravioli served with mustard sauce. Violet recommends the Rack of Lamb or Rasco Steak, a Brazilian specialty. Other entrees on the menu include Chicken Kiev, Cornish Game Hen and Beef Stroganoff. Violet's offers an excellent selection of domestic and imported wines, champagne and sparkling wines to accompany your meal. A luscious finish to your evening may include a dessert such as a chocolate cup filled with ice cream or mousse.

Violet's offers live entertainment while you dine and ample parking. Be sure to make reservations; Violet's Restaurant is quite popular, especially with the pre-theater and after-theater crowd. This romantic "Best Choice" is easy to find; it's close to Occidental College, Cal-Tech and the Ambassador on Colorado Boulevard.

THE WURST
7465 Melrose Avenue
Los Angeles, CA 90046
Tel. (213) 651-4747
Hrs: Sun. - Thu.   11:00 a.m. - 11:00 p.m.
          Fri. - Sat.   11:00 a.m. - 12:00 midnight
Also,

10874 Kinross Avenue	2832 Broadway
Westwood, CA 90024	Corner 110th/Broadway
Tel. (213) 824-9597	New York, NY 10025
	Tel. (212) 749-6190

"You haven't had the best until you've had The Wurst," and that's the truth! Before opening the Westwood restaurant in 1984, owner Robert Gura traveled throughout Europe, and specifically Germany, to scout out the best recipes for sausage, sauerkraut and potato salad. The Wurst, located on busy, bustling Melrose Avenue is the exciting culmination and success of that search.

The eclectic selection of sausages include Wurst Link, a beef sausage with Cajun spices; Smoked Kielbasa, pork sausage with black peppers; and Duckwurst, a melange of duck, chicken and cilantro. Bockwurst, Knackwurst and home made sauerkraut are standards that never fail to delight patrons. A vegetarian variety of sausage is available, made from five vegetables and nuts. Sausages are barbecued over a mesquite grill and served on a sesame French roll. The condiment bar features sweet hot mustard made with honey, whole grain and Dijon mustard; and a sweet pickle relish made of a mixture of onions, carrots and bell peppers, pickled to perfection. Take-out and catering services are available as well as studio delivery.

Co-owned by Lenny Linar and John Tesh, host of *Entertainment Tonight*, The Wurst has become a "hot spot" for good eating. One visit and you'll see why; it's alive! Juke box music, large screen TV, high-tech modern decor and abstract art make for an exciting dining locale. You won't be the first to say, "I want it in the Wurst Way."

YAFA KOSHER RESTAURANT, 647 South Fairfax, Los Angeles, CA. Tel. (213) 656-YAFA. For intimate and elegant dining at its finest, Yafa offers Continental cuisine with Israeli and Persian specialties.

ZUMAYA'S
5722 Melrose Avenue
Los Angeles, CA 90038
Tel. (213) 464-0624
Hrs: Mon. - Thu.   11:30 a.m. - 10:00 p.m.
       Friday   11:30 a.m. - 12:00 midnight
       Saturday   6:00 p.m. - 12:00 midnight
Visa, MasterCard and Diners Club are accepted.

Zumaya's is an atypical Mexican restaurant. None of the usual Southwestern adobe architecture will be found at this sophisticated gem of a restaurant. Rather, a dining salon appointed with warm accents of yellow, salmon and pink creates an ambiance of cool, crisp sophistication.

Zumaya's specialties include a combination of culinary inspirations from Baja, New Mexico and Mexico City. Antojitos include Zumaya's shellfish cocktail, tender abalone and shrimp marinated in fresh lemon juice, cilantro, onion and tomatoes and mild chiles; and its renowned Empanadas , a crispy meat turnover filled with shredded beef, tender potato slices and a mild red sauce. The list of *entradas* (entrees) are scintillating and endless. Pollo Caliente, spicy boneless chicken breast sauteed in New Mexico Red chiles and butter topped with Nopales; Carmarones al Mojo de Ajo, jumbo Mexican shrimp, butterflied and sauteed in garlic, butter and pimento are two favorites. Others include Pescado de Cilantro pesto sauce, halibut simmered in garlic butter; and Tacos de Pescado, fillets of white fish lightly coated in a special seasoning topped with cabbage and a delicious sauce and served in corn tortillas.

The service is excellent and owners Teresa Gabaldon and Emily Diaz are delighted to share the secrets of their culinary know how with patrons. "Don't let earthquakes, heat or holidays stand between you and Zumaya's."

STATIONERY

WRITE ON THIRD
8222 West 3rd Street
Los Angeles, CA 90048
Tel. (213) 658-5348
Hrs: Mon. - Sat.   11:00 a.m. - 5:00 p.m.
Visa and MasterCard are accepted.

Owner Barbara Safrin was for many years a buyer for the Super stores in Los Angeles. This was not her heart's desire, however, so after traveling extensively in Europe and Scandinavia, she returned to her hometown and decided, in 1985, to open a fine stationery and gift store.

Her experience, personal taste, imagination and ability to perceive accurately and appropriately the changing needs of her greater Los Angeles clientele have paid off. This very distinguished shop with the glass window overlooking Third Street is cool, eclectic, and displays in a very tasteful way the many types of handwoven papers and accessories. Her goal has been to supply the consumer in the Los Angeles metropolitan area with the best writing materials in the world. She's learned that people have distinct preferences as to their style and that it is her job to help them reflect that in their purchases. She also says that it's a real trend nowadays to write and to have the quality paper to write on. Her lines, then, include fine paper in a large variety of types and colors, handmade cards with wonderful bouquets and flowers entwined, frames of all kinds, journals, and playing cards from all over the world. The desk accessories are top of the line and state of the art as well. She also provides engraving or printing and ships through United Parcel Service.

If how you say it is as important as what you're communicating, chances are good that you're already a regular customer. If you aren't, you owe it to yourself to become one.

TEA ROOM

PADDINGTON'S TEA ROOM
729 North La Cienega Boulevard
Los Angeles, CA 90069
Tel. (213) 652-0624
Hrs: Tue. - Sat.   9:00 a.m. - 9:00 p.m.
         Sunday   11:00 a.m. - 7:00 p.m.
Visa, MasterCard and AMEX are accepted.

The traditional tea house as we now know it originated with the brothers Neal, who began serving tea with scones and biscuits in their renowned W.H. Smith & Sons Tea Rooms. The same sublime experience of high tea can be enjoyed at Paddington's Tea Room. Owned and operated by Julianne and Richard Gorski, natives of Paddington, Australia, Paddington's Tea Room is a warm and cozy environment in which to enjoy a delicious "cuppa."

The walls are covered with pictures of British royalty, and each nook and cranny houses treasures of tea cups, saucers, and of course the ever present, loveable, and cuddly Paddingtons. Choice blends of Fortnum & Mason's Royal of London teas are selected and served in quaint style in brown Betty tea pots accompanied by a pitcher of fresh milk. The traditional high tea, well known as a pick-me-up of the British, is the specialty of the house. Accompanied by delicacies of little sausage rolls, liver and dilled egg pâtés, finger sandwiches, fresh raw vegetables, English water crackers, savoury English pies and mouth watering scones, it is a meal and experience to delight the appetite and warm the soul.

If your "cup of tea" is coffee, you will be astounded with the fifty-six varieties of gourmet coffees available at Paddington's Tea Room, including premium Jamaica Blue Mountain blend. Located on La Cienega Boulevard in a lovely English cottage, you'll experience the time honored tradition of high tea in style. Come and join the Gorskis who understand that "having a good cuppa is most important as the grand finale of any meal."

TOUR

LAWRY'S CALIFORNIA CENTER
570 West Avenue 26
Los Angeles, CA 90065
Tel. (213) 224-6840

Hrs:	Lunch	Jan. - Dec.
	Mon. - Sun.	11:00 a.m. - 3:00 p.m.
	Dinner	Apr. - Nov.
	Mon. - Sat.	4:30 p.m. - 9:30 p.m.
	Sundays	4:00 p.m. - 9:00 p.m.
	Tours	Jan. - Dec.
	Mon. - Fri.	11:30 a.m. - 2:30 p.m.
	Shops	Apr. - Nov.
	Mon. - Sun.	10:30 a.m. - 9:30 p.m.
		Nov. - Mar.
	Mon. - Sun.	10:30 a.m. - 4:00 p.m.

Visa and MasterCard are accepted.

Lawry's California Center rests upon a 1784 Spanish land grant to the Verdugo family. In 1950, Lawry's Foods, Inc., the manufacturer of Seasoned Salt and 110 other consumer items, began acquiring the fifteen acre parcel that Lawry's occupies. 1988 will mark Lawry's fiftieth anniversary!

Free guided tours take you "behind the scenes" of the manufacturing facility, laboratories and test kitchens. They are available on weekdays and leave on the half hour. Reservations are required for groups of ten or more. After your tour, you can browse through The Gift Shop or The Wine and Gourmet Shop.

Two luncheon facilities, La Cocina, specializing in Mexican cuisine, and La Barbacoa, featuring barbecued fare, are available daily year round. In addition, Los Portales Bar and Patio serves luncheon, supper, appetizers and cocktails daily from 11:00 a.m. The Margarita Brunch is featured Sundays, 10:30 a.m. to 2:00 p.m. From April through October, The Garden Restaurant serves delicious dinner entrees, all of which include Cartwheel Salad, corn on the cob,

Sour Cream Tortilla casserole, a fresh vegetable and hot herb cheese bread.

Throughout the year, you may find a variety of special events taking place, including wine classes, festivals, entertainment features and even a beer fest. Call ahead for information pertaining to current scheduled events and for dinner reservations which are recommended, but not required. No reservations are necessary for lunch time.

Lawry's California Center promises an interesting visit where you can learn about Lawry's Foods, be entertained by strolling mariachis or other featured entertainers, dine among flower filled brick patios, and enjoy their gift and wine shops.

TOY STORES

JOYS & TOYS
7375 Melrose Avenue
Los Angeles, CA 90046
Tel. (213) 658-8697
Hrs: Mon. - Thu.   10:00 a.m. - 10:00 p.m.
      Fri. - Sat.   10:00 a.m. - 11:30 p.m.
      Sunday   12:00 noon - 8:00 p.m.
Visa, MasterCard and AMEX are accepted.

Joys & Toys proprietors Sebastian and Cheryl Giefer travel the world to find the best toys each country has to offer. "We believe toys should have aesthetic value as well as play value," says Sebastian. "If you have toys around the house why not have beautiful things which offer quality, design and education?" adds Cheryl. The Giefer's philosophy embraces the beautiful, the simple and the safe, and they have succeeded in creating an environment that is stimulating and attractive to both the child and the child within every adult.

As you enter Joys & Toys your senses will be delighted by the imaginative children's world, more compelling and creatively designed than Hollywood could summon up. At the entrance, striking modern art posters, designed for children, enthrall the eye. There are beautiful displays of Pablo Art Construction and Vilac motor bikes that could be sculptures as well as toys, in addition to handsome handcrafted European furniture. Sebastian and Cheryl make frequent trips to Italy, Germany, Austria, Sweden, England and Switzerland, searching for items they judge their customers will find most appealing. Their favorites are hand carved, hand painted originals with themes children love: familiar farm animals, unique jigsaw puzzles, modular doll houses and pull toys that teach toddlers the concept of cause and effect. For the more intellectual tyke there are museum quality art books, computer and science oriented kits, 3-D transparent picture cards and S-Point building sets. If it's a newborn you're shopping for, you won't want to miss the infant section. There are stuffed animals with music boxes inside, colorful mobiles, wooden pull toys from different countries and much more.

Joys & Toys is filled with delightful and unique surprises including the convenient extended store hours. "By far the most beautiful toy store in Los Angeles" reports *AM Los Angeles*. "Best in L.A." declares the *LA Weekly*. Joys & Toys has something for every budget; from their electric miniature Mercedes to their Bauhaus Building Sets, and computer and science oriented kits, Joys & Toys is a complete toy store for the very selective. Each item is educational, beautiful or clever, and usually, all three.

TOY PALACE
8639 Lincoln Boulevard
Los Angeles, CA 90045
Tel. (213) 645-5467
Hrs: Mon. - Sat.   9:30 a.m. - 5:30 p.m.
Credit cards are not accepted.

Think of a palace and the images that come to mind may be royalty in elegant gowns, rich colors, wonderful collectibles, and smartly uniformed guards at their posts. For all of us, young and old, palaces seems to be intriguing, magical places. The same is true for toy stores. There's a child inside of all of us, jumping up and down each time we walk into a toy store. The kid in you will gleefully enjoy the Toy Palace.

The Toy Palace's unusual collection of toys makes it a regal shop amongst the toy trade. In business since 1952, these folks are very knowledgeable on the subject of toys. Steiff Bears and other animals, both limited edition and collectibles, will awaken the child in all of us. Specialty dolls sure to turn the heads of collectors abound here. Madame Alexander and Jerri McLoud dolls grace the store with their elegant attire. There are Brio wooden trains from Sweden and armies of British toy soldiers. Burago cars are ready to race and Exin castles wait to fill fantasies. The Toy Palace also carries an excellent selection of unusual educational coloring books and games as well as a special book section.

The Toy Palace is located such that it faces the back parking lot of the shopping center. Double deck parking ensures space for all. For a diverse selection of quality toys to please any child as well as the small child within, visit the Toy Palace and take a regal walk through toyland.

WINE SHOPS

DU VIN WINE & SPIRITS
540 North San Vicente Boulevard
Los Angeles, CA 90048
Tel. (213) 855-1161
Hrs: Mon. - Sat.   10:00 a.m. - 7:00 p.m.
         Open Sundays in December
Visa, MasterCard and AMEX are accepted.

Du Vin is more than a wonderful place to select the finest wines. Owner Rene Averseng notes that his shop stands at the location of the very first outdoor dining establishment in Los Angeles, which he took over in 1979.

Allow Rene to guide you through his vast selection of wines. He stresses that customers who come to his wine shop should feel comfortable when they are buying. He will ask how much you want to spend so he can offer the very best wine at the very best price. Du Vin specializes in imported French and Italian wine, rare cognac, single malt scotch, Calvados, rum and vintage Armagnac. Rene offers a Basic Wine Collection; a wine cellar of twelve bottles. He also stocks wonderful gift baskets for all occasions, and will appraise the wine you've held for years. After you've made your selection take a chair in the trellised patio and enjoy a light lunch. It's a true delight to relax under the shady trees away from the hustle and bustle of the city. Sample the French cheese and the variety of pates, including duck liver with truffles and cognac, and the goose *foie gras*.

Du Vin Wine Shop is the perfect place to spend a balmy afternoon in Los Angeles, sipping freshly ground espresso or a glass of wine and exchanging conversation with the cosmopolitan clientele. Don't miss this "Best Choice" in Los Angeles.

WALDERS WINE & SPIRITS
6333 West 3rd Street
Los Angeles, CA 90036
Tel. (213) 937-1225
Hrs: Winter   Mon. - Sat.   9:00 a.m. - 7:00 p.m.
         Summer   Mon. - Sat.   9:00 a.m. - 8:00 p.m.
                            Sunday   10:00 a.m. - 5:00 p.m.
Visa, MasterCard and AMEX are accepted.

Located along the east side of the parking area of the Farmers Market is a wooden building reminiscent of the early California winery buildings, known as Walders Wine & Spirits. Gene and Cira Walder, purveyors of this fine shop, have been instrumental in pioneering the wine industry in the Los Angeles area by searching out the rarest and choicest wines available. Traveling extensively throughout Europe, they have selected premier wines, brandies, cognacs and spirits from France, Italy, Germany and Spain to stock in their store.

Over 750 rare wines and old vintages are housed within the 4500 square foot oak beamed building. An extensive collection of liquors are also available as well as an area devoted solely to aperitifs, rare brandies and cognacs. Gift baskets can be made to your own specifications to include wine, champagne, fresh caviar, gourmet food and fresh fruit, or choose from one of the gift packages on display. Magnum size—three liter champagne bottles; Methusalem, oversize champagne bottles; and an Nebuchadnezzar, an extra oversized champagne bottles which hold over one case of champagne are available for those extensive banquet occasions. Lunch in the enclosed restaurant serving soup, salad and sandwiches while sampling over forty wines served by the glass.

Whether you are planning a quiet intimate event or a banquet, Walders' assistants will help you in choosing that special selection to make the occasion perfect. Connoisseurs and epicureans have long ago discovered the treasures found at Walders Wine & Spirits. Why not join them by making Walders Wine & Spirits your "Best Choice."

HOLLYWOOD-MIDTOWN

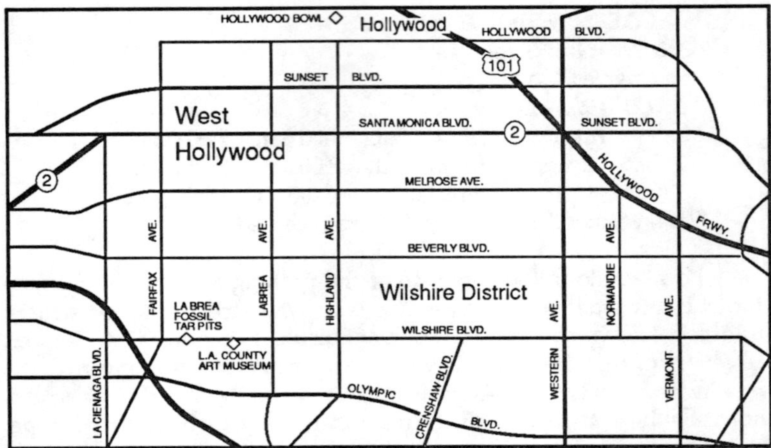

Hollywood. That's all anyone has to hear to conjure up images of glitz, movie stars, studios, bright lights, marquees and free spirited people. While Hollywood has more than its share of glamor and glitter, the truth is that much of what we associate with the community is no longer concentrated in Hollywood. In fact, if you look a bit beyond the two square miles of West Hollywood to the Wilshire District and the rest of the Midtown region we see a community of marked contrasts.

It is one of the charms of the region that record and motion picture companies lie so close to a farmer's market with fresh produce stalls. On one hand you have an emerging fashion and design industry, and on the other you have quiet middle class and Jewish neighborhoods where you can sometimes overhear the elderly speaking Yiddish.

Hollywood is not an independent city. Technically it's simply the Hollywood District of Los Angeles. It lies along the foothills of the Santa Monica Mountains, about eight miles from downtown. The district is defined roughly by La Brea Avenue on its west side, Vermont Avenue on the east, Franklin at the north, and Melrose Avenue on its south side. The opulent community of Beverly Hills lies on Hollywood's west side.

While Hollywood may symbolize glamor and fast-lane living, its roots are quite conservative. Horace H. Wilcox, a Methodist prohibitionist from Kansas, began subdividing a large tract of land at the base of the foothills in 1887. Although none of the species of American holly is native to the region, Wilcox christened his real estate development Hollywood.

In the early years Hollywood was a pious and temperate community that grew slowly. Even as late as 1896 the most exciting event of the day was the arrival of the stagecoach, which came rattling in on a dusty street. Deer would come out of the hills to Hollywood Boulevard in the mornings. Hardly a soul was aware that Thomas Edison had just invented Living Pictures, which were being shown in a theater in Los Angeles.

The era of the quiet, sober days would come to an end in 1911, when the Nester Company bought the old Blondeau Tavern at the corner of Sunset Boulevard and Gower Street and turned it into a movie studio.

The original Hollywood sign overlooking the community went up in 1923 and read *HOLLYWOODLAND* as a promotion for a fashionable subdivision in the nearby Beachwood Canyon. Each of the letters measured thirty feet wide and nearly fifty feet tall and were studded with thousands of twenty watt light bulbs. Albert Kothe, whose job it was to clamber up and down the sign to change light bulbs, lived in a little cabin behind one of the L's.

Even after the "LAND" part of the sign blew down, HOLLYWOOD symbolized the hopes and dreams of those who wanted to be movie stars. Lillian Milicent Entwhistle, a famous stage actress, was among those who came with high hopes. When it became clear to her in September, 1932 that her hopes for success on the silver

screen would not pan out, she climbed to the top of the "H" and jumped to her death.

ATTRACTIONS

• With more than four thousand acres of landscaped park land, **Griffith Park** is the largest city park in the United States. It offers the traditional park facilities such as picnic areas and children's playgrounds, but it offers much more. You'll also find hiking and bridle trails through the wooded hillsides, a miniature railroad, pony and stagecoach rides, a zoo, planetarium, astronomical observatory and an old fashioned merry-go-round.

A trail map in which the various trails are graded for their difficulty is available at the visitor's center at 4730 Crystal Springs Drive.

The **observatory** contains the largest public telescope in California and visitors can gaze into the heavens every clear evening except Monday. And no matter what the weather is like, you can star watch at the **planetarium.** You'll find the main park entrance at Vermont Avenue and Riverside Drive. For information call (213) 655-5188.

• **Travel Town,** located on Griffith Park's east side, contains a collection of airplanes, trains and a variety of vehicles on which children can climb around, including one of the city's old trolley cars. For information call (213) 662-5874.

• **Los Angeles Zoo,** in Griffith Park near the intersection of the Ventura and Golden State freeways, contains more than 2,000 animals on 113 hilly acres. The animals are kept in natural looking environments similar to their native habitats. Some of the more unusual species include mountain tapirs, emperor tamarins and red flanked duikers.

The two acre **Children's Zoo** offers children the opportunity for a close up look at a variety of docile animals such as goats, sheep, llamas, ducks and geese. For information call (213) 666-4090.

• **Barnsdall Park,** 4800 Hollywood Boulevard, sits atop a hill in a quiet spot surrounded by olive trees. The park offers the usual facilities such as picnic areas and playgrounds, but it also contains a municipal art gallery, a crafts center and the **Hollyhock House,** which Frank Lloyd Wright designed for Aline Barnsdall, an oil heiress who once owned the land. The house is one of the few Wright designed homes open to the public. For information call (213) 662-7272.

• The **Los Angeles Municipal Art Gallery** in Barnsdall Park displays works by contemporary Southern California artists. Many of the exhibits include artist's statements which attempt to explain their work. Often the exhibits focus on some aspect of the creative process, such as how artists sometimes turn everyday objects into art.

• **The Hollywood Bowl,** 2301 North Highland Ave, Los Angeles, is a natural amphitheater nestled in the Hollywood Hills and famous for its renown cultural events, such as evening symphonies and the three day **Playboy Jazz Festival.** On the grounds are picnic tables. For information on programs call (213) 876-0232.

FARMER'S MARKET

If you can't find it at the Farmer's Market, the question is do you need it? 160 individually owned shops are presented in a labyrinth like setting. Filled to the brim with fresh fruits, vegetables and seafoods, souvenirs and gifts of all descriptions, the fifty year old institution is a favorite stop for visitors from all over the world.

What began in 1934 as a cooperative venture by a group of hard pressed farmers, setting up stalls in a vacant lot bordering Los Angeles, is now an attraction that draws over 20,000 shoppers a day. The vacant lot now comprises twenty acres, features twenty-six kitchens and sports a parking lot filled with tour busses from all over the L.A. area.

Founded by Earl B. Gilmore, the Farmer's Market still has some of the original farmers and/or their families associated with the operation. A sensory experience, the Market is guaranteed to delight each of the five senses. Easily recognized by the landmark White Clock Tower, on West 3rd and Fairfax, the Farmer's Market has the air of a midwestern farming community.

Among its many attractions the Market features DuPars Coffee Shop. A popular haunt for writers, actors, artists and photographers, DuPars is touted as serving the best and the cheapest espresso and cappuccino in town. A surprising number of Farmer's Market shoppers are inhabitants of the area, which speaks highly of the selection, price and quality of the available merchandise.

A unique approach to dining is offered. Diners become akin to "galloping gourmets" as they select an appetizer from one stand, salad or soup from another, an entree from yet another stand and then top the meal off with dessert from still a different restaurant. The hungry patron can turn an ordinary meal into an international event, choosing from Chinese, Italian, French, Spanish, Cantonese or any of the other foreign flavored dining experiences.

The art galleries include displays involving European imports, capodemante flowers, portraits, hand painted ceramics, ivory, cloisonne graphics, oriental art and original oils to name a few. Browsing is encouraged, and the interested patron can virtually travel around the cultural world without leaving the Market.

A vast selection of clothing for the entire family is included within the Market's array of shops and stands. Men's and boy's fashions include neckwear, dress and sport shirts. European styles,

Hawaiian, Polynesian and Oriental clothing is offered as are sweatshirts, T-shirts, unisex fashions and sportswear. Women's contemporary designer fashions are naturally included and are as tasteful as they are reasonably priced. Shoes, sweaters, blouses, jewelry and accessories can be found throughout the Market and come in a wide variety of styles and prices.

The food offered can be anything from groceries to gourmet or health foods. Ice cream shops, produce stands and bakeries abound. Fresh fruits, either individually or as gift baskets, are available and many establishments are more than glad to ship anywhere in the world. Several different delicatessens specialize in an enticing blend of horseradishes, mincemeats, salads and special meats and cheeses. After gorging yourself on the wide variety of foods available, the dessert shops may prove to be the straw that breaks the camel's back. Fruit and cream pies may beckon, cakes and other pastries including cookies and coffee cakes will vie for attention, and the most difficult part of the experience might be choosing what to indulge in and where to put it.

Restaurants abound in the market and can be something as simple, yet as tasty as breakfast or pit barbecues, or as exotic as authentic Cajun foods and oyster bars. Hamburgers, omelettes, hot dogs and pizzas compete with falafels, sushi, tempura, seafood, Chinese and New York style deli foods.

A wide assortment of specialty shops present the ultimate in choice. Candles, crystal, Chokin art, coats of arms china and creative rubber stamps are liberally sprinkled throughout the twenty acres. Native American jewelry, fine arts, greeting cards, fresh flowers and brass items abound. The list seems endless and constantly changing as handbags, party decorations, garden supplies, even pets and pet supplies are included in the massive inventory.

Retail stores aren't the only shops available. A wide range of service oriented businesses also make the Market their base of operation. Beauty salons and barber shops, photo and automotive centers, shoe repair or shoeshine shops, pharmacies, opticians, banks, and even postal services are included among the 160 businesses.

Touted as a complete one stop shopping paradise, each and every visitor will find themselves wrapped in a sensory experience that includes touching, tasting, viewing, smelling and listening to the collage of extra special experiences. Allow plenty of time to take in the many one of a kind shops.

ACCOMMODATION

HOLIDAY INN, HOLLYWOOD
1755 North Highland Avenue
Hollywood, CA 90028
Tel.   (213) 462-7181
All major credit cards are accepted.

Hollywood's glamor attracts thousands of vacationers every year and many want accommodations near the "entertainment center of the universe." With this in mind, many choose the Holiday Inn, Hollywood.

While you stay at the Holiday Inn you'll walk the streets made famous by movies and television. You're only blocks from the legendary intersection of Hollywood and Vine and only a short drive from the sights of Universal Studios and Mann's Chinese Theater. At the end of the day, you'll relax in deluxe rooms featuring king size or double beds. Guests in wheelchairs have access to special accommodations. You may enjoy all of the major cable television channels, or gaze out at the incredible Los Angeles cityscape. On a clear day, you'll see Catalina Island across the blue Pacific Ocean. You'll want to try the wonderful meals offered at the Show Biz Cafe. Be sure to check for the Chef's surprises set out for breakfast or lunch. For a romantic evening meal, you and your partner must not miss the magnificent Windows on Hollywood Restaurant. This revolving restaurant on the twenty-third floor of the Holiday Inn provides panoramic views and outstanding meals.

The Holiday Inn, Hollywood outdoes the Holiday Inn reputation for the finest banquet and meeting facilities. Whether you're on business or on vacation, visit the Holiday Inn, Hollywood.

APPAREL

J. GERARD CLOTHES, 8575 Melrose Avenue, Hollywood, CA. Tel. (213) 657-3336. A design studio and showroom frequented by stars of stage and screen, J. Gerard Clothes carries unique designer clothes and accessories.

BOOKSTORE

SAMUEL FRENCH THEATER AND FILM BOOKSHOPS
7623 Sunset Boulevard
Hollywood, CA 90046
Tel.   (213) 876-0570
       (800) 7ACTNOW CA
       (800) 8ACTNOW US
       Toll free lines are for credit card orders.
Hrs: Mon. - Fri.   10:00 a.m. - 6:00 p.m.
       Saturday   11:00 a.m. - 5:00 p.m.
Visa, MasterCard, AMEX and Optima are accepted.
Also,
11963 Ventura Boulevard
Studio City, CA 91604
Tel. (818) 762-0535
Hrs: Mon. - Fri.   10:00 a.m. - 9:00 p.m.
       Saturday   11:00 a.m. - 5:00 p.m.
       Sunday   12:00 noon - 5:00 p.m.

In Hollywood, the movie capital of the world, actors, actresses, directors, producers and fans depend on Samuel French's Theater and Film Bookshop for their professional needs. Established in 1830 and incorporated in 1899, Samuel French's began as Play Publishers and Author Representatives. As the film industry developed, French's took on the job of supplying film actors with everything they would ever need for their craft and now can supply just about any book on performing acts.

You don't have to be an actor to enjoy Samuel French's. They have books on all your favorite movie stars and theater personalities in addition to the enormous selection of hard and soft cover books on acting technique, voice, theater theory and history, movement, improvisation and other subjects. You may learn how the greats interpret Shakespeare and create unique mime characters. Filmmakers from novices to professionals will love selecting a book on screenwriting, cinematography, editing, and lighting. Animators will find publications on technique and the history of cartoons. You'll also find Ben Nye make up and biographies on all your favorite stars, both in the theater and motion pictures.

If you can't make it to this Los Angeles "Best Choice," write or call for Samuel French's, 126 page Film Book Catalog free or the *Samuel French Basic Catalog of Plays* for $2.25 post paid; and remember there are many special events sponsored at Samuel French's, including book signings, readings and seminars.

NIGHTCLUB

THE LAUGH FACTORY
8001 Sunset Boulevard
Hollywood, CA 90036
Tel. (213) 656-1336
Hrs: Sun. - Thu.   Show starts at 8:30 p.m.
        Fri. - Sat.   Shows start at 8:00 p.m. and 10:30 p.m.
Admission is $6.00 as of this writing.

Many well known comedians began their careers at the world famous Laugh Factory in Hollywood. Visitors will discover the best new talent in the comedy business and enjoy a night of laughter in the process.

Many of today's stars come to The Laugh Factory to test out new material before they appear on *The Tonight Show with Johnny Carson* or David Letterman's show. You'll find an intimate room and walls covered with images of well known entertainers; their portraits are painted right on the brick. Customers can enjoy beer, wine or soft drinks along with hearty foods. Entertainers, including Eddie Murphy, Rodney Dangerfield, Richard Pryor, Robin Williams, Woody Allen,

Don Johnson and Julian Lennon have dropped by to see what's new in comedy. Many television shows are taped at The Laugh Factory, and you could be a member of the audience. *Fortune Magazine* and the *Los Angeles Magazine* have named this comedy spot one of the three best clubs in Southern California. There's no age limit on who can enjoy the show, though the management recommends no children under thirteen.

The Laugh Factory also offers a special guarantee: If you don't laugh, you'll get your money back. But don't plan on leaving without a smile on your face, someone might tickle you at the door.

RESTAURANTS

THE BROWN DERBY, Hollywood & Vine, Hollywood, CA. Tel. (213) 469-5151. This is the famed location where careers, romances and big business deals of the movie capital are made. The Hollywood Brown Derby opened on Valentines Day, 1929 and maintains a tradition of excellence in food and service.

COLUMBIA BAR & GRILL
1448 North Gower
Hollywood, CA 90028
Tel. (213) 461-8800
Hrs: Lunch   Mon. - Fri.   11:30 a.m. - 3:30 p.m.
        Dinner   Mon. - Thu. 5:30 p.m. - 11:00 p.m.
                    Fri. - Sat.   5:30 p.m. - 12:00 midnight
Visa, MasterCard, AMEX and Diners Club are accepted.
Rooms available for private parties.

When the celebrities, movie and entertainment executives of Hollywood want to dine they choose Columbia Bar & Grill, located on the corner of Sunset Boulevard and Gower Street. The restaurant has been part of the movie industry's history since the days of Columbia Studios, when it was the site of the Columbia Drug Store. It was there that the old movie cowboys used to anxiously await casting calls and, over time, the corner was coined Gower Gulch. Now it is the grazing grounds of the Hollywood elite.

Owned by actor Wayne Rogers along with a host of other well known producers, writers, advertisers and moguls of the entertainment industry, it has become one of Hollywood's premier restaurants. Combining the culinary talents of Chef Timothy McGrath, formal personal chef to Julie Andrews and husband/producer Blake Edwards, and the management expertise of Paul Hanley, the restaurant boasts such succulent offerings as Dungeness Crab Cakes served with a zesty Dijon mustard; Smoked Chicken Salad with seedless grapes, pecans and mixed greens dressed with honey mustard sauce; and Grilled Boneless Chicken Breast with pico de gallo. Desserts include such decadent delectables as Warm Apple Crisp, a tempting buttery confection capped with vanilla ice cream; and Lemon Sherbet in an Almond Shell, topped with Amaretto cookies and raspberry sauce.

The ambiance of the Columbia Bar & Grill is warm, sophisticated and reminiscent of a 1920s American grill, yet has a touch of contemporary Southern California architecture. A soaring skylight, plenty of greenery and the spectacular paintings by Rick Stich, Frank Stella, Jasper Johns and David Hockney provide the perfect setting for a superlative dining experience. Reservations are strongly suggested.

EL FLORIDITA RESTAURANT
1253 North Vine Street
Hollywood, CA 90038
Tel.   (213) 871-0936
         (213) 871-0968
Hrs: Lunch   Mon. - Sun. 11:30 a.m. - 3:00 p.m.
         Dinner   Mon. - Sun. 3:00 p.m. - 10:30 p.m.
Visa and MasterCard are accepted.

Set in the heart of Hollywood, El Floridita Restaurant is a replica of Cuba's legendary Floridita restaurant. El Floridita is not only the new Cuban restaurant in Hollywood, it is the only Cuban restaurant in Los Angeles. Ernest Hemingway would be pleased with this northern version of his favorite Central American spot.

Salsa and Afro-Cuban jazz and saucy Cuban food keep the action happening at El Floridita. The interior of owner, Armando Jose's place is enjoyably lush. There are mirrored wall panels throughout, soft lighting and a fresh rose on every table. Hollywood's El Floridita has a warm and friendly atmosphere. Armando Jose greets each customer like an honored friend. The waiters are efficient and attentive. The menu features tantalizing Cuban dishes of pork, chicken, red meats, seafood and Floridita specials, including Paella Valenciana. El Floridita's chef hails from Santa Clara, Cuba and has just the right touch with *criollo* spicing. Those who enjoy pork will be tempted by the Pierna De Puerco Ascado, roasted pork marinated in garlic, lemon, and spices and baked to perfection. All of the meals are served with traditional rice, beans and Cafe Con Leche.

The excitement at El Floridita goes on all evening. El Floridita attracts many Spanish speaking people and Hollywood celebrities who like the ambiance of old Havana in its heyday.

MOUN OF TUNIS
7445 1/2 Sunset Boulevard
Hollywood, CA 90046
Tel. (213) 874-3333
Hrs: Mon. - Sun.   6:00 p.m. - 11:00 p.m.
All major credit cards are accepted.
Also,
1027 West Washington Boulevard
Venice, CA 90297
Tel. (213) 399-1355

One of the fun things about dining out is trying something new, something entirely different from what you're used to. An evening at Moun of Tunis will transport you to the extravagant pleasures of the Arabian nights.

When you walk through the doors of Moun of Tunis you are entering another time and place. The exotic atmosphere, reminiscent of the Casbah, is enhanced by gleaming white walls with sky blue accents, Oriental carpets, bird cages and gleaming brass lamps. Belly dancers, both male and female, dance to lively Arabic music, while a friendly, costumed waiter sees your party to a table. Dining is a communal affair, where guests sprawl leisurely on soft pillows around a brass tray table and share the various courses. In keeping with the Tunisian tradition, there are no utensils. After you are seated, your waiter provides a Turkish towel and pours warm rose scented water over your hands. Guests then proceed to eat a delicious meal with their fingers. As in Tunisa one meal is ordered for the entire table and is shared by all. Six meals are featured on the menu, and feature authentic dishes such as Brik, a savory turnover filled with potatoes and egg, B'stilla, a spiced chicken, almond and egg pie that is baked and covered with powdered sugar, and Couscous, made with steamed wheat, vegetables and lamb.

The tastes, aromas, sights and sounds are a delight, and the service is fabulous. A dinner at Moun of Tunis is a sensual experience, a real Arabian night on the town.

YAMASHIRO
1999 North Sycamore Avenue
Hollywood, CA 90068
Tel. (213) 466-5125
Hrs: Lunch Mon. - Sun. 11:30 a.m. - 2:30 p.m.
Dinner Sun. - Thu. 5:30 p.m. - 10:00 p.m.
Fri. - Sat. 5:30 p.m. - 11:00 p.m.
Visa, MasterCard, AMEX, Carte Blanche and Diners Club are accepted.

Yamashiro was created in 1913 as an exact replica of a magnificent palace located in the beautiful mountains near Kyoto, Japan. The doors of the original "Mountain Palace" were open to dignitaries and royalty who entertained in a most comfortable and gracious manner.

During the "Golden Age" of Hollywood, Yamashiro served as a club house for the ultra-exclusive *Club of the Four Hundred*. A Hollywood landmark, its hand carved beauty and authentic architecture have been familiar in countless movies and television productions.

Today, Yamashiro preserves the tradition of elegant hospitality. The service and cuisine are applauded by many gourmet organizations and restaurant writers throughout the world. Yamashiro is designated one of Los Angeles' most romantic spots in a recent edition of the *L.A. Times*. Featuring a breathtaking hilltop panoramic view and eight acres of sculptured gardens, Yamashiro's restaurant, cocktail lounge, banquet rooms and wedding facilities are unrivaled in all of Southern California. It is the favorite of distinguished visitors and celebrities seeking a memorable dining and entertainment experience. Yamashiro's menu includes Japanese and Continental cuisine featuring such enticing items as the Lacquer Box, a combination of Chef Masa Kurihara's special selections, and the Japanese Feast, a beautiful presentation of Tempura, Teriyaki and other delicious Japanese fare. The sushi bar is excellent. The Garden

Court provides a garden setting with stage, dance floor and a complete range of banquet features in unparalleled surroundings. The new Skyview Terrace overlooks the city.

The staff of Yamashiro takes pride in offering you gracious service. Enjoy experiencing a part of old and new Hollywood at Yamashiro.

WEST HOLLYWOOD

When most people think of Hollywood, they are probably thinking of West Hollywood. In this urban village visitors find the vibrant nightlife and fashionable boutiques where one can walk out looking punk or chic.

In West Hollywood you can stroll down the Walk of Fame where the names of celebrities appear in bronze stars embedded in the sidewalk. You can compare your footprints to those of Clark Gable or Lassie, or any of nearly 160 legendary personalities whose imprint has been left in the concrete of the courtyard at Mann's Chinese Theatre.

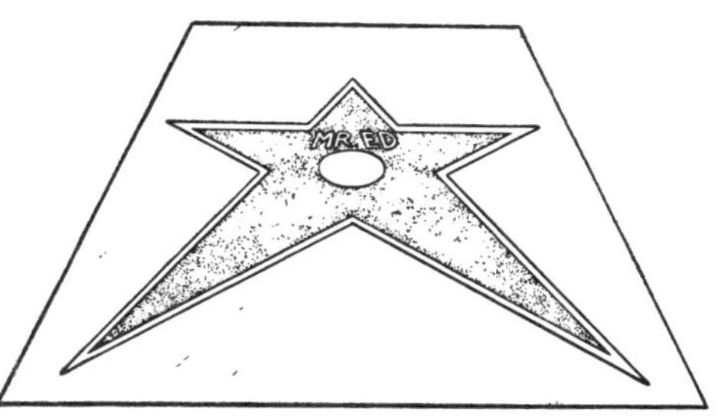

Some also compare West Hollywood with sophisticated cultural enclaves such as the Left Bank of Paris, London's Chelsea, Rome's Trastevere and New York's Soho area. West Hollywood likes to think of itself as the creative center of Los Angeles.

In addition to being a major center for entertainment, the community's boosters herald it as the "interior design capital of the Pacific Rim." There are some four million square feet of interior design show rooms in West Hollywood. The concentration of top designers and show rooms is rivalled only by Chicago and New York. This is where Arab princes come to decorate their palaces and Hollywood stars furnish the homes of their dreams.

The nightlife in West Hollywood is electric. You'll find everything from top comics to high voltage rock clubs, fashionable restaurants to late night shops, bookstores to lavish theaters.

West Hollywood has contributed to L.A.'s reputation for fine California cuisine. Restaurants such as Spago, Morton's and Trumps have led the way among the more than 100 restaurants in the city.

The shopping in West Hollywood is world class. You won't find shopping malls, but in specialty shops you will discover everything from California's new designer wear to European and Japanese styles. Sunset Plaza and Melrose Avenue are "where the next generation of fashion lovers are hanging out," according to *Women's Wear Daily*.

The two most famous streets in West Hollywood are Hollywood Boulevard and Sunset Boulevard. Both run east to west about a block apart. In the local parlance *The Boulevard* refers to Hollywood Boulevard, or "Walk of Fame." That's not to be confused with Sunset Boulevard, which is often called *The Strip*.

At midpoint on the "The Boulevard" is one of the world's most famous intersections: Hollywood and Vine. Throughout the 1930s, 1940s and 1950s this was considered the California version of Times Square. The region's greenhorn playwrights and novelists found plenty of material for their works of comedy and tragedy by observing those eccentric and idealistic folks who came by this way.

There are still remnants of the legendary Hollywood at this intersection, so if it is not what it once was, it is still well worth the effort to take the one mile stroll along The Boulevard from La Brea to Vine, where you can poke around the curiosity shops, poster shops, movie memorabilia dealers and bookstores.

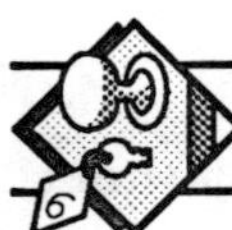

ACCOMMODATIONS

LE BEL AGE, 1020 North San Vicente Boulevard, West Hollywood, CA. Tel. (213) 854-1111. Le Bel Age is a grande classe, all suite luxury hotel with a four star rating by both AAA and Mobil. The exquisite decor is filled with original old-master paintings. The restaurant serves Franco-Russian cuisine in an outstanding setting with impeccable service.

MONDRIAN
8440 Sunset Boulevard
West Hollywood, CA 90069
Tel.   (213) 650-8999
        (800) 424-4443
        (213) 650-5215 FAX
        182570 Telex
Visa, MasterCard, AMEX, Diners Club and Discover are accepted.

The Mondrian Hotel explodes in a brilliant array of stylized color in reflection of Dutch artist Piet Mondrian. Bold and dramatic, the Mondrian is a blaze of rectangular colors set against the rolling green landscapes of Los Angeles. It defies convention in its vibrant exterior and gorgeous interior.

Huge windows frame the spectacular panoramic views from every suite. Bold combinations of yellow, black, gray, blue and red dominate the separate living and sleeping areas of the suites. A rainbow of over 2,000 works of art by contemporary artists play on the walls and byways of the Mondrian. The artistic setting of the hotel extends to the extraordinarily high level of service. Guests are greeted by a heaping basket of fresh fruit and soda water carefully arranged on a table. A host of complimentary services anticipate the needs of guests. The hotel's phone system is designed to meet the needs of business people. The three telephones in each suite give a variety of usage including conference calling. The art of fine dining is always on exhibit. The Cafe Mondrian menu is a rich palette of French and California cuisine. On The Terrace guests can dine *al fresco* with a backdrop of color and views of the city.

The Mondrian is one of the seven masterpieces within the gallery collection of L'Ermitage Hotels.

PARK SUNSET HOTEL
8462 Sunset Boulevard
Los Angeles, CA 90069
Tel. (213) 654-6470
All major credit cards are accepted.

The convenient location near some of Hollywood's most famous attractions makes the Park Sunset Hotel a top choice for accommodations. Its warm, cozy atmosphere also makes it perfect for families.

Recently refurbished, the hotel features eighty-four all new guest rooms, including one bedroom suites with fully equipped kitchens. You'll find direct dial phones with message indicator lights, a must for business people. All rooms have remote control cable television, air conditioning and an AM/FM radio. If you enjoy the sun, relax in the heated pool and on the sun deck. Women will enjoy the full service beauty salon and skin care center. Business people should take note of the excellent meeting facilities, plus they'll find the fine restaurant a pleasant setting for a business dinner or luncheon. For a late night snack, the room service is hard to beat. Before you take your well deserved rest in the king size bed, spend a moment enjoying the panoramic view of Los Angeles from your room's window. You might be inspired to visit the world famous Comedy Store, which is only half a block away.

Many other interesting attractions are only a short drive or walk away, including Century City, downtown Los Angeles, Hollywood, the Marina area, and Disneyland. Magic Mountain, Knott's Berry Farm, and Universal Studio are also nearby. For convenience, the Park Sunset Hotel is certainly a "Best Choice."

APPAREL

EXTREMZ
7377 Melrose Avenue
West Hollywood, CA 90069
Tel. (213) 653-4675
Hrs: Mon. - Sat.   11:00 a.m. - 9:00 p.m.
            Sunday   12:00 noon - 7:00 p.m.
Visa, MasterCard, AMEX, Diners Club and Carte Blanche are accepted.
Also,

La Reina Fashion Plaza   Montana Avenue
14622 Ventura Boulevard   Brenwood, CA 94513
Sherman Oaks, CA 91403
Tel. (818) 995-2905

Fashion conscious Los Angelenos will always go to Extremz when they want the latest in chic clothing, because owner John Ovanessian goes out of his way to choose the finest New York, London and Paris styles available.

His clientele is perhaps the most discriminating anywhere. They want the best and won't settle for anything less. The store itself is high fashion, with a high-tech design in black, white and gray. On display you'll find uniquely designed leatherwear for men and women, including the finest long coats, suits, jackets and accessories. Imagine yourself in one of Extremz sleek dresses or suits of silk, silk moire or wool gabardine. John and his experienced tailors will alter your ensemble to fit like a glove. Alek, Extremz' European designer, will create a garment to your taste from a wide selection of fine fabrics. You can't miss the glittering display of art deco and rhinestone, one of a kind jewelry pieces and accessories. Nearly every item at Extremz and all the displays are created by the Extremz staff. It's all in-house and exclusive.

Visit this "Best Choice" in Los Angeles and find chic elegance that can always be seen on the fashionable thoroughfares of New York, London, Paris and Rome at Extremz.

ID#___________
8605 Sunset Boulevard
West Hollywood, CA 90067
Tel. (213) 659-8081
Hrs: Mon. - Sat.   10:00 a.m. - 6:00 p.m.
Visa, MasterCard, AMEX and Carte Blanche are accepted.

The unique combination of Mediterranean, Caribbean and Southwestern influences come together at ID #______ on Sunset Boulevard. A rainbow of colorful solids and award winning prints make up the natural fabric collection of easy care and easy wear designs.

ID #______ owner Roland Kosser emphasizes attention to detail: buttons, stitching and top quality fabrics designed to last; colors, prints and fabrics that don't get dated, just better and more comfortable with wear. ID #______ specializes in cotton sheetings, denims, chambrays and French terry knits that are all machine washable. Casual, comfortable lifestyle dressing in contemporary silhouettes are offered for men, women and children. New prints, updated treatments and artistically altered fabrics bring freshness to shirts, shorts, skirts, dresses and pants every season.

Original prints on T-shirts create art for the body. Special one size garments and fashion accessories make gift giving a pleasure. Gift certificates are also available in any amount. This store will appeal to the fashion conscious consumer as well as those who just enjoy the easy styling and carefree fabrics.

MICHAEL MORRISON
8010 Melrose Avenue
West Hollywood CA, 90046
Tel. (213) 655-1700
Hrs: Mon. - Sat.   11:00 a.m. - 7:00 p.m.
Visa, MasterCard, AMEX and Discover are accepted.

If you enjoy trendy clothes and style, and if you think Rod Stewart, Mick Jagger and Diana Ross have a special, exciting look, then you should plan to visit this outrageous shop.

Australian born fashion designer and trendsetter, Michael Morrison recently opened this retail outlet to add his own brand of wit and "look" to the California scene. Having gained a reputation with his artful belts and jackets, Morrison has built a showcase for a much broader line of accessories. Still, the belts are not to be missed.

Starting with fine, thick leather, he festoons them with old coins, bits of turquoise, watch faces and other "found items." The result is both a collage and a fashion statement. To complement the belts, the store is filled with jewelry, scarves, handbags and a line of rhinestone studded denim jackets. The entire collection is a wearable tribute to Morrison's talent. You will also find a carefully selected array of designer clothing from Europe. If, after browsing through the store, you have an idea for a creation, don't hesitate to ask for a special design order.

This collection of leading edge fashions and accessories is a must for the adventurous. With a large and often startling selection to choose from, those with a desire to make a statement with their clothes will find Michael Morrison a fashion heaven.

RONNY'S MENSWEAR AND FINE SHOES
8705 Santa Monica Boulevard
West Hollywood, CA 90069
Tel. (213) 659-2830
Hrs: Mon. - Sat. 11:00 a.m. - 7:30 p.m.
Visa, MasterCard, AMEX, Discover, Diners Club and Carte Blanche are accepted.

Those who enter Ronny's Menswear and Fine Shoes emerge in the latest style and trends. Regular and new customers alike know they will find the latest in European fashion at Ronny's. Many try to imitate Ronny's avant garde look but few succeed.

Ronny's motto is "super clothes at super prices." Beautifully displayed designer clothes of very casual style to very dressy modes are offered at reasonable prices. Trust Police Unisex sweaters, Shang-Hai coats and jackets from Italy, leather jackets and pants, YSL sport coats, shoes by Capezio, leather belts and accessories are but a few of the well displayed offerings at Ronny's.

Mirrors line the shop walls so that you may contemplate your new image from all angles. The staff at Ronny's Menswear and Fine Shoes are helpful and have the special ability to assist you in coordinating an individual look. Ronny himself is always present to help with your selection. Rest assured that when you wear an outfit chosen and fitted at Ronny's, you will be on the cutting edge of fashion.

ART GALLERY

PATTI'S AFRICAN ART MUSEUM
607 West Knoll Drive
West Hollywood, CA 90069
Tel. (213) 659-3283
Hrs: Mon. - Sun.   12:00 noon - 6:00 p.m.
Visa, MasterCard and AMEX are accepted.

As you walk into Patti's African Art Museum you can feel the presence of hundreds of tribal chiefs and elders gathered together to bring us their heritage from across the centuries. Here is a museum where the entire family can learn and enjoy a slice of our world's rich history.

Set back in a quiet green patio, one building off Melrose, the African Art Museum is stocked from floor to ceiling with pieces of African folklore. Owner Patti Yeliter, or "Mama" as she is affectionately known, has collected authentic tribal artifacts from fifteen African countries. There are handwoven wall pieces, counters filled with beads and jewelry of every description, and cabinets of musical instruments and baskets, but by far the most dominant items in the museum are the masks. Hundreds of African masks of all types and sizes fill the rooms, their eyes reaching out to visitors as they wander through the gallery. These beautiful works of art include the large headdress of the Kurumbo of the Upper Volta, and large basket body masks along with various other masks used in tribal festivals of every description. In the sixteen years Patti has been in business she has become quite an expert on African arts and has lent considerable advice and props to Hollywood's motion picture and television industries.

Whether you're a collector looking for the rare and unusual, a interior decorator searching for the perfect wall decoration, or a family on vacation looking for something new and original, Patti's African Art Museum is an outstanding experience that should not be missed.

 # HAIR SALON

RUMORS
9014 Melrose Avenue
West Hollywood CA 90069
Tel. (213) 550-5946
Hrs: Tue. - Sat.   9:00 a.m. - 5:00 p.m.
           Late appointments Thursday evening.
All major credit cards are accepted.

Rumors is the place in Los Angeles that thrusts it's clientele into the modern age of beauty. With the best of everything, including hair designers, Rumors has become not only a place to beautify and enhance yourself, it has become a place to see and to be seen.

Rumors is located in a low slung, white building that is set back off of Melrose Avenue. Along with ample valet parking, the building is ensconced by windows, white railing and a bushy, green patio that makes the beauty salon a comfortable place to visit. Inside the salon everything has been done in space capsule decor. The futuristic style is in all black and white and the green panes of glass add to the sensuous feeling of well being. The salon is alive and exciting, with television screens that show video fashion shows, hair styles and fashion colors, scattered throughout the building. Rumors can fulfill your hair care needs with a complete selection of perms, styles and cuts done by the best designers available. Rumors also offers a select line of hair care products by Focus 21, Sebastian and Paul Mitchell.

Owners Warren Hjerpe and Jim Fisher, known best for their innovative hair coloring techniques as seen in major fashion magazines such as *Harper's Bazaar*, *Vogue*, and *Glamour*, work with you to shape your individual look. Their multi-color highlights let you paint texture in, creating the illusion of bigger, bouncier curls. This is a particularly effective process for people with long hair. Rumors is a fast paced, up to date beauty salon that will create the best for you. That is why Rumors is the finest and most exciting hair salon in the heart of Hollywood.

RESTAURANTS

BUTTERFIELD'S RESTAURANT
8426 Sunset Boulevard
West Hollywood, CA 90069
Tel. (213) 656-3055
Hrs: Lunch   Mon. - Fri.   11:30 a.m. - 3:00 p.m.
      Brunch   Sat. - Sun.   10:30 a.m. - 3:00 p.m.
      Dinner   Mon. - Sat.   From 6:00 p.m.
Visa, MasterCard, AMEX and Diners Club are accepted.

Butterfield's Restaurant is a rare find in the busy metropolis of Los Angeles. Originally the guest house of the John Barrymore estate, this small house has been converted into an intimate dining room and garden patio.

Butterfield's knows the changing appetite of the many visitors and Hollywood residents who frequent this gourmet jewel. It offers an eclectic mix of international and California dishes. Butterfield's award winning wine list offers a supreme variety of fine wine and champagne from Europe and California. Butterfield's also has a full bar and a large selection of dessert wines and ports. Since Butterfield's was opened in 1973, owners Michael Buckley, Dennis English, and Joy Shollenbarger, who purchased Butterfield's in 1979, have catered to world travelers. Visitors have rested in the leafy patio only yards from the famed Sunset Strip. The old brick, natural wood tables and terraces decorated with lush plants add a warm atmosphere in which to enjoy the fine food and drink. Butterfield's dining room is one of the most charming in Los Angeles with stained glass windows, woodburning fireplace and intimate seating. You'll taste the imaginative salads, the always changing appetizers, and the freshest of fish and veal dishes there.

You'll also find enough seating for all your intimate banquet needs at Butterfield's Restaurant. Visit and enjoy this outstanding Los Angeles establishment.

FRENCH QUARTER
7985 Santa Monica Boulevard
West Hollywood, CA 90046
Tel. (213) 654-0898
Hrs: Mon. - Thu. 7:00 a.m. - 2:30 a.m.
      Fri. - Sat.   7:00 a.m. - 3:30 a.m.

For fourteen years, this colorful bit of New Orleans has been a fixture in West Hollywood. The authentic design and cheerful staff generate a relaxed, southern mood that adds a special warmth to a meal. Borrowing its style from the French Quarter of New Orleans, the restaurant is an oasis in an urban desert. The sound of waterfalls combines with the soothing presence of flowers and greenery to help relax the visitor.

The extensive menu, from breakfast to dinner, is a clever mix of familiar favorites and intriguing house specialties. Tempting homemade delicacies include Eggs Mondaire, fresh poached eggs atop crisp bacon, steamed spinach, tomato slices and a toasted English muffin, smothered in Hollandaise sauce; Big Mamou's Chicken Sandwich, hot broiled breast of chicken on a squaw roll; and Lasagne Pasticcate, pasta layered with beef, Italian sausage, ricotta and mozzarella cheese. Another enjoyable feature is that breakfast is served at any time.

While waiting for your food, you can unwind at a patio table and watch the action on the boulevard or, if you wish, you can browse the many shops that are scattered throughout the building. In the hustle and bustle of Los Angeles, a visit to the French Quarter can be the perfect break. Bring a healthy appetite, as the food is good and the portions large.

THE KING'S CROISSANT
640 North Robertson Boulevard
West Hollywood, CA 90069
Tel. (213) 652-5445
Hrs: Mon. - Sat. 8:00 a.m. - 9:00 p.m.
      Sunday   11:00 a.m. - 6:00 p.m.

The British rock stars that go to the King's Croissant might feel a little homesick, but their illness is soon cured by the tasty English meat pastries that await at this restaurant, located near the swinging center of West Hollywood.

Signed photos of rock stars, black and white flooring and tables shaded by umbrellas set the tone for The King's Croissant. You'll get the same royal treatment accorded the Hollywood celebrities who make it a second home. Stars such as Robert Culp, Catherine Oxenberg, Ozzie Osbourne, and Rod Stewart are tempted by the splendid variety of stuffed pastries, such as chicken, mushroom, and cheese, the Swiss cheese and fresh tomato, and the Polish sausage with mustard croissants. Customers also enjoy whole meal bread pudding, homemade apple pie, raisin custard, sugarless muffins, and Scottish shortbread. Turnovers feature fillings made from lemon curd, cherry, pineapple, peach, and blueberry. Those with a lighter palate choose Chinese Chicken Salad or an English Garden Salad. Owner Debbie King-Stewart has always had an interest in gourmet eating. After being praised by friends, she opened her restaurant on April Fool's Day four years ago.

One of the restaurant's specialties is the "banger," a meat pastry made with pork sausage. Regulars of The King's Croissant have named the English goodie the "best banger in town." In fact, *Cable TV* in 1985, and *L.A. Weekly* in 1986 voted The King's Croissant one of the best in L.A. dining establishments.

MATUSZEK'S CZECHOSLOVAK CUISINE
7513 Sunset Boulevard
West Hollywood, CA 90046
Tel. (213) 874-0106
Hrs: Mon. - Sat.   5:00 p.m. - 11:00 p.m.
Visa and MasterCard are accepted.

In the busy scene of Hollywood restaurants, Matuszek's Czechoslovak Cuisine is a real find. The restaurant has gained a reputation for delicious traditional Czechoslovakian cooking made only from the freshest and most natural ingredients.

The restaurant is young and modern. Its clean, California look is highlighted by grays and lavenders, leafy plants and twinkling lights in the evening. Each table is decorated with a candle, which adds to the romantic mood. The food, of course, is delicious, and it's prepared with the utmost love and care. Specialties include Svickova na Smetane, marinated beef with vegetables in sour cream sauce served with flour bread dumplings and cranberry sauce. Another entree is Teleci na Hribkach, sauteed veal with mushrooms, served with rice and Czech style carrots and sweet peas. The Pecena Kachna features roast duckling with potato dumplings and red cabbage. As a starter, the Prague borscht is marvelous with its rich, creamy, smokey broth. It's chock full of vegetables and laced with sour cream.

Owners Jan and Lidia Matuszek brought all of the menu's sumptuous creations from their native Czechoslovakia. Even the wines are Czech, made from the best grapes and produced in Sonoma County. A slice of Lidia's sinful cheesecake goes well with the wine. If you're lucky, Jan will entertain you with his music, completing a wonderful evening at Matuszek's Czechoslovak Cuisine.

OSCAR'S
8210 Sunset Boulevard
West Hollywood, CA 90046
Tel. (213) 654-3457
Hrs: Lunch   Tue. - Fri.   11:30 a.m. - 2:30 p.m.
      Dinner   Mon. - Sat.   7:00 p.m. - 11:00 p.m.
Visa, MasterCard and AMEX are accepted.

Oscar's opened by demand of the English actors who stay at the Chateau Marmont Hotel directly across Sunset Boulevard when in Los Angeles. Oscar's began business on Valentine's Day over thirteen years ago to provide the "splendid food" and congenial atmosphere the British actors miss abroad.

Immediately acclaimed for being "cool, hip, cozy and completely civilized," Oscar's reinforces this assessment with healthy doses of Smoked Eel, Angels on Horseback, Fresh Dover Sole, London Mixed Grill and a full selection of beers and ale on tap. To keep things even more "civilized," an exciting and appropriately gory English murder mystery evening is given each Friday night. Saturday night finds the stiff upper lip breaking into smiles at a rousing British comedy. Light jazz punctuates the rest of the week.

Designed as an old English pub and eatery, the interior of Oscar's is divided into individual rooms connected by a corridor. The front dining room is a replica of an English bar room, the tables laid with white linen and decorated with fresh flowers. A white grand piano is set in a lovely Art Deco "music room" to the side of the bar; the windows are frosted in Art Deco designs. In the back, capering across white plaster walls, exotic birds and plants enhance the "jungle room."

Each room is individually designed to accommodate all types of private parties, whether a flamboyant celebration, or for more sedate dining. Oscar's is a place to warm the cockles of the English heart.

Those of us in the colonies will also find a good time in the "hip, cozy and completely civilized" Oscar's.

PALETTE
8290 Santa Monica Boulevard
West Hollywood, CA 90046
Tel. (213) 654-8094
Hrs: Mon. - Fri.   7:00 p.m. - 10:30 p.m.
            Lunch   Sat. - Sun.   11:00 a.m. - 2:30 p.m.
            Dinner   6:30 p.m. - 10:30 p.m.
            Club is open from 10:30 p.m. on.
Visa, MasterCard and AMEX are accepted.

Everything about Palette denotes glamor and sophistication. Though the building began humbly as a warehouse, architects Frank Israel and Bob Johnson and interior designer Anthony Machado have transformed the space into one of the serene wonders of L.A. Six giant columns on the inside of the restaurant recall ancient classical temples. At night, strips of neon lights remind you it's the late twentieth century. Machado's trademark bowling ball, fills the lines and corners of the space and injects a bit of humor.

It's no secret why people love to visit Palette; the food is excellent. Palette specializes in Russian, French, Continental, and Nouveau California cuisine. Diners often begin with a soup called Solianica, a cream of Russian delights. Appetizers include Piroshky a la Russ, an ancient Czarist recipe that dates back to Ivan the Terrible. Baltic Herring is also recommended. Entrees include Chicken Paris, featuring a plum or pineapple rolled inside the tender white meat of a chicken breast. Another entree, known as Sturgeon Brochette, offers skewered cubes of marinated sturgeon.

Designers, directors, producers and other celebrities host many of their parties at Palette. Areas are available for screenings and other events. Palette is a feast for all the senses, excellent for an evening of dining and dancing.

ROSE TATTOO
665 North Robertson Boulevard
West Hollywood, CA 90069
Tel. (213) 854-4455
Hrs: Dining Room
          Tue.-Sun.   6:30 p.m.-11:00 p.m.
          Luncheon
          Mon. - Sat.   11:00 a.m. - 3:00 p.m.
          Sunday Brunch   11:30 a.m. - 3:00 p.m.
          Cabaret
          Mon.- Sun.   5:00 p.m. - 2:00 a.m.
          Happy Hour
          Mon.- Fri.   5:40 p.m. - 8:30 p.m.
Visa, MasterCard, AMEX, Diners Club and Carte Blanche are accepted.

For luncheon and dinner in an exciting atmosphere complete with live entertainment nightly and a variety of seafood and other dishes, Rose Tattoo is the place to go. This cabaret hosts famous artists such as Linda Hopkins, Rosalyn Kind and Mara Getz, making it a place to see and be seen. Rose Tattoo is also frequented by notables such as Neil Sedaka and Robert de Niro, to name just a few.

Set back off of Robertson Boulevard in the heart of Hollywood, this charming pink stucco building gives a very stylish air to your dining experience. The patio dining is a lovely experience, with seating for thirty among the plants and flowers. If dining under the stars doesn't suit you, dine in the large, yet intimate dining room that is exquisitely decorated in pink, black and mirrors with patterned wall coverings. The crystal and linen sparkle on the tables, waiting to be filled with delicious platters of food.

Fresh fish is served daily, along with Jumbo Shrimp Cocktails and Oysters on the half shell, which are leagues above the ordinary. With a different flair, the Japanese Chicken Salad, served with snow peas, bean sprouts, ginger and sesame vinaigrette will definitely please anyone with an appetite for quality. Other delicious favorites are the Scampi Provencale sauteed in a garlic butter sauce; the Osso Bucco, served with fettuccine and gremolata sauce; and the famous rack of lamb. Most entrees are served with complimentary hors d'oeuvres. To accompany your meal, choose from an extensive wine and champagne list that would please even the most discriminate tastes.

Downstairs, the Cabaret Room hosts live entertainment and on most nights, guests who are dining are invited to go and enjoy the entertainment without having to pay a cover charge. This restaurant/cabaret provides a thoroughly enjoyable evening out. If you get a chance while you are in Los Angeles, treat yourself to a night out at the "Best Choice" restaurant, the Rose Tattoo.

SPAGO
1114 Horn Avenue at Sunset Boulevard
West Hollywood, CA 90069
Tel. (213) 652-4025
Hrs: Mon. - Sun.   6:00 p.m. - 12:00 midnight
Reservations are required.
Visa, MasterCard, AMEX and Diners Club are accepted.

Among the people who have changed Los Angeles, and a foremost influence in distinctive, contemporary cuisine, Wolfgang Puck has helped to set the style for restaurants around the country. Utilizing a blend of fresh, innovative ingredients with classical French tradition, California cuisine has emerged triumphant and is gloriously presented at Spago.

The Austrian born Puck developed his culinary skills at Hotel de Paris in Monaco and Maxim's in Paris. After attaining fame as top chef at Ma Maison in L.A., he left French cooking to establish Spago on Sunset Boulevard. The restaurant, which is light, airy and open, features a long expanse of picture windows that invite patrons to gaze out over the city lights. The chic, yet lighthearted interior, designed by Puck's wife, Barbara Lazaroff, has set the standard for many new restaurants in much the same way Wolfgang's cuisine has done. Frequented by luminaries, as well as a contingency of loyal regulars, reservations should be made as well in advance as your itinerary allows.

Like Los Angeles itself, the fare at Spago is a blend of American, French, Italian, Japanese, Chinese and Mexican cuisines, prepared with flair and imagination. Enjoy appetizers such as sauteed crab cakes with a lime herb butter and rockette salad; or wild rice and corn risotto with grilled quail. Pasta dishes such as lobster ravioli with lobster tarragon butter; or Wolfgang's famous pizzas, such as one with spicy Louisiana shrimp, sun dried tomatoes, leeks and red onions, grace the lively menu. Entrees defy choice in their ingenuity, such as roasted Alaskan salmon with ginger, black pepper and Cabernet butter; thick cut free range veal loin on a potato onion pancake with a black pepper sauce; and crisp sauteed sweetbreads on argula salad with sherry vinegar butter. Desserts such as pecan pie with cinnamon ice cream and bourbon sauce will send you into Nirvana!

Indulge in some of the finest cuisine available anywhere at the celebrated Spago. From the creations of a brilliant chef to the brilliant company you'll rub elbows with, a dining experience at Spago is sure to be a highlight of your Los Angeles adventure.

TUTTOBENE
945 North Fairfax Avenue
West Hollywood, CA 90046
Tel. (213) 655-7051
Hrs: Mon. - Sat.   11:30 a.m. - 3:00 p.m.
       Mon. - Sun.   6:00 p.m. - 11:30 p.m.
Visa, MasterCard, AMEX and Diners Club are accepted.

Tuttobene means "everything's fine," and that's the way it should be at one of West Hollywood's most distinctive restaurants. Located on Fairfax in what was formerly the Hollywood Diner, it continues a tradition started with the opening of two other Italian establishments, Panecaldo and Silvios.

"We serve Italian country cuisine," says owner Silvio De Mori. "That's modern, essential, simple, basic, and very good." He recommends the Tuna Carpaccio, thin slices of fresh tuna with lemon and extra virgin olive oil on a bed of Radicchio and Belgian endive. Once your appetite's roaring, you might try the Florentine Steak, a two to three pound Porterhouse steak prepared and grilled in the Florentine tradition. And for dessert, there are those luscious baked bananas with strawberry sauce.

Tuttobene features homemade breads and pastas, prepared fresh every day. So, you like Italian cooking, do you? We guarantee, you're going to love Tuttobene, where "everything's fine."

THE WILSHIRE DISTRICT

In contrast to the glamor of Hollywood, is its adjacent Wilshire District directly to the south. If Hollywood could be considered the entertainment center of the region, Wilshire Boulevard is the district's cultural center. Several of L.A.'s most respected museums lie within a block of each other where you can see everything from the bones of a saber tooth tiger to exquisite works of contemporary or impressionistic art.

ATTRACTIONS

• The ooze and goo of the **La Brea Tar Pits** are where many a prehistoric creature met his premature end. Both the tar pits and the museum containing the remains of the creatures are located in **Hancock Park**, at Curson Avenue and Wilshire Boulevard. Replicas of prehistoric beasts are set up at the bubbling asphalt tar pits.

• The **George C. Page Museum** contains the exhibits of fossilized animals recovered from the pits. You can see the assembled skeletons of saber tooth tigers, mastodons, wooly mammoths and camels. There's also a section where children can handle some of the sticky ooze taken from the pits. For information call (213) 936-2230.

• The **Los Angeles County Museum of Art**, 5905 Wilshire Boulevard, is a complex of three buildings surrounded by a sculpture garden. The collections range from ancient artifacts to the most contemporary of modern art.

• At the **Bing Theater** visitors can usually watch a fine film. Weekends usually bring to the museum's plazas an assortment of mimes, musicians and other outdoor performers.

• During the Depression, farmers began setting up stalls on a vacant field at 3rd Street and Fairfax Avenue. Today the **Farmer's Market** continues to thrive as both a tourist attraction and a favorite place for the locals to shop. The sprawling market covers some twenty acres and includes more than 150 shops, stores, stalls and restaurants. One can watch candy makers at work and see peanut butter being made. The two dozen or so restaurants offer all manner of American and international food. The market is closed Sundays. For information call (213) 933-9211.

ACCOMMODATION

HYATT WILSHIRE
3515 Wilshire Boulevard
Los Angeles, CA 90010
Tel.   (213) 381-7411
        Telex 677139
All major credit cards are accepted.

As anyone who has done much traveling will tell you, there is nothing that can compare with a stay at a true luxury hotel, a hotel such as the Hyatt Wilshire. A gleaming landmark on world famous Wilshire Boulevard in the heart of the city's business district, the Hyatt Wilshire has been a bastion of sumptuous, sophisticated civility for twenty-two years.

Superlative service is the hallmark of the hotel. From valet parking to the complete concierge service, a friendly, efficient, well trained staff stands ready to assist you in any way they can. The hotel has recently been totally refurbished and features a sparkling new decor in all 400 rooms as well as the lobby, main rooms and restaurant. The large rooms are decorated in subtle art deco pinks and greys and are furnished in French deco style with lacquered armoires, marble tables and potted plants, which give each room its own gentle ambiance. Those with a taste for the best in life should experience the Regency Club, a finely appointed security floor featuring a private lounge and luxurious amenities such as stocked refrigerators, bathroom televisions, lounging robes and hairdryers. Hyatt Wilshire guests may enjoy an invigorating swim in the heated outdoor pool or a workout in a fully equipped exercise center. For your dining pleasure the hotel boasts several fine restaurants. Try the superb menu of Hugo's Garden Court for an exquisite dinner or a poolside brunch. For breakfast, lunch or a late afternoon appetizer, visit g.g.'s, a modern, European style sidewalk cafe. The Cafe Carnival serves drinks and dancing to spirited music provided by a DJ.

For the discerning traveler the Hyatt Wilshire offers the perfect combination of refinement and relaxation with a matchless blend of classic and current all topped off with the unparalleled service of a world class hotel.

BED & BREAKFAST INN

WILSHIRE CREST INN
6301 Orange Street
Los Angeles, CA 90048
Tel.   (213) 936-5131
        (800) 232-7378 CA
        (800) 654-9951 US
Visa, MasterCard, AMEX, Discover and Diners Club are accepted.

Looking for charm, comfort and convenience only steps away from from Beverly Hills, Hollywood and Century City? Some place tucked quietly away in a green residential area? The Wilshire Crest Inn is a small, elegant European style hotel made to suit your needs.

The Wilshire Crest Inn is owner operated and preserves the European tradition of gracious hospitality and personal attention by a caring staff. As you approach the Inn you will notice all the bedroom windows of the lovely two story building look over the courtyard or patio. Colorful flowers and feathery green ferns fill the gardens and patio areas. The foyer is beautifully mirrored and there is a feeling of the past mixed with the elegance of the age of Art Deco. Graceful arches lead from the foyer into the parlor where you can sit in comfort on luxuriously appointed furniture. At the end of your busy day you can return to a spacious air conditioned bedroom with color TV, direct dial phone, a king, queen or double-size bed and attractive toiletries. A pleasant parlor in soft touches of mint green beckons for a quiet conversation. High tea is served in the parlor in the afternoons. The Inn is sprinkled with comfortable niches in which to relax.

The best of Los Angeles attractions are close to the Wilshire Crest Inn. The fabulous Farmers Market, Rodeo Drive, movie studios and La Cienega's Restaurant Row are but a few of the many sights to enjoy. Treat yourself to the comfort and quietness of a residential inn located a step or two away from the places and events that make Los Angeles intriguing.

WESTSIDE

Los Angeles County's Westside Region is best known for its fashionable neighborhoods, wooded canyon communities and fine beaches. True to its reputation, the Westside contains some of the most spectacular displays of opulence in America in the neighborhoods of Beverly Hills, Bel Air and Westwood.

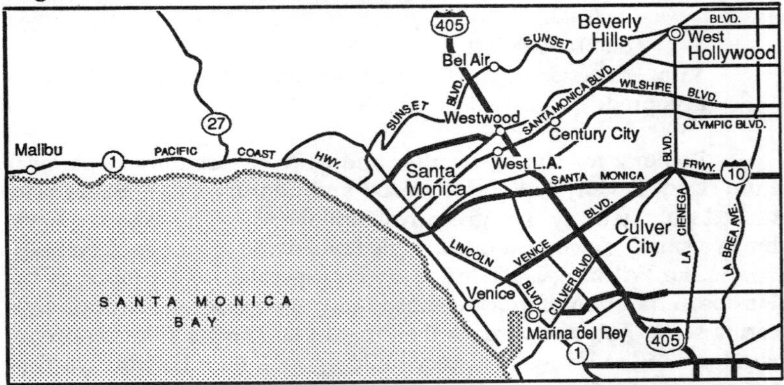

This is also the Beach Blanket Babylon region of the Santa Monica and Venice beaches. Where the boulevards wind up the south slope of the Santa Monica Mountains, more fine homes are set among the dense growth of trees. Whether it's grand homes or suntan oil slick bodies basking on the beach, the Westside region of Los Angeles County offers a visitor plenty to see and do.

SHOP 'TIL YOU DROP

Los Angeles is many things to many people. Playground, home and vacation destination; it is also super salesland and its retailing contributes heavily to the Gross National Product.

If the fashion scene is not determined in L.A. it is at least marketed to the masses. The rich and famous, middle class or mundane, tourist and traveler, man, woman and child are offered a chance to rub elbows with as diverse a mixture of "fellow shoppers" as is imaginable.

Equally diverse are the shopping locations, prices and wares displayed. From the downtown area of Los Angeles proper to the sinfully expensive, trendy and exclusive Beverly Hills area; cultures, creations and costs run the gamut almost as far as the imagination can travel.

Beverly Hills is not connected to the same reality as most of the world. Locked into a tangent of its own design, Beverly Hills boasts of its own government, once having Will Rogers as its first honorary mayor, and the "Ambassadears." Dressed in designer uniforms, these multi-lingual hostesses are available to fill a variety of functions. Walk/shop tours, registration services at meetings, conventions, group dinners and luncheons are among the services provided by highly intelligent, concerned and attractive hostesses.

From the jungle-like interior of Banana Republic to the *nouveau riche* theme of stores such as Camp Beverly Hills, this little community (33,000 residents) is an island of elegance. Intersecting Benedict Canyon Drive on the west, **Rodeo (that's ro-DAY-o) Drive** runs parallel to Beverly Drive, crossing Wilshire Boulevard before running out of steam near the Santa Monica Freeway.

On Rodeo Drive world renowned names in fashion—Gucci, Cartier, Van Cleef & Arpel and Giorgio—provide the latest in stylish, posh and expensive designs. Six figure price tags are the rule rather than the exception, valet parking is available at most of the shops, and the only apparent competition between stores is in who can give off the greater aura of grandeur.

Also within the confines of Beverly Hills, **Wilshire Boulevard** features the elite of the department store world. Established—both in price and stature—names read like a veritable Who's Who of multi-level shopping. Neiman-Marcus, Saks Fifth Avenue and Bonwit Teller are a few of the more easily identifiable establishments.

Just west of Beverly Hills is **Westwood Village**. Whereas Beverly Hills seems to have evolved into the lifestyle it represents and maintains an air of inaccessibility, Westwood Village is a manufactured environment, catering to the masses. Once a grove of sycamore trees, Westwood was founded in 1928 by an investment corporation desiring to create an unusual business district. That they did. Musicians and mimes travel the streets, sidewalk vendors dot the corners and outdoor restaurant patios provide viewers and viewees with ringside seats for the circus-like atmosphere of Westwood.

Although the store names may be less recognizable than those on Rodeo Drive, the quality of the merchandise is comparable and often represents one of a kind creations. At times surrounded by and at times surrounding the UCLA campus, this Mediterranean style development is home to a wide variety of specialty shops geared towards a wide variety of tastes.

Also located near Beverly Hills is the **Beverly Center**. Shopping with an international flair is the theme of this eight level extravaganza. Boutiques offer all the recognizable designer labels and then some, specialty food stores and restaurants feature concoctions as wild as the Los Angeles night life, and enough movie theaters to almost eclipse Broadway in New York City await. Just at the front of the Beverly Center is the Hard Rock Cafe. A diverse and youth oriented establishment, the Cafe has already made the front of T-shirts across the U.S.A.

The **Westside Pavilion** is a sprawling monolithic mall designed by many of the same architects and firms involved in the 1984 Olympics. Created to give the impression of a sunny, upbeat, urban environment the glass encased structure is located on Pico Boulevard. A traditional experience, the Pavilion features 149 different shopping attractions including a May Company and the area's only Nordstrom department store.

Over in the Pasadena-Glendale area you'll find more than the now famous Tournament of Roses Parade and the more infamous smog. At times the smog is so bad your hand can almost disappear before your very eyes. For those needing one, the smog is a good excuse to get indoors and do a little serious shopping.

The **Pasadena Plaza** is as good a place as any to dry those watery eyes, give the lungs a shot at some manufactured oxygen and shop, shop, shop. Boasting award winning art and architecture, the Plaza is rivaled, at least in shopability, by the Glendale Galleria. The **Glendale Galleria** is located on Colorado Boulevard and features Buffums, The Broadway and Nordstrom department stores, and 160 other specialty shops, stores and eateries.

The Pasadena-Glendale area is home to many cultural offerings, including the Norton Simon Museum, Pacific Asia Museum, Rancho Santa Ana Botanical Gardens, Santa Fe Railroad Depot and the world famous Huntington Library and Art Gallery. But, with all the available shopping areas why anyone would want to visit any of these is beyond the imagination.

Deeper into the heart of the San Fernando Valley there lies another galleria, this one in Sherman Oaks. On Ventura Boulevard, the **Sherman Oaks Galleria** is an upbeat indoor mall offering a myriad of restaurants, shops (over 120) and major department stores.

A few blocks away is the **Sherman Oaks Fashion Square** proudly living up to its name. The latest in fashions and yet to be fashions are adeptly presented in what is billed as the first open air shopping plaza in this particular area.

For a major touch of elegance and luxury the **Promenade Mall** on Topanga Canyon Boulevard is home to Saks Fifth Avenue, Bullock's Wilshire, Robinsons and a host of equally challenging stores and restaurants.

A partial listing of other Los Angeles area shopping centers, malls and plazas include, Century City's **ABC Entertainment Center** with its outdoors environment and first run movie theaters or

Broadwayish Schubert Theatre. The **Century City Shopping Center** serves up a healthy portion of the latest in trends, fashions and unique gifts, as well as sidewalk cafes and big name department stores.

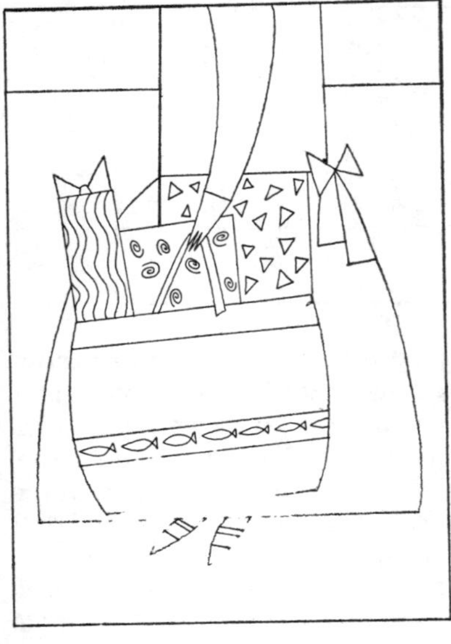

Near the Los Angeles International Airport, in Culver City, is the **Fox Hills Mall**. The major attraction in addition to May Company and The Broadway is a booth where tickets to every major cultural event in Los Angeles may be purchased. Also near the Airport is the **Manhattan Village Mall**. Beautiful may be too tame a word for this garden like shopping mall gently fanned by Pacific Ocean breezes.

The infamous last, but not least is upon the valiant Los Angeles shopper, and it is the biggie: downtown L.A. You want it, they got it; you need it, you'll find it; can't afford it, charge it. Upstairs, downstairs, on the sidewalk, in the back alley, brand name, no name. Psst! Psst, hey you! Yeah you, come here! Have I got a bargain for you.

Right smack dab in the middle, the pulsing, throbbing heart of it all stands the **Broadway Plaza**. Within its impressive girth the Broadway Plaza features the department store of the same name, a 500 room Hyatt Regency and an entire city block of upwardly spiraling shops and restaurants.

Outwardly, instead of upwardly, spiraling is the **ARCO Plaza**. Dishing out the *Subterranean Homesick Blues* to the tune of seven acres, the ARCO Plaza is one of the largest underground shopping centers in the world.

Did someone say clothes? Where else but the **Garment District**? If those words evoke the image of racks of clothing racing down crowded streets; tall, lithesome models and the rather gonzo world of fabric, fashion and fanfare, then you're right on target. The **Cooper Building** at 860 Los Angeles Street is representational of that special insanity associated with industrial garmenting. Nine floors of *haute couture* in brand name clothing and every imaginable accessory is offered at prices so low, that a trip to this area can pay for the entire trip to Los Angeles with the savings.

With the same theme, but without as much of the hustle and bustle, elbow to elbow franticness, is the **1717 Outlet** on Figueroa. If designer clothes at discount prices in a warehouse environment seems bizarre, try it. You might find it to be more bazaar.

Also in the Garment District are dozens of shops, stores and markets offering a melange of goods from around the world at discount prices. An excellent example of the endless possibilities is **the St. Vincent Jewelry Center.** The largest jewelry store in the world, St. Vincent features high quality original jewelry at the lowest possible prices.

Not to be outdone by the outlying areas, downtown L.A. boasts its own mall with the **Seventh Market Place.** Within the confines of the Citicorp Plaza, the unsuspecting shopper is whisked away to the international flavor of a European marketplace. Street vendors in authentic costumes sell a potpourri of aromatic and inspiring foods with a worldwide flavor and theme.

Esprit has made and left its mark on the fashion world and Los Angeles to the extent of opening an enormous, 30,000 square foot retail store. Once a roller rink, shoppers can visit one of the four separate and distinctive shops within Esprit. If there is such a thing, non-shoppers can enjoy the fascinating architecture of the building and its interior.

Ethnically speaking, downtown Los Angeles is unparalled in its diversity and authenticity. For south of the border flair, **Olvera Street** is part of the El Pueblo de Los Angeles State Historic Park. Looking just like the American idea of a Mexican marketplace, Olvera Street features Mexican crafts, art and foods.

Southeast Asia is represented *en force* along 1st and 2nd Streets. **Little Tokyo** offers the best in Japanese handiwork. Stretching from Main Street to Alameda, the oriental flavor is enhanced by the Japanese Village Plaza and Weller Court, both specializing in Nippon manufactured goods.

Perhaps the best known shopping area sporting an oriental flavor is **Chinatown.** Within its expansive borders, first generation Chinese, Taiwanese, Vietnamese, Cambodians, Thai and Laotians have authentically recreated the architecture, atmosphere and ambiance of their respective homelands. Herbs, pastries, jewelry and personal expressions of art and culture are available for viewing and purchasing.

Nowhere can the urge to shop be so hedonistically indulged as in Los Angeles. The sublime and the ridiculous rest side by side with the expensive and the outrageous. Price tags of $500,000 can be found just a few feet from tags marked $5.00. Gold plated Buddahs and gold and diamond necklaces harmoniously co-exist within the L.A. city limits. Marketplace to the stars, international visitors and the average shopping maniac, Los Angeles is *the* place to shop 'til you drop.

BEL AIR

Although Bel Air is not as legendary a community as nearby Beverly Hills, its sumptuous homes set in lush landscaped neighborhoods make it one of the nation's premier prestige communities. Once you drive through its white iron gateway north of Westwood off Sunset Boulevard, you'll discover that many of the homes are as impressive as those in Beverly Hills. In many cases, however, all you will see is the rooftops of the lavish homes because owners have taken great care landscaping their estates so the yards are protected from the prying eyes of passersby.

RESTAURANT

THE FINE AFFAIR
666 Sepulveda Boulevard
Bel Air, CA 90049
Tel. (213) 476-2848
Hrs: Lunch   Tue. - Fri.   11:30 a.m. - 2:30 p.m.
      Dinner   Tue. - Sun.   6:00 p.m. - 10:30 p.m.
      Sunday Brunch   11:00 a.m. - 2:30 p.m.
Visa, MasterCard, AMEX and Diners Club are accepted.

Luxuriance and romantic dining unite with premiere service and food at this prestigious restaurant, just blocks from Sunset Boulevard. Exit the San Diego freeway and moments later the valet parking cares for the car, and an experience in exceptional service has only just begun.

Flawless table side decorum is assured by the expert captain. From the time you are seated, it is clear that each table's candlelight, fresh flowers and pale pink table linens speak the word "extraordinary." Each meal is classically prepared, beginning with "Les Salades," such as La Salade de Champignons Pleurottes aux Poivres Rouges Et Verts, a mélange of French Oyster Mushrooms and multi-colored Bell Peppers sautéed with Shallots and Garlic, served on a bed of Red Leaf lettuce. Select from an impressive list of appetizers, including Spinach Angel Hair Pasta and delicately sautéed Scallops resting on a light Tomato Sauce garnished with a puree of Nicoise Olives. Fresh fillet of Norwegian Salmon with Saffron Sauce, Roast Breast of Duck, Filet Mignon, Veal Chop with a creamy wild Mushroom sauce, Loin of Lamb and other tasty specialties are prepared to excite the classical taste yet provide contemporary palates with beautiful and appealing presentations.

The Executive and Bel Air dining rooms are available for private parties in this fine restaurant. Whether you choose The Fine Affair for a party or for a romantic dinner for two, you are assured of the finest food and service. Servings are exquisitely timed and each time you leave the table, your return is greeted by an attentive waiter pulling out the chair and replacing the napkin.

BEVERLY HILLS

Palatial homes, lush boulevards and exclusive shops are all part of the Beverly Hills scene. It has long been known as the community of the stars, as well as a place where a member of the *nouveau riche* could build his Moorish palace next to a neighbor's Tudor Mansion, complete with Corinthian colonnade around the pool, and still be within minutes of one of the world's foremost business and entertainment centers.

If you're heading out on Sunset Boulevard from Hollywood, the mood suddenly changes at Doheny Drive. The glitter and glitz of the Strip's sidewalk life gives way to a more elegant backdrop of clipped lawns, manicured hedges and stately homes. Turn off on Rodeo Drive and you'll see an array of expensive specialty shops.

Beverly Hills is just eight miles west of booming Los Angeles, and just a short drive from the overnight bedroom developments of the San Fernando Valley. But, Beverly Hills residents have kept a close reign on development for decades. For many years the community required that lawns be maintained in front of homes, and

"For Sale" signs larger than one square foot were never tolerated. The community has a tradition of being very protective of its greenery. To remove any of 28,000 planted pines, acacias, palms, eucalyptus or pepper trees, one would have to gain the approval of fifty-one percent of the neighborhood, and then agree to replace it with a tree of similar age and size.

For visitors, Beverly Hills offers an opportunity to browse through exclusive shops looking at fine jewelry, furs and designer clothing. The most exclusive shops are open to customers, by appointment only, who are prepared to drop a bundle of green for a new set of threads.

Traditionally, the homes of the rich and famous have been clustered up Lexington Road, Coldwater Canyon Drive, Tower Way and Cove Way. While driving by you're more likely to see the walls and gates to these estates than the onyx pools, sunken gardens, reproduction Grecian temples, private golf courses and terraced lawns.

Over the years Beverly Hills' reputation for opulence has given rise to a thriving tour business. Although the names of the residents have changed, not much else has since the days when bus drivers guided loads of tourists through the neighborhoods announcing: "Folks, if you look to the right you'll see Eddie Cantor's home, and over there to your left is Charlie Chaplin's place. Right there is Jack Benny's house, and there you can see Fred Astaire's house, and if you look to your left..." and so on.

Sales of maps to the star's homes is still a major enterprise along Sunset Boulevard. Their accuracy is not always of the highest standards because the personalities who move into these homes almost as often move out. Will Rogers once remarked that properties change hands so fast that by the time escrow is completed for one buyer, it has been sold a dozen more times. Rogers was speaking of the real estate boom of the 1920s, but his hyperbolic wit might just as well apply today.

Tour buses still roll down streets, but the names of the people who live in the houses are not as likely to be as recognizable as in days gone by. The Trousdale Estates section of Beverly Hills is more than fifty percent foreign owned. Local real estate people say the trend is continuing with nearly seventy percent of home buyers being non-Californians and foreign nationals. Many are refugees of sorts, having left some of the world's trouble spots to live in the relative security that the walled estates of Beverly Hills has to offer.

Shoppers can have a good time in Beverly Hills, even if they can't afford a $100 pair of designer boxer shorts. The merchandise is some of the world's most expensive, as well as the most out of the ordinary. Where Wilshire crosses Beverly Hills you'll find several department stores known for their up-scale clientele. Saks Fifth Avenue, a Neiman-Marcus and the always eclectic Abercrombie and Fitch are fixtures in this area.

Rodeo Drive is the community's most famous shopping district. Many of the shops provide the wardrobes for television personalities. Any of the several restaurants with street side patios can offer the perfect vantage point from which to people watch while enjoying a bite to eat.

Beverly Hills has a long history that goes back to the days of Spanish and Mexican occupation. In the early part of the nineteenth century was the 4,500 *Rancho Rodeo de las Aguas*, or "gathering of the waters." In the early 1930s the granddaughter of one of the original Los Angeles settlers maintained a home there.

In 1854 two Americans purchased the ranch and attempts were made to settle the area, all of which failed; until 1912, when the Rodeo Land and Water Company, headed by Burton E. Green of Beverly Farms, Massachusetts, began building subdivisions. One sprang up between Wilshire and Santa Monica Boulevard, and another a little to the northwest. The lavish Beverly Hills Hotel also went up that year in what was then a bean field. Within two years the population of Beverly Hills had grown to 500. In the 1920s Beverly Hills saw a growth rate exceeding 2,500 percent.

The 1920s boom came right after Douglas Fairbanks Sr. purchased a hilltop site to build his magnificent Pickfair estate, often referred to as the Buckingham Palace of the West. Before long other celebrities followed suit, often times trying to outdo previous efforts at erecting lavish monuments to their success.

Some would grow to regret their efforts. The huge estates became something of an albatross around the necks of people who longed for simpler lifestyles. John Barrymore moved into a hilltop mansion that he later scornfully referred to as "The Chinese Tenement." Barrymore had trouble finding a buyer for the estate with three swimming pools, one of which he stocked with rainbow trout. Speaking of his attempts to maintain the property, he said, "It was a kind of nightmare, but it might appeal to somebody—maybe some actor."

ACCOMMODATIONS

THE BEVERLY HILTON
9876 Wilshire Boulevard
Beverly Hills, CA 90210
Tel.   (213) 274-7777
        (800) HILTONS
Visa, MasterCard, AMEX, Diners Club and Hilton are
accepted.

Share in the opulence of the rich and famous and make The Beverly Hilton your "home away from home." Built in 1955 by Conrad Hilton, the Beverly Hilton has earned a reputation as a deluxe hotel by providing excellent personalized service in a singularly luxurious surrounding.

Located in the heart of the social center of Los Angeles, The Beverly Hilton is close to world famous restaurants, exclusive shopping centers along Rodeo Drive and within minutes of the sandy expanses of the ocean beach or cultural attractions. The Beverly Hilton has been host to such illustrious events as the Golden Globe Awards, the Board of Governor's Ball and the American Film Institute's Life Achievement Award Presentations.

Accommodations are tastefully decorated in soft pastels and contemporary furnishings. Each guest room and suite has complimentary HBO, CNN and ESPN and your choice of six in-room movies, a small refrigerator stocked with mineral water, a well lighted work area, direct dial telephones (two in most rooms) in addition to a host of various amenities. Most rooms feature a balcony.

A choice of two heated swimming pools, a fitness center under the administration of a full time recreational director, tour information and arrangements, a beauty and barber shop, a women's boutique, a men's shop and a jewelry department are among the other various services offered at The Beverly Hilton. A full time foreign language service is offered for those guests who hail from abroad. Special attention is given to understand their many cultural differences and to ensure that their stay is memorable. Foreign exchange currencies are available through the hotel cashiers.

For the business executive, who can't always travel with computer in hand, a state of the art Executive Business Center is offered at The Beverly Hilton. It features three IBM Personal Computers ATs with IBM Color Displays, an AT&T Personal computer, modems, printers, typewriters and everything you'll need to get the job done. The center also provides secretarial, notary and stenographic assistance as well as a private office for business meetings.

Three award winning restaurants are featured at The Beverly Hilton. Trader Vic's features exotic cuisine from the South Seas in the surroundings of a nautical motif. L'Escoffier, on the penthouse level offers exquisite French entrees in a romantic setting and Mr. "H" provides a host of buffet items. A coffee shop, two cocktail lounges and an extensive room service menu are also available.

"The Renaissance of a World Class Hotel" can only be experienced at The Beverly Hilton. Make this your "Best Choice" for a home away from home.

BEVERLY WILSHIRE HOTEL, 9500 Wilshire Boulevard, Beverly Hills, CA. Tel. (213) 275-4287. This is a distinguished grand hotel in the heart of Beverly Hills, at Rodeo Drive. It has been the stopping place of royalty, dignitaries and celebrities for the past sixty years.

FOUR SEASONS HOTEL
300 South Doheny Drive at Burton Way
Los Angeles, CA 90048
Tel.   (213) 273-2222
        (800) 332-3442
All major credit cards are accepted.

The Four Seasons Hotel presents an elegance unusual in California. "This hotel is unlike any other in Los Angeles. Four Seasons is bringing an East Coast and European flavor to the city. Instead of a lot of large spaces flowing together, this hotel is like a home—you walk through spaces to get to other spaces," explains general manager Charles Ferraro.

Jade green balcony railings accent the soft beige, sixteen story residential tower. The grandeur of a European manor house and the sensuousness of Southern California combine to make the interior ambiance a balance of elegance. Guest accommodations of 285 luxuriously furnished rooms and suites are decorated in plush residential style, each with French doors leading onto a balcony overlooking Beverly Hills and greater Los Angeles. All rooms have individual climate controls, concealed remote control televisions, clock radios, refrigerated mini bars and multi-line telephones. Marble bathrooms feature television, telephone, hair dryer, lighted makeup mirrors and terry robes. Rooms with wheelchair accessibilities and free from tobacco smoke are available on request.

The executive chef oversees an international menu of fine dining in the Gardens Restaurant. The Cafe offers an informal menu. Windows Lounge provides light lunch, afternoon tea and cocktails in a sophisticated setting. A complete fitness facility is available. Meeting facilities are extensive. Four Seasons Hotel makes its own unique statement in Los Angeles. Visitors will be surprised to find this urban European elegance in casual Southern California.

L'ERMITAGE HOTEL
9291 Burton Way
Beverly Hills, CA 90210
Tel. (213) 278-3344
All major credit cards are accepted.

Hidden away in a quiet residential neighborhood in Beverly Hills, L'Ermitage is the only hotel in Los Angeles to receive the American Automobile Association's "Five Diamond" rating. It's been doing so since 1977 and there are several reasons.

It begins with a 112 suite establishment staffed by 130 trained professionals. Those suites are an orgy of opulence and fastidiously maintained. They consist of living rooms and fireplaces, stocked wet bars, dressing areas and powder rooms, private terraces and fully equipped kitchen facilities. The telephones have conference call capabilities and when you arrive, you are greeted with a basket of fresh fruit and a bottle of wine or mineral water.

The Cafe Russe is also a major factor in L'Ermitage Hotel's sterling reputation. In a setting of dark woods and original European and American oil paintings, the guest is treated to Eggs Cocotte Bordelaise, Crab Tartar, caviar with blinis and sour cream and other Gaellic delights. So, as you can see, the L'Ermitage is not for everyone. But if luxury, sophistication and Cordon Bleu cooking mean something to you, you've either already stayed at L'Ermitage and will soon return.

APPAREL

BELLI BAMBINI
8618 Melrose Avenue
Los Angeles, CA 90060
Tel. (213) 854-1996
Hrs: Mon. - Sat. 10:00 a.m. - 6:00 p.m.
Visa, MasterCard, AMEX and Discover are accepted.

Share in the Belli Bambini experience, an exquisitely stocked children's apparel shop in the full spirit of the finest European children's stores. Owner Ute Pancer's shop is roomy and gives ample space to display the exciting, unusual lines of children's fashions. Belli Bambini is the only store in Beverly Hills that carries the wonderful up to the minute Sonia Rykeil line of infants and girls fashion wear.

The breathtakingly beautiful silk party dresses of Babetta of Italy are also featured. Fine cottons and silk from Anastasia of Paris are beautifully displayed as well as charming taffetas with silver polka dots and black velvets with white lace collars. A complete sporty line for boys and girls is crafted by Delfino of Italy. Belli Bambini's infant section is a paradise for babies. Names such as Joseph Baby and Tartine et Chocolat grace the labels of exquisite baby clothes. Baby armoires are filled with handmade lace christening gowns from Spain, overnight bags, delicately knitted coverups, stockings and soft leather shoes.

Natural fibers, laces and linens, bright, jewel colored printed dresses, classic pants, shirts and ties are beautifully displayed at Belli Bambini. Outside this fantasy land of children's clothing is a shaded garden area where parents and little ones may relax and enjoy their shopping adventure at Belli Bambini.

DORAL'S PICKLES AND CREAM
125 South Robertson Boulevard
Beverly Hills, CA 90211
Tel. (213) 855-0696
Hrs: Mon. - Sat.   10:00 a.m.-5:30 p.m.
Visa, MasterCard and AMEX are accepted.

Doral's Pickles and Cream is the shop that all pregnant women dream about. Doral, the owner, has gone through four pregnancies herself and knows how hard it is to find beautiful, appropriately priced maternity clothes. Doral's offers a wide selection of merchandise and the best service a pregnant woman could ask for. Parking is ample and the shop is centrally located so you do not have to walk several blocks to get there. The inviting entrance, complete with a green canopy and lattice work around the windows, gives a charming country feel to the store. Another plus is that Doral's is located between a footwear store, and a children's clothing store, which makes your shopping easier as you do not have to walk all over town to find what you want.

This shop is filled with racks of the largest assortment of maternity wear in the country. Doral carries everything from evening wear to bathing suits and underwear. Some of the designers that are represented are Amy Ruth and Bill Frame, who design beautifully made upscale dresses and evening items; Isis, a wonderful maker of suits, dresses and pantsuits for the business woman; and Oliver Pease who designs a line of younger looking clothing for everything from work to play. Doral's even takes care of you after the baby is born with a line of nursing wear that complements a mother's need to nurse discreetly. Accessories and stockings that go with all of your outfits are also available.

Intimate and warm, the atmosphere is the ultimate in relaxation—there is even a couch to rest on. Doral's Pickles and Cream is much more than just a clothing store, it is a place where women can feel comfortable and relaxed while they are taken care of with the exceptional service that Doral and her caring staff offer. For some women the experience of maternity can be exciting and confusing, but Doral offers a very comprehensive service that is both honest and caring. Besides dressing and undressing those that have difficulty, they offer decaf, tea, snacks and even soda crackers for those with nausea. There is a broad price range from very moderate to very high so that everyone's needs can be met. If you have trouble coming in during the hours the shop is open, Doral will provide after hour appointments. Doral will custom prints birth announcements and they are the only place in Beverly Hills that offers twenty-four hour availability. Not only does Doral's Pickles and Cream offer the best maternity clothing in Beverly Hills, they represent maternity fashion at its best.

BAKERY

IL FORNAIO, 301 North Beverly Drive, Beverly Hills, CA. Tel. (213) 550-8330. The bakery offers authentic fresh Italian breads and pasteries combined with a popular Italian cafe for dining.

FURNITURE STORE

SCANDIA DOWN SHOPS
310 North Camden Drive
Beverly Hills, CA 90212
Tel. (213) 274-6925
Hrs: Mon. - Fri.   10:00 a.m. - 6:00 p.m.
          Saturday   10:00 a.m. - 5:30 p.m.
Visa, MasterCard and AMEX are accepted
Also,
17200 Ventura Boulevard 205 Del Amo Fashion Center
Encino, CA 91316   Torrance, CA 90503
Tel. (818) 995-6163   Tel. (213) 370-1560

350 South Lake 109
Pasadena, CA 91101
Tel. (818) 449-0944

People spend one third of their lives in bed. At the Scandia Down Shops, you'll find bed dressings that will make that one third of your life the best it can be.

Walk into one of the four Los Angeles area shops and browse through the wonderful collection of genuine goose down or eider down comforters. Scandia Down also offers Tussah silk or Quallofil™ as down alternatives. Scandia Down uses only the finest, lightest and strongest ticking available, so the down can breathe naturally and have enough room to expand, puff up, and loft. Scandia's best comforters feature a long-staple, Egyptian cambric cotton woven in West Germany. Scandia Down double stitches and pipes the edges of their comforters to prevent loss of down. Scandia Down offers more than comforters. You'll find fluffy feather beds and natural fill sleep pillows in all sizes. Accent pillows add a soft touch to your sofa or chair. Scandia also offers the finest in bed linens featuring hundreds of glorious patterns. Parents will find great linens and comforters for the baby's room.

Scandia Down Shops prides itself on its personalized service. They'll restore and clean your favorite down product. After a night under a luxuriously warm Scandia Down comforter, you'll never be the same.

GIFT SHOP

TESORO
319 South Robertson
Los Angeles, CA 90048
Tel. (213) 273-9890
Hrs: Mon. - Fri.   8:30 a.m. - 5:30 p.m.
       Saturday   9:00 a.m. - 5:00 p.m.
Visa and MasterCard are accepted.

Mark Krasne has created Tesoro, a unique gallery specializing in fine tabletop dishes, giftware and flatware for those discriminating in their tastes. Tableware as functional art is the concept at Tesoro.

Enter Krasne's wonderfully eclectic showroom, and you'll find a totally new focus in tabletop dressing. Krasne works with artists from Europe and America to design colors and shapes patterned after the artwork of Picasso, Miro and the themes of the American Southwest. These collectibles are well suited to the fashionable Southern California clientele who frequent his gallery. They purchase Krasne's extraordinary sandstone pieces; vases and urns in free form shapes in bold or muted colors. You may browse through his fabulous European collection of contemporary custom and handmade linens, featuring matching towels and tablecloths. Those with a nose for the unusual, visit Krasne's scent bar, featuring designer candles, room fragrances, and other potpourri.

Krasne has carefully built up a reputation for inspiring contemporary design wizards to create home accessory art forms. Tesoro is his latest showcase in artwork for the home.

 # GOURMET FOOD

THE CHEESE STORE OF BEVERLY HILLS
419 North Beverly Drive
Beverly Hills, CA 90210
Tel.　(213) 278-2855
　　　(800) 547-1515
All major credit cards are accepted.

As the name implies, The Cheese Store has the best selection of cheese on the West Coast, but they are in no way restricted to just cheeses. White and black truffles, imported Italian and Parma hams and a complete selection of hard to find French and California wines makes the store a complete, one stop shopping gourmet experience.

The entire store is kept at a cool sixty-eight degrees to ensure optimum freshness of the cheeses and other cuisine. Among the more than 500 different cheeses offered are fresh goat cheeses from France, buffalo milk mozzarella, many different Bries, Swiss, Blues and Cheddars from all over the world.

There is always something new and delectable because the owners travel to Europe three or four times a year searching for unusual and delicious things to eat. Gift baskets can be sent all over the United States, although you may be tempted to eat your purchases before you leave the store.

GRAFFEO COFFEE ROASTING COMPANY
315 North Beverly Drive
Beverly Hills, CA 90210
Tel. (213) 273-0817
Hrs: Mon. - Sun.   9:00 a.m. - 6:00 p.m.
Visa and MasterCard are accepted.

Many things have been said and written about the coffee that comes from Graffeo but it can all be summed up in one sentence: simply the world's finest coffee.

All of the Graffeo coffee beans are roasted on the premises which means that you are guaranteed the freshest coffee with a consistently high grade of flavor and aroma.

The Graffeo coffee beans are imported from Columbia, Costa Rica and New Guinea. The beans are then blended and carefully roasted. Concentrating on one vital blend, Luciano Repetto produces just three variations: Dark Roast, Light Roast and Swiss water-process Decaffeinated. This simple process has kept Graffeo a success since 1935.

HAIR SALON

CASSANDRE
9388 Santa Monica Boulevard
Beverly Hills, CA 90210
Tel. (213) 273-9918
Hrs: Mon. - Wed., Sat.   9:00 a.m. - 5:00 p.m.
       Thu. - Fri.   9:00 a.m. - 7:30 p.m.
Also,
18386 Ventura Boulevard
Tarzana, CA 91356
Tel. (818) 881-8400

The name of the game is choices. The name of the choicest is Cassandre, the salon in Beverly Hills known for superb hair design and creativity in coloring.

Cassandre is a salon for all seasons; for the young and mature, the female species, the male too. They come to Cassandre for many reasons. It is the showcase for the line of legendary Sebastian products: hair care, Sebastian Trucco make-up line, skin care, and the brand new Systema line of hair care products.

The salon is electric and eclectic in design. You enter the salon through an asymmetrical door suspended by a giant concrete triangle and move into a world of tasteful design—concrete, gold tile, mat black and grey surroundings, unusual light fixtures and bright splashes of color. You have a distinct impression of the merging of the arts, the raw streets and high fashion.

The philosophy of the dynamic owners, Phillip Carreon and Paul De Armas is unique: to train and house members of the Sebastian Artistic Team at Cassandre, Beverly Hills and to educate their clients not only to achieve the look they receive at the salon, but to create new looks for themselves at home.

Phillip and Paul together with the artistic team at Cassandre work the complete beauty spectrum including cuts, hair color, make-up, the videos and the pictures. From the bizarre and outrageous to the classic look, Cassandre has the extraordinary knack to do it all and is the trendsetter in hair style and make-up design. They are closely scrutinized by the fashion conscious world, so visit Cassandre soon.

ICE CREAM PARLOR

APHRODITE
375 North Beverly Drive
Beverly Hills, CA 90212
Tel. (213) 276-7891
Hrs: Mon. - Thu.   11:00 a.m. - 10:00 p.m.
      Fri. - Sat.   11:00 a.m. - 12:00 midnight
      Sunday   11:00 a.m. - 9:00 p.m.

Appropriately named, this specialty shop is truly an exquisite sweet shop with delicious delicacies and sensational sweets. The quality reputation that this sweet shop has earned is solely due to their award winning products. Located on busy Beverly Drive in the heart of Beverly Hills, Aphrodite has a spacious front accentuated by sheer glass panels that span across the width of the shop. Spacious and comfortable, this is the perfect place to sit and enjoy a Cappuccino, try a piece of the marvellous cheesecake, or taste the delicious yogurt and ice cream while resting after a day of shopping. The pink neon ceiling complements the glass counters, black topped stools, white patio seating and the blinking lights around the windows.

The large glass counters are filled with a luscious array of ice creams and frozen yogurt. A tall glass cabinet is filled with a mouthwatering array of cheesecakes and other specialty cakes. For something really extraordinary, try the turtle cheesecake topped with a chocolate turtle candy. And, if chocolate is what you desire, try the 1001 chocolate chip cake. Or as a gift for a chocolate loving friend, give the chess set of white and dark chocolate. Each piece can be replaced as they are eaten. Aphrodite also makes gelato shakes or smoothies in any flavor you want. Their immense selection includes several pies such as the Key Lime or peanut butter with chocolate mousse. Of their thirty-one kinds of cheesecakes, all of which weigh between five and seven pounds, Dutch apple and Praline 'n Cream are favorites.

Aphrodite treats are sold wholesale through distributors on a national scale, but the Beverly Hills store is their flagship. Aphrodite is a wonderful place to sit and enjoy the delicious quality chocolates and cakes that are produced there. Aphrodite is a sweet shop named "desire."

RESTAURANTS

ANDRE'S RESTAURANT
8635 Wilshire Boulevard
Beverly Hills, CA 90211
Tel. (213) 657-2446
Hrs: Lunch   Mon. - Fri.   11:30 a.m. - 3:00 p.m.
          Dinner   Mon. - Sun. 4:00 p.m. - 11:00 p.m.
Visa, MasterCard and AMEX are accepted.

Andre's Restaurant is a fine eating establishment that has served and satisfied customers for more than twenty-nine years. Andre's is one of the old fashioned family style restaurants that still serves good portions, has superb service, and has specialties guaranteed to satisfy any palate. It may be considered posh, but not stuffy, lavish yet comfortable.

Andre's original Lazy Susan Antipasto Tray is an excellent way to begin a dinner. Entrees include Scampi with jumbo shrimps`a la Andre, and Veal Cutlet Parmigiana. Fresh Norwegian Salmon is served daily as well as Beef Wellington and Grenadine of Beef. For lunch, the chef recommends Broiled Liver with Onions. Other luncheon selections include Cannelloni a la Ripley and Clam or Alfredo Fettuccine. Andre's will accommodate any special dish you request. After a cocktail in the bar frequented by power people and Andre's old timers, you'll take a seat in one of the four dining rooms. Two are reserved for regular dining, two are for banquets and parties.

Hangings and oil paintings cover the walls, while the finest silver and linens adorn the dark baroque furnishings. The staff is attentive and courteous. Andre, with his partner Don Medica, supervise the entire concern, and Andre prepares some of the delicious fare himself. Perhaps he'll prepare a special meal for you.

THE BEVERLY RESTAURANT AND MARKET
342 North Beverly Drive
Beverly Hills, CA 90210
Tel. (213) 274-427
Hrs: Mon. - Sun.   7:30 a.m. - 11:00 p.m.
Visa, MasterCard and AMEX are accepted.

As you walk the streets of Beverly Hills, you'll come across a tidy place that has become a favorite rendezvous for young and old. It's called the Beverly Restaurant and Market, and it features a "something for everyone" menu with a bit more variety than similar menus elsewhere.

Glass windows overlook Beverly Drive, while the entry is dominated by deli cases brimming with whole roast chickens and ducks. You'll see and smell freshly baked bread, along with an array of exotic salads from calamari to Italian ripieni. If you're staying for a meal, you'll find your table in a high ceilinged dining room where the walls are hung with vintage photographs of Beverly Hills' history. Like the luminescent beveled glass above you, everything is fresh, clean and bright. The ambiance combines the old with the new. The menu offers starters such as Rock Crab Salad with Seared Tuna Carpaccio. You can order a salad with the special house dressing; roasted walnuts in roquefort and balsamic vinegar. Specialty sandwiches include Thick Cut Beverly Cheese, with sharp Tillamook cheddar, bacon and tomato grilled in butter and Parmesan cheese. The menu features pastas such as mezzaluna, tagliatelle, and angel hair. From the rotisserie, ask for the Rosemary and Roasted Garlic Chicken.

The Beverly Restaurant and Market is always busy with many residents and visitors exploring the wonderful food in the deli cases. Like them, you can take out any of the establishment's specialties.

THE BISTRO
246 North Canon Drive
Beverly Hills, CA 90210
Tel. (213) 273-5633
Hrs: Lunch
       Mon. - Fri.   11:30 a.m. - 3:00 p.m.
       Dinner
       Mon. - Sat.   6:00 p.m. - 11:00 p.m.
Visa, MasterCard, AMEX and Diners Club are accepted.

Most people remember Billy Wilder as a great Hollywood director. But movie fans may not know he helped design The Bistro in Beverly Hills. After much first hand research in France, Wilder and the owners of this fine establishment created a place that most other restaurants look up to. Despite its California location, the restaurant refuses to become completely Californian. Diners find a decor and menu that reflects classic elegance in a turn of the century atmosphere. Etched glass mirrors and exquisitely set tables give an aristocratic feel. The restaurant is a warm and comforting place, with formal, yet friendly service by a mature, European staff. The menu offers a catholic selection of the finest European dishes. Carpaccio of Tuna is a good cold hor d'oeuvre for dinner, while Small Puff Pastry in a seafood saffron sauce makes an excellent hot beginning. Pastas include Canelloni Piemontaise. A favorite salad is the Young Spinach Leaves with bacon and warm goat cheese. Dinner entrees include Mille Feuilles of Salmon with saffron sauce, which is made of layers of spinach and steamed salmon, or Chicken Casanova, a chicken mousse with Diablo sauce. Lunch soups feature Cream of Watercress, while Capelline with fresh tomato sauce is offered as a pasta choice. For a fish lunch entree, the Eastern Lobster on a bed of tagliatelli noodles is suggested.

In all, the menu offers twelve appetizers, seven soups, five pastas, twelve salads, thirteen fresh fish and shellfish dishes, and eighteen other entrees. All these dishes are served in an atmosphere worthy of the best Parisian restaurants, making The Bistro an international "Best Choice."

THE BISTRO GARDEN
176 North Canon
Beverly Hills, CA 90210
Tel. (213) 550-3900
Hrs: Lunch   Mon. - Fri.   11:30 a.m. - 3:30 p.m.
      Dinner   Sun. - Thu.   6:00 p.m. - 11:00 p.m.
                    Fri. - Sat.   6:00 p.m. - 12:00 midnight
Visa, MasterCard, AMEX and Discover are accepted.

The Bistro Garden, a less formal sibling of The Bistro, is a place to wile away your time in a shaded garden decorated with brilliant fresh flowers. Dine on delicacies from an eclectic menu, while enjoying the chic, elegant atmosphere.

The Bistro Garden features many of the same delicious dishes as The Bistro. Some of the best appetizers include Cold Veal Tonnato, thin slices of veal with a tuna anchovy sauce. The fresh, cracked Dungeness crab is also excellent. Fresh seafood and game are specialties at this restaurant. Fish selections include John Dory sauteed with bananas and orange sections, Grilled Hawaiian Tuna with a mustard and lime sauce, and Grilled Dover Sole. Fresh game dishes include pheasant, venison and rabbit. Desserts are prime at The Bistro Garden. Choose one of the many assorted souffles, a Chocolate Raspberry Mousse Cake, Tarte Turtin, Berries Bistro or assorted fresh sorbet.

The Bistro Garden continues to grow in popularity with Beverly Hills residents and celebrities. Visit this elegant establishment and enjoy an ambiance unmatched in the Los Angeles area.

CAFE EUROPA
326 1/2 South Beverly
Beverly Hills, CA 90212
Tel. (213) 277-2200
Hrs: Lunch
      Mon. - Fri.   11:30 a.m.- 3:00 p.m.
      Dinner
      Mon. - Fri.   5:30 p.m.-10:00 p.m.
Visa, MasterCard, AMEX and Diners Club are accepted.

For contemporary European cuisine, Cafe Europa is the only place that offers satisfaction to the fullest. The reason behind the success of Cafe Europa is Chef Tonio Hipp, who surely is counted among the best chefs in Los Angeles.

A seasoned professional with an extensive European background, Chef Hipp is a member of the prestigious Chaine Des Rotis Seurs, an international epicurean society, headquartered in Paris. The restaurant itself has a delicate European flair to it with tiny white lights outlining and defining the windows and awning, and a red bougainvillea that climbs the building and cascades over the awning. The charming interior is in a pale rose theme and numerous unique fresh floral arrangements, personally created by the talented Ingrid Hipp, adorn the tables.

Cafe Europa is already famous for the Spaetzle that Toni makes from scratch, but all of the other delicacies that he makes deserve just as much, or more praise. Lunch specialties include fresh mussels; seafood marinated in tequila, orange juice, garlic and cilantro; and Swiss and Bavarian Bratwurst. Favorite starters for dinner are the Fresh Mushroom Salad, Shrimp Costa Brava, and Smoked Salmon Strudel. Cafe Europa classics for dinner are the fresh fish of the day, Extra Crispy Duckling, the classic Wiener Schnitzel, Veal Steak, Filet Mignon and Sauerbraten. If you are feeling especially European, have a cappuccino or one of the various freshly squeezed juices with your meal.

Ingrid and Toni Hipp and their staff offer friendly service that shows that they care for their customers. The feeling of a great neighborhood restaurant is a rarity anywhere, especially in Beverly Hills, but you can get it at Cafe Europa.

CALIFORNIA PIZZA KITCHEN
207 South Beverly Drive
Beverly Hills, CA 90212
Tel. (213) 272-7878
Hrs: Sun. - Thu. 11:30 a.m. - 11:00 p.m.
         Fri. - Sat.   11:30 a.m. - 12:00 midnight
Visa, MasterCard and AMEX are accepted.
Also,

Beverly Center
121 North La Cienega
Los Angeles, CA 90048
Tel. (213) 854-6555

Topanga Plaza
6600 Topanga Canyon Boulevard
Canoga Park, CA 91306
Tel. (818) 884-8858

Brentwood
11677 San Vicente Boulevard
Los Angeles, CA 90049
Tel. (213) 826-3573

A wood fired pizza oven sets California Pizza Kitchens apart from the rest of their competitors. But these restaurants have another difference in mind. With the phenomenal growth of the interesting chain, CPKs may become, as owners Larry Flax and Rick Rosenfield plan, the "Baskin-Robbins of pizza."

Although it features the classic cheese pizza, this restaurant offers gourmet dishes that would excite any pizza lover. At the top of the list is the Original Barbecued Chicken, with sliced red onion, cilantro and smoked gouda cheese. The barbecue sauce makes this one stand out. Another favorite is the Roasted Garlic Chicken, with Maui onion, chopped Italian parsley, and garlic shallot butter. Reviewers have praised the Thai Chicken pizza, with pieces of chicken breast marinated in a spicy peanut ginger and sesame sauce. Pizza aficionados enjoy their meal among a black, white and yellow tile motif while watching their order made to perfection by expert chefs, then placed in wood burning ovens. If pizza is not your preference, the menu suggests calzone. Spinach Brie is a recommended choice; light pastry stuffed with garlic, onion, spinach and Brie. Seasoned with cayenne and cumin, the dish becomes spicy. Light entrees, salads, and cheeseless pizzas are on the menu for weight watchers.

California Pizza Kitchens disavow any connection with nouvelle cuisine. They simply provide superlative, innovative gourmet pizza for the individual who wants to try something different.

CELESTINO
236 South Beverly Drive
Beverly Hills, CA 90212
Tel. (213) 859-8601
Hrs: Lunch   Mon. - Fri.   11:00 a.m. - 3:00 p.m.
         Dinner   Mon. - Fri.   5:30 p.m. - 11:00 p.m.
Visa, MasterCard, AMEX and Diners Club are accepted.

Celestino Drago grew up in Sicily on a farm where his family produced everything they ate. The food was traditional, simple and basic. Celestino has carried his family food styles into Celestino restaurant and has created a popular light Sicilian/Italian menu in keeping with today's contemporary lifestyles.

Lunches at Celestino feature delicious antipasti and insalate dishes such as Cozze e Vongole con Crostini all'Aglio; mussels and clams in a light tomato and garlic sauce. The seafood is fresh from the Pacific. Celestino excels in pasta dishes such as Cappellacci al Timo; large ravioli stuffed with zucchini and cheese, butter and thyme sauce or Capelli D'Angelo Pomodoro Fresco e Basilico, angel hair pasta in a fresh tomato and basil sauce. Main lunch entrees include Fietti di Pesce Gatto al Pepe Rosa e Senape, spring water farmed catfish fillet in a pink peppercorn and mustard sauce. The dinner menu finds the taste of love in the pasta dish Cuari di Sicilia Burro e Salvia, heart shaped ravioli stuffed with eggplant, butter and sage. The entrees feature an outstanding quail dish of Quaglie e Salsiccie con Polenta, sals Olive Nerc, quail stuffed with sausage served with grilled polenta and black olive sauce.

Celestino caters to small parties and has an excellent wine list of Italian and Californian wines. *Buon Appetito!*

CHEZ HELENE
267 South Beverly Drive
Beverly Hills, CA 90212
Tel. (213) 276-1558
Hrs: Lunch   Tue. - Sat.   11:30 a.m. - 3:00 p.m.
         Dinner   Tue. - Sun.   6:00 p.m. - 10:30 p.m.
Visa, MasterCard, AMEX and Diners Club are accepted.

Care to feel as if you've stepped into a farmhouse or village inn after a drive through the Quebec countryside? Want to be treated to country French food by a motherly *cuisine de femme* with a French-Canadian accent? Chez Helene is the restaurant for you.

Designed to resemble a cozy country inn, Chez Helene has a picket fence, potted flowers and blue shutters opened against the fresh bricks of the building. A warm welcome from a gracious hostess with a French lilt to her voice and gentle manners will greet you at the front door. Classical music and the buttery aromas of delicious French country food curl through the cozy and inviting rooms. Pewter plates and baskets of ferns and flowers highlight the woodwork.

You will be treated to provincial French dishes like you have never tasted before. Micheline Hebert, the restaurant's chef and proprietor, is a French-Canadian from Montreal and a chef supreme. She invests standard bistro dishes with a freshness and goodness that make them a new adventure. Dishes such as Chicken Liver Paté served with cornichon and toasted baguette slices; Cream of Leek Soup and, for lunch, Sausages sauteed with onions and simmered in beer with tomato and fresh basil are hearty and refreshing. Desserts range from a dense and creamy Flourless Chocolate Cake to a light, delicate Lemon Pie, not forgetting the typical Quebec dessert, the Chomeur, upside down cake with caramel or raspberry served with heavy cream.

Mme. Hebert's customers are fiercely loyal. Many of Venice's resident artists are nourished on Madame Hebert's provincial dishes and in gratitude have given her a rich collection of their works for her walls. It won't take but a taste of Mme. Hebert's cooking magic for you to take up the banner of Chez Helene.

GAYLORD INDIA RESTAURANT
50 North La Cienega Boulevard
Beverly Hills, CA 90211
Tel. (213) 652-3838
Hrs: Lunch   Mon. - Thu.   11:30 a.m. - 2:30 p.m.
                           Sat. - Sun.   12:00 noon - 3:00 p.m.
        Dinner   Mon. - Sun.   5:30 p.m. - 10:45 p.m.
All major credit cards are accepted.

Gaylord India Restaurant is an elegant East Indian restaurant located in the heart of Beverly Hills' restaurant row. Authentically costumed staff offer the guest fragrant, pungent and delicious Eastern cuisine.

The art of spice blending is performed daily, as spices from all parts of India are prepared for use in Gaylord's exotic dishes. The connoisseur of appetizers will find delight in Lamb Samosa, crisp patties stuffed with spiced minced lamb. Gaylord's daily buffet lunch includes a Tandoori oven item, two curries, three or four vegetables, rice, salads, Tandoori bread, teas and coffee. Champagne and desserts are served on Saturday and Sunday. Dinner delights include Tandoori Prawns, which are king prawns marinated in spices and roasted, and Tandoori Chicken marinated in yogurt and roasted. Baked in the clay Tandoori oven, Bengan Bhartha is a delicious eggplant dish made with onions, tomatoes and spices. Nauratan Karma covers tasty vegetables with farmers cheese, nuts and a mild cream sauce. Tandoori breads are baked to order.

Don't forget the dessert which is a delightful saffron flavored ice cream with pistachios and almonds. Indian cuisine at its finest can be experienced at Gaylord India Restaurant, an exotic "Best Choice."

THE GRILL, 9560 Dayton Way, Beverly Hills, CA. Tel. (213) 276-0615. The Grill offers quality American cuisine in a classic and timeless setting. Open Monday through Saturday, 11:30 a.m. to 12:00 midnight, The Grill will excite the palate of even the most discerning diner.

IL FORNAIO
301 North Beverly Drive
Beverly Hills, CA 90210
Tel. (213) 550-8330
Hrs: Breakfast
        Mon. - Fri.   7:30 a.m. - 11:30 a.m.
        Saturday   7:30 a.m. - 12:00 noon
        Lunch
        Mon. - Fri.   11:30 a.m. - 5:30 p.m.
        Saturday   12:00 noon - 5:30 p.m.
        Brunch
        Sunday   8:30 a.m. - 3:30 p.m.
        Dinner
        Mon. - Sat.   5:30 p.m. - 10:00 p.m.
        Sunday   3:30 p.m. - 10:00 p.m.
Visa and Master Card are accepted.

Whether you are in the mood for a wonderfully authentic Italian meal or just a taste of Pasticceria (pastries), Il Fornaio is the place to go. In 1983 this restaurant was introduced to America from Italy, where there are more than 1000 Il Fornaio bakeries. To make the foods they are well known for, the Veggetti family gathered recipes from every region in Italy. Easily recognizable with its bright blue and white awnings, Il Fornaio is centrally located on the corner of Beverly and Dayton Drives. There is table seating for forty-five and for those who want to be nearer the action, there is a pine wood counter near the cappuccino machine.

With one side of Il Fornaio containing a bakery and the other a full service restaurant, you are surrounded by savory aromas. In the bakery, where over one hundred different types of breads are sold, you may also choose from a wide selection of delectable Italian cakes, pastries and cookies. In the restaurant, you can sit down and relax for a delicious breakfast, lunch or dinner. Il Fornaio will excite the senses early in the morning with fragrances of freshly baked breads, steaming Italian coffee and such popular dishes as Uova Con Pomodoro E Basilico (eggs with tomatos and basil) and Frittelle Viennesi (pancakes with apples, pinenuts and cinnamon). The complete lunch menu includes such delights as Panzanella and Insalata Capricciosa. In the evening, as the ambiance of Italy prevails, you can dine on some of the best pasta and rice dishes found anywhere. Dinner selections include grilled fresh fish, Insalata Di Mare (squid, shrimp and mussels antipasto), and Carpaccio (a thinly sliced beef antipasto).

Il Fornaio, truly an experience in fine Italian dining, is a "Best Choice" for the Los Angeles area.

JIMMY'S RESTAURANT, 201 Moreno Drive, Beverly Hills, CA. Tel. (213) 879-2394. Jimmy's restaurant was established in 1977 by Jimmy Murphy, a well-known, and well respected host of many of the town's top restaurants. Jimmy broke all records with his fine cuisine, exquisite interior and marvelous desserts. Enjoy the piano bar nightly, along with an impressive wine list. Reservations are imparative.

L'ESCOFFIER
9876 Wilshire Boulevard
Beverly Hills, CA 90210
Tel. (213) 274-7777
Hrs: Dinner   Mon. - Thu.   6:30 p.m. - 10:30 p.m.
                              Fri. - Sat.   6:30 p.m. - 11:30 p.m.
          Music and Dancing
                              Mon. - Thu.   6:30 p.m. - 12:00 midnight
                              Fri. - Sat.   6:30 p.m. - 12:30 a.m.
All major credit cards are accepted.

Bernard Shaw once said "There is no sincerer love than the love of food." Dedicated to the works and talents of Auguste Escoffier, "The King of Chefs," this world premier restaurant features French cuisine served in an elegant European manner. Located on the penthouse level of the Beverly Hilton, overlooking the spectacular and breathtaking view of the Los Angeles area, L'Escoffier entwines sight, sense and sound to create an ambiance of romanticism.

Surrounded by muted greens and pastel peach tones, beveled mirrors, light woods and subtle marble accents, the atmosphere is elegant and scintillating. Original works of art, ranging from superbly handcrafted Oriental vases and handpainted screens to oil paintings from the nineteenth century are displayed throughout the dining area. Music is provided for both your dining and dancing pleasure by the Ben Rizzi Orchestra.

L'Escoffier offers delectable hors d'oeuvres, from French Goose Liver Paté with Truffles to Curried Seafood in Papaya. Entrees include Roasted Quail in Potato Nest with Grapes, Breast of Duckling with Grand Marnier Sauce, Steak Diane prepared at your table and a host of fish and steak platters prepared in unparalleled French style. An impressive wine list including rare vintages is featured, and a full time sommelier is at your convenience to assist you in making the right selection to complement your dinner. For a night to remember and dining at its most prestigious, L'Escoffier is the ultimate.

LA FAMIGLIA RESTAURANT
453 North Canon Drive
Beverly Hills, CA 90210
Tel. (213) 276-6208
Hrs: Mon. - Sat.   5:00 p.m. - 12:00 midnight
Visa, MasterCard, AMEX and Diners Club are accepted.

Families will love the atmosphere of La Famiglia, made warm and cozy with Tiffany style lamps. The friendly waiters will help you select from an antipasti menu that includes delicious Calamari, Shrimp Scampi, and Mozzarella Marinara. All La Famiglia's pasta is homemade and cooked to taste, and diners can choose from items including Vermicelli in a Tomato and Basil Sauce, or Cannelloni with chicken or beef. Keep an eye out for the daily pasta specials. For your entree, try one of the three daily seafood specials, including salmon or sea bass. Or try the broiled veal chop. For those watching their diet, La Famiglia offer entrees with no butter or flour, including Shrimp Scampi Principessa, shrimp poached in white wine and sauteed with grappa or aquavit and served with a sauce of sour cream, caviar, chives and white pepper.

LAWRY'S THE PRIME RIB
55 North La Cienega Boulevard
Beverly Hills, CA 90211
Tel. (213) 652-2827
Hrs: Mon. - Thu.   5:00 p.m. - 11:00 p.m.
      Fri. - Sat.   5:00 p.m. - 12:00 midnight
      Sunday   3:00 p.m. - 10:00 p.m.
Visa, MasterCard, AMEX and Diners Club are accepted.

After fifty outstanding years of business, this "Grand Master" restaurant continues to lead the way in excellence of food, service, personal warmth and concept. Every detail down to the famous Lawry's silver serving cart reflect the concern for individualized service. The restaurant's decor is definitely English featuring Georgian and Edwardian design.

Four Prime Rib cuts are served from six to sixteen ounces, each with mashed potatoes, whipped cream horseradish, Yorkshire pudding and the famous spinning salad bowl. Creamed spinach, creamed corn, buttered peas and potatoes are available as side dishes. Lawry's also has a children's menu and offers valet parking and a cocktail lounge.

Sometimes it is easy to forget how lush, tender and flavorsome a high quality cut of prime beef should be. Lawry's serves only the finest USDA Prime graded beef. Lawry's serves as a delicious reminder of the right way to serve the best cut of prime beef.

THE MANDARIN
430 North Camden Drive
Beverly Hills, CA 90210
Tel. (213) 272-0267
Hrs: Mon. - Fri.   11:30 a.m. - 11:00 p.m.
        Sat. - Sun.   5:00 p.m. - 11:00 p.m.
All major credit cards are accepted.
Also,
8386 Beverly Boulevard
Los Angeles, CA 90048
Tel. (213) 655-6115

The rich, expansive history of China is reflected in the opulent atmosphere and exquisite cuisine of The Mandarin. From the strikingly beautiful handcarved wood panels, some over 300 years old, to the quiet, efficient service, the reserved dignity of old China pervades this fine restaurant.

Located in the heart of Beverly Hills, The Mandarin features distinctive dishes of Peking, Hunan, Szechwan, Canton and Mongolia as well as specials from other regions of China. Meals are served in the Mandarin "family style" where everyone shares the entrees. The Chef suggests Tangerine Shrimp, jumbo shrimp sauteed with fresh tangerine peels; Smoked Tea Duck (duck smoked in special ovens over burning tea leaves gives this incomparable dish a crisp skin and a haunting flavor); or Mandarin Crab. Offered in season, fresh crab is sauteed in the shell with a pungent sauce of Chinese rice wine and crushed, fresh ginger, resulting in a truly fantastic dish. For a special treat, visit The Mandarin during the Chinese New Year, when the chef creates ten or more special courses to celebrate the holiday. From the valet parking to the maitre d', you will find the service excellent. Whether you're trying Mandarin Chinese food for the first time, or as an epicure wishing to discuss the philosophies of fine food, the knowledgeable, friendly staff awaits the pleasure of serving you.

In the West, the term "mandarin" has come to mean anything exquisite, stylish or exotic from China, synonymous with the best from this vast, venerable country. The owners and staff are proud to name their restaurant The Mandarin, offering the best of China for your enjoyment.

PASTEL
421 North Rodeo Drive
Beverly Hills, CA 90210
Tel. (213) 274-9775
Hrs: Lunch   Mon. - Sat.   11:30 a.m. - 5:00 p.m.
             Dinner   Mon. - Sat.   6:30 p.m. - 11:30 p.m.
Visa and MasterCard are accepted.

Not everyone has the opportunity to visit the French countryside, with its quaint homes and villages all working at a slightly slower speed than the rest of the world. In Beverly Hills, a slice of the French country side has been transported to the Rodeo Collection Shopping Center.

It's Pastel, a unique restaurant offering the best in country French cuisine. Look for Pastel on the Patio level of the Rodeo Collection. Take a seat outside on the patio so you can see and be seen.   Enjoy the lunch menu of this modern French bistro, which includes soup of the day, a mixed green salad with home dressing or a Chicken Mayonnaise salad. You must try the Mushroom a la Grecque. If you come by Wednesday, Thursday, Friday or Saturday evenings, you'll discover the Pastel specialty *prix fixe*, a total dining package. The *prix fixe* starts with large olive wood bowls overflowing with Panier de Crudites; fresh vegetables with olive oil and chopped herbs, soft white cheese and homemade duck paté. Next you're served slabs of grilled French bread ready for generous slabs of paté. For dinner choose Loin of Lamb grilled with fresh thyme. Or try the Prime Rib roasted over mesquite. After such treats, you have to sample the Chocolate Mousse served in large bowls.

You don't have to travel to France to sample the French culture. Visit Pastel, and you'll dine on food a Frenchman would savor.

PREGO
362 North Camden Drive
Beverly Hills, CA 90212
Tel. (213) 277-7346
Hrs: Mon. - Sat.   11:30 a.m. - 12:00 midnight
       Sundays   5:00 p.m. - 12:00 midnight

To say "don't mention it" in Italian, you say: *Prego!.* To say "good Italian food" in English you say: Prego! and you mention it. This light and lively restaurant has the clean look of blond wood, white tile, sleek modern art and dramatic displays of bare branches and flowers punctuated by high ceilings. A glass wall separates the handsome bar and the main dining area. An open kitchen features an oak burning brick pizza oven, a grill, a corner where the *pastaio* hangs his handiwork to dry, and a counter of mouthwatering Italian comestibles.

Italian born chef, Claudio Marchesan says, "We want to cook food with the flavor of our mother's cooking. Food that makes you smile and makes you happy." A sample of mama's happy food can be tasted in the prawn, tomato, basil, garlic, mozzarella pizza, baked with a soft and yeasty crust. Taste buds will blossom with delight when finding the Tortelloni di Magro as Burro, a dish of large delicate pasta squares, thin as crepes, filled with chard, ricotta and garnished with melted butter and fresh sage leaves. There are Spinach Noodles with Mushrooms and Cream, and Lasagnette, wide noodles with Mascarpone cheese and shavings of preserved Italian white truffle. *Belle!*

Reservations are highly suggested at Prego. Food so delicious draws eager crowds during the dining hours. This *trattoria* on the city's liveliest shopping street provides fresh, bright and casual eating at its best.

R.J.'S, THE RIB JOINT
252 North Beverly Drive
Beverly Hills, CA 90210
Tel. (213) 274-RIBS
Hrs: Sun. - Thu.   11:30 a.m. - 10:00 p.m.
      Fri. - Sat.   11:30 a.m. - 11:00 p.m.
      Sunday Brunch   10:30 a.m. - 3:00 p.m.
Visa, MasterCard, AMEX and Diners Club are accepted.

If you enjoy fine dining, you won't want to miss R.J.'s, The Rib Joint. Located in the heart of Beverly Hills only one block from Rodeo Drive, the restaurant is the "Rolls Royce of Barbecue."

Rib selections include Pork Back Ribs, Beef Ribs, R.J.'s 50/50, and R.J.'s Hickory Smoked Platter, each slow smoked over hickory wood. A favorite is the Sizzling Chili Steak, a zesty top sirloin steak, sliced at your table and smothered in the award winning house chili. Those with a bent for the unusual should try Broiled Chicken Tarragon or Fresh Smoked Duck. Sample the world famous Green Grocery, a salad bar of over sixty items, which takes three and a half hours just to assemble, three types of lettuce, two types of avocados, Hearts of Palm, tuna and sardines, spaghetti salads and a whole lot more. Giant Baked Potato features a choice of toppings, which include American golden caviar, ocean shrimp, assorted cheese, crisp strips of bacon, guacamole, salsa, chopped peppers, blue cheese, sour cream, chives, and whipped butter. Be sure to investigate the Mile High Chocolate Cake and other delectable delights on the dessert list. The Library Bar features a selection so huge that it takes a sliding library ladder to reach all the different liquors—over 500 brands and fifty different beers. Private dining in The Board Room facilitates parties of up to fourteen guests.

Sawdust strewn floors, buckets of peanuts throughout the bar area, ceiling fans and frosted deco lamps create an atmosphere for casual Californian dining pleasure. R.J.'s, The Rib Joint, "The restaurant that put the thrills in Beverly Hills" is your "Best Choice" for dining.

RANGOON RACQUET CLUB
9474 Little Santa Monica Boulevard
Beverly Hills, CA 90210
Tel. (213) 274-8926
Hrs: Lunch   Mon. - Fri.   11:30 a.m. - 2:00 p.m.
      Dinner   Mon. - Sat.   6:00 p.m. - 11:00 p.m.
Visa, MasterCard and AMEX are accepted.

Before the sun set on the Empire, British officers in Burma sipped and supped swankly at the original Rangoon Racquet Club. The finest of food and the heartiest of spirits are still the order of the day at the modern day RRC, now recreated in all its original elegance in Beverly Hills.

Gold credit cards have replaced the swagger stick, and the only epaulettes in evidence are on the uniforms of the attentive waiters and bartenders. The army officers have been replaced by men and women who wheel and deal in the worlds of finance, entertainment and international trading—while the truly powerful sup on Saturdays, and observers at lunch and dinner can hear dynasties crumble and rebuild.

Owners Manny and David Zwaaf have built today's RRC as a near replica of the old, which was frequented by Manny during his WW II service as an officer in The Princess Irene Brigade.

The bill of fare repeats some of the original's exotic Indian and hearty English favorites—but the Zwaafs have wisely made the enormous menu widely appealing with a selection of dishes from America and Europe. Industrialist C.V. Woods' prize winning chili is listed next to Chicken in the Pot, complete with matzoh ball. Tempting, classic Dover Sole follows Medallions of Sweetbreads and Crab, followed by prime steaks done to lip smacking turn. The menu is eclectic, the desserts awe inspiring and the wine list deserves your respect.

The main room, highlighted with military memorabilia and agleam with elegance, echoes the special event status of the menu— while the bar boasts an incredible evening long meal of gourmet appetizers and the town's most comely group of Yuppies of all ages.

SHANGHAI PALACE
8689 Wilshire Boulevard
Beverly Hills, CA 90211
Tel. (213) 657-5574
Hrs: Lunch   Mon. - Fri.   11:30 a.m. - 3:00 p.m.
     Dinner   Mon. - Thu.   4:30 p.m. - 10:30 p.m.
                Fri. - Sat.   4:30 p.m. - 11:00 p.m.
                Sunday   4:30 p.m. - 10:00 p.m.
     Brunch   Sat. - Sun.   11:30 a.m. - 3:00 p.m.
Visa, MasterCard and AMEX are accepted.

The Shanghai Palace marries the flavors of Cantonese and Szechwan cooking creating a bond of delicious tastes and beautiful arrangements of food. Your host, Tommy Kuan and his staff, will offer you the best in service and customer recognition.

Specialties of the The Shanghai Palace include Vegetable and Pork Dumplings lightly steamed and served with hot and sweet sauce. The Crispy Shrimp is puffed to a golden brown. The Shredded Chinese salads are served with fresh shrimp. The House Chicken is a Mandarin dish and is crispy brown outside and tender and steaming inside. The Shredded Beef in a scallion and orange sauce is a combination of sweet and spicy and the pieces are bite size and crunchy. The wine list is small but well chosen. Beautifully presented fresh fruits are offered for dessert.

The Shanghai Palace is centrally located in Beverly Hills on Wilshire Boulevard adjacent to West Hollywood, Century City and Culver City. Valet parking at night and validated parking during the day is offered. Catering services are featured and a twenty dollar minimum order will be delivered free of charge.

TRADER VIC'S
9876 Wilshire Boulevard
Beverly Hills, CA 90210
Tel.   (213) 274-7777
        (213) 276-6345
Hrs: Mon. - Sun. 5:00 a.m. - 1:00 p.m.
All major credit cards are accepted.

Encounter the exotic flavors and lure of the South Sea Islands with an evening at Trader Vic's. Located in the Beverly Hills Hilton, Trader Vic's is acclaimed as being one of the finest restaurants in California. Designed around a nautical theme, with artifacts from such faraway places as Wales, Polynesia, Peru and other South American countries, the decor creates a backdrop for an evening you won't forget.

Your adventure begins with a sample of the tropical concoctions served in the Boathouse Bar. Sample the tangy zip of such fancy cocktails as the Kamaaina, the Samoan Fog Cutter and the Tiki Puka Puka. Exquisite coral displays, bamboo basketry and Japanese glass fishing floats all tend to peak your senses, preparing you for the divine feast to follow.

The meat, fish and poultry selections served at Trader Vic's have become world renowned. Observe, from behind glass windows, how the meat is hung inside huge four feet high Chinese ovens. It is by these ovens that the succulent flavors of the meat are preserved and enhanced. These Chinese ovens have become the trademark of Trader Vic's.

Appetizers include such tantalizing choices as Crisp Calamari, Crispy Duck and Cosmo Tidbits, which is a selection of fried prawns, spareribs, Crab Rangoon and sliced pork. Choose your entree from four menu selections: From the Lakes, Rivers, and Seas; Meat and Fish From Our Chinese Ovens; Favorites from Trader Vic's, and Paké or Chinese Dishes. Highly recommended are the *mahi mahi* with macadamia nut sauce, Indonesian Lamb Roast served with Chutney Peach and Trader Vic's Peanut Condiment and Ginger Chicken which has been marinated in fresh ginger, orange peel, and soya and then roasted in the Chinese oven. For your final pleasure enjoy a Trader Vic Mudpie or an Aloha Ice Cream of vanilla with mango sauce topped with crunchy banana chips.

Take home a little of the magic and spice of the South Seas with a selection of *Trader Vic's Book of Food and Drink*, *Trader Vic's Pacific Island Cookbook* or *Trader Vic's Mexican Cookbook*. An adventure in eating unsurpassed around the globe is waiting for you at Trader Vic's. Coats are required for gentlemen and reservations are recommended. Come experience the exotic and make Trader Vic's your "Best Choice."

TUMBLEWEED
130 South Beverly Drive
Beverly Hills, CA 90212
Tel. (213) 274-5844
Hrs: Lunch   Mon. - Fri.   11:30 a.m. - 2:30 p.m.
          Dinner   Mon. - Sun.   6:00 p.m. - 11:30 p.m.
Visa, MasterCard and AMEX are accepted.

The best artists offer their own interpretation of their art and Elka Gilmore is no exception. This native of Austin, Texas, offers her own food creations, based on her roots in Texan and Mexican cookery, at Tumbleweed in Beverly Hills.

Tumbleweed food is a combination of regional Mexican dishes and Texas style slow smoked barbecue. Printed daily, the menu concentrates on those items freshest in the markets. The menu is designed to encourage you to try many kinds of dishes, which you can order in small, medium or large portions. Some of the best choices include the barbecue combination platter, which features ten different smoked meats and smoked fish of the day. Those meats, which are smoked by Gilmore herself, could include lamb ribs, pork ribs, pork loin or chicken. The menu also offers tacos done the Tumbleweed way, such as smoked pork loin with spicy chili sauce and scallions. The Navajo Taco features marinated beef tenderloin, chipotle chili and grilled onions. Desserts include Cashew Praline Pie, Almond Crisps with mixed berries and cream, and peach dumplings. You'll enjoy all these items in a whimsical country decor. A white picket fence crosses the front windows. Large, hand colored dairy cows and country folk are framed by fence posts.

Gilmore has won the grand prize at the California Seafood Challenge for two years in a row, proving that the quality at Tumbleweed is unsurpassed. But if you can't visit Tumbleweed to enjoy Gilmore's unique creations, call and order the delicious food for take out.

YANKS: A DINING ROOM AND BAR
262 South Beverly Drive
Beverly Hills, CA 90212
Tel. (213) 85-YANKS
Hrs: Lunch   Mon. - Fri.   12:00 noon - 3:00 p.m.
         Dinner   Sun. - Thu.   5:30 p.m. - 10:00 p.m.
                             Fri. - Sat.   5:30 p.m. - 11:00 p.m.
Visa, MasterCard and AMEX are accepted.

Yanks: A Dining Room and Bar is nestled in the heart of beautiful Beverly Hills. Here you will find a unique and comfortable restaurant, offering memorable cuisine at affordable prices.

Yanks has broken the "stuffy restaurant" mold with their clean style and relaxed sophistication. The seasonal menu is an eclectic update of American food with enough nostalgia to make you smile and enough flair to make you a regular customer. Begin your meal with Louisiana Crab Cakes, Garlic Tortilla Soup, fresh Corn and Crab Chowder or crispy Onion Rings. Entrees include an All-American classic, Chicken Pot Pie, Spicy Cajun Meatloaf, Soft Shelled Crabs, Grilled Salmon with mustard chive butter, Barbecued Baby Back Ribs, Crusty Mustard Rack of Lamb, and many other tasty specialties. All food at Yanks is prepared from scratch. Enjoy a fine wine with your meal, or choose from among a wide selection of drinks available from the bar. As a finale to your meal, select from several enticing desserts, including Lemon Bars, Blueberry Peach Crisp, Chocolate Nut Pudding Cake and Hot Fudge Cheesecake.

For a touch of humor, the restaurant and bar areas are separated by a section of wall that seems torn from Heartland USA. With its clapboard facade and country floral wallpaper, it reminds the diner that this is a place to relax and enjoy. On Friday and Saturday nights, Yanks features live piano music. Private parties of fifty to one hundred people are welcome at Yanks, and off-site catering is available for special occasions. For a relaxing and reasonably priced lunch or dinner, Yanks is your "Best Choice."

TANNING SALON

LE BEACH CLUB—A TANNING RESORT
998 South Robertson Boulevard, Suite 205
Beverly Hills, CA 90035
Tel. (213) 659-8301
Hrs: Mon. - Fri.   7:00 a.m. - 10:00 p.m.
      Saturday   8:00 a.m. - 8:00 p.m.
      Sunday   9:00 a.m. - 7:00 p.m.
Visa, MasterCard and AMEX are accepted.

Everyone has wanted to visit far off vacation spots where there's nothing to worry about except getting a great tan. Le Beach Club—A Tanning Resort in Beverly Hills offers great tanning, with no worries, in the Los Angeles area.

Imagine a twenty minute vacation in Bali, Hawaii, Indonesia or Italy. Le Beach Club has several rooms all focusing on one of these international themes. All the rooms are kept spotlessly clean and fresh linens are provided for every customer. Le Beach Club uses only the best equipment available. The staff prefers the SCA Wolff system, developed by Swiss scientist Friedrich Wolff. The SCA Wolff Tanning System carefully balances the sun's rays to help your skin produce the most luxurious tan possible. It works like this: A one of a kind of ray triggers the tanning process in the lower layers of the skin where a natural coloring agent is released. The agent travels to the skin's surface where a second ray transforms it to create a rich, golden tan. Professionals at the salon will recommend products by a top manufacturer to enhance your tan.

Those same friendly, courteous professionals will advise you on times and other factors that will give you the finest tan. After just a few sessions, you'll come away looking as if you've visited the hottest vacation spots in the world.

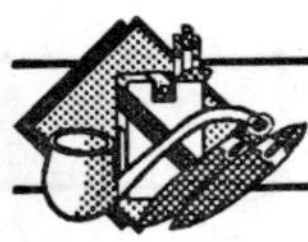

TOBACCO SHOP

NAZARETH'S FINE CIGARS
350 North Canon Drive
Le Grand Passage
Beverly Hills, CA 90210
Tel. (213) 271-5863
Hrs: Mon. - Sat.   10:00 a.m. - 8:00 p.m.
Visa, MasterCard and AMEX are accepted.

In Victorian England, men of consequence had private clubs in which they could relax, enjoy a moment of silence while reading the latest tabloid, and smoke cigars in quiet contemplation. Now, cigar connoisseurs can enjoy that same club style atmosphere and luxury at Nazareth's Fine Cigars.

Nazareth Guluzian, world traveler and cigar aficionado, has created the ultimate environment for those who appreciate a good cigar. His passion for cigars is evident in the product line he carries, which includes Romeo & Julieta, Partagas, H. Upmann, Punch, vintage Macanudo, Excalibur, Montecruz, Ramon Allones or Davidoff cigars. You will also find the finest cigar accessories, including Dupont Lighters, cigar cutters and humidors to satisfy the most discriminating clientele.

Personalized humidors are available free to clientele who buy more than thirty boxes of cigars a year. The names on these boxes include personalities such as Arnold Schwarzenegger, David Cassidy and Dirk Benedict. Come in to Nazareth's, light up, and relax in one of three leather Chesterfield sofas while enjoying a cognac, cordial, or a freshly brewed cup of espresso. "No other cigar business in the world treats the cigar connoisseur as I do." To savor the best the world has to offer in cigars, experience Nazareth's Fine Cigars.

# WINE SHOPS

ROBERT BURNS WINES
157 North Robertson Boulevard
Beverly Hills, CA 90211
Tel.   (213) 274-0033
        (213) 274-1717
Hrs: Mon. - Thu.   8:00 a.m. - 9:00 p.m.
        Fri. - Sat.   8:00 a.m. -10:00 p.m.
        Sunday   10:00 a.m. - 6:00 p.m.
Visa, MasterCard, AMEX and Diners Club are accepted.

Whether you are an experienced wine connoisseur and are familiar with such wine tasting vocabulary as bouquet, balance, harmony, breed and finesse; or are a wine novice awash in a sea of Pinot Blancs, Chardonnays and Cabernets, Robert Burns Wines will delight and astonish you. With ten years experience as a purveyor of fine wines and liquors, owner Andy Abelman can assist you in making the best selection of wine for whatever occasion you may be planning.

Boasting one of the largest selections of fine wines in the greater Los Angeles area, Robert Burns Wines is also known for its sterling reputation and exceptional service. An extensive selection of California wines and champagnes are stocked in addition to the latest arrivals from Europe and around the world. Enjoy perusing the stacks of wines from all over Europe, or browsing through the wide assortment of spirits, fine old Ports and liquors. If staying in the local Beverly Hills area, Andy will be more than happy to send your selection to your hotel or to custom design a delightful gift basket to take with you.

Located on Robertson Boulevard, Robert Burns Wines has ample off street parking for your convenience. Delivery service is available for both office and residence. Frequented by celebrities who trust in the superlative quality and expertise at Robert Burns Wines, you too can enjoy the nectar of the gods. Make Robert Burns Wines your "Best Choice."

THE WINE MERCHANT
9701 Santa Monica
Beverly Hills, CA 90210
Tel. (213) 278-7322
Hrs: Mon. - Sat.   9:30 a.m. - 6:30 p.m.
Visa, MasterCard and AMEX are accepted.

Grand Master Dennis Overstreet owns the most prestigious wine and spirits store on the west coast. Located in Beverly Hills and known as the "Tiffany's" of wine stores since 1973, Dennis Overstreet devotes his business to serving the elite of southern California real estate, entertainment moguls—from producers, directors, celebrities, oil tycoons to musicians, writers, composers, great wine collectors and, of course, everyone who likes wine.

The Wine Merchant boasts of having more than a two million dollar wine inventory, which includes the great Bordeaux and Burgundies, as well as California's and Italy's best.

Overstreet's expertise in wine and flair for presentation lends itself to the most gorgeous custom gift baskets in the country. Customers call from all over the United States, Japan, Canada and neighboring countries to fulfill their gift sending needs. For those who cannot shop at the store, there is the Wine-of-the-Month Club where members receive, by mail, monthly newsletters and wines selected by Mr. Overstreet.

The Wine Merchant is also a famous landmark for providing perfect atmospheric conditions—continuous fifty-eight degree temperature and eighty-five percent humidity—for wine storage. Beneath his store lies a wine cellar where Overstreet's customers store their precious liquid. Millions of dollars worth of shredded money from the Mint is scattered throughout the wine cellar, which is far more effective than the conventional means in warding off unwelcome rodents.

The Wine Merchant specializes in wine and services and Dennis Overstreet brings a sense of adventure and real enjoyment to the experience of wine. Selected by *Market Watch* as one of the top ten wine retailers in the country, Overstreet and his staff strive to maintain his outstanding reputation.

BRENTWOOD

Brentwood is one of Los Angeles County's upscale communities. It lies along the south slope of the Santa Monica Mountains between Westwood and Pacific Palisades.

 **ART GALLERIES**

DEL MANO GALLERY AND STUDIO
11981 San Vicente
Los Angeles, CA 90049
Tel. (213) 476-8508
Hrs: Tue. - Sat.   10:00 a.m. - 6:00 p.m.
Visa, MasterCard, AMEX and Diners Club are accepted.
Also,
33 East Colorado Boulevard
Pasadena, CA 91105
Tel. (818) 793-6648

Del Mano Gallery and Studio showcases multifaceted collections consisting of artwork by over 250 American artists and craftspeople. Each month, new artists are featured, and seven major exhibitions are held throughout the year.

Jan Peters and Ray Leier have chosen fine examples of contemporary American crafts in precious metals, ceramics, blown glass, exotic woods, metal and fiber art. The gallery offers unique services such as corporate acquisitions, gift buying, appraisals, worldwide shipping, special presentations, art installations, consultations, guest lectures and will commission custom work to your specifications.

These excellent services, in addition to the hand chosen selections which are so imaginatively presented, demonstrate Ray and Jan's commitment to showcasing and supporting "The Fine Art of American Craft."

TWO BEARS GALLERY
153 South Barrington Place
Los Angeles, CA 90049
Tel. (213) 476-0998
Hrs: Tue. - Sat.   11:00 a.m. - 5:00 p.m.
Visa and MasterCard are accepted.

As the demand rises for art with a Southwestern flair, more and more galleries are specializing in this uniquely American style. A "Best Choice" in this arena is Two Bears Gallery, which offers jewelry, furniture and other items that reflect a Southwestern ambiance.

Every item at Two Bears Gallery is created by contemporary artists who are either Native American or closely aligned with and knowledgeable about the culture. All items are chosen with an eye toward the unique. The gallery represents Larry Yazzie, one of the top Native American sculptors. He works in alabaster, bronze and other media. Also featured are masks by Lillian Pitt, a Yakima Indian from Oregon. Pitt is one of the few artists who fire masks in an Angama oven. One of the most interesting groups of works come from Turza and Andy Shows. Called Tirzah jewelry, the bolos, collars, necklaces, pins, buckles, bracelets and other items feature bronze inlaid with semi-precious stones. The Tirzah artists work with turquoise, mother of pearl, malachite, jet, pipestone and melon shell. Only bears are represented in the Tirzah designs. Visitors will also find carved wooden bears by Drew Kristel, as well as hand painted traditional Native American symbolic designs. Other items of note include square drums once made by the Sioux and handmade gourds decorated with feathers, stones, arrowheads and other designs.

Two Bears Gallery stocks many other types of items in its small, well appointed store. Much of the merchandise makes wonderful gifts.

GIFT SHOP

SALUTATIONS, LTD.
11640 San Vicente Boulevard
Los Angeles, CA 90049
Tel. (213) 820-6127
Hrs: Mon. - Sat.   10:00 a.m. - 6:00 p.m.
Visa and MasterCard are accepted.

Salutations, Ltd. is the brainchild of owner Carey Krevoy, who got her inspiration for this unique store featuring gifts and tabletop accessories after reading a book called The Perfect Setting. Personalized custom gift baskets are offered as a special sideline, and Carey has served many celebrity and studio clientele.

Dinnerware selections are primarily handcrafted from Metlox earthenware to Eiegen's Terracotta, Mackenzie-Child's majolica, and other assorted domestic and imported ceramics and accessories. In addition is an extensive array of linens to coordinate. Other items, such as imprinted silk flowers, scented candles and candle holders, Italian desk accessories and stationery, picture frames, vases and a wide variety of personal home fragrance, provide a generous field of possible choices for the gift giver. Carey also stocks Country French and Southwestern furniture, Mexican pottery, jewelry, and artifacts, Zapotec pillows, and kilim rugs patterned after the Santa Fe influence.

Carey travels extensively in her search for unique items for her customers. She combines a natural talent for finding just the right thing with perceptive instincts in guiding her customer's selections for gift giving or in helping them attain a special style of their own. Salutations, Ltd. offers customers the opportunity to make great impressions!

RESTAURANT

MASON'S
11500 San Vicente Boulevard
Brentwood, CA 90049
Tel. (213) 826-5666
Hrs: Lunch   Mon. - Fri.   11:30 a.m. - 2:30 p.m.
      Dinner   Mon. - Thu. 6:00 p.m. - 10:30 p.m.
                 Fri. - Sat.   6:00 p.m. - 12:00 midnight
Reservations are recommended.

It is said that in California there is a new fad born every minute. Mason's offers a refreshing break from the norm. As you enter the tranquil atmosphere of this plush restaurant, you will find the elegance and timeless appeal of a private club.

A favorite haunt of celebrities, Mason's exudes tradition and substance. This posh tone is evident in the professionally experienced staff. The cuisine is contemporary continental with a refreshing selection of fresh and seasonal foods. Lunch features appetizers of Beluga Caviar, Oysters on the Half Shell and Spicy Squab with Mushrooms. Salad choices range from a classic Chilled Lobster Salad to a Shredded Duck Salad with Cucumbers and Green Onion. There are several sandwiches, pastas and other entrees offered at lunch. Among the favorites are a Grilled Tuna, Eggplant and Pepper Sandwich, Mason's Sticky Rigatoni, Grilled Salmon with Caviar and Mint, and Roast English Rump Steak with Cabernet Sauce. Dinner might begin in the lounge, which features live piano music nightly. The dinner menu offers an enticing selection of appetizers, including Fresh Dungeness Crab, California Field Salad, Sauteed Foie Gras and Sweet Corn Salad, and Mixed Seafood Salad. Choose from an assortment of fresh dinner entrees, such as Grilled Salmon, Grilled Veal Chop with Black Pepper Sauce, Grilled Lamb Rack with Spicy Minted Rice and Sauteed Veal Sweetbreads. As you might expect, there are excellent desserts and a nicely balanced wine list to complement your meal.

Whether dining in the main dining room or on the patio, the ambiance at Mason's offers comfort and a sense of tradition. For private parties, Mason's will accommodate you in style. In Brentwood, Mason's is your "Best Choice" for fine cuisine.

TANNING SALON

LE BEACH CLUB—A TANNING RESORT
11761 San Vicente Boulevard
Brentwood, CA 90049
Tel. (213) 820-2710
Hrs: Mon. - Fri.   7:00 a.m. - 10:00 p.m.
      Saturday   8:00 a.m. - 8:00 p.m.
      Sunday   9:00 a.m. - 7:00 p.m.
Visa, MasterCard and AMEX are accepted.
Also,
2520 Overland Avenue   11915 West Pico Boulevard
Rancho Park, CA 90064   West Los Angeles, CA 90064
Tel. (213) 202-0415   Tel. (213) 479-4044

If anything separates the California look from any other, it's a deep rich tan. But even in the southern part of the state, the sun doesn't shine all the time. For a fine tan all year round, Le Beach Club—A Tanning Resort is a certain "Best Choice."

Le Beach Club provides all the latest in tanning services and supplies at rates that might surprise you. Unlike many other salons, Le Beach Club offers tanning rooms focused around themes. Indoor beach bums can choose the Bali Room, the Indonesian Room or the Hawaiian Room. The Italian Room features wicker furniture and authentic art. All rooms give sun worshippers the feeling of being at an international resort, where you relax and forget about your cares. Le Beach Club features tanning equipment developed by German scientist Friedrick Wolff. Under the SCA Wolff system, the sun's rays are duplicated and scientifically balanced to help your skin tan, not burn. The tanning professionals at the salon will recommend times and provide assistance that will help you obtain the most luxurious tan possible.

The staff will also recommend a fine line of tanning and moisturizing products by a top manufacturer. All rooms, including the stand up rooms, are kept scrupulously clean and fresh linen is always provided. Enjoy Le Beach Club's complimentary mint while you melt away the stress and strain of the day.

CALABASAS

This little town overlooking the San Fernando Valley retains a rural and homey atmosphere that seems fitting for a former stagecoach stop. In keeping with its down home flavor, quite a few of the townspeople in Calabasas own horses. The town's name dates back as far as the late 1700s when it was the name of a local rancheria. *Calabasas* is the Spanish word for "pumpkin." The community celebrates the vegetable for which it is named every autumn with the popular Pumpkin Festival.

RESTAURANTS

GAETANO'S RISTORANTE
23536 Calabasas Road
Calabasas, CA 91302
Tel. (818) 716-6100
Hrs: Lunch   Tue. - Fri.   11:30 a.m. - 2:30 p.m.
       Dinner   Tue. - Thu., Sun.   5:00 p.m. - 10:00 p.m.
                   Fri. - Sat.   5:00 p.m. - 10:30 p.m.
Visa, MasterCard and AMEX are accepted.

Beautiful strains of Italian melodies float gently through bougainvillea bedecked rooms. Reflected candlelight flickers in cut glass window panes. Petals from fuchsia silk flowers drop quietly on the red brick floor. Wine glasses clink in private toasts of special moments. This is the ambiance of romance and charm of which Gaetano Palmeri is justly proud.

Once a garage in old Calabasas, Gaetano's Ristorante is now a perfect place for a romantic lunch or dinner or even a wedding. Upon entering Gaetano's you encounter a dark mahogany bar beautifully reflected in mirrors. Peach colored tablecloths echo the soft coloring of the wall hangings. Attention is given throughout Gaetano's to create and maintain the feeling of being in Italy. Gaetano has prepared an Italian menu as carefully as he has created a genuine Italian ambiance. Once a customer hears the specials of the day they rarely order off the menu. Consider a dish of Cioppino on a bed of linguini with a variety of seafoods, or homemade pasta such as Ravioli stuffed with chicken, raddichio, ricotta cheese, butter and sage or Ravioloni stuffed with porcini mushrooms, veal, fresh tomatoes and basil sauce. The wine list is extensive and encompasses Italian, French and California wine.

Gaetano Palmeri loves to see his guests enjoy themselves. Through his ristorante he has created a place made for romantic dining experiences. Many a starry eyed toast has been lifted at Gaetano's Ristorante. *O mia belle amore!*

SADDLE PEAK LODGE
419 Cold Canyon Road
Calabasas, CA 91302
Tel.   (213) 655-9770
        (818) 340-6029
Hrs: Dinner
        Wed. - Sat.   6:00 p.m. - 11:00 p.m.
        Sunday   5:00 p.m. - 11:00 p.m.
        Brunch
        Sat. - Sun.   11:30 a.m. - 3:00 p.m.
Visa and MasterCard are accepted.

Looking for a gorgeous rustic setting and a dinner of Frontier American dishes elevated to high cuisine? Saddle Peak Lodge has been a favorite in the Santa Monica Mountains area for over fifty years, but it has been only recently renovated into a million dollar restaurant. Saddle Peak was acquired by entrepreneur and restaurant magnate Al Ehringer, who gutted the interior of the structure and turned it into a stunning new multi-level mountain lodge.

The lodge has retained its original Western ambiance. The ceilings are high and the exposed timbers are wrapped in rawhide. Western paraphernalia is displayed on the walls. A huge stone fireplace dominates the main room. The renovation of the menu is the second outstanding transformation at Saddle Peak. Leading the Western *haute cuisine* are appetizers such as salmon cured in vodka and tarragon and served with a heap of thinly sliced red onions. Salmon Cooked in a Paper Bag will catch your attention on the fish menu. The main emphasis at Saddle Peak is placed on game entrees. You have your choice of meals such as a Brace of California Quail with Cheese Corn Crepe, broiled and served with a juniper sauce, or perhaps you would prefer Texas Black Boar Chops, sauteed and served with Indian peaches and crisp homemade noodles.

Saddle Peak Lodge is a place where dining is at it's very best; a place where you will find "Bountiful Country Dining."

CENTURY CITY

The former back lot of the Twentieth Century Fox film studio is today a gleaming modern city of high rise office buildings, fashionable department stores, trendy boutiques and luxury condominiums. It has attractive boulevards adorned with sparkling fountains and lush landscaping. You will discover casual cafes and fine restaurants and even some first rate entertainment and night spots at Century City.

Located west of Beverly Hills, Century City's promoters claim it is one of the world's most widely recognized and rapidly developing business districts.

Among the leisure and entertainment opportunities available is the ABC Entertainment Center which offers three levels of restaurants, theaters and retail outlets. The 1,800 seat Shubert Theatre features some of the best Broadway shows.

# ACCOMMODATIONS

CENTURY CITY INN
10330 West Olympic Boulevard
Los Angeles, CA 90064
Tel.   (213) 553-1000
         (800) 553-1005 CA
Visa, MasterCard, AMEX, Diners Club and Discover are accepted.

In a city renowned for its world class hotels and accommodations, the Century City Inn blends a contemporary California style with classic European charm, creating a unique and intimate atmosphere in lodging and hospitality. Brilliant sun filled rooms, rich in warmth and color, are thoughtfully prepared and appointed to meet the needs of today's sophisticated traveler. Perfect for business, ideal for pleasure, the Century City Inn offers an exclusive sense of privacy and all the character one would expect of a fine hotel.

You'll stay in dramatic loft-suites, featuring elegant spiral staircases, cathedral ceilings and a variety of amenities designed for a sense of luxury and residency. All rooms feature a microwave oven, refrigerator, remote control television, video cassette player, remote control air conditioning and heating, and a ten cup coffee maker complete with a selection of freshly ground coffee and premium teas. You'll also find a safe, a robe, a whirlpool tub, a **complimentary breakfast** and morning newspaper. Commercial guests appreciate the unique business center, which features an IBM personal computer, a typewriter, a copier and a FAX machine.

Guests are welcome at the nearby ABC Entertainment Center for a game of tennis. After a busy day, enjoy one of many fine dinner selections from the Century City Inn's room service, or experience the glamor and excitement of L.A.'s prestigious Westside.

J. WILLARD MARRIOTT AT CENTURY CITY
2151 Avenue of the Stars
Los Angeles, CA 90067
Tel.　(213) 277-2777
　　　(800) 228-9290
Visa, MasterCard, AMEX, Diners Club, JCB and Discover
are accepted.

Opened in June of 1988, the J. Willard Marriott is the corporation's elegant first step into the rarefied world of super luxury. Standing on the high ground of Century City, the stepped towers echo the clean lines of California Deco.

From the landscaped courtyard to the 375 guest rooms and suites, the sense of luxury is everywhere. Rich fabrics and soft tones, coupled with the generous use of marble and other stones achieve a sense of European style and elegance. Special touches are abundant, with fine artwork, armoires, wood paneling and antiqued brass in the guest rooms enhancing the European ambiance. Every room and suite has a balcony, with views stretching from the Pacific shore to the San Gabriel Mountains. The thoughtfulness of design and decor is extended to the service philosophy. A twenty-four hour concierge staff offers full room service, valet service and shoe shines. Limo service, swimming pools and a health club with men's and women's saunas, are further evidence of the attention to detail and luxury. The J. Willard Marriott facilities also include the 4,000 square foot Grand

Salon, which is available for receptions or banquets; a beauty salon; a boutique and specialty shops. As a final touch, there is JW's Restaurant and Lounge, where a delightful gourmet menu is enhanced by the serenity of a garden view.

J. Willard Marriott is ideally located for sightseeing or shopping excursions. Disneyland, UCLA, Rodeo Drive and the Getty Museum are nearby, as well as easy access to other Los Angeles attractions. There is no doubt that with all it offers, the J. Willard Marriott at Century City is a "Best Choice."

RESTAURANTS

HARRY'S BAR AND AMERICAN GRILL
2020 Avenue of the Stars
Los Angeles, CA 90067
Tel. (213) 277-2333
Hrs: Lunch   Mon. - Sat.   11:30 a.m. - 3:00 p.m.
        Dinner   Mon. - Fri.   5:30 p.m. - 10:30 p.m.
                        Sat. - Sun.   5:00 p.m. - 10:00 p.m.
        Late Supper from 10:30 p.m.
Visa, MasterCard and AMEX are accepted.

For a trip to Italy, without leaving the United States, take a trip to Harry's Bar. It's an exact replica of the Harry's Bar in Florence, Italy and you'll feel like you've been transported to the old country. When you taste the food there will be no doubt you are in Italy.

Harry's pasta is homemade, the fish is fresh and they serve superb Venetian and Florentine specialties. The food is authentic Northern Italy. They won the *Third Annual Los Angeles Basil Festival Award* with Harry's Fettuccine al Pesto. They offer lunch specialties and fresh fish catch of the day and a whole menu of Italian dishes you may be hard pressed to pronounce. The menu represents the best in Northern Italian dishes: Prosciutto d'Anatra, homemade duck prosciutto, Linguini Rosse con Gorganzola e Pindi, beet pasta with gorganzola and pine nuts and Scaloppine alle Bacche di Senape e Balsamico, veal with basalmic vinegar and mustard.

The bar is very European with its high walnut counter and tall wooden stools. The intimate dining rooms are enhanced by warm colors. Harry's has recreated the wonderful natural pink illumination that surrounds the city of Florence. For authentic Northern Italian food, visit Harry's. It's a little bit of Italy in Los Angeles.

STAGE DELI OF NEW YORK
10250 Santa Monica Boulevard
Los Angeles, CA 90067
Tel. (213) 553-DELI
Hrs: Breakfast
        Mon. - Sun.   6:30 a.m. - 10:30 a.m.
        Sun. - Thu.   6:30 a.m. - 12:00 midnight
        Fri. - Sat.   until 2:00 p.m.
Visa, MasterCard and AMEX are accepted.

The hottest new deli in Los Angeles is really a fifty year grande dame of New York delis. The Stage Deli of New York has revolutionized the Los Angeles deli scene. The Stage, as it is affectionately called, is a faithful replica of New York's famous Stage Deli. The original Stage Deli has been a New York tradition since 1937. It was founded as The Delicatessen of the Performing Arts by Russian emigré Max Asnas. Max made the best sandwich in town.

The Los Angeles Stage Deli has replicated its New York counterpart down to ordering the pastrami, corned beef, tongue and other sandwich meats from the same meat purveyor used in Manhattan. The main difference between a sandwich from New York and L. A. is, of course, the size! A double decker from the Angel City's grill is twice the size of any comparable sandwich seen anywhere. Screen and stage entertainers, radio, television and musical personalities and a host of other famous people have created their favorite combination sandwich for The Stage's menu. You can choose a Frank Sinatra, triple decker with turkey, salami, imported Swiss cheese, cole slaw and Russian dressing or Robin Williams, with a little tongue and a lot of bologna, pastrami, cole slaw and Russian dressing.

The service is very good with just a twinge of New York attitude thrown in for atmosphere's sake. The Stage Deli offers authentic deli food from chicken soup to incredible sandwiches to their specialty of the house: Brooklyn Egg Creams. Don't miss this "Best Choice" when visiting the Los Angeles area.

MALIBU

Lying along the Pacific Coast Highway, west of Pacific Palisades, Malibu is an unincorporated area of L.A. County that extends along the coast for some twenty-seven miles. The Malibu Colony is an exclusive community inhabited by movie stars, musicians and other celebrities. Johnny Carson, Larry Hagman and Barbara Streisand are among those who have opted to enjoy the clean air and good life along the beach.

Malibu is one of the county's most picturesque spots, where mountain peaks rise 2,000 feet above the coastline, providing a wealth of opportunities for hikers, cyclists and horseback riders on the many trails that wind through the canyons and park lands.

The cost of living in Malibu is high. A modest beach bungalow sells for several hundred thousand dollars. And beach view mansions go for as much as several hundred million dollars. In recent y ears, those who have lived on the beach have been beset with a series of natural disasters. Heavy beach erosion and high tides have claimed several homes. And fire is a constant threat in the canyons during the tinder dry summer months.

Visitors can enjoy the wide variety of dining experiences along the Malibu coastline. Most of the restaurants in the Malibu Colony overlook the beach and prices range from moderate to expensive. Recreational pursuits include fishing, sailing and surfing, a sport made famous in old Beach Boys tunes.

Human occupation of Malibu goes back at least 7,000 years; it was the home of the Chumash and Gabrielino people. In fact, the name Malibu comes from the Chumash word, *Maliwu*, meaning "place along the cliff," which is what they named their village at the mouth of the Malibu Canyon.

In 1887 Frederick and May Rindge purchased what had been a Spanish land grant. The couple spent the rest of their lives fighting to prevent construction of a public highway along the coast. Rindge went as far as to build his own private twenty-mile railroad to prevent the Southern Pacific Railroad from doing so. At that time the only access to the ranch was by boat or horseback. May Rindge continued the fight after her husband's death, hired armed guards to keep trespassers out and had construction sites dynamited. Eventually she exhausted her financial resources in court battles. In 1929, the state opened the Pacific Coast Highway.

Malibu became the exclusive domain of the famous when May Rindge began leasing her property to writers and entertainers such as Barbara Stanwyck, John Gilbert and Dolores Del Rio, who built summer cottages along the beach. Rindge continued to develop the area throughout the 1940s. In the 1960s and 1970s development skyrocketed with the building of houses, condominiums, shopping centers and mobile home lots in the Malibu area. Fortunately, the state and county agencies also acquired beach and park property for public use.

ATTRACTIONS

• **The Malibu Lagoon Museum**, 23200 Pacific Coast Highway, is set in a 1928 Spanish style beach house built for Frederick Rindge's daughter, Rhonda, on a thirteen acre site overlooking the Malibu Lagoon, beach and Malibu Pier. The spectacular tile work was crafted by artisans Mrs. Rindge recruited in Europe to establish a tile and pottery manufacturing operation. Exhibits include artifacts, rare photographs, maps, documents and books depicting Malibu's colorful history. The house is sometimes used for filming television programs, including sections of Dallas. For information write Malibu Lagoon Museum, 23200 Pacific Coast Highway, Malibu, CA, 90265. Tel. (213) 456-8432.

• Located in the 2300 block of Pacific Coast Highway is the **Malibu Pier**. It's a popular spot for fishing and watching surfers. A bait and tackle shop rents fishing gear and one can take a charter excursion from the pier. Anglers reel in bass, halibut, yellowtail and rock fish. The original 400 foot pier was built by Frederick Rindge in 1893 to serve as a loading dock for ranch supplies.

• The **J. Paul Getty Museum** at 17985 Pacific Coast Highway is one of the nation's finest art museums containing collections of Roman and Greek art, as well as European masterpieces from the Middle Ages, Renaissance and Baroque periods. In 1945 oil baron Getty purchased a sixty-five acre citrus farm in Malibu where he kept his ever growing art collections in a ranch house. In 1968 Getty began work on a new building, which would be a reproduction of a lavish country villa that had been buried by the eruption of Mount Vesuvius in A.D. 79. Getty died in 1976, leaving a trust that will enable the museum to continue to acquire art for its thirty-eight galleries and gardens. For information call (213) 458-2003.

• **Malibu Lagoon State Beach,** at Pacific Coast Highway and Cross Creek Road, is a 166 acre recreational facility that includes the **Malibu Bluffs** and **Malibu Lagoon.** The beach is a favorite surfing spot because of the strong southwest swells that refract around a rock reef at Malibu Point and break over a gently sloping sandy bottom. Facilities include volleyball courts, parking and rest rooms. The lagoon is a small brackish estuary at the mouth of Malibu Creek. It supports salt marsh plant life and is used by migratory birds for resting and feeding. More than 200 species of birds have been seen here including great horned owls and belted kingfishers.

• Named for the spaced-out character in the Doonesbury comic strip, the **Zonker Harris Accessway** provides public access to a beach that has no beach facilities. The accessway is at 22548 Pacific Coast Highway.

• **Las Tunas State Beach,** one mile west of Topanga Canyon Road, is a narrow and rocky beach that offers good diving access to an offshore reef that's home to spiny lobsters and halibut. Anglers fish there for perch and California corbina. For information call (213) 457-9891.

• **Topanga State Beach** is a mile long sandy beach where the Topanga Creek empties into the Pacific. A popular sunbathing beach, swimming and surfing is good here, too. Facilities include rest rooms. The beach is located down the coast from Las Tunas State Beach. For information call (213) 451-2906

• **El Pescador State Beach**, 32900 block of Pacific Coast Highway, offers a parking lot, rest rooms and picnic tables on the bluff. A trail leads down the bluff to a sandy ten acre beach.

• **La Piedra State Beach**, 32700 block of Pacific Coast Highway. Although *La Piedra* means stone in Spanish, this is a fine sandy beach, perfect for sunbathing and swimming. You'll find picnic tables and rest rooms on the bluff.

• **El Matador State Beach** 32350 block of Pacific Coast HIghway, is eighteen acres of beach facilities that includes a panoramic view of the coast and the Channel Islands. A picnic area and trails, along which a variety of flowering plants thrive, are available. Surf fishing and scuba diving are popular activities here.

• **Zuma County Beach**, on the 30,000 block of Pacific Coast Highway is more than 100 acres of white sand beach, making it Malibu's largest and most popular beach. Joggers, sunbathers, swimmers and surfers come here by the thousands each month.

RESTAURANTS

BEAURIVAGE
26025 Pacific Coast Highway
Malibu, CA 90265
Tel. (213) 456-5733
Hrs: Lunch   Mon. - Fri.   11:30 a.m. - 3:00 p.m.
         Dinner   Mon. - Sun.   5:00 p.m. - 11:00 p.m.
Visa, MasterCard and AMEX are accepted.

From the shore of the Mediterranean Sea to the shores of our own Pacific Ocean comes one of the most varied cuisines in the world. The incredibly diverse dishes of France and Italy await you at BeauRivage.

Nestled at the base of the Malibu Mountains, BeauRivage is patterned after the charming inns of Southern Europe. There is a casual old world ambiance in the blossoming flowers and gently sloping hillside surrounding this comfortably elegant restaurant. Their menu is exceptional, featuring the homemade pastas and heavenly light sauces of Mediterranean Europe. Begin with a tantalizing appetizer such as Mouclade au Curry, made with fresh mussels, curry sauce, apples and cream, followed by their special chilled California

Soup made with clam broth, scallions, avocado, tomato, cucumber and bay shrimp. Next try one of the BeauRivage's superb salads, such as their Insalata Frieolore made with crisp Belgian endive, avocado, watercress, radicchio and chutney dressing. For your entree the chef recommends either the Singuire Pollo, a pasta dish made with smoked chicken and mushrooms, or Baby Salmon in Sorrel Sauce. And finally for a perfect end to a perfect dinner, be sure to try one of the BeauRivage's luscious homemade desserts. Besides the regular menu they also offer from eight to fourteen daily Blackboard Specials such as bouillabaisse, homemade pasta specials and fresh fish dishes of all types. Owners Daniel and Luciana Forge are proud of their many fresh game dishes such as venison, wild boar, mallard duck and quail which are offered in season. They also offer a weekend Champagne Brunch with an exciting menu all its own. From the many herbs and spices grown right on the property to the fish brought daily fresh from the sea, every dish at BeauRivage is made from fine quality ingredients with an eye toward perfection.

Daniel and Luciana invite you to join them at BeauRivage overlooking the enchanting shores of the Pacific for a dining experience you'll remember for a lifetime.

MALIBU ADOBE
23410 Civic Center Way
Malibu, CA 90265
Tel. (213) 456-2021
Hrs:　Lunch　　　Tue. - Sat.　　11:30 a.m. - 2:30 p.m.
　　　Dinner　　　Mon. - Sun.　6:00 p.m. - 10:00 p.m.
　　　Sunday　　　Brunch　　　11:30 a.m. - 2:30 p.m.
Visa, MasterCard and AMEX are accepted.

Few bits of decorating are as different as a 700 year old, twenty foot high cactus skeleton. But then, Malibu Adobe contains one of the most striking decors of any trend setting restaurant in Southern California.

Actress Ali MacGraw has designed a Santa Fe style interior that reflects the high taste of luminous owners bearing names such as Dustin Hoffman, Bob Newhart, Tony Danza, Randy Quaid, Stacy Keach and Alan Ladd, Jr. Gourmets come in to try the Malibu Adobe's extensive menu while relaxing in an atmosphere that features an unfinished pine ceiling, terra cotta tile floors, Native American pottery, exotic plants, and tables draped with cornflower blue tablecloths. Enjoy a cocktail at the large bar, and choose a seat at the upper level balcony that overlooks the entire restaurant. The restaurant's menu contains some of the best hot and spicy dishes that California and Southwest cooking traditions can produce. There's grilled swordfish with picante pineapple-banana salsa, grilled ahi tuna with poblano pesto, and quesadillas with wild mushrooms and fresh goat cheese. Another favorite is flautas of grilled chicken and roasted corn, served with ancho-tomatillo sauce and creme fraiche.

In addition to the Southwest style, general partner James Palmer has paid homage to the Malibu surfing tradition by displaying huge sepia toned photographs of surfers. Palmer and the owners of Malibu Adobe invite you to enjoy Malibu and the best of the Southwest.

SAND CASTLE
28128 Pacific Coast Highway
Malibu, CA 90265
Tel. (213) 457-2503
Hrs: Breakfast   Mon. - Sun.   6:00 a.m. - 12:00 noon
      Brunch   Mon. - Sun.   9:00 a.m. - 3:00 p.m.
      Lunch   Mon. - Sat.   11:00 a.m. - 4:00 p.m
                   Sunday   12:00 noon - 3:00 p.m.
      Sunset Dinner
                   Mon. - Sat.   5:00 p.m. - 7:00 p.m.
                   Sunday   4:00 p.m. - 7:00 p.m.
      Dinner   Sun. - Thu.   5:00 p.m. - 10:00 p.m.
                   Fri. - Sat.   5:00 p.m. - 11:00 p.m.
Visa, MasterCard, AMEX, Diners Card, and Carte Blanche are accepted.

The next time you're watching an episode of *The Rockford Files*, look closely, you may see Jimmy McDonald seating one of his guests at a table overlooking the breathtaking Malibu Beach. Jimmy has been in the restaurant business for twenty-five years and at this location for fifteen. All those years of experience have paid off for Jimmy, his customers and the ever popular Sand Castle restaurant.

Jimmy's sense of adventure and his commitment to keep his many repeat customers coming back for more prompts him to add entrees to his menu. He now has fifty, ranging from abalone and Beef Wellington to Chicken with Peppercorn Sauce. The day starts early at the Sand Castle with a spectacular sunrise and the 6:00 a.m. fisherman's breakfast of fresh squeezed orange juice, homemade biscuits, and a wide variety of omelettes, waffles, pancakes and eggs.

The high quality service and food continues into lunch with its broad menu including escargots, soups, salads and sandwiches as well as complete entrees such as Fresh Catch of the Day, scallops in white wine sauce and red snapper with avocado, cheese and tomato sauce. Meat and poultry are also available. For an extra special treat enjoy the daily champagne brunch with six specials to choose from, all with a refillable glass of champagne. An early sunset meal will give you your choice of six or seven entrees at an extra reasonable price. Dinners feature authentic Bouillabaisse and a wide variety of seafood, beef and chicken delicacies. A choice from the dessert cart will add to your enjoyment.

The breathtaking view, excellent prices and extensive and versatile menu make this a "Best Choice." The next time you feel like taking a trip on an ocean liner on dry dock, stop by the Sand Castle. If it happens to be during the summer you can take advantage of the snack bar available on the beach serving the best in burgers, fries, soft drinks and wine.

SPLASH, THE RESTAURANT
6800 Westward Beach Road
Malibu, CA 90265
Tel. (213) 457-5521
Hrs: Sun. - Sat.   5:00 p.m. - 12:00 midnight
Visa, MasterCard and AMEX are accepted.

Fly away to your own special hideaway on the beach at Malibu. Splash, The Restaurant, is an idyllic, secluded establishment located across from Westward Beach, nestled into a hillside. There is a feeling of being on an island. Splash is a place for romance, a special evening or private place to dine with friends.

Splash's menu offers all-time favorites. Madras style curries are a popular choice. They are served mild or hot as you wish. You can choose from Boneless Chicken Curry or Jumbo Shrimp Curry, both served with saffron rice, mango chutney and coconut. Homemade pasta dishes include Rigatone Dudley's for Two, rigatone stuffed with veal sausage and broccoli in an Alfredo sauce. The Caesar salad is prepared tableside and has won rave reviews from critics near and far. Tableside cooking is a specialty at Splash and there is a bountiful catch of fresh fish daily. Desserts are a specialty and include ice creams such as Caramel Pecan, Chocolate Raspberry, White Chocolate Chip and Amaretto. Fresh kiwi, raspberry or strawberry sorbets make a refreshing end to a Splash meal. Cafe Diable finishes a romantic meal with a flash of flame. It is a coffee with Sambucca, Grand Marnier, Myer's Rum and an orange peel studded with cloves which, when ignited, imbues the essence of the orange into the drink.

The wine list at Splash is comprehensive; including twenty champagnes, excellent white Burgundy, twenty-four Chardonnays and twenty-four Cabernets ranging from current to great vintages. Splash, The Restaurant, was formerly The Whale Watch Restaurant and its location is an official whale watching station.

MARINA DEL REY

As its name implies, Marina del Rey is the king of the boat harbors. The community enjoys the largest manmade small craft harbor in the world. This is home to some 6,000 privately owned yachts and another 3,000 boats in dry dock. The harbor area covers 375 acres of land and more than 400 acres of water. Marina del Rey is also known as something of a young and affluent single's community.

Although Marina del Rey is not known as a beach community, it does have a public beach at the end of Basin D that is open all year. Admiralty Park, extending along Admiralty Way between Lincoln Boulevard and Washington Street, commands an excellent view of the marina. The community also offers several fine restaurants, some with spectacular views of the harbor.

In addition to boating, many of Marina del Rey's visitors enjoy cycling, roller skating, tennis and jogging. The stores also offer a variety of shopping experiences. Visitors during the Christmas holidays will be treated to an evening parade and many of the marina's boats will be decked out with lights and Yuletide decorations.

The harbor area was once known as the Playa del Rey inlet, where the Los Angeles River emptied into the ocean. The first marina was established by a real estate speculator in the 1880s, but was abandoned when the real estate market collapsed a few y ears later. Oil was discovered there in the mid-1920s, but the swampy wetlands made oil exploration unprofitable. In 1954, Congress authorized dredging the wetlands for construction of a recreational harbor. And, in 1962, the harbor was opened to the public.

ATTRACTIONS

• **Fisherman's Village**, with its cobbled dockside walkways and weathered shingle sided buildings, resembles a New England fishing village. It extends along the waterfront with shops, restaurants and galleries. Also available are boat charters, rentals, fishing licenses, bait and tackle. For more information on cruises contact the Boat House by calling (213) 822-1152.

• **Ballona Wetlands**, along Ballona Creek, south of Marina del Rey, serves as a refuge for migratory birds and a breeding habitat for several endangered species. A nature interpretive center operated by the Audubon Society has been proposed, but in the meantime the wetlands offer a prime opportunity for bird and wildlife viewing.

ACCOMMODATION

MARINA BEACH HOTEL
4100 Admiralty Way
Marina del Rey, CA 90292
Tel. (213) 301-3000
      (800) 882-4000 US
      (800) 8-Marina CA
All major credit cards are accepted.

For a quiet stay in genteel surroundings overlooking the yacht harbor, the Marina Beach Hotel is a "Best Choice." Just five miles from the Los Angeles International Airport, the hotel offers a convenient retreat from the hubbub of Los Angeles.

It features 300 guest rooms and a breathtaking view of the Palos Verdes Peninsula and Malibu coastline. The lights of Century City and downtown Los Angeles can be seen at night. Each guest room has its own balcony. Standard amenities range from the morning newspaper to a concierge. There is a VIP floor for Signature Club guests which provides bar service and continental breakfast. The hotel's Stones Restaurant serves gourmet continental cuisine. LaCour is a terrace cafe that offers more casual dining. The hotel is well suited for professional business meetings. Just across the street is an inland beach and it is a short walk to the ocean.

The Marina Beach Hotel is stylish and spacious. It offers a haven of luxury complete with sea breezes. It is centrally located to many points of interest in Los Angeles and has convenient freeway access. If you are looking for a quality establishment, where you can vacation in a relaxed, refined atmosphere, look no further than the Marina Beach Hotel.

DIVING SHOPS

MARINA DEL REY DIVERS
2539 Lincoln Boulevard
Marina del Rey, CA 90291
Tel. (213) 827-1131
Hrs: Mon. - Fri.   10:00 a.m. - 7:00 p.m.
       Saturday   10:00 a.m. - 6:00 p.m.
       Sunday   10:00 a.m. - 4:00 p.m.
Visa, MasterCard and AMEX are accepted.

Come away for a day on the magical isle of Catalina. Visit this gorgeous chunk of paradise by land and explore the underwater sea gardens. Experience the clear blue water of the Pacific Ocean at its finest. Marina Del Rey Divers offers one day boat trips to Catalina Island. With their expertise and experience you'll see all the special spots, both above and below the water, that have given this picturesque island its reputation.

Marina Del Rey Divers, run by R.A. Buck, Steve Cooper and a cockatiel named Rambo, extends a full array of diving activities and teaches a complete range of diving classes, from beginning to advanced. They also help coordinate local diving club activities. Diving trips range from one day trips to Catalina Island to longer trips to places like Australia's coral reef and Cozumel. They maintain a diving equipment shop. Whatever your diving needs, they are able to supply you with the right gear and full equipment rental. Be sure and get your name on their monthly newsletter mailing list to keep abreast of upcoming events.

If you like to scuba dive within an easy going, fun atmosphere with the security of being accompanied by top notch divers and instructors, then contact the Marina Del Rey Divers for your next dive.

RESTAURANTS

EDIE'S DINER
4211 Admiralty Way
Marina del Rey, CA 90291
Tel. (213) 823-5339
Hrs: Mon. - Sun.   24 hours
Visa, MasterCard and AMEX are accepted.

Remember the fifties, when girls wore bobby sox, cool guys drove convertibles and the local malt shop was where everyone gathered for a sandwich and shake and danced to the juke box? If you find those memories nostalgic, you'll enjoy Edie's Diner. It's almost as good as a time machine. The booths and counter tops are red, the floor is black and white checkerboard, and there are tabletop juke boxes.

You can get real, honest to gosh, American food here, just like the old malt shops used to make burgers, malts, meatloaf sandwiches, french fries. They even make old fashioned soda and root beer floats! For breakfast Edie's has great combinations like lox, eggs and onions, three egg omelettes and corned beef hash. Dinners include Edie's "Blue Ribbon Meatloaf," spaghetti and meatballs, turkey dinner and top sirloin. The soups are homemade and mighty delicious.

Their motto is "God bless America...and Edie's Diner too!" It's all American, right down to the story of how the diner got started. Edie won big money in a bowling tourney back in New Jersey. She decided to move out west and open her dream diner. For an old fashioned, all American meal, stop at Edie's Diner and enjoy the good old days all over again.

GULLIVER'S
13181 Mindanao Way
Marina del Rey, CA 90292
Tel. (213) 821-8866
Hrs: Dinner   Mon. - Fri.   from 5:30 p.m.
      Lunch   11:30 a.m. - 2:30 p.m.
Visa and MasterCard are accepted.

The enchantment of the eighteenth century and times of Jonathan Swift are captured in this traditional English roadside inn. American cuisine is graciously served in a warm, comfortable environment replete with saucy waitresses.

Prime Ribs of beef are Gulliver's specialty. Dinner includes a hearty creamed soup of the day, or salad of hearts of romaine garnished with chopped eggs, cherry tomatoes, baby bay shrimp, with a delicate vinegar and oil dressing. Included are Spinach Souffle, Yorkshire Pudding, whipped horseradish sauce, *au jus*, and Gulliver's famous creamed corn. Desserts are ala carte and sinfully delicious. The menu includes an assortment of entrees including fish, poultry, veal and steaks.

The dinner guest is surrounded by a museum of leaded glass pieces, pewter and ceramic objects, bric-a-brac, and a vast collection of old prints of Hogarth, Rowlandson and the prolific Gulliver illustrators. Waitresses at Gulliver's are carefully selected and trained. Their floor time is described as being "on stage." The employee's locker room is a theatrical dressing room, even to the traditional make-up mirrors. Waitresses work a four day week so they will be alert and rested. Flippant dialogue between the women and their table guests is assured. Gulliver's is a place you will want to tell your friends about!

PACIFIC PALISADES

Seventeen miles west of Los Angeles, along jagged shoreline cliffs, Pacific Palisades serves as another coastal community for the well to do. Its spectacular ocean views and fresh ocean air made it a popular resort area in the 1860s with vacationers from Los Angeles.

From the 1920s through 1940s this beach community, which had become a center for educational and recreational gatherings, became the region's cultural center. Writers, artists, actors and architects came to Pacific Palisades to pursue their talents. The architect's efforts are evident in some of the buildings. John Entenza, the editor and publisher of *Arts and Architecture* magazine, helped focus the talents of the architects who developed some of the most advanced modernist styles. The Case Study House Program, which was under way from 1945 to 1960, encouraged architects to make use of the latest building techniques and materials.

Cultural variety was brought to Pacific Palisades when followers of Parmahansa Yogananda, an Indian religious leader and founder of the Self-Realization Fellowship, built a non-denominational open air temple at 17191 Sunset Boulevard. Visitors meditate and stroll through the gardens where a spring-fed lake is surrounded by lawns, native chaparral and exotic plants.

ATTRACTION

• **Will Rogers State Beach,** 16000 block of Pacific Coast Highway, is a three mile long sandy beach that offers swimming, diving, surfing and surf fishing. Perch, halibut and bonito are often caught from the shore. A bike path and pedestrian promenade extend along the length of the shore from Chautauqua Boulevard to Temesca Canyon Road. For information call (213) 394-3266.

RESTAURANT

GLADSTONE'S
17300 Pacific Coast Highway
Pacific Palisades, CA 90272
Tel. (213) GL-4-FISH
Hrs: Sun. - Thu.   7:00 a.m. - 11:00 p.m.
      Fri. - Sat.   7:00 a.m. - 12:00 midnight
Visa, MasterCard and AMEX are accepted.

Located "On the beach where Sunset Boulevard meets the ocean blue Pacific," Gladstone's is the ultimate in seafood cuisine and fine dining, California style. From the overturned lifeboat which serves as a covered entry, to the nautical decor appointed with brass and copper fixtures, rough wood planking and live lobster tank, the ambiance is one of warmth and romance.

Among the featured catch of the day is Gladstone's award winning clam chowder, She crab soup and oysters on the half shell. Gladstone's World Famous Marine Salad provides a melange of ocean shrimp, snow crab, avocado, tomato and hardboiled egg; and Cioppino features a San Francisco fisherman's stew of fresh fish, clams, mussels, crab and shrimp in a rich pungent tomato and vegetable broth. If it's fish you desire, Gladstone's has it. All seafood is fresh, and lobsters, clams, and oysters are picked live before being cooked to your preference. As with all Bob Morris' restaurants, diners will be astounded with the "overabundance" of portions and selections. The Mile High Chocolate Cake and Piece of Cake are among the decadent desserts. Be sure to sample the wonderfully delectable ice cream spirits, concoctions and cocktails.

An outside deck and broad expanses of windows provide an eclectic view of the ever changing panorama of the Pacific Ocean and serve to heighten your palate. So, steer a course to Gladstone's, one of the "Best Choices" in seafood and fine dining that California has to offer.

SANTA MONICA

Long regarded as the "Coney Island of the West," Santa Monica retains much of the flavor of a time when going to the seashore was associated with quick dips and roller coaster rides. Today, families still flock to Santa Monica's fine beaches, located just fifteen miles west of downtown L.A. And, you can still ride the old carousel on the municipal pier on weekends; although some of th e old ring toss and shooting galleries have been replaced with video arcades.

About a third of the pier was washed away in 1983, but its quaint backdrop continues to be used by film makers looking for an old timey setting. The pier also offers a variety of seafood restaurants to call a time out from the day's activities and watch the action. If you want to enjoy the beach, but don't want to get sand in your shoes, you'll find a bike path you can walk along.

Long before Santa Monica was developed into a community, it was regarded as a special spot by the Spanish, at least special enough for Gaspar de Portola to establish a camp here during his 1769 expedition. Legend has it that the priest who accompanied Portola was so taken by the waters, he was moved to think of the tears Saint Monica shed for her heretic son, Saint Augustine.

For many years the area was used as ranch land, but in 1875 developers saw its potential as a railroad terminus if a town and wharf could be developed. The Southern Pacific Railroad later bought the land, but destroyed the wharf so it would not compete with its established wharf facility at Wilmington to the south.

The Long Wharf was built in 1894 and Santa Monica became a busy commercial port. About the same time, trolley service from Los Angeles arrived, making the trip to Santa Monica's beaches, bath houses and amusements irresistible to inland residents.

In the 1960s, as Santa Monica was becoming increasingly urbanized, a downtown pedestrian mall was developed. And, in 1980 a strikingly beautiful shopping mall with glassed in galleries was built.

ATTRACTIONS

*   **Palisades Park**, at Ocean Avenue between Colorado and Adelaide, stretches for two miles through palm trees on the top of eroding cliffs, offering panoramic views of the ocean. A remnant of the past is the old **Camera Obscura** near Arizona Street, which is open daily. The visitor center in the park hands out brochures and maps of Santa Monica.

*   The **Santa Monica State Beach** is one of California's most popular beaches, with its wide sands that stretch for three miles south, from Will Rogers State Beach to Venice City Beach. Picnic facilities, volleyball courts and a playground are available. Just south of the pier was the original "Muscle Beach." Although it was a hangout for bodybuilders and circus performers, the name originally referred to the shellfish that attached themselves to the pier pilings. Today Venice Beach lays claim to the term "Muscle Beach." In the 1920s this stretch of sand was known as the Gold Coast, an apparent reference to the celebrities such as Cary Grant and Mary Pickford who built cottages there.

ART IN SANTA MONICA

There has long been a spiritual relationship between the ocean and many, if not most, artists. Perhaps it is the awesome, uncontrollable force or the mysterious nature of the tides that ebb and flow that connects artists and the sea.

Located on the western coast of California, Santa Monica lies just a few miles west of Los Angeles. To be precise, Santa Monica is only twelve miles from Hollywood and eight miles from L.A. International Airport. In spite of this closeness, the broad glistening beaches of the picture perfect Santa Monica Bay remained fairly deserted for many years. It wasn't until the Santa Monica Freeway was completed that the first influx of permanent residents, commuters to the city, began to occupy the virgin beaches with a jumble of houses and automobiles.

As with any growth, once started there was little stopping, or even slowing, the mass exodus from L.A. and the introduction of the intrepid commuter to the pristine shores of Santa Monica. A community sprang up overnight and seemed to establish its identity by building Palisades Park and catering to the city folk, much to the dismay of a blossoming artist's colony.

This artist's colony had been tentatively elaborating on its newly formed presence throughout the fifties and sixties. Well known, and even famous artists, had sought the seclusion of the isolated coastline to work uninterrupted. Edward Kienholz, Richard Diebenkorn, Ed Moses, Claire Falkenstein and a host of lesser known artists had established what was to become known as the Greenwich Village of the west coast.

In the seventies there seemed to be a resurgence of "civilization" in the area as new and more expensive homes were built, and the city folk threatened to regain the strangle hold they had periodically exercised. Fortunately, that trend seems to have been reversed and once again, Santa Monica is on the verge of becoming an artistic, if not a cultural mecca.

Several new galleries have opened in a five block long section of downtown Santa Monica. The exposure they now offer to resident artists, as well as the drawing power they may have on future resident artists, could easily revitalize the aesthetic qualities of the community.

Part of the contribution of past and present artists has been the many murals that enhance the downtown area. Along **4th Street and Ocean Park Boulevard** as well as in the heart of the city, giant renditions, including *Another Magical Sunset in Santa Monica*, by Gilbert Lugan and *Unbridled*, which depicts the horses of the carousel at Palisades Park breaking free and running down the beach and bigger than life marine animals, add to the citiy's allure.

The Santa Monica Arts Foundation is in the process of establishing and maintaining a **Natural Elements Sculpture Park** which will occupy a two mile stretch of the beach. One of the first pieces of public art already established is entitled *The Singing Chairs.* Shaped like those used by lifeguards, the chairs are capped by wind organs which play whenever breezes waft in from the ocean.

The **Santa Monica Museum of Art** has been recently completed and is a showcase for area artists including Stanton Macdonald-Wright, John Cage, Richard Diebenkorn and Sam Francis. The building is a renovation rather than a new construction, and the included artwork is international, as well as local in scope. Other area museums are the **Heritage Museum** which features period displays of furnished rooms dating from 1890, and **Angels Atticx** which offers antique doll house exhibits. Both buildings are worth viewing in and of themselves for their architectural design.

Finally, under the direction of artist James Caswell, **Correia Art Glass,** a factory specializing in three dimensional glass sculptures, offers tours as well as sales of museum quality pieces. This factory accents the **Santa Monica American Glass Art Gallery.** Operated by founder Thomas Crane, the gallery features a variety of glass pieces destined to become heirlooms.

Santa Monica's art colony has managed to pull off a resurgence of, and a commitment to, the arts. Just as the tide in Santa Monica Bay is a constant ebb and flow, so it seems is the emphasis on the arts within this community. Fortunately for the local artists, the tide appears to be in.

ACCOMMODATIONS

THE HUNTLEY HOTEL
1111 2nd Street
Santa Monica, CA 90403
Tel.   (213) 394-5454
          (800) 556-4011 US
          (800) 556-4012 CA
Visa, MasterCard, AMEX, Diners Club, Carte Blanche,
Eurocard and Access are accepted.

When traveling to the Los Angeles area, those who wish individual attention will find the Huntley Hotel in Santa Monica to be a "Best Choice." This top rated hotel in the heart of one of the most beautiful towns on the California Coast is only two blocks away from the Pacific Ocean.

The Huntley Hotel is small enough to be intimate but large enough to provide all the amenities of a full service establishment. Choose from 210 rooms, all featuring luxurious queen beds. Most rooms offer views of the Pacific or the nearby mountains. Amenities include laundry/valet service, beauty salon, meeting rooms, free parking and room service. A glass elevator runs up the front of the hotel to Topper's, the hotel's Mexican/California cuisine restaurant, which is a romantic spot for cocktails or a sunset dinner. In the evening, the panoramic view of the ocean from Catalina to Malibu is spectacular. Topper's always has two happy hours; one after work and another after the theater. On Sundays, Topper's lays out a lavish brunch buffet with a wide and unusual assortment of fare. After the meal, sun on the beach or walk to any of Santa Monica's fine shopping areas. Joggers will appreciate the miles of scenic jogging paths that overlook the ocean and the beach.

The Huntley Hotel brings together the best of Santa Monica: small town ambiance, clean ocean air and a quiet lifestyle. It's no wonder that guests return many times over.

MIRAMAR SHERATON
101 Wilshire Boulevard
Santa Monica, CA 90401
Tel. (213) 394-3731
All major credit cards are accepted.

Miramar provides the accommodations and Mother Nature provides the view. The sparkling blue Pacific Ocean spreads out almost literally from the doorstep of the hotel. Cool ocean breezes attract summer visitors from warmer climates, and warm winter days are a haven for visitors from the north.

The Miramar Sheraton is refreshingly small in comparison to other world class hotels. It houses 305 luxurious guest rooms and sixty-one beautifully decorated suites. However, its comfort, service and access to exciting activities is plentiful indeed. Miramar Sheraton is a great hotel for the individual vacationer or groups looking for the perfect meeting place.

The climate and surroundings of Santa Monica provide the Miramar visitor with unsurpassed recreational activities. The Santa Monica coast is one of California's most beautiful beaches. Sunning, surfing, sailing and swimming are unlimited. Motor trips along the Pacific Coast Highway are outstanding. Joggers and bicyclists will enjoy the six jogging and bicycling paths along the beautiful Palisades Park. Specialty shops in the town offer purchases from caviar to kites, from paintings to high fashion items. For those who would rather look than purchase, excellent museums are within close proximity of the Miramar. The historic Miramar Sheraton is a relaxing, fun place to be.

ANTIQUE SHOP

MAIN STREET GALLERY
2803 Main Street
Santa Monica, CA 90405
Tel. (213) 399-4161
Hrs: Mon. - Sun.   11:00 a.m. - 6:00 p.m.
Visa, MasterCard and AMEX are accepted.

For many people, the modern miracle of Japan, with its high technology and constant growth, is all they know of this world power. Few people realize that only a short time ago, Japan was a feudal land.

It is to this earlier era of Japanese culture that Main Street Gallery owner Jean Concoff takes us. Walking among the various pieces of cultural history offers a new perspective on Japan. A mystical sense of the past is present in the drawers of an ancient apothecary chest, the remnants of herbs still visible. Throughout the gallery, brick walls and bamboo accents create an atmosphere that adds warmth and charm to the various antiques. Craftsmanship and functional form, the legendary hallmarks of modern Japanese products, are shown to be parts of cultural heritage. Everything that is shown was created for use in Japanese daily life, with none of the items made for export. There are tools, shop signs, dolls, shrines, garden doors and furniture. All items are from eighty to two hundred years old.

Jean Concoff, whose frequent trips to Japan and obvious reverence for the culture are the source of the collection, sees to it that all pieces are in original condition and of the best quality. She has also developed a love for the clothes of modern Japanese designer Issey Miyake, and carries his clean lined Plantation label. The clothing and antiques at Main Street Gallery offer a unique and interesting bit of Japan. Jean will be happy to include your special request as part of her next buying trip.

APPAREL

THE AdDRESS
1116 Wilshire Boulevard
Santa Monica, CA 90403
Tel. (213) 394-1406
Hrs: Mon. - Sat.   10:00 a.m. - 6:00 p.m.
          Thursday   10:00 a.m. - 8:00 p.m.
          Sunday   12:00 noon - 5:00 p.m.
Visa, MasterCard and AMEX are accepted.

Here's good news for shoppers with Dom Perignon taste and a tight budget. The fashion resale business is booming in Southern California and The AdDress leads the way. You'll find new and resale clothing, all at discounted prices, though the quality is as high as any top rated New York or Los Angeles boutique. Labels with such names as Chanel, Armani, Sonia Rykiel, Chloe, Anne Klein and Oscar de la Renta abound at The AdDress.

The fashion conscious, the career women and the downright smart shopper can trust entrepreneur Maureen Clavin's fashion savvy. They might find a $1,500 Adolpho suit for less than $100. A $5,000 Fabrice hand beaded gown might sell for one-tenth the original price. In addition to dresses, customers will find beautiful jackets and coats, and new items come in all of the time. Regular patrons, frequenting the store on Wilshire Boulevard in the heart of Santa Monica are continually impressed with the inventory. The shop's contemporary California architecture features a four pillared archway entrance and blooming plants in antique planters. Customers are greeted with cheese, wine and coffee, as though they had entered someone's cozy living room. The elegance of the store complements the elegance of the clothing, which is displayed along the walls so that shoppers have plenty of space to browse.

Personalized service helps to make The AdDress a success. Consultants cater to the store's valued clients, and friendly sales people are on hand to help create a whole new look with clothing gently worn by the chicest women in Southern California.

COTTON RAINBOW
2408 Wilshire Boulevard
Santa Monica, CA 90403
Tel. (213) 828-1945
Hrs: Mon. - Sat.   10:00 a.m. - 6:00 p.m.
Also,
156 South Beverly Drive
Beverly Hills, CA 90212
Tel. (213) 859-7328
Visa, MasterCard and AMEX are accepted.

Cotton Rainbow is aptly named, for a rainbow of colors is exactly what you see when you walk in. Kjersti Durow opened Cotton Rainbow because she preferred to wear natural fiber clothing and found it difficult to locate good quality cotton clothes.

Her store is full of 100% cotton clothes, all machine washable, hand dyed and original designs. The designs are hers. Kjersti has a unique flair for designing comfortable, fashionable, yet functional garments. Cotton Rainbow carries clothes for all ages, from newborns to adults. You will find the garments bright and cheerful with a distinctive look to them. Kjersti's designs are soft, comfortable and easy to wear. The store carries garments in all types of cotton from batiks to cotton knits. As part of the special services, Cotton Rainbow will ship any order, anywhere, via UPS.

Whether you are shopping for yourself or looking for a gift, you will find something just right for the occasion. You'll know you are at the Cotton Rainbow when you see the big neon rainbow on the outside of the building. Be prepared, it's bright and colorful on the inside. Just walking into the store with all its colors makes you feel happy.

MÜDRA
2818 Main Street
Santa Monica, CA 90405
Tel. (213) 396-1211
Hrs: Mon. - Sun. 10:00 a.m. - 6:00 p.m.
All major credit cards are accepted.

In 1971 Müdra owners Bob and Kay Miller developed a line of women's cotton clothing that is pre-shrunk, color fast and requires no ironing. The full line of women's fashions comes in thirty different styles and fourteen different colors.

The collection includes jackets, blouses, vests, obi-sashes and pleated and pull on pants. They will layer and mix to allow you many imaginative looks. The color schemes are deep, rich, no fade shades of peach, jade, chocolate, teal and many more. Müdra also has ten talented artists who hand paint unique paintings on selected garments.

Müdra is a Sanskrit word meaning a state of being. At Müdra the Millers have not only created a state of being, but a state of comfort and fashion that is sure to endure.

PILAR'S II
108 Santa Monica Boulevard
Santa Monica, CA 90401
Tel. (213) 394-2214
Hrs: Mon. - Sun. 10:00 a.m. - 8:00 p.m.
Visa, MasterCard, AMEX, Diners Club and Discover are accepted.

When it's "fun in the sun" weather and you are in Southern California, you naturally head for the beach. Sometimes it is difficult to find beachwear with pizazz that also compliments your figure. At last there is a store that carries a large, stylish selection of beachwear to fit everyone's needs and shape.

Pilar's II, located on Santa Monica Boulevard just off the famous Santa Monica Ocean Park, has a phenomenal collection of swimwear from around the world. The store carries sixty lines of brand name fashions. Whatever your size, whatever your style, you will be pleased with the choices available. From petite to size "D" cup, junior sizes, women's sizes and half sizes, there are individual suits and swimsuit sets in all the latest fabrics. You can mix and match both designs and sizes. Pilar's II has a swimwear selection capable of accommodating the diverse needs of most people.

Owned and run by Ursula Lopez, the shop is located in a brand new building that has a distinct Italian feel. The store itself is very contemporary. Ursula has a flair for fashion. You will enjoy her hand selected lines of beachwear. If you can't find it at Pilar's II, it probably isn't available. For outstanding prices and the best selection around, stop by Pilar's II and treat yourself to a great look.

SARA
1324 Montana Avenue
Santa Monica, CA 90403
Tel. (213) 394-2900
Hrs: Mon. - Fri.   10:00 a.m. - 6:00 p.m.
         Saturday   10:00 a.m. - 5:00 p.m.
Visa, MasterCard and AMEX are accepted.

The world of beauty and exotic luxury that all women deserve can be found in Sara, a unique apparel and gift store on Montana Avenue. Jewelry, accessories, imported gifts and clothing are available for gift giving or for your own enjoyment.

Sara features, among other things, a wonderful selection of jewelry. Treasures vary from American Indian to Asian antique along with selected contemporary artists such as Consuelo Campos who composes one of a kinds out of onyx, ivory, turquoise, lapis and other semi-precious stones in sterling silver settings. Tibetan Buddhas, Chinese porcelains, Indonesian artifacts and Philippine baskets are part of the gifts hand selected by Sara Schifrin, who opened the store in 1981. Her clothing line is a wonderful mixture of American selections and exotic finds, such as Balinese cultural clothing, which Sara brings back from her travels. Divine jewelry, antiques and art objects, purses, belts and hats create an unusually wide range of accessories from which to choose. The caring staff is available to help the customer with wardrobe consulting, alterations or gift wrapping.

When shopping for a special gift or unique clothing, stop at Sara. This delightful store offers something for everyone.

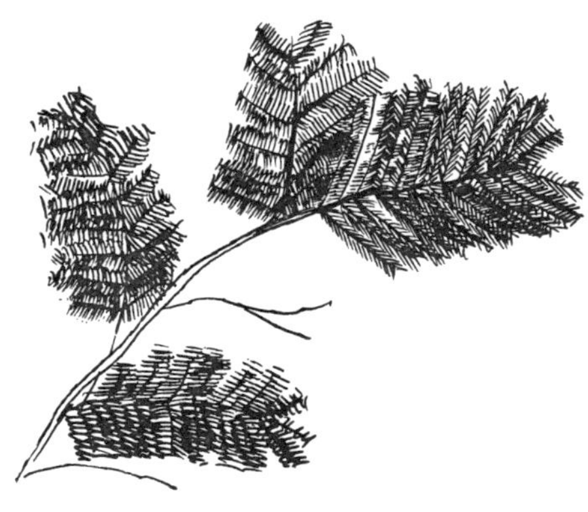

ART GALLERIES

AMERICAN GLASS ART GALLERY
3110 Main Street
The Courtyard
Santa Monica, CA 90405
Tel. (213) 399-1515
Hrs: Tue. - Fri.   10:00 a.m. - 6:00 p.m.
          Saturday   11:00 a.m. - 5:00 p.m.
          Sunday   12:00 noon - 5:00 p.m.
Visa, MasterCard and AMEX are accepted.

Thomas Crane opened the first and only art glass gallery featuring strictly American artists. Across the country, there are only a handful of other glass art galleries. American Glass Art Gallery is housed in a new three story brick building with exposed steel rafters and track lighting over the unique displays of glass sculptures.

Computerized, synthesized glass sounds provide the background music, "Sounds From Glass." Thomas realized his dream in the creation of this gallery in response to the fact that glass art is currently viewed as a craft, rather than the legitimate art form it is. He likens this to "a beautiful woman who has to prove herself before she is taken seriously." To this end, he has provided a neutral decorating scheme in shades of grey as a backdrop for the multi-colored glass art objects that are portrayed in different shapes and textures. Some of these glass works are opaque, others are transparent.

Vases, jewelry, sculptures, paperweights and ornaments are some of the various forms of glass art highlighted in the gallery. Thomas personally designed a patriotic red, white, and blue Christmas ornament. The ornament is the first American Collectors Ornament, a new one will be released annually and will be designed by a prominent American in the field. The first ornament completed was sent directly to the White House, an appropriate gesture in that the ornament has a strictly American heritage.

B-1 GALLERY
2730 Main Street
Santa Monica, CA 90405
Tel. (213) 392-9625
Hrs: Mon. - Sun.
          Call for hours.

Opening in 1984, B-1 Gallery has developed emerging and mid-career artists, while offering art collectors and the community provocative, often ground breaking exhibitions of up and coming sculptor and painter's work.

Located in the Ocean Park area of Santa Monica, this unique gallery enjoys diversifying its installations within its intimate space, at times spartan and reverent; alternatively, other curations are crowded and salon stacked. Each effectively showcases fine exhibitions. The gallery specializes in important contemporary art from Los Angeles and New York, and is widely recognized for its collection of L.A. Chicano art. Featured as well are master print works by Andy Warhol, David Hockney, Jim Dine, Keith Haring and Carlos Almaraz. You'll also see pieces by L.A. master printmakers Richard Duardo and Efram Wolff. B-1 Gallery represents Frank Romero, who is known for his paintings and wood constructions; Michele Roberts' paintings and monoprints; Robert Delgado's oils on canvas, board and paper, and Stephen Douglas' paintings and drawings. You'll find neon, glass and steel constructions by Craig French, mobiles by Brad Howe and ceramics by Leo Limon.

B-1 Gallery also sponsors educational exhibitions, panel discussions and lectures. Owner Robert Berman has functioned as auctioneer and organizer for charity auctions in conjunction with Los Angeles cultural institutions. Director Kristina Van Kirk has written articles on contemporary L.A. art for international art publications. B-1 Gallery also has a publishing division which has produced several critically acclaimed editions available through the gallery. The variety of work and activities make this gallery a "Best Choice" in Santa Monica.

THE CLAYHOUSE
2909 Santa Monica Boulevard
Santa Monica, CA 90404
Tel. (213) 828-7071
Hrs: Mon. - Thu.   10:00 a.m. - 7:00 p.m.
      Fri. - Sat.   10:00 a.m. - 5:00 p.m.
      Sunday   12:00 noon - 4:00 p.m.
Visa, MasterCard and AMEX are accepted.

Those of us with an appreciation for fine art know that today's ceramic art continues a tradition thousands of years old, beginning with simple clay bowls and other items, to elaborate designs of museum quality. One shop that combines practical ceramic art with a touch of the creative spirit is The Clayhouse in Santa Monica.

At The Clayhouse you'll find a large space divided into two sections. The front section features a showcase for displaying an extensive selection of handcrafted vases, casseroles, teapots and mugs. You'll also find Christmas ornaments, contemporary crafts, decorative wall masks, large decorator urns and blown glass. The gallery puts on regular shows of artists working in the medium. Owners Ken Catbagan and Natalie Neith have collected the works of more than 140 artists for display. In the back, students of the art will enjoy working in the gallery's studio. Students may take classes provided by The Clayhouse or they can rent wheels, kilns and other equipment on an hourly or monthly basis. Catbagan and Neith say they offer the classes to help keep the art growing. They want to work for a professional approach to ceramic art and The Clayhouse provides some of the best and most complete training facilities in Southern California.

Catbagan and Neith say pottery has become one of the last affordable art forms. Visit The Clayhouse, and you'll see not only the best in art, you'll become part of the tradition.

DOROTHY GOLDEEN GALLERY
1547 9th Street
Santa Monica, CA 90401
Tel. (213) 395-0222
Hrs: Tue. - Sat.   10:30 a.m. - 5:30 p.m.

The Dorothy Goldeen Gallery is an ideal place to experience and enjoy the most lauded contemporary artists working today.

Visitors will discover the latest trends in sculpture and painting at this important Santa Monica gallery.

From the outside the gallery appears modest. Once inside, the space is grand, lit by the natural light that streams through the windows. Each room flows into the next, allowing for optimum viewing of the art. The aesthetic of the gallery is warm, humanistic and poetic with both figurative and abstract works available. Color is emphasized. Viewers will find paintings, sculpture and works on paper in many different mediums. The gallery represents a distinguished group of artists who exhibited internationally and have been collected widely by major institutions and private collectors. Most of the artists are mature in their careers. The gallery also has several young, emerging artists. Represented artists are Robert Arneson, Fletcher Benton, Cheryl Bowers, Squeak Carnwath, Roy DeForest, Michael Dvortcsak, Charles Ginnever, Robert Hudson, Oliver Jackson, Terence La Noue, Dennis Leon, Donald Lipski, Nathan Oliveira, Nam June Paik, Ed Paschke, Janis Provisor, ZiZi Raymond, Italo Scanga, Larry Thomas, John White, Allee Willis and Robin Winters.

The Dorothy Goldeen Gallery should be a definite stop on your journey through contemporary art in the Los Angeles area. The gallery is very professional and will welcome your visit.

JAMES CORCORAN GALLERY
1327 5th Street
Santa Monica, CA 90401
Tel. (213) 451-4666
Hrs: Tue. - Sat.   11:00 a.m. - 5:00 p.m.
Credit cards are not accepted.

Art connoisseurs often want to support local artists as these men and women break new ground in their chosen medium, be it painting, sculpture, mixed media, or perhaps something entirely new. At the same time, these connoisseurs want access to classic works and traditions. The James Corcoran Gallery in Santa Monica offers both traditional greatness and support for area artists.

Two years ago, after fourteen years in West Hollywood, Corcoran moved his gallery to its present Santa Monica location. Art lovers walking into James Corcoran's gallery will be pleased not only with the collection of works by Picasso, O'Keeffe, De Kooning and others, but also by the gallery's new building, designed by architect Max Gordon. His high ceilings illuminate the works with warm natural light, and maximize the emotional impact of the artist's work. Some might say the gallery space is a work of art in itself. Corcoran is committed to maintaining high standards in carefully choosing works to show, and features a new exhibit beginning on the first Saturday of the month. Some of the premier Southern California artists Corcoran has shown include Peter Alexander, Eric Orr, Joe Goode and Steve Galloway.

Sometimes called "the dean of Santa Monica's growing art gallery community," Corcoran strives to find the best artists he can for the discriminating art lover. Connoisseurs can support local artists and maintain contemporary traditions, as well as enjoying the best works of art.

KARL BORNSTEIN GALLERY
1658 1/2 10th Street
Santa Monica, CA 90404
Tel. (213) 450-1129
Hrs: Tue. - Sat.   11:00 a.m. - 5:00 p.m.

The history of creative art has often been played out in the physical spaces left by industry. From the lofts of New York and Paris to the warehouses of Seattle and Dallas, working artists have found large, affordable studio and gallery space.

This is also true of the Karl Bornstein Gallery, which is located in a light industrial area of Santa Monica. The area is fast becoming a center for contemporary art and artists in Los Angeles. The gallery reflects this fact in its polished concrete floors and stark white walls. Skylights and track lighting are the only intrusions on the displayed works. As one of the fifteen members of the Santa Monica Art Dealers Association, the gallery has expanded its focus to include a sense of public education and the nurturing of artistic careers. In line with this attitude, the list of artists represented by the gallery is as diverse and eclectic as the contemporary art world itself. From the politically charged enamel paintings of Tom Jenkins to the minimalist sculpture of George Geyer, one will find the best works of Los Angeles artists on display. Other artists and their styles include the architectonic and factory paintings with text of Lawrence Gipe, environmental sculpture of James Turrell, the surrealist inspired paintings of Leonard Koscianski, urban sculpture of Michael Davis and landscape paintings of Larry Gray.

Yet the gallery also exhibits works of other American and European artists, believing that their perspective and philosophy add a welcome dimension to the gallery and the community as a whole. In the fall of 1988, there will be a showing of New German Abstract painters and sculptors featuring such renown artists as Gunter Forg, Eberhard Bosslet, Gerhard Merz, Helmut Dörner and Georg Herold. To put yourself in touch with the contemporary art scene in Los Angeles, this is a great starting point.

LAKOTA GALLERY
2814 Main Street
Santa Monica, CA 90405
Tel. (213) 392-3422
Hrs: Tue. - Sun. 11:00 a.m. - 6:00 p.m.
      Fri. - Sat.   11:00 a.m. - 10:00 p.m.
Visa, MasterCard and AMEX are accepted.

The picture windows, white beamed ceiling and plank floors are appropriate accents to the Southwestern Contemporary works featured at this new gallery. They combine with the bold colors and vibrant forms on display, in a testament to the strength and appeal of this native style.

Every piece seems to produce a feeling of environmental and cultural influence. Many of the works draw directly from the mythology of Indian lore. This influence is enhanced by the fact that five of the gallery's artists are Native Americans. The represented artists work in a variety of media. One can find both oil and acrylic pieces as well as ceramics, sculptures, stone carvings and steel kinetic works. Artists represented at Lakota Gallery include painters Len Agrella, Darren Vigil, Reina, Theodore Villa, Don Stambler and C.J. Wells, mythological ceramist and sculptor Susi Nagoda Bergquist, oil pastel artist Amy Cordova, Southwestern furniture craftsman Timothy Curtis, ceramic sculptors Glen La Fontaine, Gene and Rebecca Tobey, steel kinetic sculptor Frederick Prescott, wood carver David Fischel, stone carver John Redtail Freesoul and bronze sculptor Heyoechkah Merrifield.

With the mass production of many products that claim to be Southwestern in origin, it is left to galleries and museums to preserve the true influences and artworks of this inspiring heritage. The artists of Lakota Gallery represent the finest expression of that creativity.

MERGING ONE GALLERY
1547 6th Street
Santa Monica, CA 90401
Tel. (213) 395-0033
Hrs: Tue. - Sat.   10:00 a.m. - 5:00 p.m.

Contemporary art thrives in the energetic air of California and there's no better place to see the finest work to date than at Merging One Gallery in Santa Monica. The gallery's light and space make it the perfect exhibition area for The Golden State's most shining talent.

Dedicated exclusively to contemporary art, Merging One has gained a wide reputation for showcasing important emerging and established artists. Directness and experimentation separate California contemporary artists from others in the field, as can be seen in works by abstractionists Camille Cornelius and Joe Doyle, as well as in the glass and light sculptures of Ray Howlett. You'll also see work by new abstractionists such as Linda Kallan. Works by new classicist sculptors Jeff Laudenslager and Ed Saenz are well represented, as are pieces by whimsical sculptor Todd Rich and painter/printmaker Diana Wong. The gallery's architecturally designed white walls and natural wood plank flooring combine a contemporary sensibility of elegance and understatement with an appreciation of California's light and openness.

With two exhibition areas plus a beautifully landscaped sculpture garden, unique to the area, visits to Merging One Gallery are always invigorating.

RUTH BACHOFNER GALLERY
926 Colorado Avenue
Santa Monica, CA 90401
Tel. (213) 458-8007
Hrs: Mon. - Fri.   9:00 a.m. - 5:30 p.m.
          Saturday   10:00 a.m. - 5:30 p.m.
          Thursday evening until 8:00 p.m.
AMEX is accepted.

Ruth Bachofner Gallery specializes in contemporary painting, sculpture and work on paper by veteran, mid-career and emerging artists from California and New York. To give its "stable" of artists in-depth exposure, the gallery maintains an active schedule of one and two person exhibitions that change every four to five weeks. Gallery artists include Craig Antrim, Karl Benjamin, Stanley Boxer, Jean

Edelstein, Stephen Greene, Stephen Kafer, Brock Klein, George Page, Leo Robinson, Joan Thorne, Selina Trieff and Margi Weir. The gallery also handles a plethora of work on consignment by artists at various stages in their careers. So, if you wish to make an acquisition, be sure you ask to see what's in the "back room."

The staff at Ruth Bachofner Gallery takes seriously its role in helping to illuminate the world of contemporary art, and they are always delighted to assist the nascent collector or art devotee to find just the piece of art they may be searching for. To this end, considerable effort is spent keeping abreast of changes and developments on the local, national and international art scenes. The staff knows exactly what trends are worth following, which artists are worth watching and what prices are worth paying for particular works of art.

You will certainly enjoy viewing art in this gallery's spacious, light filled contemporary environment. Ruth Bachofner and staff are always available to help, and you will soon understand why this gallery enjoys a reputation of the highest regard.

SHOSHANA WAYNE GALLERY
1454 5th Street
Santa Monica, CA 90401-2470
Tel. (213) 451-3733
Hrs: Tue. - Sat.   10:00 a.m. - 5:00 p.m.
Visa and MasterCard are accepted.

Shoshana and Wayne Blank took over what once had been an old Beach Boys recording studio and hired architect Scott Johnson to design an interior masterpiece that would complement the masterpieces they planned to hang on the walls. The final effect is indeed a masterpiece.

The gallery has been broken into several subtle spaces, from large to intimate. Natural light comes from the generous skylights above, complemented by halo track lighting. Concrete unfinished floors and huge, rough hewn columns merge with natural wood rafters on the high ceilings, providing perfect punctuation to the smooth, white gallery walls.

The gallery features fine artists, many of whom have never been shown in the Los Angeles area. Included in a long litany of accomplished names are, Polish artist Bogdan Perzynski, sculptor Colin Gray from Santa Barbara, Houston based sculptor and minimalist Bob Bourdon, and Deborah Remington, who studied with

Clifford Still in San Francisco. If you're looking for a rich selection of emerging artists, visit the Shoshana Wayne Gallery.

TAOS INDIAN TRADING CO.
230 Santa Monica Boulevard
Santa Monica, CA 90401
Tel. (213) 395-3652
Hrs: Mon. - Sat.   11:00 a.m. - 7:00 p.m.
       Sundays   12:00 noon - 6:00 p.m.
       Also by special appointment.
Visa, MasterCard, AMEX and Diners Club are accepted.

David Lewis has assembled an impressive collection of Native American artifacts, headdresses, pottery, wood and stone carvings, woven baskets, silver jewelry and North and Southwestern Indian oils and lithographs in a compact, organized gallery.

An expert in Indian folklore, you will want to allow plenty of time to browse through his collection and listen to David recant various legends. David got his start by attending trade fairs across the Southwest. He won several awards during 1987 for best displays of pottery, wood carvings and jewelry. Each piece in his collection is uniquely individual, irreplaceable, and comes with its own certificate of authenticity.

David conducts private showings by appointment, and offers worldwide shipping and overnight mail service. In addition to the various artwork, postcards and books on Native American artifacts are also available for sale. You won't want to miss this gallery where over fifty-three tribes are represented.

GIFT SHOP

NATURE'S OWN
2736 Main Street
Santa Monica, CA 90405
Tel. (213) 392-3807
Hrs: Sun. - Tue.   11:00 a.m. - 6:00 p.m.
        Wed. - Thu. 11:00 a.m. - 9:00 p.m.
        Fri. - Sat.   11:00 a.m. - 11:00 p.m.
Visa, MasterCard and AMEX are accepted.
Also,

El Paseo, No. 27   Stearn's Wharf, 217
Santa Barbara, CA 93101 Santa Barbara, CA 93101
Tel. (805) 965-2869   Tel. (805) 965-4040

488 Alisal Road
Solvang, CA 93463
Tel. (805) 688-2456

Most people think of geology and paleontology as something very dry, like the dusty soil scientists have to dig through to get at their stones and fossils. Step into a unique shop in Santa Monica called Nature's Own, and you'll be infected with the same enthusiasm for ancient things that inspired owner Jeff Marshall.

Jeff's uncle introduced the sciences of geology and paleontology many years ago in Jeff's Wisconsin boyhood home. With this love, he displays buried treasures from the earth, including many museum quality fossil and mineral specimens. Amateur rockhounds will revel in Marshall's collection of nature's own works of art, including minerals such as amethyst, tourmaline, malachite, quartz crystals, and the rare lavender and purple colored sugilite from Nambia. Decorators looking for that unusual wall hanging might consider a fossilized fish millions of years old. Or, select a turtle shell from South Dakota that's thirty-six million years old. Perhaps a forty to sixty million year old rhinoceros tooth would make an unusual paperweight. Customers will find almost incomprehensible the fossils upwards of half a billion, yes, billion years old, and rocks two and a half billion years old.

Of course, visitors to Nature's Own are invited to take some of earth's history home with them, perhaps in the form of an educational kit for children. They'll gain the same enthusiasm Jeff has, and see the sciences of geology and paleontology as exciting and rewarding.

HEALTH AND FITNESS

STUDIO WEST DANCE AND EXERCISE
1211 Montana Avenue
Santa Monica, CA 90403
Tel. (213) 451-1814
Classes are offered seven days a week, call for a schedule.
Visa and MasterCard are accepted.

Whether you are thinking of entering an exercise or dance program for the first time, or are looking to continue at an advanced level, Studio West has a class that is right for you. They offer a full range of classes for all age groups and levels of experience, in a warm and inviting setting that makes exercising a pleasure.

Located in a beautiful and spacious building that was used as a dance studio in the 1920s, the now remodeled studio includes natural wood floors, plenty of lighting, high ceilings and air conditioning. This provides the perfect backdrop for the well structured, carefully choreographed classes available at Studio West. Choose from beginning, intermediate or advanced classes in such areas as high and low impact aerobics, stretch and tone, yoga and jazz. Children are welcome to join classes in ballet, jazz, tap or karate. Special classes are also held at the studio, including pregnancy classes and recovery classes for mother and child. To offer this wide range of classes, Studio West employs some of the most experienced exercise and dance instructors in the Los Angeles area. In addition to the training they receive from the studio, all instructors have extensive backgrounds in their individual areas of expertise.

A large variety of programs, thorough preparation, convenient, comfortable surroundings, and exceptionally well trained staff all combine to make your experience both enjoyable and beneficial. Do your body a favor and visit Studio West soon.

RESTAURANTS

BELLE VUE FRENCH RESTAURANT
101 Santa Monica Boulevard
Santa Monica, CA 90401
Tel. (213) 393-2843
Hrs: Lunch
        Mon. - Sat.   11:30 a.m. - 3:30 p.m.
        Dinner
        Sun. - Thu.   4:30 p.m. - 9:30 p.m.
        Fri. - Sun.   4:30 p.m. - 10:00 p.m.
        Brunch
        Sunday   12:30 p.m. - 3:30 p.m.
Visa, MasterCard, AMEX, Diners Club and Carte Blanche are accepted.

A beautiful view is just the beginning of what the fine French restaurant, located across the street from the ocean and the Santa Monica Palisades has been offering customers for more than fifty years. Just twenty-eight years ago the "new" management of Belle Vue, the Pilloni family, added their touch, which included executive chef Robert Laly. Every day of the week, customers who want the very best enjoy French cuisine provençal with an emphasis on fresh fish and seafood as well as continental dishes and daily specials, all at reasonable prices.

If you're looking for something to make Sunday special, Belle Vue's sumptuous champagne brunch should be on your agenda. You'll have a choice of Lobster Thermidor or Parisienne, omelettes, crepes, Calamari and more. You'll enjoy the warm ambiance of the newly remodeled building with its abundance of rich warm wood, stained glass accents and blue and white lace linens. The old world setting is perfect any time of the day. For lunch or dinner you'll be treated to a choice of fourteen appetizers including the house specialty, Pâté Maison. A wide range of salads include vegetable, meat and seafood delights. All complete dinners are served with salad and a selected choice of appetizers. Gifts from the sea include swordfish, frogs legs and poached salmon. For meat eaters, there are Tournedoes of Beef Tenderloin, Sweetbreads in Patty Shell, Sautéed Rabbit and Grenadine of Beef Chasseur. A Bouillabaisse, carefully watched over by Chef Robert, is served on Friday only; it includes a salad and is served in a tureen at your table. Last but not least are desserts made fresh daily by Chef Laly, including English Trifle, tarts, chocolate mousse, Meringue Bombe and Croque En Bouche plus more on the pastry cart. An exemplary selection of domestic and imported wines, coffee drinks and a full bar are at your disposal.

For an afternoon or evening filled with romance, fine food, drink, and the fresh breeze off the ocean, come to the Belle Vue French Restaurant. Satisfied customers have been doing so for half a century.

CHINOIS ON MAIN
2709 Main Street
Santa Monica, CA 90405
Tel. (213) 392-9025
Hrs: Lunch   Wed. - Fri.   11:30 a.m. - 2:00 p.m.
         Dinner   Mon. - Sun.   6:00 p.m. - 10:30 p.m.
Visa, MasterCard, AMEX and Diners Club are accepted.

Austrian born Wolfgang Puck honed his culinary skills at Hotel de Paris in Monaco and Maxim's in Paris. After achieving fame as top Chef at Ma Maison in L.A., he established Spago on Sunset Boulevard. Puck is once again dazzling the connoisseurs of gourmet cuisine with *gastronomie extrordinaire* at the most recent addition to his culinary empire, Chinois on Main.

The restaurant is a study in visual interest and features a twelve foot expanse of windows, framing a garden of bromeliad, dendorobrium and oncidium orchids. Designed by Wolfgang's wife, Barbara Lazaroff, Chinois on Main is a unique harmony of Japanese accents and contemporary Art Nouveau architecture.

For those who desire the exceptional, the fare at Chinois on Main is a masterful blend of East and West. Appetizers might include a scintillating selection of warm, sweet, curried oysters with cucumber sauce and salmon pearls; or sauteed goose liver with plum wine sauce complemented by fresh pineapples. Dare to inspire your palate with an entree such as whole sizzling catfish stuffed with ginger; or barbecued salmon with marinated black and gold noodles and watercress sauce. Not to be outdone, desserts such as Mandarin chocolate cake with raspberry citrus sauce defy definition.

Join the luminaries who flock to world renowned Wolfgang Puck's latest triumph in order to savor his brilliantly original creations, and indulge in some of the finest cuisine to be found anywhere at Chinois on Main.

THE CHRONICLE, SANTA MONICA, 2640 Main Street, Santa Monica, CA. Tel. (213) 392-4956. The Chronicle is located in a beautiful old Victorian house in the heart of Santa Monica. This restaurant offers outstanding continental cuisine and excellent service.

CUTTERS RESTAURANT
2425 Colorado Avenue
Santa Monica, CA 90405
Tel. (213) 453-3588
Hrs: Lunch
      Mon. - Sat.   11:30 a.m. - 3:00 p.m.
      Dinner
      Mon. - Thu. 5:00 p.m. - 11:00 p.m.
      Fri. - Sat.   5:00 p.m. - 12:00 midnight
Visa, MasterCard and AMEX are accepted.

One of the hottest Friday night meeting places on Los Angeles' West Side is Cutters Restaurant. On any given Friday, you'll see "beautiful people" celebrating the end of the work week with a meal and a cocktail at this mingling spot.

A large bar with the largest selection of liquor in Los Angeles attracts many of this restaurant's regulars. Some come specifically for the bar's specialty: single malt Scotch. There's plenty of excitement in the air as people crowd into the huge lounge area and two dining rooms, all decorated to reflect California's casual lifestyle. The Art Deco touches add a unique aura to Cutters Restaurant. The restaurant offers some of the best pastas and sauces in L.A. Cutters' fresh pasta is fettuccine, made daily from whole eggs, semolina and durum flour. Pasta selections include Spinach Tortelloni with Tomato-Basil Cream Sauce and Fresh Parmesan. The restaurant is also proud of its seafood selections. One of the most popular choices are Steamed Quilcene Bay Petite Manila Clams with wine butter sauce. The clams are flown in twice weekly from the Quilcene Bay on Hood Canal in Washington State. Another seafood specialty is Columbia River Salmon, mesquite grilled with toasted hazelnut butter, fresh tarragon butter or fresh basil-garlic butter.

Cutters' chocolate souffle is a truly sinful dessert, and one of the many reasons this restaurant is a "Best Choice" in Santa Monica.

IVY AT THE SHORE
1541 Ocean Avenue
Santa Monica, CA 90048
Tel. (213) 393-3113
Hrs: Lunch   Mon. - Fri.   11:30 a.m. - 3:15 p.m.
     Dinner   Sun. - Thu.   5:30 p.m. - 11:00 p.m.
                  Fri. - Sat.   5:30 p.m. - 11:30 p.m.
     Late Breakfast Saturday   11:00 a.m. - 3:15 p.m.
     Late Breakfast Sunday   10:00 a.m. - 3:15 p.m.
     Bar opens   Mon. - Sun.   5:00 p.m.
Visa, MasterCard, AMEX and Diners Club are accepted.

For outstanding drinks and fabulous freshly grilled seaside fare, escape to Ivy at the Shore. Immerse yourself in a true 1930s tropical paradise. Old ceiling fans circle overhead; swaying Bermuda palms, hibiscus and gardenias thrive in the open air patio; and you are waited on by a friendly "beachy" staff while relaxing in vintage rattan chairs. Welcome to Ivy at the Shore.

A collection of big band records play in the background, courtesy of co-owner, Lynn von Kersting, whose father played with Benny Goodman. She and her partner, Chef Richard Irving, have assembled food and drink that emphasizes freshness and quality. Appetizers include Caesar Salad, garden grown Tomato, Basil and Mozzarella Pizza and Fresh Louisiana Crabcakes. Entrees range from familiar favorites such as Mesquite Grilled Fresh Tuna and New York Steak with homemade steak sauce to fresh Pacific Coast Lobster Tacos with homemade tortillas, served with fresh Lopez Ranch Corn, barbecued and cut off the cob. Not to be missed as a side order are the delicious Maui Onion Rings.

Drinks reminiscent of Havana in the 20s are shaken to order at the bar and incorporate only fresh ingredients. No bar mixes or sugar is used. Try a romance cocktail such as Rum Boogie, Fresh Santa Maria Raspberry Daiquiri or a delicious garden grown Mexican Lime Margarita, and other refreshing drinks prepared with or without alcohol.

On Ocean Avenue in Santa Monica, with a view of the Pacific, Ivy at the Shore is right across the street from the famous Pacific Palisades Park. For an outstanding lunch, dinner or late weekend breakfast (try the homemade fresh blueberry pancakes) escape to Ivy at the Shore.

THE MARQUIS WEST
3110 Santa Monica Boulevard
Santa Monica, CA 90404
Tel. (213) 828-4567
Hrs: Mon. - Fri.   11:30 a.m. - 2:30 p.m.
       Mon. - Sat.   5:30 p.m. - 10:30 p.m.
       Sunday   4:30 p.m. - 9:30 p.m.
Visa, MasterCard, AMEX, Diners Club and Carte Blanche are accepted.

Set in a baronial atmosphere right from the Middle Ages, The Marquis West offers the best in Northern Italian cuisine and seafood. The late Louella Parsons described Chef Pietro's Fettuccine Alfredo as "better than you'll find in Rome," and that's how it's been since the fine dining establishment first opened its doors in 1977.

In addition to its fine fare, The Marquis West is also famous for its fine service. The waiters and captains have been recruited from among the finest restaurants in Europe, the United States and South America. Their dedication matches that of the chefs and the result is a potpourri of pasta dishes, a Linguine Mediterranea for which the shrimp sacrificed themselves willingly, and a ravishing Ravioli Bolognese. Seafood choices include Lobster Fra Diavolo, sauteed with olive oil, shallots and white wine and served in the shell; Mussels Marinara; Sea Bass; Bouillabaisse Riviera, Gamberoni Marquis and Fillet of Red Snapper Supreme.

It's very popular, The Marquis West, so you'll want to make reservations. Valet parking is also provided. So for the finest in Northern Italian dining, it's The Marquis West, a tradition since 1977.

MERLIN MC FLY'S
2702 Main Street
Santa Monica, CA 90405
Tel. (213) 392-8468
Hrs: Sun. - Thu.   11:30 a.m. - 12:00 midnight
       Fri. - Sat.   11:30 a.m. - 1:00 a.m.
       Bar open till 2:00 a.m.
Visa, MasterCard, AMEX and Diners Club are accepted.

Merlin, the great magician of Arthurian legend, would stand in awe of this spectacular restaurant. If you are in Santa Monica and would like to put a little magic in your life, don't hesitate to stop at Merlin McFly's.

As you approach the building, you will get an idea of the wonders inside by studying the great windows that adorn its facade. There are ten of them, each depicting a famous magician. Each stained glass scene is a masterwork that took over four hundred hours to complete. As you enter, through stained glass doors sporting top hatted skeletons, be sure to take a moment to survey the interior design. The large curved bar is made of hand carved mahogany and Mexican onyx. The bar stools and table stands are of cast aluminum. Original posters of the 30's and 40's decorate the walls. The whole restaurant is a tribute to the creative mind of designer Mike Leeds. Once you settle in, you have a choice of several enticing menu items. Meals can begin with soups, salads or appetizers, including fresh Soup of the Day, Chinese Chicken Salad, Tostada Grande, an Artichoke with Garlic Mayonnaise or Lemon Butter, or Chicken Strips. Merlin McFly's is famous for its burger selection, but sandwiches or pizza are also available. Choose from a varied selection of entrees, including Fettuccine with Chicken and Broccoli, served in a Parmesan Cream Sauce and garnished with Cashews, homemade Ravioli or Cannelloni, Grilled Lemon Herb Chicken, Soft Tacos Al Carbon and a fresh fish special daily.

To complement your magical meal, several house magicians perform table side illusions nightly. It would be giving away much of the fun to describe the various happenings that regularly occur here. But be assured that magical things await you at Merlin McFly's.

MICHAEL'S RESTAURANT
1147 3rd Street
Santa Monica, CA 90403
Tel. (213) 451-0843
Hrs: Lunch   Mon. - Fri.   12:00 noon - 2:00 p.m.
       Dinner   Mon. - Fri.   6:30 p.m. - 10:00 p.m.
       Brunch   Sat. - Sun.   10:30 a.m. - 2:00 p.m.
Visa, MasterCard, AMEX and Diners Club are accepted.

Pioneers are sometimes hard to find in this era of copy cat fast foods and even fine restaurants, but in Santa Monica those with a more discriminating palate can dine at a restaurant that led the way in the trend of sophisticated American dining with strong roots in French culture.

Michael's Restaurant features the finest haute cuisine in perhaps all of Southern California. Run by business and creative entrepreneur Michael McCarty, who started the business in 1979 at the ripe old age of twenty-five, Michael's features contemporary elegance with service unsurpassed. More than 300 articles have been written about this gourmet's delight and nine years later Michael's is still making news. Sit in the lush garden patio and terraced courtyard after examining the fine art that decorates the restaurant's interior. Sample the menu, sometimes called "California French," which features the freshest possible provisions from all over the world. For an appetizer, try the Gravlax Cafe des Artistes, marinated Norwegian salmon with a sauce of dill, mustard and mayonnaise, and served with toasted brioche slices. For your entree, order the grilled marinated quail, squab or duck breast with a variety of stock reduction and wine sauces.

Not only the gourmet, but the up and coming entrepreneur will appreciate how McCarty has created and nurtured this fine restaurant. All his top people rose from the ranks, and his restaurant ranks among the best California can serve.

THE OAR HOUSE/BUFFALO CHIPS
2941 Main Street
Santa Monica, CA 90405
Tel. (213) 396-4725
Hrs: Mon. - Sun. 11:30 a.m. - 2:00 a.m.
Visa and MasterCard are accepted.

Do you like a bar or restaurant where you and your friends can hang out, have a drink, some good conversation, munchies and maybe dance? Then you'll love The Oar House/Buffalo Chips. It was started back in the sixties by a group of airline pilots who wanted a place to hang out on their evenings off in Los Angeles.

The Oar House/Buffalo Chips offers good tunes, food and drink in a casual laid back atmosphere. Located in a gray building embellished with big white oars, the inside of the Oar House will surprise you. It's packed with hundreds of antiques and artifacts hanging from walls and suspended from the ceiling. The floor is covered with sawdust. At Buffalo Chips there are lots of video games and good, inexpensive, self service food. The Oar House is where the real action is. Dancing and general carousing can be found here from about 7:30 p.m. on. Only brand name liquors are served. The menu includes burgers and fries, pizzas, sandwiches, salads and munchables.

Monday night is golden oldies night with classic fifties and sixties rock 'n' roll music. Tuesday, Thursday and Sunday nights are burger madness nights, with burgers and fries at nearly half price. Wednesday is south of the border night and Thursday is no pants night with quality spirits served at reduced prices for everyone wearing shorts. And don't forget happy hour, every day from 7:30 p.m. to 9:00 p.m. For good times, good food and good drinks, visit The Oar House/Buffalo Chips.

RENEE'S COURTYARD CAFE
522 Wilshire Boulevard
Santa Monica, CA 90401
Tel. (213) 451-9341
Hrs: Lunch   Mon. - Sat.   11:00 a.m. - 3:00 p.m.
      Dinner   Mon. - Sat.   6:00 p.m. - 10:00 p.m.
                  Sundays   5:30 p.m. - 9:30 p.m.
      Brunch   Sundays   10:30 a.m. - 3:00 p.m.
Visa, MasterCard, AMEX and Diners Club are accepted.

One of the oldest houses in Santa Monica, an ivy covered brick building circa 1900, has been converted to a wonderful restaurant reminiscent of a European chalet, Renee's Courtyard Cafe. Visible from the street only by a large green awning with the name emblazoned on it, patrons wind their way down from the sidewalk through a flower filled courtyard patio brimming with inviting tables and chairs tucked among potted trees, shrubs and a bubbling fountain.

An intimate setting ideal for private parties, Renee's Courtyard Cafe displays a treasured antique doll collection, books, and pictures in addition to the unique architectural features such as the handpainted, stenciled woodwork and leaded glass windows. The privacy afforded and the superlative cuisine by Belgium-trained chef, Steve King, makes Renee's Courtyard Cafe a popular retreat for many celebrities such as Barbara Streisand, Richard Dreyfus, Gene Wilder, John Cuzak, Robin Williams, Gilda Radner, Harvey Korman, Pamela Sue Martin and many others. Recommended entrees include Dijon Chicken, Veal Marsala, the nightly specials and any of their highly acclaimed seafood dishes. An irresistible dessert is the Blackout Cake, a chocolate masterpiece served with hot fudge and whipped cream.

Perhaps the most intriguing delicacy, not included on the menu, is Renee's handwriting analyses. She continues to analyze customer's handwriting upon request "to their amusement and amazement!" Even without the analysis, Renee makes you feel right at home with her friendly personality. Reservations are encouraged to ensure your dining comfort.

TAKA SUSHI RESTAURANT
1345 2nd Street
Santa Monica, CA 90401
Tel. (213) 394-6540
Hrs: Summer hours
         Lunch
         Mon. - Fri.   11:45 a.m. - 2:30 p.m.
         Dinner
         Mon. - Thu.   5:30 p.m. - 11:00 p.m.
         Fri. - Sat.   5:30 p.m. - 12:00 midnight
         Sunday   4:30 p.m. - 10:00 p.m.
Visa, MasterCard, AMEX, Diners Club and Carte Blanche are accepted.

If you like Japanese food, but feel you can't speak above a whisper in a typical, staid sushi restaurant, try eating at the Taka Sushi Restaurant for a modern approach to traditional Japanese food. At Taka Sushi you can cut loose and enjoy yourself. They play new wave and reggae music and put on a laser light show in the evenings.

It's twenty first century all the way at Taka Sushi with its high tech, stylized look. Lots of glass, a black tiled floor, overhead spotlights and original paintings by Muramara Kydo whet your appetite for traditional sushi and Japanese dishes, as well as more modern recipes such as sushi pizza. If you still have room left, be sure and try some of their deep fried ice cream.

The Taka Sushi Restaurant has successfully fused the modern high tech American environment with traditional Japanese cuisine to create a fun and relaxed atmosphere Americans relate to easily. For what may be an adventure of a lifetime, visit the Taka Sushi Restaurant.

THIRD STREET PUB AND GRILL
1240 Santa Monica Mall
Santa Monica, CA 90401
Tel. (213) 395-7012
Hrs: Mon. - Sat.   11:30 a.m. - 2:00 a.m.
          Sunday   11:30 a.m. - 12:00 midnight
AMEX is accepted.

If you enjoy the cozy atmosphere of a neighborhood pub, and talking with friends over a good brew, Third Street Pub and Grill offers such a setting in the middle of busy Los Angeles. Located just a couple of blocks from the beach in the recently revitalized Santa Monica Mall, this bar and grill is a short walk from the big hotels in the area as well.

Built from the ground up with oak and brass, the place has a warm homey feel to it. In the true pub spirit, they carry over sixty varieties of imported beer, ten on draft and have plans for more. The pub also offers a choice of wine by the glass. Third Street makes great burgers with all the trimmings. They also have soup and fresh fish daily. If you're still hungry there is Chocolate Mousse Cake for dessert.

Third Street Pub's slogan is "The Sportsman's Bar" and it's decorated with sports trophies, plaques and professional football team pennants. It is a comfortable, unpretentious place with an easy neighborhood bar feel to it. Treat yourself to a pleasant afternoon or evening sipping a new imported beer and enjoying some conversation and perhaps a little people watching too.

VALENTINO
3115 Pico Boulevard
Santa Monica, CA 90405
Tel.   (213) 829-4313
          (213) 829-4314
Hrs: Lunch   Friday   12:00 noon - 3:00 p.m.
          Dinner   Mon. - Sat.   5:30 p.m. - 12:00 midnight
Visa, MasterCard, AMEX and Diners Club are accepted.

Visitors to Santa Monica hoping to try one of the top restaurants in Southern California, if not the whole United States, won't want to miss Valentino. Diners will enjoy the recent new look of the restaurant, displaying an elegant atmosphere equal to the top notch cuisine.

Gourmets will be amazed by the incredible variety available at Valentino. It's impossible to list all the daily specials, and owner Piero Selvaggio says he sometimes wishes he didn't have a menu at all. That way, customers could trust him to decide for them. Perhaps you could try that, and let Piero choose from such exotic dishes as Fried Squid with Ricotta Cheese Fritters, Grilled Swordfish with Maui Onions, or Grilled Pigeon with Polenta and Porcini Mushrooms. Or he might choose for you a roast leg of veal or lamb with a reduction sauce of red wine and stock. Whether or not you trust Piero to select your meal, you can trust he'll give the freshest ingredients available, including some flown in daily from Italy. Some of those items include white and black truffles when they're in season, Italian mushrooms, cheeses, olives and virgin olive oils. Don't forget Italy's famous wines. Valentino has more than 1,300 wines, Italian and otherwise, to choose from.

The award winning Valentino is often considered at the forefront of Italian cookery in the United States. Try Valentino and meet Piero, and you won't misplace your trust.

WARSZAWA POLISH CUISINE RESTAURANT
1414 Lincoln Boulevard
Santa Monica, CA 90401
Tel. (213) 393-8831
Hrs: Mon. - Sun.   5:30 p.m. - 10:30 p.m.
Reservations are recommended.
All major credit cards are accepted.

Warszawa was first established in Berkeley by Polish born Elina Lejman. Warszawa met with instant success and when Elina's husband was transferred to Santa Monica, Elina brought her restaurant with her. Warszawa is intimate and homey, separated into several small dining rooms furnished with vibrant handwoven rugs and brilliantly colored Polish theater posters.

The menu is as rich in texture, color and intriguing content as the decor. Elina has arranged a large menu of Polish specialties, lightening the sturdy meat and dumplings cuisine, which evolved in a country of harsh winters, to make it compatible with Southern California's climate. Are you ready for an appetizer of hot dried plums wrapped in bacon and garnished with walnuts; followed by a cold borscht, called Chlodnik, beautifully pink, made with cucumbers, yogurt, scallions, fresh dill and lemon? The pierogis are outstanding. They are delicate pasta shells stuffed with meat, cheese, mushrooms or potatoes and lightly fried in butter or steamed, served with sour cream and fresh vegetables. A dessert of poached pear in vanilla cream and cranberry kisiel will pleasantly finish your meal.

As you relax with your companions after a Warszawa meal listening to classical music, (on Sunday to live music, a pianist and violinist) you may want to raise your glass in tribute to the Polish people and, in particular, to their chefs.

WAVE RESTAURANT AND BAR
2820 Main Street
Santa Monica, CA 90405
Tel. (213) 399-9114
Hrs.   Lunch   Tue. - Sat.   11:30 a.m. - 2:30 p.m.
       Dinner   Sun. - Thu.   6:00 p.m. - 12:00 midnight
                   Fri. - Sat.   6:00 p.m. - 1:00 a.m.
       Brunch   Sunday   11:30 a.m. - 2:30 p.m.
Visa, MasterCard, AMEX and Diners Club are accepted.

If you are looking for flavorful food in a friendly atmosphere, Wave Restaurant and Bar is the place for you. With two covered patios, a very popular bar, contemporary decor and exciting food, this restaurant is California style personified.

Where else would you find a palm tree as the center accent of the dining room? The tree, an abundance of fresh flowers and art works, are all expressions of an up-beat and high energy style that is both clever and casual. The food is hearty, varied, and different without being trendy. The menu offers hot and cold appetizers, such as Crab Cakes, traditional Carpaccio with a two day marinade, and Select Domestic Caviars. The salad favorite features Smoked Oriental Duck with Shitaki mushrooms. Pasta dishes include Seafood Ravioli and Fettuccine with Black Forest Ham. The pizzas available include one known as the Daily Tidal Wave and another with Smoked Chicken. Wave also offers a large selection of fish entrees, such as Lobster with a trio of Caviar Potatoes, Tiger Shrimp in Wave Pesto and Mesquite Grilled Ahi Teriyaki. Oakwood roasted meat entrees include Breast of Duck with an Apricot Riesling sauce and Rack of Lamb. A well structured wine list complements the menu. Top off your meal with a chocolate or raspberry mousse, a fresh fruit tart, cold Amaretto souffle´ or a chocolate truffle.

Seldom does a restaurant offer such a well crafted mixture of style, ambiance and good food. Wave Restaurant and Bar offers a California contemporary dining experience you are sure to enjoy.

WILDWINGS CHICKEN CAFE
1415 Santa Monica Open Air Mall
Santa Monica, CA 90401
Tel. (213) 393-0986
Hrs: Mon. - Fri.   8:00 a.m. - 8:00 p.m.
       Sat. - Sun.   11:00 a.m. - 6:00 p.m.
All major credit cards are accepted.

Would you like to find a place where you can get delicious, innovative meals at reasonable prices served in a fresh clean atmosphere with enough light so you can see what you're eating? For a totally new and unique concept in dining try the Wildwings Chicken Cafe.

Wildwings is located in the revitalized Third Street Mall in Santa Monica. A fresh concept, brought to fruition by owner Mitch Kobara, Wildwings dishes up gourmet food, at a fast food pace, in his indoor/outdoor restaurant. He serves delicious chicken cuisine in many flavor variations. There are chicken wing drummettes served sesame style, or in a Milano Sauce of garlic, wine and imported cheese, or Red Hots in a fiery barbecue base with freshly minced parsley and many more. Mitch creates "special" dishes each week so there is always something new to try. Wildwings also offers a choice of simple desserts and espresso and cappuccino to accompany dessert or for a perfect coffee break.

For a new experience in gourmet food, Wildwings Chicken Cafe is the place to go. You'll enjoy the creative food, the reasonable prices and the delightful atmosphere.

YE OLDE KING'S HEAD
116 Santa Monica Boulevard
Santa Monica, CA 90401
Tel. (213) 451-1402
Hrs: Restaurant   Mon. - Sat.   11:00 a.m. - 11:30 p.m.
                    Sundays   12:00 noon - 1:30 a.m.
       Pub   Mon. - Sat.   11:00 a.m. - 1:30 a.m.
                    Sundays   12:00 noon - 1:30 a.m.

Known as California's meeting place for the British, Ye Olde King's Head has a genuine air of a British pub. Built and run by Birmingham born Phil Elwell and wife Ruth, the pub and restaurant has been a popular spot for fifteen years.

Westside

Having served as a location for many T.V. and film productions, Ye Olde King's Head is, nevertheless, best known as an enjoyable place to bend an elbow with a pint of many brews from all over the commonwealth.

Step into the restaurant and enjoy a selection of award winning British foods. The fish and chips are world renowned. The emphasis is on quality and value. Good food, good drinks, good conversation will be found at Ye Olde King's Head. No one ever visits this place just once.

TOY STORE

IMAGINE
1001 Montana Avenue
Santa Monica, CA 90403
Tel. (213) 395-9553
Hrs: Mon. - Sat.   10:00 a.m. - 6:00 p.m.
Visa and MasterCard are accepted.

Andrea Wolman, a former schoolteacher, brought her love of children into play when she opened Imagine, a children's toy and gift shop. "Imagine" this: Children are actually encouraged to play with the merchandise, and Andrea willingly opens any package for demonstration purposes!

Andrea has traveled extensively during the four years since she opened Imagine in her search for creative, unique and artistic items for children ranging in age from infant through preteen. Her comprehensive inventory includes such items as art, science and outdoor supplies, magician's kits, infant's building blocks, inflatable toys, dinosaurs, play dough, stencils, puzzles, clothing, blankets and bedside lamps, crib mobiles, baby carriers, lunch boxes and "spill proof" cups, and toys from over twenty different countries. Her toy selection features durable, engaging toys bearing brand names such as Lego, Brio, Fischer-Price, Battat infant toys from Canada, and French Corrolle dolls.

Andrea offers many services including personalizing book plates, birth announcements, calling cards and gifts. Due to her originality, her dedication to providing a unique children's store and her warm personality, she is enjoying well deserved popularity through an increasing customer clientele.

TOPANGA

The wooded countryside of Topanga Canyon rests below the divide between the coastal watershed and the San Fernando Valley. Mineral springs were once a main attraction to the area, while Topanga Beach served as a shore colony where some of the older homes were built by movie people, many of whom later moved on to Malibu.

RESTAURANT

INN OF THE SEVENTH RAY
128 Old Topanga Canyon Road
Topanga, CA 90290
Tel. (213) 455-1311
Hrs: Lunch   Mon. - Fri.   11:30 a.m. - 2:30 p.m.
        Dinner   Mon. - Sun. 6:00 p.m. - 10:00 p.m.
        Brunch   Saturday   10:30 a.m. - 3:00 p.m.
                   Sunday   9:30 a.m. - 3:00 p.m.
Reservations are required for dinner.
Visa, MasterCard, AMEX, Diners Club and Discover are accepted.

Just a few minutes off the busy Ventura freeway, diners will find one of the most calming eating experiences in Southern California. More a retreat than a restaurant, Topanga's Inn of the Seventh Ray treats you to food and atmosphere guaranteed to elevate ones awareness of higher things.

The restaurant's location adds to the spiritual experience. It's a renovated church, once thought to be the retreat of Aimee Semple McPherson. Twelve years ago, a husband and wife team took the old church and planned an environment within a natural setting that's conducive to relaxation and a creative dining experience. Every aspect of the Inn of the Seventh Ray accomplishes this, from the babbling brook that flows past the tables, to the menu that features only the most natural of ingredients. All food is prepared from scratch with items totally free of preservatives and other chemicals. Specialties include vegetarian dishes and free range chicken. Nouvelle style sauces complement many menu selections. The menu includes soups made from cream and nut milk bases and herbs grown on the property. Many diners choose the Seventh Ray Salad, a blend of fresh greens tossed tenderly with a mystical dressing from the Master Alchemist's files.

Los Angeles diners have named the Inn of Seventh Ray one of the area's most romantic restaurants. You'll most likely agree, as you bask with your dinner partner in the high violet vibrations among the winter sounds of the courtyard fountain.

VENICE

For the truly off beat, there is Venice, a beach community with a long history of bizarre and outrageous folks bent on experimenting with lifestyle. In Venice you'll find the eclectic collection of punkers and a motley assembly of non-conformists.

Venice began to take on its own character in 1904 when a cigarette magnate, Abbot Kinney, purchased 160 acres of coastal marsh land with the idea of developing a community modeled after Venice, Italy, complete with canals and Italian gondoliers. The novelty drew visitors to the community's beach front rococo promenade where they could sit in sidewalk cafes or attend lectures and concerts.

When cultural events waned in the 1920s, the main attraction became roller coasters, casinos and bathhouses, and Venice fell into a state of disrepair. The sewage system fouled the canals, so most were filled in. As rents became more affordable, Venice drew a contingent of poets, writers and artists. In the late 1950s Venice was Southern California's beatnik capital; in the 1960s it was a haven for hippies.

At present, Venice is becoming more up-scale and the gentrification of its neighborhoods is putting increased pressure on the lifestyle of long time resident writers and artists.

ATTRACTIONS

• Popular for swimming, surfing, diving and kite flying, the three mile long **Venice Beach** was one of the first Southern California beaches to employ full time professional lifeguard protection. An asphalt walkway that runs parallel to the beach is a popular people watching spot. A medley of performers, artists and street merchants make their way down the promenade, as do folks on roller skates, skateboards and bicycles. Nearby, visitors can rent skates and bicycles.

• **Venice Fishing Pier**, at the foot of Washington Street, offers food concessions and an area for strolling, roller skating and fishing. A bait and tackle shop is located at the end of the pier.

ART GALLERY

L.A. LOUVER GALLERY
55 North Venice Boulevard
Venice, CA 90291
Tel. (213) 822-4955
Hrs: Gallery
      Tue. - Sat.   11:00 a.m. - 5:00 p.m.
      Office
      Mon. - Fri.   9:00 a.m. - 6:00 p.m.
Also,
77 Market Street
Venice, CA 90291
Tel. (213) 822-4955

The small coastal community of Venice boasts a long history as one of the most vital artistic centers in California. The L.A. Louver Gallery was opened thirteen years ago, committed to introducing an international art perspective.

The gallery features works of emerging American artists from such diverse areas as Washington and rural Texas, as well as from Los Angeles, New York and Chicago. In addition, they show art work from contemporaries in London, Wales, Paris, Rome, Berlin and Melbourne. This blending of international talent and stylistic statement creates an exciting forum for contemporary art. L.A. Louver Gallery's show rooms offer an inspiring and relaxed environment in which to view the art pieces. The gallery's impressive list of artists includes names such as Terry Allen, Comenico Bianchi, David Hockney, Bernd Koberling, Ed Moses, David Nash and William T. Wiley. Amenities offered by the gallery include a photography and catalogue reference library and frequent production of catalogues about their artists in conjunction with exhibits. L.A. Louver Gallery also participates with privately funded arts foundations, universities and museums on commissions and other projects.

The artistic fusion that has centered in Venice and has been so thoughtfully and thoroughly nurtured by the L.A. Louver Gallery offers a refreshing view of contemporary art. Take the time for a visit to this "Best Choice" gallery. Call ahead for information on current exhibits.

BED & BREAKFAST INN

THE VENICE BEACH HOUSE, #15 30th Avenue, Venice, CA. Tel. (213) 823-1966. Located a half block from Venice Beach and the boardwalk, this 1911 landmark house has ten elegant bedrooms and suites. Serving a full Continental breakfast this bed & breakfast offers style and location.

RESTAURANTS

72 MARKET STREET OYSTER BAR AND GRILL
72 Market Street
Venice, CA 90291
Tel. (213) 392-8720
Hrs: Lunch
          Mon. - Fri.   11:30 a.m. - 2:30 p.m.
          Brunch
          Sunday   10:30 a.m. - 2:30 p.m.
          Dinner
          Sun. - Thu.   6:00 p.m. - 10:30 p.m.
          Fri.-Sat.   6:00 p.m. - 11:30 p.m.
Visa, MasterCard and AMEX are accepted.

In 1984, film producer Tony Bill, restauranteur Julie Stone, actor Dudley Moore, architect Tony Heinsbergen and chef Leonard Schwartz opened this well known restaurant. Often graced by famous regulars such as Robert Duvall, Goldie Hawn, Bruce Willis and David Byrne, this contemporary restaurant has a menu influenced by both American and European palates.

Choosing which room to dine in is almost as hard as the choice of what to have for dinner. Architecturally more interesting, the front room contains the cocktail and oyster bars and includes some seating for dining. With varied materials and textures creating a contemporary atmosphere along with sculpture-like partitions and brick walls, the decor is as inviting as the cuisine. The back room is larger and a little more formal. Carpeted in a red and grey pattern, with cream walls, rattan and cane chairs, this room is uplifted with a large display of original art. This includes a full length, smoked glass, mirrored sculpture which provides a backdrop for the baby grand piano that is played nightly, and often by Dudley Moore.

"The Ultimate", as praised by *Vogue Magazine*, is the Market Street Meatloaf with Spinach and Mashed Potatoes. But, if a full meal is not what you want, you can order oysters on the half shell, broiled oysters with pesto and salsa, or chilled crayfish with spicy garlic mayonnaise from the Oyster Bar. From the kitchen, the landmark starters are the Heart of Romaine with creamy Iowa Maytag Bleu Cheese dressing; or the Kick-Ass Chili with corn bread and condiments. Favorite desserts are the pecan pie, gratin of bananas and berries, mosaic of three chocolates, peach cobbler and rice pudding.

If, after your meal, you are still starved intellectually, you can see the Market Street Series once a month on Saturday afternoon from October through July. This is a series of lectures from a diverse group of individuals that have made outstanding contributions in their fields. Some past lecturers have been George Plimpton of the Paris Review, author E.L. Doctorow and monologist Spalding Gray. Individual lectures are available by subscription and offer wine, hors d'oeuvres and fascinating conversation. 72 Market Street Oyster Bar and Grill is much more than a restaurant partially owned and frequented by celebrities; it is a restaurant with the kind of menu that would allow you to eat there every day and still enjoy the excellent dishes. Most importantly though, they have created a feeling of comfort, relaxed ambiance and hospitality together with intelligence, class and style in which you can thoroughly enjoy yourself.

HAL'S BAR AND GRILL
1349 West Washington Boulevard
Venice, CA 90291
Tel. (213) 396-3105
Hrs:　Mon. - Fri.　11:30 a.m. - 1:30 a.m.
　　　Sat. - Sun.　9:00 a.m. - 1:30 a.m.
　　　Brunch　9:30 a.m. - 3:00 p.m.
Visa, MasterCard and AMEX are accepted.

In the heart of Venice, just four blocks from famous Venice Beach, you'll find a white, stone walled landmark. Hal's Bar and Grill resembles a fine, contemporary art gallery; the stately white interior walls are hung with works by well recognized contemporary artists.

The ambiance is further enhanced by exotic floral displays, skylights, polished concrete floors and soft music.

A visit to the full bar allows time to absorb the art and architecture. Once seated, the wine list, featuring carefully chosen California and French wines, initiates this supreme culinary experience. Try an appetizer such as Poached Oysters in Cream Sauce, or Fried Zucchini Blossoms. For dinner, choose from an extensive menu which includes Norwegian Salmon, Grilled Chicken Breast with shiitake mushrooms and thyme glaze, and New York Steak. Lunch includes a variety of salads, including House Cobb Salad, Grilled Shrimp Salad and Grilled Breast of Chicken Salad. For the more hearty appetite, choose the Grilled Steak Sandwich, Grilled Half Chicken or an Omelette with potato, leek and bacon. All entrees can be prepared to accommodate special dietary needs.

Be sure to save room for one of Hal's desserts. Everything is prepared fresh daily, and can include custardy flan, chocolate espresso cake or a fruit tart. Hal's Bar and Grill offers a unique "Best Choice" dining experience in Venice.

REBECCA'S
2025 Pacific Avenue
Venice, CA 90291
Tel. (213) 306-6266
Hrs: Mon. - Fri.   5:30 p.m. - 12:00 midnight
       Sat. - Sun.   5:30 p.m. - 2:00 a.m.
Visa, MasterCard, AMEX and Diners Club are accepted.

In California, Venice has always been the focal point for the avant garde. In lifestyle, in creative arts and in entertainment there has always been room for the next trend. Bruce and Rebecca Marder, after establishing the popular West Beach Cafe, decided to open another restaurant across the street.

Architect Frank Gehry designed the interior, an eclectic blend of visuals that are as much entertainment as they are art. One can observe the giant alligators and octopi that adorn the ceiling, while sipping a cerveza, margarita or exotic fruit juice. With an emphasis on freshness, the food captures the wonderful traditional flavors of Mexico and brightens them with this influence. The kitchen serves six soups, including a Shrimp and Jalapeño classic and a wonderful Tortilla Chicken Soup. For an appetizer, one can choose made to order Ceviche, Abalone Cocktail or Oysters and Clams on the half shell. Twelve different tacos and burritos are offered, including

Carnitas, Sea Bass and Shrimp. Other menu selections include Shrimp or Steak Tamales, Spinach or Lobster Enchiladas and Quesadillas. Comidas de la Noche feature Leg of Lamb Adobo, Charred Pacific Swordfish, Tuna and Lobster, Filet Mignon and a tempting variety of meat stews. For a refreshing after dinner treat, try the Lime or Apple Tart, Fig Sorbet, Chocolate Bread Pudding or Flan.

Rebecca's is a restaurant that has become a favorite of locals and a must for visitors. While the atmosphere is trendy and fun, the outstanding food is assurance that this restaurant is your "Best Choice" in Venice.

WEST BEACH CAFE
60 North Venice Boulevard
Venice, CA 90291
Tel. (213) 823-5396

Hrs:	Breakfast	Tue. - Fri.	8:00 a.m. - 11:30 a.m.
	Lunch	Tue. - Fri.	11:30 a.m. - 2:45 p.m.
	Dinner	Mon. - Sun.	6:00 p.m. - 10:45 p.m.
	Brunch	Sat. - Sun.	10:00 a.m. - 2:45 p.m.
	Pizza	Mon. - Sun.	11:30 p.m. - 1:00 a.m.

Visa, MasterCard, AMEX and Diners Club are accepted.

Take a break from the activity of Venice Beach and the Boardwalk, and enjoy the relaxing atmosphere and high quality food at West Beach Cafe. From breakfast to late night pizza, this is a very exceptional restaurant.

The term "transportation cuisine" is used to describe the food. Transportation services have allowed the mixing and matching of fresh, unusual ingredients from California and all over the world. The menu is based on a foundation of freshness and creativity. For example, breakfast can range from bacon and eggs and omelettes to Salmon Eggs Benedict and Chorizo and Scrambled Eggs. The lunch menu features a delightful variety of selections, including Mexican Sea Bass Tartare, Grilled Pacific Tuna Sandwich and Linguini Fini with Saute´ Mexican Shrimp. Dinner entrees are even more interesting, with dishes such as Ravioli of Braised Pork and Raddichio, Grilled Lake Superior White Fish, Braised Lamb Shank in Red Wine and Dry Aged Prime New York Steak. West Beach Cafe features an excellent wine list and tantalizing desserts to complement your meal.

In an open and sunny interior, set off by exceptional art works, Bruce Marder and his staff have established a very high standard of food and service. If you enjoy excellent cuisine in a contemporary atmosphere, you owe it to yourself to try this "Best Choice."

WESTLAKE VILLAGE

Created in the mid-1960s, along the shores of a manmade lake, this planned community lies along the Los Angles-Ventura County line beside Highway 101. It's set in a valley within the Santa Monica Mountains. Westlake Village's 24,000 residents enjoy a public golf course, three tennis clubs, community pools, and more than thirty-three miles of bicycle trails. The community contains nine neighborhood shopping malls, a community hospital and a pleasant smog free environment.

 # ACCOMMODATION

HYATT WESTLAKE PLAZA
880 South Westlake Boulevard
Westlake Village, CA 91361
Tel.　(805) 497-9991
　　　(800) 238-9800 CA

For a great getaway spot in the Los Angeles area, you'll find the **Hyatt Westlake Plaza** perfect. Located midway between Los Angeles proper and Santa Barbara, it offers a desirable retreat from the city's hubbub. The Hyatt Westlake features 264 guest rooms in a luxurious setting of Spanish villa architecture nestled among landscaped grounds. It has the distinction of being the only luxury hotel in the Conejo Valley.

Hyatt Westlake is equipped to host business meetings and conferences with suites, meeting rooms, classrooms and catering capacity as well as providing outstanding accommodations and all the amenities that make a vacationing guest feel like royalty. The hotel offers a "night to remember package" which is priced reasonably, and includes accommodations for two people, for one and a half days, a pair of cocktails in the hotel lounge, a thirty-two dollar credit at either of the hotel restaurants and a complimentary bottle of wine or champagne. There is live music and dancing to complete your evenings. The two hotel restaurants are both excellent. Daniel's offers gourmet cuisine and has been touted as the best dinner spot in the area. La Terraza offers more casual dining with buffets and a garden setting.

Relaxation, sports and entertainment await you at the Hyatt Westlake Plaza. Excellent dining and first class accommodations and a host of amenities provide you with a truly regal getaway.

RESTAURANT

BOCCACCIO'S
32123 Lindero Canyon Road
Westlake Village, CA 91361
Tel. (818) 889-8300
Hrs: Lunch   Mon. - Fri.   11:30 a.m. - 2:30 p.m.
         Dinner   Mon. - Sun.   5:30 p.m. - 10:30 p.m.
Visa, MasterCard and AMEX are accepted.

When you want to celebrate a special occasion or spend a memorable night on the town, head for the ultimate in fine dining and intimate luxury at Boccaccio's along the shores of Westlake.

A Mediterranean style restaurant facing Westlake, Boccaccio's offers European elegance in a tranquil, romantic setting. The menu reflects the Mediterranean influence with a variety of French and Italian dishes. As you sit down at a candlelit table you might contemplate beginning with an appetizer of Brazilian Salad, California Goat Cheese Salad, or Oysters on the half shell. For an entree you might try Les Crevettes Mâitre Escoffier, fresh shrimp sauteed with shallots, chives and sherry, served with black and white pasta; Aiguillette de Boeuf, beef tenderloin roasted with Xeres sauce; or Carre D'Agneau Persille, a roast rack of lamb served with creamed shallots. For something truly special the chef suggests the Crispy Culver Duck served with the day's selection of sauces which might include cherry, orange or raspberry. Desserts are homemade pastries featuring fresh fruit tarts with custard and tarte tartin, or an upside-down apple cake served with fresh whipped cream. There is also a full bar and an excellent wine list.

Definitely not a place to hurry through a meal, the food, the service and the ambience are unsurpassed. You'll find that an evening at Boccaccio's is an evening to be remembered.

WEST LOS ANGELES

The San Diego Freeway (Interstate 405) cuts through the heart of a section of L.A. called West Los Angeles. As one of the fastest growing areas, it has seen a new high rise center go up along Olympic Boulevard and enjoys being surrounded by several upscale residential communities such as Beverly Hills, Westwood and Brentwood.

# APPAREL

LINGERIE FOR LESS
2251 South Sepulveda Boulevard
West Los Angeles, CA 90064
Tel. (213) 477-1898
Hrs: Mon. - Sat.   10:00 a.m. - 6:00 p.m.
Visa and MasterCard are accepted.
Also,

3823 Foothill Boulevard	17572 East Colima Road
Pasadena, CA 91107	Puente Hills, CA 91748
Tel. (818) 351-4297	Tel. (818) 964-8842

Lingerie for Less has sensuous wearables from the basic to the exotic and specializes in designer and famous maker lingerie for up to seventy percent off regular retail store prices.

A sense of frolic pervades the store. Color, music, excitement and fun make shopping for lingerie a special treat. Choose from a large selection of bras, panties, teddies, camisoles, robes, nightgowns and daywear as well as such items as shoulder pads and potpourri. You'll find an excellent selection of Naughty and Nice labels as well as designer brand hose which are displayed in colorful, imaginative ways. Lingerie accessories make your underwear wardrobe complete.

The service at Lingerie for Less is special. Attentive salespeople are ready to help you with a smile, and owner Kevin Cassidy has created an exciting store where underwear is both sensual and very wearable. Gift certificates are available and there is plenty of free parking. So whether you are feeling naughty or nice, choose your next "hot item" from Lingerie For Less.

RESTAURANTS

THE APPLE PAN, 10801 West Pico Boulevard, Los Angeles, CA. Tel. (213) 475-3585. For more than forty years, The Apple Pan has been serving some of the best hamburgers and fresh fruit pies.

GOOD STUFF BURGERS
11903 West Olympic Boulevard
West Los Angeles, CA 90025
Tel.   (213) 477-9012
          (213) 477-9011
Hrs: Mon. - Fri.   7:30 a.m. - 9:00 p.m.
          Saturday   10:00 a.m. - 5:00 p.m.

The 100% beef hamburger and Hollywood are venerable traditions in Southern California. At Good Stuff Burgers, you'll find an equal measure of both. Dennis Hopper knows the place, and so does Sean Penn, Emilio Estevez and other rising stars who come to renew their love affair with American graffiti. If the sunny skylight interior, with its green, pink and purple neon lights, mural of painted palm trees and tall purple tables don't make a "fan" of you, as well, then the menu will most certainly do it.

How does an avocado, bacon, and egg "stuffie" sound to you? Do you like wheat cakes smothered in fruit? Are you a vegetarian? Then how about Chad's Favorite, which starts with sliced turkey on a veggie patty smothered with mozzarella cheese and all the trimmings, stacked high on a wheat bun? Are you a salad freak? Then try the Good Stuff Salad, with lettuce, cucumber, sprouts, tomato, carrots and a choice of dressing. If your taste runs to the exotic, you might sample the Teriyaki Chicken Sandwich. Of course, there's your basic Good Stuff, a charbroiled ground turkey or beef patty served on a whole wheat bun.

It's your opportunity to dine with the stars and if the likes of Dennis Hopper, Sean Penn and Emilio Estevez know a fantastic meal when they eat one, chances are, so will you.

LA GRANGE, 2005 Westwood Boulevard, West Los Angeles, CA. Tel. (213) 279-1060. La Grange presents an excellent traditional French Normandie-Provencial cuisine. The delightful dishes are served in a warm and comfortable atmosphere with moderate prices.

WINE SHOPS

BRIGG'S WINE BISTRO
10800 West Pico Boulevard #114
West Los Angeles, CA 90064
Tel. (213) 470-3745
Hrs: Mon. - Fri.   10:00 a.m. - 9:30 p.m.
       Saturday   10:00 a.m. - 7:00 p.m.
       Sunday   11:00 a.m. - 6:00 p.m.
Visa, MasterCard and AMEX are accepted.
Also,
BRIGG'S BRENTWOOD
13038 San Vincente Boulevard
Los Angeles, CA 90049
Tel. (213) 395-9997
Hrs: Mon. - Sat.   9:00 a.m. - 7:00 p.m.
       Sunday   11:00 a.m. - 4:00 p.m.

During the past fifteen years, the foreign and domestic wine industry has seen an increase of producers. This development has generated a challenge for the experienced as well as the neophyte wine lover. Where can one find a broad selection and informed help?

Fortunately, in the Los Angeles area there are two choices, Brigg's Wine Bistro and Brigg's Brentwood. With over twenty-five years of experience in fine wines, they have gained a reputation for their knowledge and selection. Whether you prefer red or white, sparkling or still, imported or domestic, they offer a wide selection for your palate. They are also able to help with rare and hard to find vintages. There is a full selection of spirits and liqueurs, including a wide variety of miniatures. If you wish to taste before you buy, Brigg's

Wine Bistro sells wine by the glass. If you need something special to go with your wine, try the caviar. The selection includes Sevruga, Osetra and Beluga. Brigg's Wine Bistro also serves light lunches and dinners as well as food to go. In addition, Brigg's is well known for their picnic baskets, which come complete with glasses, wine bag, dishes, cheeseboard, cloth napkins, corkscrew and cheese knife, all in a wonderful wicker basket. For gift giving, choose from a selection of fine varietal wines that can be personally labeled with any message you desire. These delightful gifts can be ordered by telephone.

Visit either Brigg's location for the finest in wine and cuisine. Or have a feast delivered free locally, compliments of Brigg's Wine Bistro and Brigg's Brentwood.

THE WINE HOUSE
2311 Cotner Avenue
West Los Angeles, CA 90064
Tel. (213) 479-3731
Hrs: Mon. - Sat.   10:00 a.m. - 7:00 p.m.
        Sunday   12:00 noon - 6:00 p.m.
Visa and MasterCard are accepted.

Many people would like to make their hobby their profession. The staff at The Wine House in West Los Angeles have done just that. Because they love their work so much, you'll get the best advice concerning wine and the finest service.

The Wine House stocks the largest selection of fine wines in Southern California. Its unusual location, in a former warehouse decorated in a "no frills" style, make possible savings that are passed on to customers. You'll find racks and racks of wine from all over the world, including eighty releases of German wines. The store offers the finest varietals California wineries produce, but the store specializes in lesser known European vintages from the Alsace, Loire, the Rhone Valley and Spain. The store has the largest selection of Italian wine on the West Coast plus a fair selection of old and rare wines. The Wine House also features a large selection of spirits, liqueurs, single malt Scotch, Cognac, Armagnac, *eaux de vie* and *grappa*. Beer lovers will delight in the selection of 250 brews, including hard to find Belgian ales. Enter your name on their mailing list and you'll receive a monthly newsletter announcing new releases and up-coming wine tasting events.

Their newsletter also announces a schedule of the Wine House's seminars and classes, which are offered three times a week, covering a vast array of wine topics. General Manager Chris Sandin says that's the best part of his business: introducing people to the joys of wine.

WESTWOOD

Westwood, a section of West Los Angeles, is a community in its own right; a kind of a college town, with all of the cultural and intellectual stimulation the adjacent University of California at Los Angeles has to offer. The campus, located just north of Westwood, provides a huge park-like environment to stroll through. Don't miss the outdoor sculpture garden where you'll find fine works of modern art. Because UCLA is a world class university, foreign nationals of all sorts converge here.

The Westwood "village" section has much to offer, stimulating visitors with a dozen movie theaters, varied restaurant fare and several book stores. Mimes, magicians and strolling minstrels liven up the streets at all hours of the day, creating a kind of Greenwich Village scene.

ACCOMMODATION

WESTWOOD MARQUIS HOTEL AND GARDENS
930 Hilgard Avenue
Los Angeles, CA 90024
Tel.   (213) 208-8765
        (800) 421-2317
All major credit cards are accepted.

Some say the Westwood Village and Beverly Hills area is the best part of Los Angeles. Without a doubt, it is one of the most unique and interesting parts of Los Angeles. One of this area's most noted qualities is the elegant and gracious lifestyle of the residents and their gorgeous luxury homes. The Westwood Marquis offers you the same elegance and luxury of the surrounding area.

Located along the perimeter of the Bel Air Estates, this hotel features 258 individually decorated one, two and three bedroom suites. There is a penthouse floor with seventeen suites and butler service. The hotel offers health spa facilities, an exercise room featuring universal equipment and twenty-four hour room service. A concierge staff will assist guests with dinner reservations, theater tickets, secretarial service and other special requests. Complimentary limousine service is available to surrounding areas and Beverly Hills. The award winning Dynasty Room restaurant represents the ultimate in Continental cuisine while the Garden Terrace restaurant is noted for its lavish luncheon buffet and renowned Sunday brunch.

The Marquis Gardens offer an outdoor respite from city life. A picturesque garden with flowering shrubs and grassy knolls seclude the winding pathways which lead to one of two heated pools. The hotel is adjacent to the UCLA campus and within walking distance of the theaters, shops and restaurants of Westwood Village. The San Diego Freeway and LAX are easily accessible and Beverly Hills and Rodeo Drive are minutes away, as are the famous beaches of Venice and Malibu. Whether you are one of the rich and famous or merely would like to be, you'll enjoy the utter luxury and elegance of the Westwood Marquis.

ENTERTAINMENT

THE WESTWOOD PLAYHOUSE, 10886 Le Conte Avenue, Westwood, CA. Tel. (213) 208-4107. Musicals and dramas are regularly scheduled in this 498 seat professional theater. Performers vary from Ella Fitzgerald to Ian McKellan.

GIFT SHOP

CONTEMPO WESTWOOD CENTER - GIFTS, 10886 Le Conte Avenue, Westwood, CA. Tel. (213) 208-4107. Their gift gallery is stocked with Scandinavian crystal such as Ittila, Orrefors and Homegard. You'll find ceramic dinnerware by Arabia and Artzberg, stainless flatware by Stelton, contemporary jewelry by local artists, Navajo jewelry and crafts from around the world.

RESTAURANTS

BON APPETIT CAFE AND JAZZ
1061 Broxton Avenue
Westwood, CA 90024
Tel. (213) 208-3830
Hrs: Mon. - Thu.   11:00 a.m. - 12:00 midnight
      Friday   11:00 a.m. - 1:00 a.m.
      Saturday   12:00 noon - 1:00 a.m.
      Sunday   5:00 p.m. - 12:00 midnight
Visa, MasterCard, AMEX, Diners Club and Carte
Blanche are accepted.

Bon Appetit Cafe and Jazz is your "Best Choice" for both Jazz entertainment and fine California cuisine. Located in the heart of Westwood, Bon Appetit has been a family owned restaurant since 1971. In 1984, Jazz was added and the combination has been a hit.

The food at Bon Appetit is always fresh and prepared with health in mind. Begin your meal with a delicious appetizer, such as Oysters on the Half Shell, Stuffed Mushrooms or Steamed Clams in Beer. The menu features a wide selection of fresh seafoods, including Marinated Grilled Salmon Steak and Blackened Swordfish Steak Cajun Style. For a special treat, try the Boston Style Bouillabaise, prepared with fresh salmon, halibut, lobster tail, clams, shrimp, crab legs and more. Pasta is freshly made, and served in tantalizing dishes such as Linguini with Fresh Bay Scallops and Shrimp and Herb Fettuccine. The most popular pasta dish is Seafood Fettuccine, a savory blend of crab, shrimp, salmon, snapper and mushrooms. Bon Appetit also offers three pasta dishes in which the sauces contain no butter or cream. Also featured on the dinner menu are salads, including Oriental Chicken Salad and crisp Eclectic Salad. Diners with a heartier appetite will find a tempting variety of selections, including Fresh Culver Long Island Duckling, Spicy Chicken with Sun Dried Tomatoes and Pasta, Choice Midwestern Steaks and Veal.

The Jazz shows feature emerging and established Jazz Fusion groups. The club has gained an international reputation that draws the best groups available. The club offers music seven nights a week with the shows changing nightly. With its unique ability to produce both quality food and entertainment, this club is a natural for a great night on the town.

STRATTON'S
10886 Le Conte Avenue
Los Angeles, CA 90024
Tel.   (213) 208-8886
        (213) 208-1358
Hrs: Lunch   Tue. - Sun.   11:30 a.m. - 2:30 p.m.
       Dinner   5:30 p.m. -10:00 p.m.
Visa, MasterCard, AMEX and Diners Club are accepted.

Are you visiting Los Angeles, love gourmet food and don't know where to go for an exemplary meal? Look no further than Stratton's. This restaurant is a gourmet's delight. With entrees for simple to the exotic, Stratton's can tantalize your taste buds, whatever your mood.

Begin with an appetizer of Duck with Wild Mushroom Linguini or Snails in Puff Pastry. Then, on to the entrees, which include fresh fish, succulent steak, roasted chicken and duck. The house specialty is Beef Wellington, classically prepared with fresh tarragon Bernaise. For dessert, there is a cart full of sweet delectables. There is a choice of coffees, espresso, cappuccino and decaf to finish your meal.

Stratton's has an ambient but stately atmosphere. The dining room is impressive with its high ceiling and exposed stone walls. Tapestries, oil paintings and hunting trophies decorate the walls. An oriental carpet and wing back leather arm chairs give the place a warmth that is reminiscent of an old English gentlemen's club. There are strains of classical music in the background. Whether you stop in for a glass of wine or come for a full dinner and dessert, you will be pleased with the excellent food, superb service and old English atmosphere Stratton's has to offer.

STRATTON'S GRILL
1037 Broxton Avenue
Los Angeles, CA 90024
Tel.   (213) 208-0488
        (213) 203-1358
Hrs: Sun. - Thu.   11:30 a.m. - 11:00 p.m.
       Fri. - Sat.   11:30 a.m. - 12:00 midnight

Housed in a former bank building that has been transformed into a turn of the century Victorian era American saloon, Stratton's

Grill sports black and white tiled floors and a huge rectangular bar in the center of the room of polished gray marble and Honduran mahogany. Columns rise to meet the high ceilings of patterned tin tiles. A dramatic staircase leads to the balcony and the upper dining area. The walls display mounted game trophies and period prints.

Stratton's menu includes a wealth of selections from appetizers to pasta. Entrees such as fish, chicken and steaks are prepared over a mesquite wood grill. They boast an extensive list of American and European wines in addition to a full bar of premium liquors. Your sweet tooth will succumb with delight to the choices of dessert delectables.

Stratton's Grill is very particular about the quality of food they serve: "Everything at Stratton's Grill is made fresh daily, using the highest quality ingredients available." For good food and drink of uncompromising quality and ambient atmosphere treat yourself to a dining repast at Stratton's Grill.

WESTWOOD FETTUCCINE BAR, 1553 Westwood Boulevard, Los Angeles, CA. Tel. (213) 473-5728. Westwood Fettuccine Bar features eighteen different pastas and thirty-five different sauces. They also serve antipasto, veal and chicken specialties.

SOUTH BAY

The South Bay is a land known for its wealth of sunshine, coastal waters and varied beach activities. Although on a somewhat smaller scale than the beach communities to the north, the South Bay offers plenty of opportunities for fine, L.A. style, surfing, swimming and sunbathing. The communities of Redondo Beach, Hermosa Beach and Manhattan Beach are most commonly associated with the South Bay fun in the sun lifestyles, but just to the south, and around the bend of the lush Palos Verdes Peninsula, you'll dscover an assortment of ocean and marina related recreational opportunities at San Pedro and Long Beach.

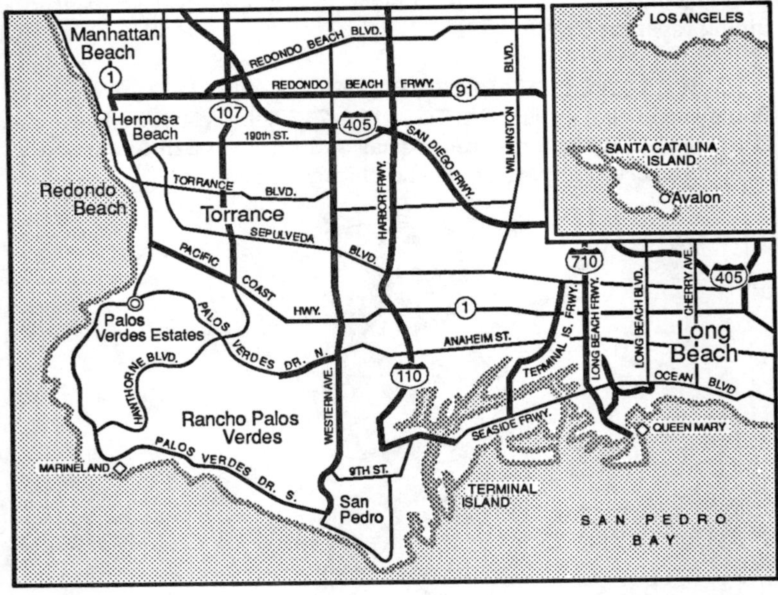

Visitors to this region will enjoy jazz clubs, ocean view dinner houses, broad grassy parks, a variety of museums and plenty of opportunities to stroll along the water's edge.

The area is frequently the jumping off point for those setting out on an ocean going adventure, whether it be a twenty mile cruise across the San Pedro channel to Santa Catalina Island with its crystal clear waters and varied wildlife, or an around the world excursion.

The South Bay area is also home to Los Angeles' aerospace and aviation industries; with a history spanning from early prop driven transport and fighter aircraft to today's super sophisticated missile and satellite development.

PARKS IN LOS ANGELES

• Set in the Santa Monica Mountains, **Malibu Creek State Park** is 5,000 acres of wooded canyons, chaparral covered hillsides and volcanic outcroppings. Within the park are a lake and several streams.

Malibu Creek is believed to be the state's most southerly steelhead spawning run. This preserve is the home of golden eagles, raccoons, foxes, bobcats and a rare mountain lion. So varied is the landscape it has been used as a filming location for everything from *M*A*S*H* to *South Pacific*.

Until 1974, the 2,000 acre canyon was owned by Twentieth Century Fox, then called Century Ranch. Although the land now belongs to the state, television series, commercials and movies are still filmed here. For visitors, the park is a good place for picnicking, horseback riding and hiking.

Hiking trails connect Malibu Creek State Park with both **Topanga State Park** and **Will Rogers State Park**. A small nature center is open on weekends. A campground is also being developed for the near future. A group campground is available in the **Tapia County Park**, which lies entirely within the boundaries of the larger state run facility. For more information contact Malibu Creek State Park, 28754 Mulholland Drive, Agoura. Tel. (818) 705-1310.

• A twenty-foot waterfall cascades into a pond set among tiger lilies and stream orchids. No, this is not a move set, but just one of the remarkable sites within the pristine 9,000 acre **Topanga State Park** in the Santa Monica Mountains. Hikers have their choice of thirty-five miles of trails and fire roads that twist through canyons and over ridges

covered with oak woodlands. The 1.5 mile **Santa Ynez Canyon Trail** leads to the waterfall. Facilities include hike-in and equestrian campsites, a picnic area and restrooms. Rangers and park docents frequently lead educational hikes. For more information call (818) 706-1310. The park entrance is at 20825 Entrada Road, Topanga.

• What was once a ranch owned by "Cowboy Philosopher" Will Rogers is a State Park. Located above Sunset Boulevard in the Santa Monica Mountains, **Will Rogers State Historic Park** includes a museum, polo grounds and hiking trails that lead to the adjacent Topanga State Park.

Rogers built the ranch in 1928 as a home for himself and his family. The grounds and the ranch house have not been changed since Roger's death in 1935 in an Alaskan plane crash. The house contains Rogers memorabilia and family possessions. You'll find the park entrance in the 14000 block of Sunset Boulevard outside of Pacific Palisades.

• Concerts and Shakespearean plays are sometimes performed in the outdoor amphitheater of the **Peter Strauss Ranch**. At other times, the sixty-four acre recreational area, operated by a private, non-profit nature preservation organization, offers hiking trails and picnic facilities. You'll find steep hillsides covered with chaparral and scrub oak. Great blue herons are sometimes seen along Triunfo Creek.

The property was first developed in 1923 as a private retreat with an aviary, fruit trees and zoo. It was a popular resort in the 1940s and contained what was then the largest swimming pool west of the Rockies.

Docents offer nature walks and conduct tours through the park. The ranch was named for Peter Strauss who purchased the land in 1977. In 1983 the Santa Monica Mountains Conservancy acquired the ranch and opened it as a park. The facility is open to the public on the first and third weekends of every month, and at all other times by reservation. For information call (818) 706-8380. The ranch entrance is at Mulholland Highway and Troutdale Road, Agoura.

• **Rocky Oaks** is one of several parks in the Santa Monica Mountain National Recreation Area administered by the National Park Service. Located in upper Zuma Canyon, the 200 acre park is full of trails that wind their way past spring wild flowers. On selected weekends rangers lead hikes along the trail. There's also a peaceful picnic area surrounded by stands of coast live oak. Brush rabbits and coyotes make their homes in the chaparral area of the park.

One of the unique features of the preserve are the volcanic rock formations. The distinctive pillow basalt formations were caused as lava flowed onto the sea floor millions of years ago, creating the rounded shapes for which the formation gets its name.

Facilities include restrooms and parking. Rocky Oaks is located at the corner of Mulholland Highway and Kanan Dune Road, Agoura. For information, call (818)-3770.

• **Paramount Ranch**, another unit of Santa Monica Mountain National Recreation Area, is a 336 acre parkland featuring oak woodland, chaparral, rolling grassland and its own wild west town, which was built as a movie set and is still used to film television shows, commercials and movies.

Weekend visitors can go on one of the tours that lead through the nature preserve and movie set. The ranch is just 2.5 miles south of the Ventura Freeway at Connell Road and Mulholland Highway. For information call (818) 888-3770.

• **Castro Crest**, located off Pacific Coast Highway at the end of Corral Canyon Road, is an 800 acre facility featuring hiking trails, including a four mile loop with sweeping views of the coastline. From the trail you should be able to see the Channel Islands and the distant Santa Susana Mountains. Much of the park is comprised of reddish and purple sandstone embedded with smooth round rocks. For information on guided tours call (818) 888-3770.

For more information on **Los Angeles County Parks** call (213) 738-2961.

Information on lands administered by the National Park Service is available by writing **National Park Service, 22900 Ventura Boulevard,140, Woodland Wills, CA 91364. Tel. (818) 888-3770.

BELLFLOWER

Bellflower lies inland from the coast about halfway between Los Angeles and Long Beach. The community was established in 1906 by F.E. Woodruff who christened his new town Sommerset. The United States Post Office Department rejected the name because of the existence of a town named Sommerset in Colorado. An orchard of bellflower apples in the north section of a ranch in this town was the source of the community's name.

RESTAURANT

MAGDALENA'S
17818 Bellflower Boulevard
Bellflower, CA 90706
Tel. (213) 925-6551
Hrs: Lunch   Tue. - Fri.   11:00 a.m. - 3:00 p.m.
         Dinner   Tue. - Thu.   5:00 p.m. - 9:30 p.m.
                           Fri. - Sat.   5:00 p.m. - 10:00 p.m.
Visa and MasterCard are accepted.

Bellflower has not been known for fine dining until Magdalena's proved that people will respond to an excellent restaurant regardless of where it is located. Magdalena's features a tempting French menu that changes daily. Owner Stephen White has created a restaurant destined to rival any of his Los Angeles competitors. He was trained at a Three Star restaurant in Paris, and California gourmets have enjoyed his culinary talents at Le Biarritz in Newport Beach.

The contemporary French menu changes daily, offering eight to ten appetizers, five salads, sixteen entrees and several dessert choices utilizing organic herbs and produce and the freshest seafood and game from Texas, such as black buck antelope, wild boar, pheasant, Sitka venison, rabbit and squab. Possible appetizer options may be the Smoked Salmon Tart with steamed spinach and a creamy scallop sauce or the Beggar's Purse featuring smoked free range chicken, goat cheese, wild boar bacon, Dijon mustard and herbs with a red wine sauce. An exotic salad of pheasant, duckling and chicken with greens and a creamy horseradish dressing will be a sure temptation. Entrees range from Black Angus filet mignon to fresh quail, boned and stuffed with veal and pistachios. All entrees are served with a choice of dinner salad or soup *du jour*. Magdalena's outstanding wine list was honored by *Wine Spectator Magazine* with the "Best Award of Excellence," and offers over 350 fine wines plus wine by the glass. No meal at Magdalena's would be complete without dessert. You might try a Grand Marnier Soufflé or a decadent Belgian White Chocolate Torte.

Magdalena's will accommodate large parties and catering is available. An innovative menu is also offered at lunch Tuesday through Friday from 11:00 a.m. to 3:00 p.m. For contemporary French cuisine and atmosphere, visit this gem in the heart of Bellflower.

BELMONT SHORE

A popular boating and recreational section of the city is Belmont Shore, located between the Belmont Pier and the Alamitos Peninsula to the south. There's always something going on at the sailboat launching ramp at the foot of Claremont Place and the Belmont Plaza Olympic Pool hosts a number of competitive aquatic events including the NCAA Water Polo Championships in November. Nearby, discover volleyball courts and parklands.

ATTRACTION

• The **Belmont Pier**, at the foot of 39th Street, is a 1,620 T-shaped structure where you can fish, rent a skiff or just enjoy the sights. Facilities include a bait and tackle shop, a snack bar, parking and restrooms. For information call (213) 434-6781.

APPAREL

A RUNNING EXPERIENCE
5304 East 2nd Street
Belmont Shore, CA 90803
Tel. (213) 439-6876
Hrs: Mon. - Fri.   10:00 a.m. - 9:00 p.m.
      Saturday   10:00 a.m. - 6:00 p.m.
      Sunday   11:00 a.m. - 5:00 p.m.

Whether you are a serious runner, a casual jogger or occasionally take brisk walks, A Running Experience has something to help you do it better. Owner Pat Patterson has an extensive background as a runner and university track coach and has been working with his own team for the past two years. The knowledge he has gained over the last sixteen years reflects in the selection and quality of running wear and accessories in his store.

All the salespeople receive extensive training in proper fit and function of running shoes. They will talk with you about the amount and type of exercise you do and perform a careful examination of your foot before picking out a shoe for you. It is not unusual for passersby to see customers jogging up and down the sidewalk in front of the store while one of the salespeople watches their stride and running style. Pat sees to it that the shop staff keeps up with the constant change in designs and material in sport shoes. A Running Experience carries a wide selection of running wear and accessories, as well as active sportswear, and even rugby boots and clothing.

They have a great selection of books including some very hard to find European publications, videos and training aids for runners. They even have running strollers for moms on the go. The most valuable product they have is the free advice and time they give to all their customers. It is their experience and background and their willingness to share that makes A Running Experience a "Best Choice."

EL SEGUNDO

Stretching along the shore of Santa Monica Bay just south of the Los Angeles International Airport is the city of El Segundo. From its name, you might think this coastal community has a past dating from the days of Spanish Occupation. Although the name *El Segundo* means "the second" in Spanish, the term actually refers to the name of Standard Oil Company's second oil refinery in California, so named in 1911.

Today El Segundo continues to play a major role in the oil industry, serving as a major port for shipping petroleum products pumped from tankers offshore, through pipes, to an oil pier.

In this industrial environment the endangered El Segundo blue butterfly survives, a remnant of the once extensive El Segundo Dunes. The tiny blue and orange butterfly feeds on a rare species of wild buckwheat that grows on the dunes within the Chevron Refinery complex.

RESTAURANT

CAPISTRANO BAR AND GRILL
1440 Imperial Highway
The Embassy Suites Hotel
El Segundo, CA 90245
Tel. (213) 640-1070
Hrs:　Lunch　　　　Mon. - Sat.　11:00 a.m. - 5:00 p.m.
　　　Dinner　　　　Mon. - Sun.　5:00 p.m. - 10:00 p.m.
　　　Lounge bar open until 11:00 p.m.
Visa, MasterCard, AMEX, Diners Club and Discover are accepted.

As more and more people are watching their waistlines and cholesterol levels, many restaurants cater to special dietary needs. The Capistrano Bar and Grill, located at the Embassy Suites Hotel in El Segundo, is especially sensitive to changes in the public's eating habits. Many of the restaurant's selections meet the American Heart Association's fat and cholesterol standards. Capistrano Bar and Grill's staff can also prepare dishes for those watching their sodium intake.

Whether you are dieting or not you can always be sure of fine dining at Capistrano Bar and Grill. Appetizers include Hot Dungeness Crab and Artichokes with fresh baked bread. Pasta dishes include the very spicy Cajun Fettuccine made with fettuccine noodles, sliced chicken breast and a Cajun sauce. The Roasted Garlic Prawns is a delightful seafood dish, while Jake's Chicken is a popular poultry choice. A traditional Jamaican preparation, Jake's Chicken features a boned half chicken marinated in fresh lime juice and spices, and basted with spicy mango sauce. Meat dishes include Grilled Lamb with Fresh Rosemary Crust. Try the homemade Key Lime Pie for dessert.

This restaurant is a first choice among many of the area's businessmen for power lunching. They mingle in the spacious lounge with the international travelers who stay at the hotel and enjoy the Spanish influence of the decor. Waterfalls, plants and brick tile floors complete the scene at the Capistrano Bar and Grill.

HERMOSA BEACH

The city of Hermosa Beach is situated on the Santa Monica Bay between the neighboring beach communities of Manhattan Beach and Redondo Beach. It was developed at the turn of the century as a residential community, but after completion of the Pacific Electric Railway in 1903, Hermosa Beach quickly became a family resort for Los Angeles residents drawn to its wide sandy beach.

ATTRACTIONS

• **Hermosa City Beach** provides parking, restrooms, volleyball courts and offers opportunities for swimming and surfing. The **South Bay Bicycle Trail** continues past the beach from neighboring Manhattan Beach. Fishermen try their luck for surfperch , spotfin croaker and shovelnose guitarfish, the last being s sort of ray. For information call (213) 372-2166.

• The **Hermosa Beach Municipal Pier** at the foot of Pier Avenue is a 2,140 foot long facility that includes restrooms and a bait and tackle shop. Anglers can fish for halibut, mackerel and opaleye. This is an excellent spot for watching gulls, coots and pelicans.

GIFT SHOP

THE PAPER MOON
1048 Hermosa Avenue
Hermosa Beach, CA 90254
Tel. (213) 379-0093
Hrs: Mon. - Sun.   10:30 a.m. - 6:30 p.m.
Visa, MasterCard and AMEX are accepted.

It's one of those gift shops that must be seen to be believed and once you're inside, you'll likely be there quite awhile. The name of the business should not connote anything illusory because this tightly packed gift boutique is much more than, "only a paper moon."

You'll recognize it by its brown and green awning and the white wood carvings atop the building. The entire storefront glows pink and orange when the sun is setting and there are thirteen feet of lighting resembling a vine of flowers, with each blossom a different color. Inside, there are three skylights and two mystical paintings in the store itself. Every shelf, nook and cranny is crammed with the familiar, the not so familiar, the puzzling and the bizarre. It's where Garfield the cat romps, where antiques from the early twentieth century hold bath soap displays; where T-shirts reflect the unpredictable eclecticia of the Southern California lifestyle; and where just about the time you think you've seen it all: a stuffed animal or a Billy Bird soap dish quietly suggests that you've only just begun.

Service includes personalized paper products and items ranging in price from fifty cents to considerably more than that. So if it's something a little unusual (or maybe even strange) you're looking for, you know where to come, don't you? Drop in and hang on tight to your imagination.

RESTAURANTS

THE BOTTLE INN
26 22nd Street
Hermosa Beach, CA 90254
Tel. (213) 376-9595
Hrs: Mon. - Fri.   6:00 p.m. - 9:30 p.m.
        Fri. - Sat.   6:00 p.m. - 10:30 p.m.
Visa, MasterCard, AMEX and Diners Club are accepted.

For over thirteen years The Bottle Inn has been providing authentic Italian cuisine in the style and manner of a traditional Italian trattoria. The prevailing ambiance is one of charm and quaint elegance reminiscent of the Old World. Two small intimate dining salons and a main dining room are appointed in Mediterranean decor, high back wooden chairs and Spanish/Italian wood and chrome chandeliers.

Appetizers of stuffed calamari, veal stuffed mushrooms and escargot are flavored with over sixteen spices to heighten your palate for the delights to follow. Among the notable entrees is Veal Villa Borghese in a creamy brandy sauce, fresh mushrooms, zucchini and water chestnuts. Pasta offerings include Quattro Formaggi, a marriage of imported Gorgonzola, Fontina, Mozzarella and Parmigiano; and Tortellini Alla Panna, veal and chicken stuffed pasta, cream sauce and imported porcini mushroom. Three specials daily are offered in addition to the standard menu. Whimsical desserts include such delights as English truffles and mascarpone cheesecake.

For the *piece de resistance*, sample a selection of award winning wines, which includes a vintage 1967 Brunello di Montalcino. A sommelier will assist you in making the perfect selection from a listing of over 400 wines. Winner of a myriad of awards from the California restaurant and wine associations, The Bottle Inn is a "Best Choice" for Italian cuisine.

GOOD STUFF ON THE STRAND
1286 Strand
Hermosa Beach, Ca 90254
Tel. (213) 374-2334
Hrs: Summer   Mon. - Sun. 7:00 a.m. - 9:00 p.m.
       Winter   Mon. - Tue. 7:00 a.m. - 3:00 p.m.
                    Wed. - Sun. 7:00 a.m. - 9:00 p.m.
Visa and MasterCard are accepted.

"It's not just a restaurant, it's an adventure," is one of the slogans owner Cris Bennett uses when describing Good Stuff on the Strand. Frequented by actors, surfing champions, professional biking teams and motion picture crews, Good Stuff has an aura of unpredictability.

There are some things about the restaurant that are highly predictable, such as the quality and healthy nature of the food and the energetic friendly service. These are just a few of the reasons Good Stuff on the Strand has been voted Best Outdoor Cafe by *Easy Reader* and *Beach Reporter* as well as being written about in the *L.A. Times, Playboy* and *Esquire*. Breakfast is the specialty at Good Stuff so bring your appetite and try their whole wheat pancakes with fruit and some fresh squeezed orange juice, or the Island Breakfast, tender white fish, two eggs, rice pilaf and toast. For lunch or dinner you might try Marco Polo, fresh broccoli wrapped in sliced turkey, topped with Hollandaise and served with rice pilaf; or the Calamari Steak, served with a generous helping of Pasta Parmesan. Don't forget to check the specials board.

Royal blue tablecloths, the brick archway leading to the patio and autographed menus on the wall, by stars such as Bruce Willis, George Brett and David Lee Roth, complement the full "healthy" menu. As they say around Good Stuff, "You've tried the rest, now eat the best."

THE HABASH CAFE
233 Pacific Coast Highway
Hermosa Beach, CA 90254
Tel. (213) 376-6620
Hrs: Mon. - Sat.   11:00 a.m. - 9:30 p.m.
Visa and MasterCard are accepted with a $10 minimum order.
Beer and wine are served.

"Man does not live by bread alone, but by every word that proceedeth out of the mouth of God." So it was written in the ancient times and so now, it is the motto by which Hanneh and Naoum Habash prepare and serve their authentic Arabian cuisine.

Ironically, The Habash Cafe didn't start out featuring the food of Old Jerusalem, but instead, began as a hamburger eatery. Hanneh, ("Mama," as she is known to her customers) gradually introduced Arabic seasonings and spices to the traditional American menu and would also cook Palestinian dishes for her children. Custmers caught the exotic aromas emanating from the kitchen, tried the fare and finally convinced her to add them to the other offerings. Now, the cafe is a favorite gathering place for homesick Arabs and everyone else with a passion for Pita bread, Falafel and a host of other entrees one just does not expect to find along the Southern California Coast. Among them are humos, tabuleh, grape leaves, cottage rolls, kibby, lamb dishes, baklava and Arabic coffee.

The cafe itself is light and airy. Peach and lime dominate the decor. It is, however, the heart which sees over all. The family has sponsored 10K races and participates each year in the Fiesta de las Artes. It was also among those restaurants featured in *Los Angeles Magazine's* silver anniversary and *Elmer Dil's Favorite Restaurants Under $10.00*. A South Bay tradition since 1969, it's The Habash Cafe, where man does not live by bread alone.

LONG BEACH

With first class visitor and entertainment facilities, Long Beach is the second largest city in Los Angeles County. Known for its aerospace industry and international shipping port, Long Beach also offers attractions such as the Queen Mary luxury liner and Howard Hughes' gargantuan Spruce Goose seaplane.

Throughout the 1980s the city has undergone massive redevelopment. Some major projects include the demolition of six city blocks for a major shopping mall, construction of two new marinas, the Shoreline Village with its complex of hotels, shops and restaurants connected by a shuttle ferry, and the newly refurbished Long Beach Convention and Entertainment Center which contains some of the most important performing art facilities in the state. Long Beach's harbor facilities make it a popular embarkation point for cruises and excursions to Santa Catalina Island.

A popular boating and recreational section of the city is Belmont Shore, located between the Belmont Pier and the Alamitos Peninsula. The protected Alamitos Bay, to the south, offers small craft sailing, paddling in rented kayaks, or just lying on the sandy beach. The Seaport Village features shops and restaurants along the jetty entrance. Naples, a residential neighborhood consisting of three islands in Alamitos Bay, boasts walkways along canals and attractive palm lined streets.

The city of Long Beach is a spicy combination of a new, flashy atmosphere and the historical past. Accommodations include major hotels and the distinctive fourteen story Villa Rivera apartment building. The flavor of Long Beach's Spanish heritage is alive, as evidenced by the stucco and red tiled buildings along Ocean Boulevard. The restored Monterey style adobe, built in 1844 on the old Rancho Los Cerritos, is now a museum.

Long Beach was part of the 1784 Nieto Spanish land grant and later the Los Cerritos and Los Alamitos ranchos under the Mexican occupations. The area was developed into an ocean resort in 1881 as Willmore City, but was incorporated as the City of Long Beach in 1897. Throughout the early part of the twentieth century visitors came to enjoy the amusement park and beaches. A building boom followed the discovery of oil at Signal Hill in 1921. So much oil was removed from the region, that by the 1950s the water table dropped and created problems with irregular land settling.

ATTRACTIONS

•   **Shoreline Aquatic Park**, at Shoreline Drive and Pine Avenue, is a grassy, landscaped park that surrounds an artificial lagoon where camping, fishing and picnicking can be enjoyed. Facilities include bicycle paths and a full service seventy site RV campground. For information call (213) 437-0375.

•   The **Downtown Shoreline Marina**, at Shoreline Drive and Linden Avenue, includes the **Shoreline Village** offering marinas, shops, restaurants and a restored 1906 merry-go-round salvaged from San Francisco's old Playland at the Beach amusement park. Fishing platforms are available at the western breakwater. For information call (213) 437-0375.

•   **Long Beach City Beach** is a wide sandy beach, also called Long Beach Strand, which begins east of the downtown area and extends for several miles past Belmont Pier. Offshore breakwaters built in the 1940s transformed what had been a surf pounded beach into a protected swimming area. Beach facilities include restrooms and volleyball courts. The old **Lifeguard Headquarters** at the foot of Cherry Avenue contains a lifeguard museum. For information call (213) 437-0375.

•   **Bluff Park**, along Ocean Boulevard between 20th Place and Redondo Avenue, offers a grassy bluff-top park with a view of San Pedro Bay.

•   **Bixby Park**, a ten acre facility at Junipero Avenue and Ocean Boulevard contains a playground and picnic area.

•   Art lovers will enjoy the **Long Beach Museum of Art**, located at the west end of Bluff Park. It is open Wednesday through Sunday from noon to 5:00 p.m. For information call (213) 439-2119.

•   The **Marine Stadium**, at Appian Way and 2nd Street, is a narrow two mile long body of seawater behind Alamitos Bay. Used for the 1932 Olympic rowing races, the Marine Stadium continues to host competitive water sport events including waterskiing and drag boat competitions. It's also used for a variety of recreational activities. The Marine Stadium includes a protected sandy beach called **Mother's Beach**.

• **The Colorado Lagoon**, located at Appian Way and 4th Street, is a manmade tidal lagoon featuring a sandy beach and swimming area. The lagoon was built along with the Marine Stadium waterway for the 1932 Olympics. For further information call (213) 594-0951.

• **Recreation Park**, just north of the Colorado Lagoon, contains a picnic area in a eucalyptus grove.

• **Marine Vista Park** offers a grassy open area with baseball and soccer fields between Colorado Lagoon and the Marine Stadium.

ACCOMMODATIONS

HOTEL QUEEN MARY
1126 Queensway Drive
Long Beach, CA 90801
Tel. (213) 435-3511
Visa, MasterCard, AMEX, Diners Club and Carte Blanche are accepted.

When it came to elegance, the old British ruling class never left home without it. That was especially true when traveling on the Queen Mary, now permanently docked in Long Beach. In this masterpiece of understated British elegance, charm and grace was what made it a great ship, as well as what now makes it a great hotel.

The ship is considered one of the most luxurious ocean liners ever to ply the Atlantic. Today, the Hotel Queen Mary offers the romance and excitement of an ocean cruise without your leaving port. The 365 staterooms, located in what was the first class section, are the largest rooms ever built in a ship. They feature all of the amenities of a first class hotel room. Each room is authentic in its decor, right down to the polished wood paneling, the brass hardware and the Victorian furnishings. The ship's deluxe suites are just as they were when the ship first sailed. The Royal Suite includes two bedrooms, a sitting room, two baths and maid's quarters. Shopping aboard the Queen Mary can be a special experience. Piccadilly Circus, the original shopping mall for first class passengers, features The Gallery, offering gourmet kitchenware, and Queen Mary's Doll House, a toy store and gift shop.

The successful blending of the Hotel Queen Mary's impeccable service and novel decor makes her the consummate choice for meetings, banquets and receptions. Meeting rooms can accommodate 10 to 1,000 people for banquets, meetings and trade shows. There's even a wedding chapel. The ship's Grand Salon is the largest ballroom ever to grace an ocean liner. Live entertainment is another special feature of the hotel. Guests enjoy colorful shows throughout the summer and holiday seasons. Even if you can't return to a time when this great ship sailed the seas, at Hotel Queen Mary you can experience the magnificent legend she has left.

HYATT REGENCY-LONG BEACH
200 South Pine Avenue
Long Beach, CA 90802
Tel.   (213) 491-1234
        (800) 228-9000
Visa, MasterCard, AMEX, Diners Club, Discover and Carte Blanche are accepted.

Dare to demand the best. From the stunning view of the Pacific Ocean to the affluent luxury of your accommodation, you can experience the finest that Long Beach has to offer at Hyatt Regency-Long Beach.

All 521 rooms, nineteen suites and fifty-two Regency Club rooms offer a magnificent view of the ocean, harbor marina, or lagoon. Tastefully decorated and offering the best in contemporary comfort, each accommodation features complimentary HBO, ESPN and pay per view in-house movies. Women travelers will appreciate the makeup mirrors and hair dryers available for their use. Robo-bars in each room provide liquor, beer, snacks and soft drinks. Non-smoking floors are also available. The Regency Club features two private floors with its own exclusive lounge, express elevator, complimentary breakfast and hor d'oeuvres at twilight. Among the list of amenities, Hyatt Regency-Long Beach features a fitness center, an outdoor heated swimming pool, a therapeutic pool and a jogging course. Babysitting and a concierge to assist in making arrangements for sightseeing tours highlighting the best "hot spots" in the Long Beach area are examples of the exemplary services at the Hyatt Regency-Long Beach.

The Emerald Cafe offers guests a choice of casual dining while enjoying the dazzling view of the Hyatt Regency's rippling lagoon. A more formal and intimate dining experience is available in the

Beacon. A dramatic ocean view complements the culinary creations of specialty dishes and seafood. Both the Beacon Lounge and the Lobby bar feature live entertainment. The Beacon also features a unique champagne Sunday brunch, the first in Long Beach. Banquet and convention facilities are also a specialty at the Hyatt Regency-Long Beach. In addition to providing its own exclusive convention facilities, the Hyatt Regency-Long Beach is adjacent to the Long Beach Convention and Entertainment Center.

Hyatt Regency-Long Beach is situated only minutes away from some of Southern California's exclusive attractions. The Spruce Goose and the Queen Mary can be seen directly across from the hotel itself and Shoreline Village is within walking distance; or take the complimentary tram which runs between the hotel and village. Excursions to nearby Catalina Island can be arranged, and of course, Disneyland, Knott's Berry Farm, and Marineland are all within hailing distance. For the "Best Choice" when in Long Beach, make it the Hyatt Regency.

SHERATON LONG BEACH AT SHORELINE SQUARE
333 East Ocean Boulevard
Long Beach, CA 90802
Tel. (213) 436-3000
Visa, MasterCard, AMEX, Diners Club and Carte Blanche are accepted.

The spectacular Sheraton Long Beach is part of the new Long Beach multi-use complex, Shoreline Square, and is located directly across the street from the Long Beach Convention and Entertainment Center. The hotel is four blocks from the Pacific Ocean in the heart of the downtown redevelopment area and nine miles from the Long Beach Airport.

Sheraton Long Beach at Shoreline Square has the largest ballroom in the city, offering nearly 13,500 square feet of space. There are eight additional meeting rooms adding another 5,000 feet of meeting space. Six hospitality suites and two tastefully appointed executive boardrooms complete with ocean views make the Sheraton Long Beach the ultimate in full service hotels for meetings. The sixteen story building holds 462 guest rooms, including twenty-nine suites. The hotel also offers the largest square footage of parking area of any hotel in the Los Angeles area.

The Sheraton Long Beach offers experienced concierge service to assist you in dinner and club reservations, limousine service and travel arrangements. Sheraton Long Beach is within walking distance of the ocean, is close to the famous Queen Mary and Spruce Goose and near Shoreline Village and its turn of the century seaside shopping. Catalina Island is just a short sail away and of course the Long Beach Convention and Entertainment Center is a step across the street.

APPAREL

FOOT LOOSE
East 2nd Street
Long Beach, CA 90803
Tel. (213) 434-9001
Hrs: Winter   Mon. - Fri.   10:00 a.m. - 7:00 p.m.
                  Saturday   10:00 a.m. - 6:00 p.m.
                  Sunday   11:00 a.m. - 5:00 p.m.
      Summer   Mon. - Fri.   10:00 a.m. - 9:00 p.m.

You have to be impressed with a woman who has 275 pairs of shoes in her own closet. You may think "This is a woman who loves to shop." You would be right. Once we talked with owner Barbara Franks, we weren't sure whether she opened Foot Loose to sell clothes or have an excuse to shop for them. Either way, the result is great.

What makes Foot Loose so great is Barbara's love of shopping. She is up at "the Mart" once or twice a week and regularly sees twenty to thirty lines of clothing a day. She looks until she sees something that is perfect for the store. This devotion to shopping, shopping, and more shopping makes the inventory at Foot Loose a real find. There is a great array of contemporary styles and accessories, from dresses to swimsuits, shorts to leather gloves, all at surprisingly low prices. Barbara also stresses the quality of the merchandise. Every shipment coming into the store is inspected to make sure the material and workmanship is the same quality as the display line was.

We would be remiss if we forgot to mention the shoe department. It is not only impressive in the front of the store, but there is a substantial back stock, so they are sure to have the right size.

LANDMARK

QUEEN MARY/SPRUCE GOOSE
1126 Queensway Drive
Long Beach, CA 90801
Tel. (213) 435-3511
Hrs: Mon.- Sun. 10:00 a.m. - 6:00 p.m.
Visa, MasterCard, AMEX, Diners Club, Carte Blanche and
Eurocard are accepted.

Take one of the greatest legends of the sea and put it alongside its counterpart in aviation and you have a multi-faceted entertainment complex like no other in the world. The Hotel Queen Mary and the gargantuan Spruce Goose come together in Long Beach Harbor to offer a multitude of shopping, dining and entertainment opportunities.

Ever since the city of Long Beach acquired the Queen Mary in 1967, it has stood as one of the most popular landmarks in Southern California. After a multi-million dollar restoration effort, the ship was opened to the public in 1971. Millions have experienced the romance of the ship. Shipboard activities include a tour through specially designed exhibits which feature replicas of original staterooms, crew's quarters, a children's playroom and the first class drawing room. The thirty-five ton propeller was balanced with such precision that it can be turned with the touch of a hand.

Every bit as amazing as an engineering feat is the ship's neighbor, the Spruce Goose, the great flying ship that Howard Hughes designed to transport World War II troops above the U-boat infested waters of the Atlantic. Its cargo bay would have held 750 men and two Sherman tanks had it ever been placed in operation. The plane is housed in an immense domed building, the largest of its kind in the world. Surrounding the plane are a variety of exhibits and audio-visual presentations describing its construction and its one and only flight.

One cannot exaggerate the immensity of these two attractions. Seeing both of them will fill a day. The Londontowne Village, a nineteenth century style English village within the complex, will tempt browsers. Restaurants and cafeteria style eating concessions, conveniently placed within the complex, will refresh you during a long and memorable day of sightseeing.

RESTAURANTS

ALISIO'S, 5199 East Pacific Coast Highway, Long Beach, CA. Tel. (213) 597-1323. Alisio's has fine French Continental cuisine with an extensive wine and liquor list. Outdoor patio or intimate restaurant dining is available.

JIMMY'S FISH & GRILL, 6563 East Pacific Coast Highway, Long Beach, CA. Tel. (213) 594-9479. Quality seafood at reasonable prices, patio dining and premium wines by the glass are available at Jimmy's.

MCKENNA'S CREEK
6575 East Pacific Coast Highway
Long Beach, CA 90814
Tel. (213) 598-7725

Hrs:	Lunch	Mon. - Fri.	11:00 a.m. - 3:00 p.m.
	Dinner	Sun. - Thu.	4:30 p.m. - 11:00 p.m.
		Fri. - Sat.	4:30 p.m. - 12:00 noon
	Sunday Brunch		10:00 a.m. - 3:00 p.m.

McKenna's Creek is fashioned after an 1800s distillery. The floors are made of slats from the old McKenna Distillery whiskey vats. From pulley fans to wooden kegs, old lamps and brass rails, everything looks authentic. A 1922 flatbed Ford has been converted into a large salad bar. An authentic looking copper still is on display near the entry. It is, however, a replica crafted by Southern California metal artists. There are several dining rooms in which to enjoy your meal. The Parlor Room is a replica of an 1890s sitting room; the Hunt Room is cozy with a fireplace and brass accents; and the Green Room is decorated with ferns, foliage, skylights and a cobblestone floor.

The food at McKenna's Creek is terrific. Lunch favorites range from special sandwiches such as Cajun Prime Rib Sandwich to salads. The Crab n' Cheddar, chunks of crab meat and cheddar cheese on grilled sourdough bread is delicious and very popular. Dinner offers chicken, beef, lamb and seafood specialties. Combinations, such as top sirloin and Louisiana hot shrimp are popular. The jumbo Cajun style Tiger Shrimp are a deliciously different treat. Desserts are made on the premises. Sample such delights as Chocolate Eclair Experience or New York Style Cheesecake.

McKenna's Creek has received both the Los Angeles and Orange County Restaurant Writer's awards for nine years. You will enjoy the total dining experience, from the authentic decor to the award winning food.

THE MUSTARD SEED
5624 Atlantic Avenue
Long Beach, CA 90805
Tel. (213) 422-6090
Hrs: Lunch   Mon. - Fri.   11:30 a.m. - 4:00 p.m.
        Dinner   Mon. - Sun.   5:00 p.m. - 11:30 p.m.
Visa, MasterCard, AMEX, Discover and Carte Blanche are accepted.

Many people have read the New Testament passage written by Matthew which says: "If you have faith as the grain of mustard seed, nothing will be impossible." These wise words inspired Walter and Susan Urweider to give up working for others and create The Mustard Seed, a fine restaurant located off the beaten path near Long Beach.

Every facet of the restaurant marks it as a "Best Choice." Lace curtains trim the half frosted front windows. A mixture of antique styles decorate the interior, making it feel like a 1920s mansion. A pair of skylights illuminate each of the two dining rooms, both furnished with antique chairs and tables. Collages of antique paintings, mirrors and antique china plates decorate the walls. You feel as if you're home, even though the restaurant can care for up to 120 people. The Mustard Seed offers one of the best salad bars in Southern California. It's so good, in fact, many diners make the salad their entree. Ten to fifteen specials are served daily, mostly fresh fish. Other specials include duck, venison, roast leg of lamb, wild boar, and chicken with a variety of stuffings. Sauces are made the old fashioned way, beginning with a stock pot. On Fridays, a special shrimp, chicken, or sausage gumbo is featured. The chef also offers Cafe de Paris, an incredible butter sauce served in only a very few establishments around the world. The restaurant also features wine by the glass and imported beers.

The restaurant has won the coveted Holiday Travel Award and has even been given the Key to the City Award by the mayor of Long Beach. Make your reservations now, and you'll be inspired to give the staff kudos when you visit The Mustard Seed.

PANAMA JOE'S
5100 East 2nd Street
Long Beach, CA 90803
Tel. (213) 434-7414
Hrs: Mon. - Sun. 11:30 a.m. - 11:00 p.m.
Visa, MasterCard and AMEX are accepted.

Award winning Mexican food with freshly squeezed juices added to every fresh fruit margarita are just some of the reasons why you should dine at Panama Joe's. Owners Steve and Rick Loomis have used their twenty-five years of restaurant experience to create four delightful Panama Joe's outlets in the south coast area. The Mexican motifs are enhanced by big screen television sets for sports buffs, offering a comfortable and casual setting and excellent food.

Winner of the Silver Medal Award from the *California Restaurant Writer's Association* for the past five years, some of their succulent menu items include daily fresh seafood specials, shrimp and crab enchiladas, sizzling fajitas, chile Colorado, chile verde, and Steve's original recipe for the now famous Mexican pizza.

You'll find only the best at Panama Joe's. Savor one of their delicious cocktails at an original antique bar that was built by Brunswick in 1901 and shipped here from New York. The bar enhances the structure on 2nd Street that was built in 1931 and won an award for the beautiful manner in which the Loomis' restored it. Panama Joe's remains a treat on all levels of enjoyment.

SAHARA RESTAURANT, 5333 East 2nd Street, Long Beach, CA. Tel. (213) 439-1518. This is the oldest Lebanese restaurant in Los Angeles County. Tried and true lamb and vegetarian dishes developed over the years are featured.

SIR WINSTON'S RESTAURANT
Aboard the Hotel Queen Mary
1126 Queensway Drive
Long Beach, CA 90801
Tel. (213) 435-3511
Hrs: Dinner   Sun. - Thu.   5:30 p.m.-10:00 p.m.
                      Fri.-Sat.   5:30 p.m.- 11:00 p.m.
       Lunch   Mon.-Sun.   11:30 a.m. - 2:30 p.m.
Visa, MasterCard, AMEX, Diners Club and Carte Blanche are accepted.

No doubt more than a few shipboard romances began amid the soft lights and sumptuous surroundings on the Queen Mary. And no doubt more will follow because Sir Winston's Restaurant continues to offer dinner guests a chance to experience a legend and begin a memory on the world's most luxurious ship.

Sir Winston's, commanding a spectacular view of the harbor, offers a deftly prepared cuisine in a romantic atmosphere. The restaurant is comprised of a series of rooms enriched with large framed mirrors and the warm hues of mahogany paneling. Although the restaurant attracts out of town visitors, most of its clientele comes from within the Long Beach community, which speaks of Sir Winston's consistent quality. The food can best be described as "French continental with a touch of California." Dinner at Sir Winston's includes a carefully selected choice of entrees prepared in unusual ways, using one of a kind ingredients. One house specialty is medallions of milk fed veal with an apple Armangnac sauce. Among the special appetizers are shrimps with champagne vanilla sauce.

As you enjoy your meal, a violinist strolls among the tables or you might be seated by the popular piano bar. So, for a legendary experience in dining, board the elegant Queen Mary for the unparalleled Sir Winston's Restaurant.

WILLIAMSBURG RESTAURANT & BAKERY
355 East 1st Street
Long Beach, CA 90802
Tel. (213) 590-0220
Hrs: Restaurant Mon. - Sun.   11:30 a.m. - 8:30 p.m.
       Bakery   Mon. - Sat.   6:00 a.m. - 8:30 p.m.
                   Sunday   11:30 a.m. - 8:30 p.m.
Credit cards are not accepted.

Return to the charm and elegance of the late eighteenth century's American Colonial period at the Williamsburg Restaurant. Steeped in the gracious tradition of its namesake, the famous, authentically preserved colonial village, Williamsburg, Virginia, the fine establishment will add a new dimension to your travels with a dining experience the entire family will treasure.

Williamsburg Restaurant's decor, based upon extensive research, consists of exquisite Early American replicas and antiques, and is singularly complemented by an extensive menu prepared in "Ye Olde" tradition—flavorful, nutritious and extraordinarily fresh—at a surprisingly moderate cost. No expense was spared in the creation of the 3.5 million dollar establishment, grandly styled to capture the essence of the Colonies. White shuttered bay windows underlined with wooden flower boxes, brick walls and carriage lamps beckon guests into another era. Inside, handcrafted brass chandeliers hang from moulded coffered ceilings, and furnishings of cherrywood made into reproductions of Chippendale originals carry you to another time and place. Early American costumed staff members see to diner's needs with friendly, courteous Old World hospitality. The delicious fare offered by the Williamsburg, prepared by skilled chefs, is presented buffet style; guests choose from a vast, freshly prepared array of entrees and vegetables, which are ultimately served to you at table. Prepared in an "alta shaam," a low temperature, high moisture process, such selections as classic roasted turkey with corn bread stuffing, juicy prime rib, delicate ham and succulent corned beef are all the more delectable. Hearty home style soups, fragrant breads and crisp salads complement your dining experience and desserts and beverage, including wine or beer, are included in the moderate price. The desserts are heavenly and include freshly baked fruit or cream pies in a variety of flavors. The Williamsburg Bakery is open early for breakfast and also offers a delightful menu filled with much of the tantalizing fare offered in the restaurant.

Private dining is available for group meetings of over twenty. There is ample validated indoor parking, to be entered from Elm Street. Signs show the way. An elevator will transport guests down one floor and into the lobby. Enjoy the best of two worlds; twentieth century convenience combined with the gracious hospitality and hearty fare of Early Americana at Williamsburg Restaurant, a pioneer in fine dining.

MANHATTAN BEACH

Primarily a residential community whose inhabitants work in nearby aerospace and technological firms, Manhattan Beach lies twenty miles southwest of Los Angeles and faces about one and a quarter miles of ocean shoreline. Throughout the community of 33,000, neighborhood shopping areas are found where you can shop for everything from beachwear to dinner jackets.

The original business district is on Manhattan Beach Boulevard and Manhattan Avenue, adjacent to the pier. You'll also find shops on the north end of town, along the Sepulveda Corridor, and on the east side at Aviation and Artesia. Only a few years ago, the shopping mall at Rosencrans and Sepulveda was the Standard Oil Tank Farm.

Manhattan Beach was planned as a seaside resort in the late 1890s and was named by its developer, Stewart Merrill, a New Yorker who thought well enough of Manhattan Island to share its moniker with this newly established community. The main part of the town was situated on a low bluff above the ocean and featured narrow streets and wooden and stucco bungalows. In 1927 a concrete "boardwalk," known as the Strand, was completed. Visitors also grew to enjoy the numerous bath houses and pavilions.

Annual events in Manhattan Beach include the **Chamber of Commerce Art Festival**, the **Grand Prix Bicycle Races**, the **International Surf Festival** and the **Old Hometown Fair**. For information about these and other events, call the **Manhattan Beach Chamber of Commerce** at (213) 545-5313.

ATTRACTIONS

• **Manhattan State Beach** follows the entire shoreline of the city of Manhattan Beach. Once a narrow beach, it benefitted from construction of a breakwater in 1938 at Redondo Beach. A paved cycling path follows an old electric railway right of way. The beach attracts swimmers, surfers and anglers. Facilities include parking, restrooms, wheelchair ramps and volleyball courts.

• The **Manhattan Beach Municipal Pier** at the foot of Manhattan Beach Boulevard has a pavilion that houses the **Roundhouse Marine Studies Lab**, where you'll find displays of marine life. Anglers who fish from the pier take in catches of halibut, walleye surf perch and mackerel.

ACCOMMODATION

RADISSON PLAZA HOTEL AND GOLF COURSE
1400 Parkview Avenue
Manhattan Beach, CA 90266
Tel.　(213) 546-7511
　　　(800) 228-9822

The newest in luxury hotels in the South Bay area, the Radisson personifies elegance and gracious hospitality. From the marble lobby to your room, attention to detail has created an exceptional hotel. The Radisson Plaza features 400 elegantly appointed guest rooms, each with a sitting area, individual climate control and special amenities.

The hotel is located in the seaside community of Manhattan Beach, conveniently close to the Los Angeles International Airport and a casual bicycle ride to the ocean. The hotel's Califia Restaurant offers award winning French gourmet cuisine in an elegant, sophisticated ambiance. The Terrace Bistro offers casual dining with a garden view and an outdoor terrace dining area. At The Waves, you can enjoy dancing in the evening as well as a drink with friends. The Radisson offers beautiful accommodations for business meetings and conferences. There are 18,000 square feet of banquet and conference space available. The Radisson has a full service health spa and exercise room as well as its own golf course.

Water fountains, palm trees and landscaped acreage surround the hotel to providing an island paradise atmosphere. Their goal is to create a gracious hotel center with all the special touches of a fine resort. For those who appreciate luxury and elegance, the Radisson Plaza will meet your expectations.

GIFT SHOP

ONCE UPON A QUILT
312 Manhattan Beach Boulevard
Manhattan Beach, CA 90266
Tel. (213) 379-1264
Hrs: Mon. - Sat.   10:00 a.m. - 6:00 p.m.
      Sunday   12:00 noon - 5:00 p.m.
Visa and MasterCard are accepted.

If the shop carried quilts alone, it would be worth experiencing. Owner Jacquie Williams, a fashion design major in college, began making them in her home and over a period of years, joined with other award winning artists whose work she appreciated to put together an assortment of gifts which reflect her own expanding creative consciousness.

Once Upon a Quilt can be recognized by its pink and green trim storybook shop front with a huge picture window and green dutch doors. The motif continues inside with white washed walls, solid hardwood floors and an overall cozy country atmosphere with a distinctly American Southwest touch. The quilts are there, of course, antique, new, and made to order, but now they are complemented by ceramic fish in bright colors, cows, frogs, pigs, cats, hearts, watermelons and dinosaurs. There's even a line of jewelry made from computer parts and Jacquie recently added a line of dish towels and aprons with cacti and chili peppers embroidered on the front. The wine bottle covers look like Indians and she's also now carrying a very unique line of Native American dolls with hand drawn faces. There are also "Hotbots," decorative hot water bottles in a variety of animal designs, and an assortment of clocks, lamps and ceramics from Santa Barbara.

This is a "must see to believe" kind of place where you can plan on being more than a little surprised when you get there. That's Once Upon a Quilt, a blue ribbon buying adventure.

RESTAURANT

SAUSALITO SOUTH RESTAURANT
3280 Sepulveda Boulevard
Manhattan Beach, CA 90266
Tel. (213) 546-4507
Hrs: Lunch   Mon. - Fri.   11:00 a.m. - 2:30 p.m.
      Dinner   Mon. - Sat.   5:30 p.m. - 11:00 p.m.
                   Sunday   5:00 p.m. - 9:00 p.m.
      Brunch   Sunday   10:00 a.m. - 2:30 p.m.
      Seafood Bar   11:00 a.m. - 10:30 p.m.

California's north/south split personality is nowhere more evident than at Sausalito South, which combines the quaint getaway atmosphere of Northern California with the chic style of Los Angeles.

You may be a long way from that sunny town of Sausalito on the San Francisco Bay, but there's plenty here to remind you of it: the sunshine on the outdoor patio, glass all around, the rich thick beamed ceilings, hanging plants, flowers and the taste of terrific Pacific seafood. Yet, there's some of the good life of Los Angeles, such as the best of locally grown jazz enjoyed by a fashionably attired clientele. As you savor all of this, crack into a northern Dungeness crab, flavorfully enhanced by chef Bob Serna's own mustard sauce. The pastas are magnificently blended with shrimp, scallops, calamari and spices. The imprint of Northern California comes through with the outstanding Cioppino and Steak a la Sausalito. Sunday brunch is a real indulgence with free flowing champagne.

Even if you've never been out of Southern California, you can still enjoy a little of the north. Just remember, don't call it "Frisco." Somebody up there might be listening.

PALOS VERDES ESTATES

The Spanish term for "green trees" was included in the names of two of the five communities located on the Palos Verdes Peninsula: Palos Verdes Estates and Rancho Palos Verdes. Another community, occupying the base of the peninsula on its north side, is Rolling Hills Estates. This peninsula separating the Santa Monica Bay and the San Pedro Bay was first developed in the 1920s as a subdivision of posh estates. Palos Verdes remains one of the most elegant regions in L.A. County and its residents enjoy some of the most spectacular and lush scenery on the Southern California coast.

The city of Palos Verdes Estates became incorporated in 1939 and had been designed in part by landscape architects Frederick Law Olmstead and John Olmstead. Many of the early houses were lavish Spanish Colonial Revival style structures with access to equestrian and hiking trails. Peacocks, introduced by one of the early residents, now roam throughout the area.

Just to the south of Palos Verdes Estates is Rancho Palos Verdes, which was developed as a residential community in the late 1940s. The community occupies seven and a half miles of coastline and includes the area known as Abalone Cove and Portuguese Bend. On several of the community's bluff tops flowers, grains and vegetables are grown. Up until the early 1980s, the hills, bluffs and canyons were the home of a rare Palos Verdes blue butterfly. Residential development and the removal of native perennial plants the butterfly was dependent upon lead to its extinction.

ATTRACTIONS

• The **Palos Verdes Shoreline Preserve** extends along the entire 4.5 mile shoreline of Palos Verdes Estates and includes 130 acres of undeveloped bluff top park land. Foot paths within the preserve are steep and sometimes hazardous, but they offer fine scenic views of the rocky shore. Divers, surfers and hikers particularly enjoy the preserve. **Lunada Bay** features a rocky beach accessible by a steep trail off Paseo Del Mar near Oakley Road. For information on the preserve call (213) 378-0393.

- The **Point Vicente Park and Lighthouse**, along Palos Verdes Drive in Rancho Palos Verdes, overlooks the offshore kelp beds and rocky shore far below. The park is situated on the bluff top of Point Vicente, where the **Point Vicente Interpretive Center** features geological and marine life displays, as well as exhibits on the Gabrielino Indians. The 1926 vintage lighthouse is open to the public on Tuesday and Thursday afternoons. Other facilities include a picnic area and a bluff top trail. For information call (213) 377-5370.

- The **Abalone Cove Ecological Reserve**, on Palos Verdes Drive South, Rancho Palos Verdes, is an eighty acre interpretive area that comprises the offshore waters, tide pools, and several beaches lying at the base of 180 foot cliffs. Bluff top trails lead past stands of cactus. Just beyond the surf, bottlenosed dolphins pass during their spring and fall migrations. The **Upper Beach** is a manmade beach built in Abalone Cove during the 1930s for a resort hotel, now in ruins. The **East Beach** is a natural sandy beach at the east end of Abalone Cove. Nearby **Smuggler's Cove**, which gets its name for the role it played in the days of Prohibition, has small sandy beaches. Facilities include picnic areas, a playground, restrooms and parking. For information call (213) 545-4502.

RESTAURANT

LA RIVE GAUCHE
320 Tejon Place
Palos Verdes, CA 90274
Tel. (213) 378-0267
Hrs: Lunch   Tue. - Sat.   11:30 a.m. - 3:00 p.m.
      Dinner   Mon. - Sun.   5:30 p.m. - 10:00 p.m.
      Brunch   Sunday   11:00 a.m. - 3:00 p.m.
Visa, MasterCard, AMEX, Carte Blanche and Diners
Club are accepted.

As you sit by the window at La Rive Gauche, you can almost imagine you're dining along the River Seine. The excellent food, exceptional service and uncommon ambiance are reminiscent of the great restaurants of Paris.

A warm, intimate, candlelit restaurant where each table is beautifully set with French floral design china, La Rive Gauche offers a lavish lunch menu with such appetizing dishes as Oysters Rockefeller, fresh oysters grilled to perfection with spinach and a brandy cream sauce; Duck Salad, julienne of duck with pine nuts, endives, French green beans and raspberry dressing; and Fillet of Sand Dabs sauteed and served with a creamy butter lemon sauce. Every item on the menu is made fresh daily of the highest quality ingredients. For dinner the chef suggests an appetizer of Pâte Maison followed by Vichysoisse. For an entree, Roasted Duckling sauce du jour, or Norwegian Salmon with dill cream sauce are recommended. Beside the regular menu, La Rive Gauche offers fifteen daily specials. Rated by *Wine Spectator* as possessing "One of the *best* wine lists in America," owners Andre Martin and Andre Moreau proudly serve over 1,200 labels. Apart from the superlative fare, the restaurant features an outstanding staff whose service and professional, caring attitude are known nationwide.

Everything at La Rive Gauche, including the food, the wine, the service, even the atmosphere, is of the highest quality. It is the kind of restaurant to which one returns again and again.

REDONDO BEACH

Redondo Beach's residents like to brag that they have one of the most scenic beach communities between Santa Barbara and San Diego. It's a claim that can be easily supported with a stroll along the top of the cliffs on the Esplanade. A breathtaking view stretches from Malibu to Palos Verdes.

Among the pleasures of this town is watching the magnificent sunset while enjoying a dinner or cocktails at one of the beachfront restaurants and listening to jazz. The community is laid out in a fairly compact fashion so you can easily walk to most attractions, or as some do, bike or skate. If all you want to do is relax, you'll find plenty of room on the beach under the warm sun. The community even has a salt water swimming pool, which the locals call "The Plunge."

Redondo Beach is home to a wide variety of annual events and contests. For serious runners the internationally famed **Super Bowl Sunday 10k Run** is popular. For the not so serious, watch the annual **waitress relay races** in which teams of swift footed waitresses, in full costume, carry trays of drinks in a real show of fast service.

Redondo Beach was established in 1881 during a land boom, stimulated by a rate war between the transcontinental railways which brought hordes of newcomers to Southern California. A narrow gauge railway connected the city with L.A. in 1888. After the first wharf was completed in 1890, Redondo Beach became a small seaport. A fashionable hotel located near the harbor, Hotel Redondo, open its doors in 1891. To promote a new salt water swimming pool, community leaders sponsored a surfing exhibition in 1907 that featured Hawaiian surfer George Freeth, who was called "the man who walked on water." Freeth's demonstration was probably the first appearance of surfing on the west coast.

ATTRACTIONS

• 	King Harbor, west of Harbor Drive, offers opportunities for swimming, boating and fishing. The harbor area also includes several good restaurants. Cyclists may enjoy the paved bike path that follows the perimeter of the harbor. During the winter whale migration, one can take a whale watching charter. For further information call the harbor master's office at (213) 372-3566.

- The **Redondo Beach Municipal Pier** and the adjacent **Monstad Pier** at the foot of Torrance Boulevard, offer a pleasant venue in which to fish, dine, shop or stroll along their long promenade. The 250 foot Monstad Pier extends from the southern end of Municipal Pier. A new fishing promenade has been constructed at the seaward side of the Monstad Pier, which links it with the middle of the Municipal Pier. There are also a variety of shops and restaurants located on the two piers. Anglers can try their luck fishing for bonito, yellowtail, halibut and surfperch. They'll find gear and advice at the bait and tackle shop on the Monstad Pier.

- **Redondo State Beach**, which lies off the Esplanade, is an eighty-five acre sandy beach popular for swimming, surfing, fishing and sun bathing. Facilities include restrooms and volleyball courts. For information call (213) 3272-2166.

ACCOMMODATIONS

PALOS VERDES INN
1700 South Pacific Coast Highway
Redondo Beach, CA 90277
Tel.   (213) 316-4211
          (800) 352-0385 CA
          (800) 421-9241 US
Visa, MasterCard and AMEX are accepted.

When the Palos Verdes Inn was first built in 1960, it was known as The Plush Horse Inn, and it was virtually the only quality hotel in the South Bay. It catered to legislators, actors, chief executive officers and others of taste and discrimination. A recent three and a half million dollar renovation and a name change have only enhanced the Inn's reputation for service and distinction.

It is now the home of the award winning Chez Melange Restaurant which features entertainment and banquet facilities for groups to 150. HERTZ Rent-a-Car is there, and a year round pool, spa and sun decks complete with lush landscaping. The Inn boasts 112 spacious guest rooms, many overlooking some of L.A.'s best beaches. Complimentary bicycles for the thirty miles of bike trails are also available.

Free transportation to local attractions, shopping and dining, baby-sitting service, beach towels and arrangements with a private tennis club and private health club, limousine service to both round out an experience deserving of those who keep the wheels of industry, commerce, entertainment and government turning not only in California, but throughout the nation. For contemporary Golden State decor and the kind of service you've come to expect from only the finest of hotels, call for reservations and see for yourself why the Palos Verdes Inn remains a quality hotel of the highest caliber.

PORTOFINO INN
260 Portofino Way
Redondo Beach, CA 90277
Tel.　(213) 379-8481
　　　(800) 468-4292 CA
　　　(800) 383-2993 US
Visa, MasterCard and AMEX are accepted.

Whether you're a landlocked mariner or you're thinking about putting to blue water in search of adventure and fine lodging, you'll be greeted by champagne and chocolate covered strawberries when you arrive.

At the Portofino Inn, each room has either an ocean view or a panorama of the 233 slip King Harbor Marina. First constructed in 1963, the Portofino Inn, has recently undergone a $6 million renovation and now includes a fine restaurant and conference table slated to open in late summer.

Complimentary bicycles, access to the sports center, health spa and racquetball club, full bath amenities including robes, mini-bars, room service and call waiting on all phones are also included.

Sheer California elegance, the lobby is terra cotta, with green marble desks and counters, large overstuffed furniture in peach, sand, plum and teal. A three story atrium ceiling and wall extend to the water's edge, where a grand piano sits against the sunset. The motif extends to the bleached pine furnishings with a coral cast, and each room is equipped with remote control color television, refrigerators, bars and a jacuzzi. For the seasoned salt, or those whose hearts are stirred, Neptune's Kingdom, come to the Portofino Inn and enjoy romance by the sea.

SHERATON AT REDONDO BEACH
300 North Harbor Drive
Redondo Beach, CA 90277
Tel.　(213) 318-8888
　　　(800) 325-3535
All major credit cards are accepted.

Have you ever slept overlooking the ocean? For a restful night's sleep in a beautiful location, visit the Sheraton in Redondo Beach. Overlooking the ocean and the King Harbor Marina, this hotel offers elegant surroundings and a leisurely atmosphere, giving you the best of contemporary Southern California.

Located a convenient distance from the Los Angeles International Airport and downtown Los Angeles, the Sheraton features 339 luxury guest rooms. The Redondo Beach area offers many sunny California activities from scuba diving, sailing, deep sea fishing and windsurfing to jogging and biking trails. The Sheraton rounds out the area's recreational opportunities with its own exercise room, tennis court, recreation deck and swimming pool. Restaurants proffering a variety of cuisine abound within easy walking distance of the hotel. The hotel is situated for easy freeway access to amusement attractions such as Disneyland, Knott's Berry Farm, the Queen Mary and the Universal Studios Tours as well as the Hollywood Park horse racing track and the Galleria Shopping Center.

In addition to boasting a completely new facility, the Sheraton offers a full range of amenities to serve your every need. They have recreational sports facilities, handicapped facilities, hotel restaurant, newsstand, gift and sundries shop, game room, full service beauty salon, lounges, meeting and conference rooms and much more. Treat yourself to relaxation and enjoyment of the blue Pacific Ocean while staying in the luxury of a gorgeous new hotel. You will appreciate the beautiful setting and excellent service provided by the Sheraton.

CHARTERS

PACIFIC CHARTERS
555 North Harbor Drive
Redondo Beach, CA 90277
Tel. (213) 374-4015
Hrs: Mon. - Sun. 9:00 a.m. - 5:00 p.m.
Visa, MasterCard and AMEX are accepted.

Remember the grand sailing ships of old and the many stories, legends and fish tales about sailors and the sea? Ever wondered what it was about the ocean that had sailors so completely captivated? Come sail with Pacific Charters and find out.

Pacific Charters has an entire fleet of boats available to rent. If you need a skipper to navigate, they have those too. Sailboats, yachts and motor launches are ready and waiting to match your needs. Would you like to try some deep sea fishing? Pacific Charters has sport fishing charters. Have you always dreamed of sailing a trimaran? Well, now you can. The Pacific Charters folks also have a complete yachting sales center. They also offer a full series of classes, from basic sailing to celestial navigation. How about treating yourself to a meal on the high seas? The Pacific Charter offers both a lunch and sunset cruise. It's a perfect setting for a romantic interlude.

Whether you are a recreational sailor out for an overnight sail or if you like to race and want to test the performance of a different mono-hull design or if you simply want learn the allure of the ocean, Pacific Charters has the right boat for you.

GIFT SHOP

THE CONNOISSEUR
201 Torrance Boulevard
Redondo Beach, CA 90277
Tel. (213) 374-9768
Hrs: Mon. - Fri.   8:30 a.m. - 5:30 p.m.
        Saturday   10:00 a.m. - 4:00 p.m.
Visa, MasterCard and AMEX are accepted.

Have you ever had the dilemma of choosing an original gift for someone who seems to have everything? Do you ever search for that business remembrance with a special touch? The Connoisseur is a unique wine shop that supplies personalized gifts of select wines.

They boast a collection of premium wines and champagnes from the best of outstanding wineries in Northern California. Each bottle bears a label inscribed with your personal message and comes packed in handsome wooden gift boxes. A wide selection of gift items such as hand engraved crystal glasses, cheeses, nuts, pate's, wine mustards, liqueur flavored fudges and gourmet delights accompany the wine. They offer shopping by mail or telephone as an adjunct to visiting their store. They will ship your gift anywhere in the United States.

Whatever the occasion may be, wedding, business gift, anniversary, bar mitzvah, a remembrance for a friend back home or something unique for the person who has everything, The Connoisseur offers an excellent assortment of hand selected wine and champagne. A premium wine bearing a label with your personal inscription is the ultimate in elegance, and a truly distinctive gift. Plan to visit The Connoisseur for an unsurpassed experience in gift giving.

MARKET

QUALITY SEAFOOD
130 South International Boardwalk
Redondo Beach, CA 90277
Tel.   (213) 372-6408
        (213) 374-2382
Hrs: Mon. - Sun. 9:00 a.m. - 7:30 p.m.
Visa, MasterCard, AMEX and personal checks are accepted.

It's the largest fish emporium in the South Bay and whether you intend to take it with you or eat it on the premises, you're in for an extraordinary piscatorial experience.

Located on the Redondo Beach International Boardwalk, it also includes Isoko Japanese Restaurant and Quality Seafood Fish Market restaurant. Isoko's, which resembles a traditional Japanese Inn, has an extraordinary Sushi bar. If you prefer, Quality will cook your fish market selection for you and you'll enjoy eating it on the premises. Quality Seafoods, which occupies eight storefronts and goes back thirty years as a family operation, includes row upon row of cold cases with fresh fillets and steaks. Tank after tank of live shellfish, a lively crab, lobster and crayfish section and counters of smoked fish give indisputable credence to their motto, "If it swims, we have it." They'll also pack fish in blue ice for shipping, smoke it on the premises, or steam it for eating there. They'll also cook any fish exactly as you order and throw in corn on the cob and coleslaw for a nominal extra.

It's been a family tradition since great grandfather Petar Dragich arrived from Yugoslavia in 1897, so there should be no doubt Pete Dragich and Ann Johnson, brother and sister, know their fish. Whether you're looking for Dungeness crab, New Zealand cockles, salmon or sushi, you'll want to make the trek to the Redondo Beach Pier. Bring your appetite with you and plan on spending some time with them.

RESTAURANTS

CAPTAIN KIDD'S
209 North Harbor Boulevard
Redondo Beach, CA 90277
Tel. (213) 372-7703
Hrs: Summer   9:00 a.m. - 10:00 p.m.
         Winter   9:00 a.m. - 9:00 p.m.
Visa, MasterCard, AMEX, Diners Club and Carte Blanche are accepted.

Imagine sitting in a glass enclosed patio overlooking a marina, watching the sailboats or the sun drift below a horizon. Imagine enjoying this resplendent view and dining on fresh fish cooked to perfection. The location is the Redondo Beach Marina and the place is Captain Kidd's Fish Market and Restaurant.

You'll find a trip to Captain Kidd's downright inspiring. This excellent restaurant began as a fish market with a small snack bar. Customers would ask the fish market to cook the fish they were purchasing. Through the years, customers not only wanted their fish cooked, but wanted to eat it there, too. As the demand grew so did Captain Kidd's.

Several dining rooms have been added, and there are four ways to dine at Captain Kidd's. They will gladly prepare any piece of fish you choose from their fish market. Let them know if you want it charbroiled, pan fried or deep fried. You can also order from their regular menu or their daily specials; or pick out your choice of live shellfish from the tanks and Captains Kidd's will steam them for you. Captain Kidd's has two patios for outside dining. For seaside eating that can't be beat, you'll find Captain Kidd's is a wonderful Southern California experience.

CHEZ MELANGE
1716 Pacific Coast Highway
Redondo Beach, CA 90277
Tel. (23) 540-1222
Hrs: Sun. - Mon.   7:00 a.m. - 12:00 midnight
Visa, MasterCard and AMEX are accepted.

People often think of Southern California as a melting pot, with its mix of cultures, but rarely does a restaurant symbolize so much of what California is than Chez Melange at the Palos Verdes Inn in Redondo Beach. The menu is a veritable stew of all the world has to offer in food, in one place.

Owners Michael Franks, an expatriate Englishman, and Robert Bell, the cuisine creator, purchased what they call "an old, tired cafe" in 1982 after falling in love with the place's huge kitchen. They've remodeled the cafe little since then, though it has a decidedly upscale decor. Reflecting many of their customers, the restaurant has a fast paced feel, with its constantly changing menu, though some selections reappear frequently. On any given day, a diner could sample a breakfast that includes eggs grilled English-style with homemade sausage, or a breakfast burrito with chorizo sausage. For lunch, diners can choose Southern Fried Chicken Salad with fresh corn, served with a salad in buttermilk ranch dressing. Evening meals feature fresh biquette sea bass grilled with sauteed asparagus and whole oyster mushrooms. After dinner, try some of Chez Melange's homemade ice cream flavored with whiskey or tequila.

For those who like their drinks straight, visit one of Chez Melange's two bars. In either place, you'll mix with others from Southern California's melting pot.

LE BEAUJOLAIS
522 South Pacific Coast Highway
Redondo Beach, CA 90277
Tel. (213) 543-5100
Hrs: Lunch   Mon. - Fri.   11:30 a.m. - 3:00 p.m.
       Dinner   Mon. - Sun.   5:30 p.m. - 10:00 p.m.
       Brunch   Sat. - Sun.   10:00 a.m. - 3:00 p.m.
Visa, MasterCard, AMEX, Diners Club and Carte Blanche
are accepted.

Le Beaujolais strives for perfection. Upon entering the totally refurnished and redesigned restaurant, you'll know that owners Andre

Moreau and Andre Martin demand the very best in the total dining experience. They've even refurbished the kitchen to their custom specifications.

The finest, freshest ingredients are utilized in the preparation of the classic French cuisine, and Mr. Moreau personally supervises the kitchen. Menu selections include such creative brunch dishes as poached salmon with tarragon cream sauce; sauteed sweetbreads with Madeira sauce and wild mushrooms; and a warm chicken breast salad. Lunch and dinner menus feature creative hors d'oeuvres, fragrant soups, and an excellent selection of meat, fish and fowl dishes. Recommended are such entrees as venison with grand veneur sauce; and poached fresh scallops in a pastry shell with lime sauce. All desserts are homemade by a pastry chef. Le Beaujolais' premium wines may be selected from the restaurant's list of 1,400 labels, including California, German and French vintages. The oldest wine on the list is a 1928 Chateau Lafite Rothschild. For cognac lovers, the restaurant has an 1893 Bas Armagnac De Cavaillan.

Le Beaujolais' warm and friendly decor is well suited to the enjoyment of a fine meal. There are two intimate dining rooms, one small and intimate, the other just a bit larger. The elegant, yet informal rooms feature rich velvet chairs and tables covered with white tablecloths. A romantic lamp lights each table, which is set with fine china in a classic French design. Patrons have made this gourmet's delight a true success.

MILLIE RIERA'S SEAFOOD GROTTO
1700 Esplanade
Redondo Beach, CA 90277
Tel. (213) 375-0531
Hrs: Lunch   Mon. - Sat.   4:00 p.m. - 10:00 p.m.
      Dinner   Sun. - Thu.   4:00 p.m. - 11:00 p.m.
      Brunch   Sunday   10:30 a.m. - 3:00 p.m.
Visa, MasterCard and AMEX are accepted.

The scene is high atop the Esplanade, the view is the glorious Pacific Ocean, the time is Labor Day, 1946. There Millie and Joe Riera envisioned an authentic seafood grotto patterned after the legendary Fisherman's Wharf of San Francisco. The grotto would give tribute to seafood prepared with original recipes from the Riera family and those imported from Italy, Sicily and the shores of the Mediterranean.

Millie Riera's Seafood Grotto became a reality and has remained unchanged through four successful decades of operation.

Patrons can be assured of enjoying the finest quality fish and seafood anywhere. A selection of eight to fourteen types of fresh fish is available daily. Abalone is collected by Millie's own divers and is processed on the premises. Thursday through Saturday evenings customers can enjoy a succulent seafood dinner and be entertained with romantic live music. Millie's well stocked wine locker features California Chardonnay.

Millie Riera's Seafood Grotto was established on the philosophy of serving only the finest of seafood and this principle has never changed in forty years.

ROLLING HILLS ESTATES

Rolling Hills Estates occupies the base of the Palos Verdes peninsula on its north side. This peninsula separating the Santa Monica Bay and the San Pedro Bay was first developed in the 1920s as an elegant subdivision of posh estates.

GIFT SHOP

CHERI DAVID
550 Deep Valley Road
Rolling Hills Estates, CA 90274
Tel. (213) 377-5777
Hrs: Mon. - Fri.   10:00 a.m. - 9:00 p.m.
     Saturday   10:00 a.m. - 6:00 p.m.
     Sunday   12:00 noon - 5:00 p.m.
Visa and MasterCard are accepted.

If you're looking for something different in antique furniture and other treasures, this quaint, 2500 square foot shop located on the third floor of the Palos Verdes Courtyard Mall is absolutely worth consideration.

Its traditional American exotica and the primitive pine furniture, antique bird cages, scents and soaps by Crabtree & Evelyn, sterling silver and other heirloom jewelry, contemporary country graphics, baskets and dried flowers are all part of a proud inventory. Cheri David is also intensely proud of her service. Some of her clientele has been with her since the beginning in 1974 and, as any discriminating customer knows, they don't keep coming back unless they're thoroughly satisfied.

One half of the store contains individual rooms, each depicting a different country perspective and filled with treasures of an era. The other half is one large expanse of beautiful furniture, larger gifts, and lighting fixtures which hang from heavy timbered beams throughout. Cheri also carries the works of local artists and a uniquely rustic line of greeting cards. So if your taste runs to the traditional and yet different, it's Cheri David, to whom loyal customers mean more than the dollar.

SAN PEDRO

Situated on the Palos Verdes Hills overlooking one of the world's busiest ports, San Pedro commands attention as a city with international flavor and charm. The community offers museums, parks, fine dining and shopping. The Cabrillo Marina and Recreation Complex is a 370 acre development featuring 1,500 small boat slips, bike and walking paths, restaurants, shops, a hotel, beaches, a fishing pier, a museum and tide pool areas. San Pedro is also an embarkation point for cruises to Santa Catalina Island.

The Chamber of Commerce refers to San Pedro as the "Cruise Ship Capital" of the West Coast. The Los Angeles World Cruise Center in San Pedro is in fact the second busiest cruise port in the United States and is the home port for the famous *Love Boat*. Those who happen to visit between December and March can take a popular whale watching cruise from San Pedro to get an up-close look at the annual migration of the California gray whale.

The San Pedro townsite traces its heritage to 1542 when Portuguese explorer Juan Cabrillo claimed it for Spain and named the bay the *Bahia de los Fumos,* or "Bay of Smokes," a reference to the many hillside campfires of the Gabrielino people. The bay was renamed San Pedro in 1602 by Spanish explorer Sebastian Vizcaino. Later the Spanish established two missions in the area, making the bay an important regional port whose significance continues to this day.

ATTRACTIONS

- **Cabrillo Beach**, located at the end of Stephen M. White Drive, is actually two sandy beaches created in 1929 with the dumping of dredged material along the base of the San Pedro Breakwater. Fishermen can try for bonito and perch . Facilities include picnic tables, restrooms and a boat ramp. For information call (213) 832-1179.

- The **Point Fermin Marine Life Refuge**, between Point Fermin and Cabrillo Beach, consists of a half mile long stretch of seashore waters and tide pools. Access for diving and tide pool observation is through Cabrillo Beach.

- **Fisherman's Wharf**, at Berth 73, is home to San Pedro's colorful fishing fleet and also a popular venue for photographers or anyone else looking for a chance to absorb the sights and sounds of a working commercial fishing facility.

- The **Los Angeles Maritime Museum**, at the foot of 6th Street, is housed in the old ferry building and features artifacts from ships, models and paintings by renown marine artists.

- **John Gibson Park**, adjacent to the Maritime Museum, provides a satisfying vantage point from which to observe harbor traffic.

- The **Cabrillo Marine Museum**, 3720 Stephen White Drive, features thirty-four marine life aquariums. Among the impressive exhibits is a kelp forest tank, wave tank, a touch tide pool and a sandy beach. For information on the museum, or any of its many educational programs and tours of the nearby Point Fermin Marine Life Refuge, call (213) 548-7562.

- The **Point Fermin Lighthouse and Park**, at Gaffey Street and Paseo Del Mar, overlooks the rocky coastline and the city's nine mile long breakwater. The thirty-seven acre park is landscaped with stands of fig trees and facilities include a playground, picnic tables and parking. The national headquarters of the **American Cetacean Society** and Community Center is next to the lighthouse building and has information on whales and dolphins. The lighthouse, built in 1874 , now serves as a private residence.

- A sort of bayside version of Hollywood's "Walk of Fame," the **San Pedro Sportswalk**, along 6th Street and Harbor Boulevard, honors sports celebrities with bronze plaques embedded in the sidewalk.

    •   The **Angels Gate Park**, at Gaffey and 35th Street, is 160 acres of parkland overlooking the ocean off Point Fermin, in addition to the harbor complex. It has picnic areas, basketball courts, and a military museum open weekend afternoons.

BED & BREAKFAST INN

THE GRAND COTTAGES
809 South Grand Avenue
San Pedro, CA 90731
Tel. (213) 548-1240
Visa, MasterCard, AMEX and Diners Club are accepted.

One more bit of color has been added to San Pedro's famous Grand Avenue as Marylyn Ginsburg extends her Grand House Restaurant to include The Grand Cottages. Three restored, spacious 1920s cottages offer inviting decor, quiet spaces, private porches and a patio garden for travelers seeking a bed and breakfast close to the harbor.

Each cottage is the same in size while varied in decor. White wicker furniture padded with dusty rose pillows eases the guests into relaxation in one cottage, the close Pacific ocean inspires a nautical theme in another and soft greens reflect the restful garden patio outside the door of the third cottage. All are spacious, and each has a living room, dining nook, bedroom with queen size bed, walk-in closet and old fashioned deep tub. Two cottages have the classic Murphy bed for a third guest. Fireplaces take the chill off, on misty seaside mornings and TVs with VCRs are provided along with a tape of the movie *Swing Shift*, starring Goldie Hawn, since The Grand Cottages were a part of the movie.

Smart travelers planning on using the San Pedro Port facilities check into The Grand Cottages the evening before they sail. They dine at The Grand House Restaurant and then retire to one of the comfortable cottages for a good night's sleep before leisurely boarding the next day. The close proximity to the cruise ships and the new Los Angeles Cruise Ship Terminal are among the many San Pedro coastline attractions accessible from this bed and breakfast.

The Grand Cottages offer a quiet, restful place close to all the color and history of Old San Pedro and surrounding environs.

RESTAURANTS

THE GRAND HOUSE
809 South Grand
San Pedro, CA 90731
Tel. (213) 548-1240

Hrs:	Lunch	Tue. - Fri.	11:30 a.m. - 2:30 p.m.
	Afternoon Cafe´	Tue. - Fri.	2:30 p.m. - 5:00 p.m.
	Dinner	Tue. - Sun.	6:00 p.m. - 9:30 p.m.
	Brunch	Sunday	11:00 a.m. - 2:00 p.m.

Visa, MasterCard, AMEX and Diners Club are accepted.

The Grand House on Grand Avenue is a grand dining experience. Marylyn Ginsburg took on a challenge seven years ago and renovated an old San Pedro family home into a restaurant and folk art shop. Her effort paid off. The Grand House is an award winning restaurant with a staff of award winning people.

Marylyn's approach to her customers and staff is the key to the Grand House's success. Working closely with the local community, Marylyn has garnered awards for her community work. She has motivated her highly talented staff into great culinary achievements. The Grand House cooking staff keeps its ever-changing menu alive with imagination, with the seasons determining the ingredients of the menu dishes. Dinner fare may run from game venison flown in fresh from New Zealand to Grilled Shark with basil-mint aioli and a changing choice of two special soups. Surprise desserts such as rosehips ice cream and the ever popular chocolate Amaretto macadamia nut whipped cream torte keep diners delighted.

The walls of The Grand House are sprinkled with original artwork which changes every two months. Upstairs in The Grand House, Marylyn has created a tiny and intriguing folk art shop full of objects she has gathered through her travels and the help of her many artist friends. In addition, Marylyn purchased property next to the restaurant which she has recently restored into three cozy bed and breakfast cottages. Travelers can now have a leisurely gourmet dinner and then relax with a comfortable night's sleep and be ready for an unhurried business meeting or tour the next day. The Grand House, and all that goes with it, is a grand adventure well worth the trip to San Pedro.

NIZETICH'S
1050 Nagoya Street, Berth 80
San Pedro, CA 90731
Tel. (213) 514-3878
        (213) 831-2347 (banquets)
Hrs: Lunch
         Monday, Wed. - Thu. 11:30 a.m. to 2 :00 p.m.
         Dinner
         Monday, Wed. - Sun. 5:30 p.m. - 9:00 p.m.
         Open Tuesdays in December
Visa, MasterCard and AMEX are accepted.

It's said that "to share one's table is to share one's wealth." That's the philosophy behind Nizetich's, a family run restaurant that offers the best of European cuisine in a setting that's elegant and friendly. The lovely restaurant reminds the diner of a beautiful Mediterranean villa and offers the same kind of ambiance. Two of the family members, both interior decorators, created a seating arrangement that offers a gorgeous waterfront view from any one of the restaurant's tables. Fresh flowers adorn every table, and the colors complement the warm tones in each of the dining rooms, including the outside dining area. The color scheme combined with the family artifacts and paintings that are interspersed around the dining areas give the diner a classic but comfortable feeling in which to dine.

The chefs prepare items from a simple and definitely European menu. Appetizers include an antipasto platter, which features salami, provolone, prosciutto, roasted red peppers, and a variety of other treats. Salads include Nizetich's Salad, which is made of beefsteak tomato, Maui onion, avocado, anchovies and vinaigrette. Entrees range from Papa's Beef Stew to a buttery Calamari Meuniere. Mrs. N's Fried Shrimp is an excellent fish selection. It is pan friend shrimp served with french fries. The dessert menu offers Josetta's Banana Cake with ice cream sauce, among several other delicious items. A specialty of Nizetich's are their banquets which are catered from a large set menu.

While you taste the wonderful menu selections, enjoy the quiet dinner music. Later on, livelier music is featured. Watch the goings on in the harbor as you sip that last drop of coffee with a loved one, or a stranger with whom you've shared the wealth of Nizetich's.

OLSEN'S RESTAURANT
589 West 9th Street
San Pedro, CA 90731
Tel. (213) 832-7437
Hrs: Lunch   Mon. - Sat.   11:30 a.m. - 2:30 p.m.
        Dinner   Mon. - Sat.   5:00 p.m. - 10:30 p.m
                          Sunday   4:00 p.m. - 10:00 p.m.
Visa, MasterCard and AMEX are accepted.

Olsen's Restaurant has a dining tradition that extends fifty years. Patrons have found dining here as comfortable and relaxing. The dining salon is appointed in aquatic motifs and includes two six foot high fish aquariums, one round and one triangular. Hurricane lamps on each table add a sparkling effect to a delightful repast.

Many of the recipes remain as they were originally featured in 1938. Over fifty different entrees are included on the menu; thirty-two of them are seafood selections. Patrons flock from miles around to sample the steamed Finnan-Haddie with chopped hard boiled egg and parsley butter. Among the catches of the day are Pacific Swordfish, Lobster Thermidor, Crab Newburg and Curried Shrimp. Beef selections include prime rib of beef, several varieties of steaks and Chateaubriand. Other favorites are jointed fried chicken, Southern style, served with real mashed potatoes and country gravy, pork chops, lamb chops, veal cutlet and Veal Oscar. The restaurant features a wine machine that allows it to serve wine by the glass. The wine list includes twelve California whites, eight reds, two imports and select champagnes.

Olsen's Restaurant has become the favorite eatery for residents of San Pedro and the Palos Verdes Peninsula and has been a constant recipient of the Southern California Restaurant Writer's Association's Dining Award. Many patrons have frequented the restaurant for years and have become like family. Come and join in the fun.

PAPADAKAS TAVERNA
301 West 6th Street
San Pedro, CA 90731
Tel. (213) 548-1186
Hrs: Lunch   Fridays   11:30 a.m. - 2:00 p.m.
      Dinner   Mon. - Sun.   from 5:00 p.m.
Visa and MasterCard are accepted.

A zest for living marks the Greek outlook on life and you can get a taste of that energy at Papadakas Taverna in San Pedro. Greek restaurants are filled with light, which is expressed through the restaurant's delicious food and spirited service.

Owner John Papadakis shows love for his customers by offering a traditional warm word and kiss. A devotee of Greek heritage, he was inspired by a trip to his ancestral homeland when he was twenty-three to create the Papadakas Taverna. In the beginning, John did all the cooking while his wife Donna prepared the appetizers. Today, the restaurant is world renowned for its authentic Greek cuisine and no nonsense atmosphere. It is divided into large rooms separated by a long chrome railing and the tables are covered with blue and white tablecloths. Greek pillars support statues, while one wall has photographs of John's family. Appetizers include Keftethes, lamb meatballs, and Dolmathes, stuffed grape leaves. The dinner menu features Arni Frikase, a filet of lamb braised with artichoke and avgolemono, and Moushari Sti Skara, white veal loin chop charbroiled. Don't be surprised if the waiters grasp arm to shoulder and break out into a Greek dance. Joyful Greek music fills the air, as well as the luscious fragrance or rosemary, garlic, and roasting meat dripping with juices.

The staff spends much time giving travel directions to this certain "Best Choice," because people from all over the world eat there. Papadakis Taverna is truly blessed by its people and its fare, and as John's uncle would say, "God Bless America!"

SANTA CATALINA ISLAND

Twenty-two miles off the shore of Southern California is the glittering island of Santa Catalina, where a host of island adventures await visitors who cruise or fly to its shores.

Part of Santa Catalina Island's charm is its quaint resort town, Avalon, but the island's rugged backcountry nature preserves also make it a special place to visit. The city of Avalon is nestled in the steep hills of Avalon Canyon, named after the mythical island valley in Camelot. The resort town is known for its old fashioned country atmosphere, and for pleasant weather, sport fishing and access to great fishing, boating and diving. The island's most famous landmark is the old circular casino. Constructed in 1929, the building now houses a museum.

Among the host of outdoor activities to enjoy are cruises around the island's fifty-four miles of shoreline that pass rock swhere a chorus of seals sometimes serenades passing cruise boats with vigorous barking. You can stay dry and discover the undersea life of the California State Marine Preserve by taking one of the glass bottom boat trips offered in summer. Tours of the nearly seventy miles of mountain interior can also be arranged.

Animals most commonly seen on the island are the introduced species of goats, deer, pigs and bison that have the run of the interior. The bison are the descendents of a herd brought to the island in 1924 for the filming of a western movie. Native wildlife include the Catalina quail, bald eagles and the elusive Channel Island fox. The local waters support bass, opaleye and garibaldi. Pilot whales and porpoises can sometimes been seen offshore.

The island's pleasant marine climate has been enjoyed by human beings for at least 4,000 years, according to the archeological record that includes the remains of villages. Cabrillo landed on Santa Catalina in 1542, naming the island San Salvador. In the early 1800s

Russian and Aleut fur traders came from Alaska to hunt the abundant sea otters. In the late 1800s Catalina served as a lay over for smuggled Chinese laborers, and was later used as a base for Prohibition era smugglers.

The island's potential as a resort was well understood by George Shatto, who purchased the island in 1867 to develop Avalon as a tourist community. He rented tent spaces around Avalon to vacationers, but set aside the remaining land for cattle and sheep ranching. In the 1890s another company took over ownership to develop the island as a pleasure resort. It was William J. Wrigley, Jr., of chewing gum fame, who purchased the island in 1919 with the intention of preserving the island's unique natural resources. Today most of the land is under the stewardship of the non-profit Santa Catalina Island Conservancy.

To find your way to Catalina Island you may fly from either Los Angeles International Airport, Long Beach Municipal Airport or from the heliport on Harbor Scenic Drive near the Queen Mary. You may also arrive by sea from the Catalina Air Sea Terminal in San Pedro, across Harbor Boulevard, the Catalina Terminal off the Golden Shore Terminal in Long Beach or the Newport Boat Terminal at the Balboa Pavilion in Balboa.

For further information on the Santa Catalina Island, call the **Santa Catalina Island Conservancy, (213) 510-1421.**

ATTRACTIONS

• **Avalon** is Santa Catalina Island's only city. Incorporated in 1914 it has a year round population of 1,030 which grows to more than 10,000 in the summer months, as well as attracting many thousands of tourists each year.

• **Little Fishermans Cove at Two Harbors** offers seaside camping, tables, showers, fresh water, camp and snorkle gear rental, a restaurant and saloon. Year round public transportaion is available. For reservations call (213) 510-0303.

•   **Catalina Passenger Service** provides transportation to and from Catalina Island. It departs from Balboa Pavilion in Orange County. For more information call (714) 673-5245.

ACCOMMODATIONS

ATWATER HOTEL, 125 Sumner, Avalon, CA. Tel. (213) 510-1788. This economically priced hotel welcomes families and is only a half block away from the beach.

HOTEL VILLA PORTOFINO, 111 Crescent Avenue, PO Box 127, Avalon, CA. Tel. (213) 510-0555. This charming hotel and ristorante is located on the ocean front. Hotel Villa Portofino offers first class European style accommodations that are especially attractive for vacationers and honeymooners.

APPAREL

BUOYS & GULLS, 407 Crescent Avenue, Avalon, CA. Tel. (213) 510-0416. This men's store features quality resort and beach attire. Buoys & Gulls is open seven days a week, year round.

THE WHALE'S TALE, 233 Sumner, Avalon, CA. Tel. (213) 510-1097. This shop features exclusive dresses, casual wear, swimwear, shoes and accessories.

DIVING SHOPS

CATALINA DIVERS SUPPLY, at Pleasure Pier, Box 126, Catalina, CA. Tel. (213) 510-0330. This full service dive shop offers mobile dive stations at Casino Point Underwater Park and snorkeling at Scuba and Lovers Cove Submarine Gardens.

GIFT SHOPS

CARLOTA'S MEXICAN SHOP, Metropole Market Place, PO Box 1218, Avalon, CA. Discover clothing, giftware and jewelry from Central America and Indonesia at Carlota's Mexican Shop.

PERICO GALLERY, Metropole Market Place, Oceanfront, Avalon, CA. Tel. (213) 510-1342. This shop offers art and gifts unique to Catalina Island.

GOLF AND TENNIS

CATALINA ISLAND GOLF AND TENNIS COURTS, #1 Country Club Drive, Avalon, CA. These public courts offer rental equipment for both golf and tennis, a nine hole golf course and a pro shop. It is located three blocks from the bay.

RESTAURANTS

CAFE PREGO, 603 Crescent, Avalon, CA. Tel. (213) 510-1218. This award winning restaurant offers seafood, steak and Italian food at reasonable prices. Cafe Prego serves cocktails and has a fine wine list. Breakfast is featured Saturdays and Sundays.

SALLY'S WAFFLE GAZEBO, Pleasure Pier, Avalon, CA. Tel. (213) 510-0355. Sally's serves incredible waffles and omelettes, as well as a variety of sandwiches and specialty burgers.

THE UPSTAIRS PLACE, 417 Crescent, PO Box 1899, Avalon, CA. Tel. (213) 510-0333. Fabulous charbroiled fish and chowder can be enjoyed while dining at The Upstairs Place overlooking the bay. This is Avalon's oldest seafood restaurant.

TORRANCE

Just south of Redondo Beach is the community established in 1911 by Jared S. Torrance, whose dream it was to design the ideal industrial and residential community. He commissioned renown landscape architect Frederick Law Olmstead to design the city as architect Irving J. Gill went to work designing many of the first buildings.

ATTRACTIONS

• **Torrance State Beach** is a sandy beach enjoyed by surfers and divers. Facilities include restrooms, parking and the twenty mile long **South Bay Bicycle Trail** that ends here. For information call (213) 372-2166.

• **Miramar Park**, located at Paseo de La Play and Calle Miramar, is a 1.5 acre grassy park and garden area overlooking Torrance County Beach.

ACCOMMODATION

TORRANCE MARRIOTT
3635 Fashion Way
Torrance, CA 90503
Tel.   (213) 316-3636
         (800) 228-9290
Visa, MasterCard, AMEX, Carte Blanche and Diners Club are accepted.

The Torrance Marriott is a sleek new seventeen story luxury hotel, located in the heart of Southern California's South Bay area; home of blue chip aerospace, automotive, high-tech industries and the world's largest enclosed shopping complex, the Del Amo Fashion Center.

This stunning hotel offers 487 guest rooms including eleven luxurious suites, two elite concierge floors and over 16,000 square feet of flexible meeting space, to suit any size or type of function. Convention and catering staff professionals are available from preparation to conclusion. Dining and entertainment needs are met with the four dining rooms and lounges. The Garden Court offers informal fare, Jasmine's is intimate, elegant dining, Cristobal's provides a sophisticated, bi-level lounge and the Lobby Bar is a cozy place for relaxing. Recreation is found in the fully equipped health club with saunas, large indoor and outdoor pool and hydrotherapy spa with sun deck and patio.

Disneyland, Knott's Berry Farm, Hollywood and The Forum,the Queen Mary and the Spruce Goose are close by. Torrance Marriott is only twenty minutes away from Los Angeles International Airport and twenty minutes away from Long Beach Airport.

KITCHEN SUPPLIES

COOKIN' STUFF
22217 Palos Verdes Boulevard
Torrance, CA 90505
Tel. (213) 371-2220
Hrs: Mon. - Sat.   10:00 a.m. - 6:00 p.m.
          Sunday   12:00 noon - 5:00 p.m.
Visa and MasterCard are accepted.

With over 20,000 items, a veritable melange of cookware, Cookin' Stuff ranks as the most completely stocked store in L.A. County. Gadget lovers will have a field day sorting through garlic presses, bean stringers, poppy seed grinders, gelato makers and eight different types of ice cream makers.

Those customers with home gardens, who enjoy processing their own food, can find water bath canners. Some of them are large enough to do your whole garden at once. Also in stock are food dehydrators, vacuum-pressure packing machines and smokers that are easily set up in the backyard and capable of smoking sausages, jerky, poultry and fish.

With over 10,000 square feet of store space, Cookin' Stuff has everything for the cook from palace premier to pushcart peddler. Fourteen years in business has given them the expertise it takes to provide a total cookware store.

RESTAURANTS

CURRY HOUSE
21215 Hawthorne Boulevard
Torrance, CA 90503
Tel. (213) 540-8980
Hrs: Lunch   Mon. - Sun. 11:30 a.m. - 2:00 p.m.
      Dinner   5:30 p.m. - 9:30 p.m.
Visa and MasterCard are accepted.

Would it surprise you that, today in Japan, curried dishes are a national favorite? It's true. A recent poll, taken in Japan, showed that ninety-five out of a hundred people love curry dishes. Japanese curry dishes are made of vegetables and meat and served over cooked rice. For authentic Japanese food, including Japanese curry dishes, plan to visit the Curry House.

Their chef has been a continental chef in Japan for ten years. He serves a wide variety of dishes from tofu hamburgers to Japanese spaghetti and an array of curry dinners. You will find the oriental version of spaghetti refreshingly unusual. The Curry House has meal options for both the meat eater and the vegetarian. The Curry House also has a bar. Happy hour is from 5:30 p.m. - 7:00 p.m. Monday through Friday. In addition to the regular bar drinks you can enjoy Japanese beer and Saki here as well. The restaurant can provide private banquet facilities for large groups.

Located in the Village Del Amo Shopping Plaza, Curry House is easy to find. For a cuisine that is a unique, but oh so good, treat yourself to a meal at the Curry House.

RESTAURANT MARENGO
24594 Hawthorne Boulevard
Torrance, CA 90505
Tel. (213) 378-1174
Hrs: Lunch   Mon. - Fri.   11:30 a.m. - 2:00 p.m.
      Dinner   Mon. - Sat.   6:00 p.m. - 10:00 p.m.
                   Sunday   5:00 p.m. - 9:00 p.m.
Visa, MasterCard and AMEX are accepted.

If you are a romantic at heart, love quaint restaurants with secluded tables, real tableclothes, soft lights, gallant waiters, strains of soft music in the background and continental cuisine at very reasonable prices, then head for the Restaurant Marengo.

Amid a distinctive Napoleonic setting, the Restaurant Marengo is probably the South Bay's most romantic restaurant. It is a consistent winner of the South Bay First Plate Award and has been rated three stars by the Los Angeles Restaurant Writers Association. Restaurant Marengo offers French cuisine with a continental flare. You can choose from delicacies such as Escargots Bourgignon or Fresh Mussels Poulette or soup, salad or crepes made to perfection. They offer five to six entree specials each evening in addition to the basic menu. Desserts includes exquisite souffles of different flavors and after dinner coffees of Irish, French, Swiss, Italian or Napoleonic accent.

If you enjoy romantic meals, reminiscing about old flames and old friends, and if you love elegant French cuisine, then don't miss Restaurant Marengo.

SAN FERNANDO VALLEY

In spite of movie studios and television production companies, it took the emergence of Valley Girls to make the San Fernando Valley famous. Most non-southern Californians had never heard of this region, generally regarded as a sprawling bedroom community. But, when Moon Unit Zappa released her hit record *Valley Girl* a few years ago, the world tuned its ears to the distinctive lingo of well heeled, middle class suburban teenage girls who shuffle through the shopping malls using words such as "vicious, tubular, and awesome," or uttering expressions of disagreement such as "bag your face." No longer would the Valley be without some kind of identity.

Any place that can produce its own linguistic derivative of the English language must have identity, even if some are uncharitable enough to think it's "grody to the max." The Valley is often the butt of jokes, giving the impression it is something of a smog filled cultural wasteland whose population spends most of their waking lives outside of the Valley. Impressions can be deceiving. True, many of San Fernando Valley's million and a half residents spend most of their time working and playing outside of the 220 square mile region, much of it on the freeways during rush hours; but, the Valley is much more than a bedroom for Los Angeles. Its commercial districts, entertainment centers, fine restaurants and cultural institutions all prove that the Valley has come into its own.

The motion picture industry is well entrenched in the San Fernando Valley. Disney, Universal, Warner Brothers and Columbia Pictures all own studios there. Celebrities such as Cybill Shepherd, Bob Hope, Dennis Weaver and Chad Everett make their homes there. As a business area, it stands as one of the area's leading business districts. In fact, there is more business employment in the Valley than in seventeen states, and jobs have been increasing faster than the population.

The leading business communities are Van Nuys, North Hollywood and Chatsworth. Van Nuys also ranks as an industrial community as well, whereas Woodland Hills, Encino and North Hollywood serve as the leading financial centers of the region. Although many of the communities are technically districts of the City of Los Angeles, the region could easily stand on its own. If the Valley were a single city, it would be the sixth largest city in the nation, just behind Houston but ahead of Detroit.

The San Fernando Valley, located just beyond the Santa Monica Mountains, was once a major agricultural area. In not much more than a single generation, orange groves have given way to sprawling housing tracts and shopping malls.

Except during rush hours, the freeways put most valley residents within easy reach of Los Angeles, as well as the recreational opportunities of the Santa Monica Mountains. To get a feel for the region, drive the twenty-two mile canyon along Mulholland Drive, which winds between the Los Angeles Basin and the San Fernando Valley, with spectacular views of the communities below. Many of the turnouts have served as park and smooch spots for generations of adolescent couples.

Below, on the seventeen mile stretch of Ventura Boulevard that travels from Studio City to Woodland Hills, an impressive array of clothing and novelty shops, including one that specializes in art deco objects and a book store that features murder mystery paraphernalia await the intrepid visitor to San Fernando Valley.

ATTRACTIONS

• The **Andres Pico Adobe** is one of the oldest homes in the Los Angeles area. Mission San Fernando Indians built the the adobe around 1834; it is completely restored and furnished in the style of the area. The surrounding twenty acres of parkland are pleasant to stroll through. The adobe, open on weekends, is located at 10940 Sepulveda Boulevard in Mission Hills.

• **Mission San Fernando Rey de Espana** was founded in 1719 and is open for self guided tours of the church and its workshops, resident quarters, wine vats and gardens. Take the Golden State Freeway to San Fernando Mission Boulevard. The mission is located at 15151 San Fernando Mission Boulevard in Mission Hills and is open daily.

BURBANK

Anyone who remembers the old *Laugh-In* television show, or seen the re-runs on cable TV could not forget the frequent, if insincere, references to "Beautiful Downtown Burbank." To set the record straight, Burbank is not the antithesis of "beautiful." It has its charms, but it's only fair to point out that "beautiful" is something of an exaggeration.

Nevertheless Burbank has much to offer visitors. This is one of the world's most important entertainment centers. More recording studios, movie and television production facilities are located in Burbank than anywhere else. You can take a tour of of the Burbank Studios, visit the Warner Brothers and Columbia film lots and even sit in on a session of the Tonight Show, sometimes hosted by Johnny Carson himself.

In addition to being a center for television and film production, Burbank has an unusually high concentration of aviation and aerospace firms. Lockheed builds the Navy's primary long range anti submarine patrol plane here, and at a high security "off limits" facility the corporation assembles a sophisticated tactical reconnaissance aircraft here. Other aviation firms include Menesco Inc., which build aircraft landing gear and Webber Aircraft, which specializes in airplane interiors.

Burbank, located along Interstate Five between Sun Valley and Glendale, was first laid out in 1887 on the Provedencia Rancho. Many of its downtown streets are aligned with the boundaries of the former Spanish land grant ranch. The city name comes from Dr. David Burbank, a dentist who was one of the community's subdividers.

ATTRACTIONS

- The **NBC Television Studio Tour**, located at 300 West Alameda Street, Burbank, takes you backstage and through the huge broadcasting complex. Visitors see everything, from the makeup department to displays of special effects. The tour takes about and hour.

CLUB

LOS ANGELES EQUESTRIAN CENTER
480 Riverside Drive
Burbank, CA 91506
Tel. (818) 840-9063
Hrs: Mon. - Sun.   7:00 a.m. - 10:00 p.m.
Visa, MasterCard and AMEX are accepted.

The Los Angles Equestrian and Polo Center is recognized as the finest equestrian and indoor arena polo facility in the United States. The Center provides a first hand glimpse into the famous Southern California lifestyle.

If you are a star watcher, you will enjoy knowing many Hollywood celebrities board their horses at the Center, attend the riding and polo school and play on the celebrity polo teams. The

Center is also home for some US Olympic Equestrian Events and the Professional Polo Association and the American Polo League. The Center provides riding trails within Griffith Park, the largest park within a city in the world. You can rent horses at the Center. These ponies are trail horses so they know their way around and you won't get lost. The finest in polo classes are offered at the Center. The school has a special offer for those who visit Los Angeles for a week or more: You can have an introduction to polo, five lessons with horse and polo equipment including helmet, mallets and riding boots.

Major horse shows and polo games take place throughout the year and many of the events are free. Call the Center for schedules. Visit the Dominion Saddlery shops where you can purchase everything equestrian and polo for the rider, the player, the horse and yourself. The Los Angeles Equestrian and Polo Center is conveniently located in Burbank with easy access to the Ventura Freeway and Golden State Freeway. The Center is housed on seventy-five lush green acres in the middle of Griffith Park.

GOURMET FOOD

THE PICCADILLY SHOP
2011 West Burbank Boulevard
Burbank, CA 91506
Tel. (818) 842-2324
Hrs: Monday   10:00 a.m. - 5:00 p.m.
         Tue. - Sat.   10:00 a.m. - 8:00 p.m.
         Sunday   12:00 noon - 8:00 p.m.
Visa and MasterCard are accepted.

Bangers, Roly Poly, tea cakes, pickled onions and mustard pickle will warm the cockles of any Britisher's heart and peak the delight of a Yankee too! Situated in the heart of movie land The Piccadilly Shop is a British shopping experience.

All types of English and Scottish foodstuffs can be purchased or phone ordered from this charming market. Holiday Christmas cakes, plum puddings, Scottish shortbread, jams, marmalades, crackers, candies and cookies jam the shop's shelves. Fresh foods include Scottish meat pies, Cornish pastries, scones and tea cakes. The freezer holds delectables such as English style gammon steaks, jam

Roly Poly, kippers and haddock. Good ceramic teapots can be found here (don't forget to rinse the pot out with boiling water each time you brew a pot of tea!). Tables and chairs are provided for customers to sit and browse through their favorite English newspaper.

The Piccadilly Shop is warm, homey store where shoppers can enjoy browsing for delicious edibles from Britain.

RESTAURANT

THE RIDING AND POLO CLUB RESTAURANT
480 Riverside Drive
Burbank, CA 91506
Tel. (818) 841-5981
Hrs: Lunch   Mon. - Sat.   11:00 a.m. - 3:00 p.m.
       Dinner   Tue. - Sat.   5:00 p.m. - 10:00 p.m.
       Country Breakfast Buffet
                      Saturday   7:00 a.m. - 11:00 a.m.
       Champagne Brunch
                      Sunday   10:30 a.m. - 3:00 p.m.
Visa, MasterCard and AMEX are accepted.

Though the Riding and Polo Club Restaurant is a public eating house, you have the feeling that you've been invited to a private, special club. People come dressed in riding clothes, jeans or suits which lend a casual air to the restaurant. The Riding and Polo Club Restaurant specializes in early California classic cuisine.

The lunch menu sports sandwiches with "equine" names such as The Open Range, a turkey sandwich, or The Longhorn, a patty melt with Swiss cheese and onions grilled on rye or The Filly, a tuna salad sandwich. At dinner choose from such dishes as Scallops Monterey, shrimp with a special garlic salsa, Calamari Monterey Style and Bouillabaisse California. Saturday morning Country Style Breakfasts feature a hearty selection of regional down home favorites. Sunday Champagne Brunch offers a spectacular array of fresh salads, seafood, roasted and carved meats, eggs, crepes and Belgian waffles cooked to order, as well as a complete selection of desserts. The wine list is extensive and has an excellent selection of California wines.

The Riding and Polo Club Restaurant provides catering at the The Los Angeles Equestrian Center. The Center provides beautiful rustic, outdoor settings for weddings, company picnics, anniversaries and all other special occasions. The polo season runs from April to December and during the Saturday evenings matches The Riding and Polo Club offers a pre-game buffet and during the game buffet.

ENCINO

Although a major residential community, the number of banks and other financial institutions make Encino a leading financial center for the Valley. The name Encino is from the Spanish word for a species of oak trees. In 1769, the Spanish explorer Portola jotted a note on a large oak tree that remains standing at the corner of Louise Avenue and Ventura Boulevard. The 1,000 year old tree has an eight foot thick trunk that supports branches spreading some 150 feet.

Another distinction of this community is that its most famous resident, Michael Jackson, has made it his home. The town is also proud of their own Lori Cole, the girl next door who has won six ladies arm wrestling world championships since 1980.

ATTRACTION

• **Los Encinos State Historic Park**, located one block north of Ventura Boulevard, offers a peaceful five acre park containing the restored buildings of the Valley's first rancho, including the nine room adobe ranch house. The grounds with duck pond and scattered farm equipment make for an ideal picnic spot.

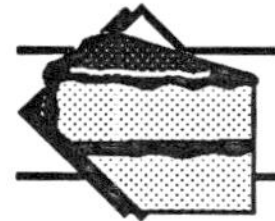

BAKERY

NICOLOSI, 17540 Ventura Boulevard, Encino, CA. Tel. (818) 784-0922. Enjoy French and Italian patisseries of distinction. Catering for all occasions is offered.

CANDY STORE

THE COCOA MAN, 17200 Ventura Boulevard, Encino, CA. Tel. (818) 788-COCO. A most unusual chocolate shop specializing in chocolate catering for all occasions.

GIFT SHOP

THE JEWISH QUARTER, 15605 Ventura Boulevard, Encino, CA. Tel. (818) 906-1133. The Jewish Quarter deals in marvelous Israeli artwork, glass, books and all kinds of gifts.

HEALTH AND FITNESS

PARADISE DANCE AND AEROBICS
16571 Ventura Boulevard
Encino, CA 91316
Tel. (818) 986-1626
Hrs: Mon. - Fri.   7:00 a.m. - 10:00 p.m.
      Saturday   7:30 a.m. - 6:00 p.m.
      Sunday   8:00 a.m. - 3:00 p.m.
Visa and MasterCard are accepted.

Opened in March of 1987, Paradise Dance and Aerobics is staffed by highly trained teachers of dance and aerobics. The professional quality of teachers and facilities creates a studio within the swing of contemporary fitness and dance.

The spacious, airy interior holds large studios as well as a child care studio. Dancewear can be purchased in the Bird of Paradise dancewear boutique. A refreshing time out can be taken at the cappuccino and fresh juice bar, and a lovely outdoor patio is available to enjoy the warm California sun. Ease sore muscles with a soothing professional massage or work on your tan in the sunbed room. You may find yourself working out alongside a star, as many well known personalities of television and screen use Paradise's facilities. The studios are also used for auditions and commercials.

Certainly any studio which is used by the famous Joffrey Ballet to train its scholarship students will offer the best there is. And that is exactly what Paradise Dance and Aerobics does.

MARKET

DOMINGO'S, 17548 Ventura Boulevard, Encino, CA. Tel. (818) 981-4466. This is an exciting market where you can shop for Italian specialties: wines, cookies, cheeses, fresh pasta, homemade sauces, individualized gift baskets and much more.

RESTAURANTS

FORTE'S
16911 Ventura Boulevard
Encino, CA 91316
Tel. (818) 990-3377
Hrs: Lunch   Mon. - Fri.   11:30 a.m. - 2:30 p.m.
          Dinner   Mon. - Thu. 5:00 p.m. - 10:00 p.m.
                      Fri. - Sat.   5:00 p.m. - 11:00 p.m.
Visa, MasterCard, AMEX, Diners Club and Carte Blanche are accepted.

For Italian continental cuisine, your "Best Choice" is Forte's. This "little bit of Italy," is easy to find; just take the Balboa exit off the Ventura Freeway, look for the cream colored stucco building with blue trim and enter a warm and inviting haven of culinary delight.

Leading the list of inspirational cuisine selections is Hot Antipasto with mozzarella and shrimp; Calamari and Scungilli Salad with a special dressing; and Stracciatella Romana, a spinach egg drop soup. Patrons with a preference for the exceptional may order Linguine Alla Lamberto with pink sauce, shrimp, cream and cognac; or Pollo Alla Picolina, prosciutto, mushrooms, garlic and white wine.

Pasta dishes are prepared fresh and the desserts include such delights as Bananas Foster and Zabaglione. All entrees as well as many desserts are finished table side with gusto and flair. An eclectic wine list features the best of vintages from California, France, Italy and Germany. Aperitifs, domestic and imported champagnes, sparkling wines and cocktails are available to complement your entree.

Live entertainment is featured nightly in the lounge featuring a four piece combo accompanying various vocalists. Popular standards and easy listening music provide for relaxing dinner pleasure or for an evening of dancing. Valet parking is provided and reservations are suggested to ensure an evening of fine dining and entertainment.

LALO AND BROTHERS
17237 Ventura Boulevard
Encino, CA 91316
Tel. (318) 784-8281
Hrs: Tue. - Fri.   12:00 noon - 3:00 p.m.
       Tue. - Sat.   6:30 p.m. - To close
Visa, MasterCard, AMEX and Diners Club are accepted.

Lalo and Brothers is one of the most elegant restaurants to be found in the valley. Its excellence is formed in part by the multi-ethnic menu, dedication to creativity and professionalism and the emphasis on originality and health awareness. The restaurant is set in the Plaza del Oro among leafy patios, flowering gardens and splashing waterfalls. Parquet floors reflect the marvelous art work hanging on the walls.

Lalo and Brothers have set the stage for creative cooking in an environment which is both serious and joyous, elegant and exuberantly fun. The "brother team" is formed by different personalities who obviously have the right chemistry to produce this outstanding restaurant concept. Beyond the quality and freshness of the food, the originality of the menu makes dining a delight. Your "first flavors" may come to you in the form of Cajun Popcorn or Crispy Blue Corn Taquitos of Chicken "Tikin Xik" with Guacamole and Tomatillo Salsa. The entrees defy description. There is Seared Salmon with Scallops and Basil Butter or Chinese Duck sauced with 101 Raisins and 2 Color Cloves. The Mesquite Grilled dishes can be addictive; consider the Cajun Prime Rib with French Fried Yams and Token Vegetables. The finale comes for dessert via Death by Chocolate.

The freshness and beauty of the surroundings, the creative menu offerings and enthusiasm place Lalo and Brothers on the leading edge of excellent Southern California eateries.

MON GRENIER
17th year at this location.
18040 Ventura Boulevard
Encino, CA 91316
Tel. (818) 344-8060
Hrs: Mon. - Sat.   6:00 p.m. - 10:00 p.m
Reservations are a must and are available from 10:00 a.m.
Visa, MasterCard and AMEX are accepted.

Mon Grenier translates to "my attic" in English. The entire restaurant resembles a plush French attic that's perfect for a romantic evening. Fresh flowers decorate tables covered with cloths the color of roses. In the center of the room, an antique Viennese chandelier creates an elegant ambiance.

The menu is also quite elegant and seduces you into sampling classic French dishes. Appetizers of Escargots au Roquefort and the Mon Grenier Petit Puff, small brioches stuffed with pureed avocado, baby shrimp, crabmeat and covered with a light champagne sauce are a tantalizing beginning to any meal. Salads include the Santa Barbara Salad with poached and chopped Santa Barbara shrimps, clams and mussels. The calamari for this dish is tossed in a light olive oil garlic dressing. Main courses include the Saumon en Croute and Loin of Venison marinated in Cabernet Sauvignon and served with Cabernet Sauvignon lingonberry sauce. Many of these items are also available through the restaurant's off-site catering service.

Desserts are made fresh daily and include five Nelly and Chrissy Lion different styles of cheesecake and several different fruit dishes. You can taste many of these items in a different setting if you choose to join Chef André Lion on one of his special gastronomic tours of Belgium and France. If you visit Los Angeles, you can visit a bit of France at Mon Grenier.

TEMPO RESTAURANT
16610 Ventura Boulevard
Encino, CA 91316
Tel. (818) 905-5855
Hrs: Sun. - Wed. 11:00 a.m. - 12:00 midnight
       Thu. - Sat.   11:00 a.m. - 1:00 a.m.
Visa, MasterCard and AMEX are accepted.

Avner and Ygal Sharoni transplanted themselves from Israel and brought with them a cuisine which represents their culture at its most flavorful. The Tempo menu offers exciting recipes of Middle Eastern and Mediterranean origin with influential Greek and Turkish touches.

The Sharonis agree that a more accurate description of their establishment would have been coffee house, cafe or even a "tiny Falafel stand." But size and cramped quarters were not to be considered when patrons discovered the delightfully exquisite cuisine served from Tempo's menu. The restaurant has grown over the years and facilities have become more spacious, the atmosphere more sophisticated. The menu is expansive and includes such mouth watering temptations as the Shwarma Special, which combines rotisserie broiled lamb and turkey with sautéed mushrooms, onions and zucchini, served either in a pita or on a bed of rice and fresh vegetables. Among the vegetarian selections offered on the menu, eggplant is a prominent staple.

Tempo now boasts a piano bar and four dining areas, including a street front patio for viewing the comings and goings along Ventura Boulevard. The menu still offers the same quality and generous portions the original group of enthusiastic patrons found so enticing. From the variety of salads, entrees or desserts, guests are sure to find dining at Tempo a venture into the sumptuously unusual.

NORTH HOLLYWOOD

If you are heading into the Los Angeles area from the north, by way of Interstate Five, an exit marked "North Hollywood" is likely to catch your eye. You might think "This where I get off to stroll down the Walk of Fame, the Sunset Strip or enjoy a soda at Schwab's Drug Store." Wrong. You're still in the San Fernando Valley and the Hollywood Hills. A couple other communities lie between North Hollywood and the "real" Hollywood.

Nevertheless, there is a concentration of television and film production operations in the immediate area. Max Sennett, producer of the Keystone Cops, had a production facility in North Hollywood, later taken over by Republic Productions which filmed many of its popular Westerns during the 1930s there.

The Academy of Television Arts and Sciences is scheduled to move into a new facility at Lankershim and Magnolia boulevards in 1989. That complex will feature production facilities, offices, a Television Hall of Fame, retail shopping outlets and a hotel.

North Hollywood is also something of a financial center for the region and was one of the first communities in the area to enjoy the benefits of urban core redevelopment efforts that began in the late 1960s and continue to this day.

ENTERTAINMENT

THE PALOMINO CLUB
697 Lankershim Boulevard
North Hollywood, CA 91605
Tel. (818) 764-4010
Hrs: Mon. - Sat.   11:00 a.m. - 2:00 a.m.
          Sunday   4:00 p.m. - 7:00 p.m.
          Live Entertainment   9:00 p.m.
Visa, MasterCard and AMEX are accepted.

When you hear the names Johnny Cash, Waylon Jennings, Marty Robbins, Jerry Lee Lewis and Linda Rondstadt, you usually associate them with Nashville's Grand Ole Opry House. But The Palomino Club has been the stomping ground to luminaries of the Country/Western entertainment scene since its birth in 1951. Named when a stunt man rode up and hitched his Palomino to a hitching post outside, The Palomino Club has become one of the premier and prominent music clubs in the United States.

No longer catering to strictly Country/Western entertainers, the club boasts a long and prestigious list of performers. A sampling of billboards include the Pretenders, Neil Young, Elton John, George Thorogood, The Pointer Sisters, Bruce Willis; and the list goes on. The club as been used as a backdrop and locale for TV movies and shows, host to fund raisers, private parties and even wedding receptions. Live entertainment is featured nightly (please call for a schedule). The Palomino Club restaurant features a hearty selection of Western Americana cuisine and includes steak sandwiches, burgers, and barbecued baby back ribs. A full bar is available to complement dinner selections and entertainment.

Experience a slice of Americana, California style. Rub shoulders with members of the entertainment industry and have the time of your life at The Palomino Club.

FURNITURE STORE

ARTE DE MEXICO
5356 Riverton Avenue
North Hollywood, CA 91601
Tel. (818) 769-5090
Hrs: Mon. - Sat.   8:30 a.m. - 5:30 p.m.
       Sunday   10:00 a.m. - 5:30 p.m.
Also open by appointment.

For years Arte De Mexico has been the special secret of a knowledgeable group of television producers, interior designers, architects, hotel and restaurant owners and certain lucky home owners. Located at the end of a quiet street in North Hollywood, this business is the leading Southwestern furniture and accessories supplier in the nation.

It all started more than twenty years ago when owner Jerry Stoffers visited Mexico. Taken by the skill and versatility of the native craftspeople, he loaded his van and returned to Los Angeles, where he sold the goods on street corners. Today it takes seven warehouses to hold his finds. It is said that a one day tour of his inventory is equivalent to several years of touring Mexico. Buying here is almost like strolling through a Mexican marketplace or bazaar. Purchases are handled by "pickers" and assembled in a holding area for later review and pricing. And what a selection from which to choose! Antique wooden doors, pottery, furniture, mirrors and lighting fixtures are among the variety of handmade items.

Years have been spent developing relationships with craftspeople, which enables Arte De Mexico to obtain the best pieces being produced. It also allows them to offer custom design and crafting of a wide variety of items. In many ways, this incredible assembly is a museum of ancient and modern crafts where the creativity and spirit of a whole culture is laid before you. But here, unlike a museum, you can take it home with you.

GOURMET FOOD

ANN'S DUTCH IMPORTS
4357 Tujunga Avenue
North Hollywood, CA 91604
Tel. (818) 985-5551
Hrs: Tue. - Sat.   10:00 a.m. - 5:30 p.m.
          Sunday   11:00 a.m. - 3:00 p.m.
Visa, MasterCard and Bank America Card are accepted.

Ann's Dutch Imports is a large store on shady Tujunga Avenue in the heart of Studio City and North Hollywood frequented by many known and yet unknown stars. As you walk in you immediately sense the homey aura of this delightful piece of Holland set down in sunny California.

At the front of the store are tables and chairs where you can sit to enjoy a piece of delicious Dutch honey cake or Dutch cheese, liverwurst or some other delicacy. All around are stands filled with a variety of Dutch Indonesian groceries, spices, gourmet foods and imported Dutch cheeses such as Gouda, Leiden, Edam and Farmers. In the freezer are homebaked items from goulash to herrings in wine sauce. There are delicious Dutch biscuits of Verkade, creme filled mocca wafers, vanilla wafers, creme crackers and Rusks. Puddings abound; chocolate, vanilla room, almond, each more delicious than the next. Every type of licorice is available, along with fruit drops flavored mint, strawberry, cherry, blackberry and more. And, there is chocolate, chocolate, chocolate. Ann will make up gift packs and ship via UPS anywhere in the States. Especially popular are her holiday packs of almond rings, almond tarts, Stollen, marzipan, raisin bread, rolls and Spek-koek. A variety of blue Delft pottery from Holland graces a wooden stand and beckons to be purchased. A copius variety of Conimex spices and condiments from Indonesia line the walls. Last but not least are the rows of imported cookware, including casseroles, frying pans, stewpans, rice steamers and woks of all sizes.

An extensive mail order list of all items from Ann's shop is available by writing to Ann at the above address. You will long remember sitting down in Ann's little bit of Amsterdam and sipping aromatic coffee in between nibbling slices of mouthwatering Dutch honey cake.

RESTAURANTS

LE PETIT CHATEAU
4615 Lankershim Boulevard
North Hollywood, CA 91602
Tel. (818) 769-1812
Hrs: Mon. - Fri.   11:30 a.m. - 10:30 p.m.
          Saturday   4:30 p.m. - 11:00 p.m.
Visa, MasterCard, AMEX and Diners Club are accepted.

Le Petit Chateau is a landmark restaurant in the heart of Hollywood. A French country restaurant, Le Petit Chateau is much frequented by producers, directors and movie stars.

Styled in the classic French Chateau manner, Le Petit Chateau is noted for its two graceful spires, a unique design in Hollywood. Dark wooden beams and walls highlighted with brass and French blue and white pottery invite the diner to intimate seating. A vintage French menu ranges from sandwiches for lunch to Broiled Petit Filet Mignon for dinner and everything in between. Les Salades include Salade Neptune and Salade de Poulet Petit Chateau with chicken, mushrooms,tomatoes and hearts of palm, all lightly tossed with Le Petit Chateau's house Caesar dressing. Classic Caramel Custard and Le Cafe d'Amour with brandy complete a Le Petit French country meal.

The professional, courteous staff is proud to serve you excellent French country cuisine. Le Petit Chateau can accommodate parties of up to fifty people. Dine with the stars at Le Petit Chateau.

MAISON GERARD
4100 Cahuenga Boulevard
North Hollywood, CA 91602
Tel. (818) 766-3841
Hrs: Mon. - Fri   11:00 a.m. - 11:00 p.m.
          Saturday   5:00 p.m. - 12:00 midnight
Visa, MasterCard, AMEX, Diners Club and Carte Blanche are
accepted.

Take a trip to the French countryside and enjoy a sublime
dining experience at Maison Gerard. Maison Gerard features an
eclectic selection of provincial French cuisine reminiscent of the inns
of Alsace, Provence and Bourgogne. Peg and groove wooden plank
floors, antique settees, mirrors and antique lamps create an ambiance
of sophistication and elegance. A flow through fireplace in the main
dining salon adds warmth and intimacy to your dining experience, all
at reasonable prices.
      Culinary creations will delight connoisseurs of gourmet cuisine.
Of notable mention is the petite onion soup au gratin; prepared from
an original recipe with only the freshest of ingredients. Specialties of
the house include Rognons Au Madere; veal kidneys cooked in port
wine with mushroom. Cassoulet Toulousain, large white beans, lamb,
port sausage and ham with melted cheese in a casserole is another
favorite. Other culinary inspirations include Brochettte of Scallops,
and Chateaubriand. Entree selections include a myriad choice of
country style specialties, seafood, fowl meats, sandwiches, pastas, and
omelettes n' eggs. A fine selection of wine and a full bar is available to
complement your dinner. Exotic coffees such as Cafe Gerard, Cafe
Royal, Cappuccino and Irish coffee are a perfect finale to a perfect
feast.
      Oscar Wilde once said, "I have very simple taste, I am satisfied
with only the best." He would have been absolutely delighted with
Maison Gerard. Conveniently located near Universal Studios,
Hollywood Bowl, Universal Amphitheater and the Pangages Theater,
Maison Gerard is a "Best Choice" in fine dining in the Los Angeles
area.

SALOMI INDIAN & BANGLADESH RESTAURANT
5225 Lankershim Boulevard
North Hollywood, CA 91602
Tel. (818) 506-0130
Hrs: Mon. - Thu.   12:00 noon - 2:30 p.m.
                         5:00 p.m. - 10:00 p.m.
      Friday   12:00 noon - 2:30 p.m.
                         5:00 p.m. - 11:00 p.m.
      Saturday   5:00 p.m. - 11:00 p.m.
      Sunday   5:00 p.m. - 10:00 p.m.
Visa, MasterCard and AMEX are accepted.

It's authentic, delicious, ethnic Indian cuisine served in a recreation of elegant India. Plush red carpets, richly flocked wallpaper, ornately carved arches and multi-colored crystal chandeliers over the large dining room softly resonate with traditional Eastern music.

In this exotic setting, you'll find Tandoori Bread, Lamb Tikka, Shikh Kabab, and a wide assortment of beef or lamb, and egg and vegetable curries. The fish curries are exquisite and if you like yours on the spicy side, ask about the Shrimp Vindaloo. There are always great compliments about their Persian Chicken Biryani and, as with all other complete dinners, it comes with a choice of any curry, chicken, lamb or beef, Keema, vegetable or shrimp. The meals are served with Papadoms, Mulligatawny Soup, Pilao Rice, condiments, dessert and tea or coffee. You'll also have the chance to enjoy mangoes, Lychee, Gulab Jaman and a large selection of wine and beer. There is, as well, a full bar.

So whether you're trying to recapture your own Bombay, New Delhi or Bay of Bengal heritage, or simply shopping around for the new, unusual and sublime, it's the Salomi Indian & Bangladesh Restaurant, authentic Eastern dining in traditional elegance. Take out is always available.

NORTHRIDGE

Located just north of Van Nuys and east of Encino, Northridge was the first community surveyed in a series of developments in the San Fernando Valley that began in 1910. Back then, the newly completed Owens Valley water project had just made it possible for large numbers of people to live in the region. Northridge enjoys the academic stimulation of nearby California State University at Northridge.

PARTY SUPPLIES

PARTY WORLD, SOUTHERN CALIFORNIA
8754 Yolanda
Northridge, CA 91324
Tel. (818) 993-7717
Hrs: Mon. - Fri.   9:30 a.m. - 5:30 p.m.
        Sunday   12:00 noon - 5:00 p.m.
Visa and MasterCard are accepted.

Party World specializes in mass merchandising of party goods at discount prices. Everything you could possible think of and many things that you may not have thought of are available at Party World.

Party World is a one stop party goods shopping center which sells at the lowest possible prices. You can purchase every thing from a two cent party favor to an assortment of piñatas, party accessories, helium filled mylar balloons, Vltron favors, classic Mickey Mouse and the Sesame Street images. Selections of all items are vast and merchandise supply seems endless. Plates and napkins come in twenty solid colors, twenty-six birthday patterns, twenty-nine general patterns, eight wedding designs, six baby shower motifs and five bridal shower selections! Anything which goes on top of a party table is available in a multitude of designs and selections. Bulk gift wrapping is sold by the running foot and dispensed "on your honor" from self-serve rolls. Gift boxes are especially delightful. Boxes come with Panda bears climbing up the sides, or in the shape of Victorian buildings or fashioned into little trains and engines.

Party World does custom invitations for weddings, Bar Mitzvahs, birthdays, or any special event. Party World has ten locations in the Los Angeles area and is considering franchising in the near future. Party World will challenge any price in the city and will either meet or go lower than any other discount store in the Los Angeles area. For one stop shopping at the lowest discount prices, Party World is the best.

RESTAURANT

JEREMIAH'S RESTAURANT
19229 Parthenia Street
Northridge, CA 91324
Tel. (818) 993-5990
Hrs: Lunch
      Mon. - Fri.   11:30 a.m. - 2:30 p.m.
      Dinner
      Sun. - Thu.   5:00 p.m. - 10:00 p.m.
      Fri. - Sat.   5:00 p.m. - 11:30 p.m.
      Cocktails
      Mon. - Fri.   11:30 a.m. to close
      Sat. - Sun.   4:30 p.m. to close
Visa, MasterCard and AMEX are accepted.

Jeremiah's opened in 1979 and rapidly became a popular dining spot for local residents. The warm, comfortable restaurant has many booths surrounded by plants, brass and stained glass. The multi-level design creates an intimate setting in which to enjoy terrific food. The menu will please you with its reasonable prices and extensive selection.

The lunch entrees offered include such delicacies as Lobster Quiche, Sizzling Chicken Luau, marinated strips of chicken breast with fresh vegetables and pineapple, and Prime Rib Stew, among others. A selection of delicious Prime Steak Burgers, sandwiches such as the Beefeater Grill and the Country Club Croissant as well as soups, salads and fresh pastas round out the luncheon menu.

The dinner menu offers many wonderful choices, from appetizers to desserts. You might want to begin your meal with Mozzarella Marinara or Steamers, fresh clams steamed in Chardonnay, butter and garlic. Then choose from one of the many steak, prime rib, chicken or fresh seafood dishes. There is a selection of "Lite Entrees" for the less than hearty appetite or for those who want to be sure to have room for Mud Pie, New York Cheesecake, or one of the other delicious desserts. The extensive selection and reasonable prices, combined with the comfortable atmosphere and excellent service make Jeremiah's a dining experience everyone will enjoy.

SHERMAN OAKS

Sherman Oaks is a suburban community situated on US 101 between Encino and Glendale. The Sherman Oaks Galleria on Ventura Boulevard contains more than 120 specialty shops and is a favorite haunt of Valley Girls. The community's name comes from General M.H. Sherman, who liked oak trees and was responsible for bringing the railroad there.

APPAREL

BOYS WILL BE BOYS
14962 Ventura Boulevard
Sherman Oaks, CA 91403
Tel. (818) 986-2697
Hrs: Mon. - Fri.   10:00 a.m. - 8:00 p.m.
        Saturday   10:00 a.m. - 6:00 p.m.
        Sunday   11:00 a.m. - 5:00 p.m.
Visa, MasterCard, and AMEX are accepted.
Also,
2230 Glendale Galleria   2530 San Bicente Boulevard
Glendale, CA 91210   Santa Monica, CA 90402
Tel. (818) 409-0931   Tel. (213) 451-9423

Sandy Latt, owner of three locations of Boys Will Be Boys clothing stores, is the answer to mother's prayers regarding vast selections of quality boy's apparel in stores designed to appeal to both mother and son. Sandy knows, from past experiences trying to outfit her own three sons, how difficult it is to find just the right thing in just the right size that will meet a mother's standards in quality and care requirements, and also please the boy's sense of personal taste and his desire to get the shopping done with as little discomfort and as much haste as possible.

Boys' clothing, in most stores, has traditionally taken a back corner next to the men's department and has too often been understocked, outdated and overpriced. Boys Will Be Boys caters specifically to boys between the ages of three and fifteen. Sandy supplies most of the boy's clothing for network television shows, and carries complete lines of boy's wear, from active sportswear to school clothes to suits. A tailor is available for free alterations, as is an on-site barber to complete the personal head to toe service. Phone orders are accepted and Sandy will ship her merchandise wherever you like. Her stores have a high-tech decorating scheme that is clean, smooth and upbeat.

Originally a small operation based out of a garage, her ideas and sensibly priced quality clothing have garnered her so much success she has three locations, with others coming in the future. Treat yourself and that special boy of yours to a store where he knows he comes first, Boys Will Be Boys.

DAVID AND ROD'S DESIGNER FASHIONS FOR LESS
14082 Ventura Boulevard
Sherman Oaks, CA 91423
Tel. (818) 784-9319
Hrs: Mon. - Thu., Sat.   10:00 a.m. - 6:00 p.m.
          Friday   10:00 a.m. - 7:00 p.m.
Visa, MasterCard, AMEX and Diners Club are accepted.

Cheap chic seems an appropriate term when describing David and Rod's Designer Fashions. High fashion items are offered at savings of fifty to seventy percent. Add to this an energetic and friendly staff and you have a shopping experience both economical and comfortable.

In order to ride the fashion wave, any store must constantly turn its inventory over. One of the best ways to maintain the necessary turnover is to offer quality fashions at an affordable price. At David and Rod's trend setting names can be found at a price everyone can afford. The interior of the boutique is divided into three sections, a sportswear, special occasion section and a sample sale room. Each section features a completely different line of quality fashions with one common denominator, low prices. Dresses, suits, handbags, jewelry and other accessories are all one of a kind.

It is possible to look stunning and "never pay retail prices again." It is also possible to treat yourself and your pocketbook at the same time. The secret of finding a bargain is knowing where to look, let David and Rod's Designer Fashions for Less prove it to you.

EUROPEAN KIDS
13604 Ventura Boulevard
Sherman Oaks, CA 91423
Tel. (818) 907-9449
Hrs: Mon. - Sat.   10:00 a.m. - 6:00 p.m.
All major credit cards are accepted.

Looking for an unusual baby gift? European Kids has a splendid selection of quality clothing and accessories that any mother would treasure.

When Janice Quals became a mother, she realized how difficult it was to find distinctive and unusual clothing for her children. Everything seemed the same. That's when she became interested in children's clothing from Europe. At first it was just a hobby, and a challenge. She received many compliments on the way her children were dressed. She told her friends and acquaintances that it wasn't just the way the clothes looked (great), but the quality of the clothing that attracted her. Eventually she decided to open a store and that's how European Kids got its start.

The store is set up perfectly for the busy mother. There is a playpen full of toys to keep kids occupied while Mom shops. The decor is bright and cheerful. The staff is knowledgeable and courteous.

European Kids is gaining a reputation for stocking the finest in European fashions for children and adolescents. There are many lines of finely crafted clothing in sizes ranging from newborn to fourteen. The most popular clothing at European Kids is the Scalabre line from France. And Elefanten shoes from Germany are always in demand. Need your purchase gift wrapped? European Kids has a fabulous gift wrap service. You won't soon forget the caring and knowledgeable service from European Kids.

JEAN'S STARS' APPAREL
15136 Ventura Boulevard
Sherman Oaks, CA 91403
Tel. (818) 789-3710
Hrs: Tue. - Sat.   10:00 a.m. - 6:00 p.m.
Visa, MasterCard and AMEX are accepted.

Your dreams of owning an expensive, glamorous wardrobe come true at Jean's Stars' Apparel, a resale clothing shop where elegance meets affordability. Women often leave the boutique with thousands of dollars worth of designer clothing, without spending thousands of dollars.

Opened in 1958, Jean's Stars' Apparel is the oldest resale clothing shop in Los Angeles. Specializing in such designers as Adolfo, Saint Laurent, Anne Klein, Missoni and hosts of other top fashion names, the landmark boutique has become well-known in the celebrity and fashion world as a place to both buy and sell clothing. Women fly from all over the country to buy clothes from Jean's, but such extravagance is warranted when an $8,000 Galanos evening dress sells for $450 and a pair of $300 shoes can be priced as low as $2.50. The merchandise at Jean's is not only of the highest quality, it is in the latest styles as well. There have been instances when women shopping at Jean's have recognized clothing they bought the day before at major boutiques and department stores. Suits and dresses bought in Europe periodically wind up at Jean's before the rest of the line has reached the United States. Much of the designer clothing at Jean's has never been worn. In fact, some garments at Jean's still have hang tags from designer fashion shows where they were originally purchased.

Amidst the racks of glamorous apparel prevails a warm, cozy atmosphere, created by the charming owner, Janet Snyder, and her mother, Jean, who founded the shop. The two offer tea and cookies to their customers, many with whom they have developed a personal relationship over the years. Although the shop has an established celebrity clientele, Jean's attracts women from all backgrounds as it offers clothing for all occasions, including formal, professional and casual. Offering exclusive attire at accessible prices, Jean's Stars' Apparel caters to every woman's whims and fantasies.

RICK PALLACK
4554 Sherman Oaks Avenue
Sherman Oaks, CA 91403
Tel. (818) 789-7000
Hrs: Mon. - Fri.   10:00 a.m. - 8:00 p.m.
      Saturday   10:00 a.m. - 6:00 p.m.
      Sunday   11:00 a.m. - 6:00 p.m.
Visa, MasterCard and AMEX are accepted.

At Rick Pallack in Sherman Oaks, fashion conscious men will find the finest store that offers the largest selection of fine men's wear in Los Angeles and also features complete wardrobe coordination. Celebrities, politicians and executives from all over the world depend on Rick Pallack for all their fashion requirements. Rick Pallack screen credits are seen daily on the best dressed television shows and

The wardrobe coordinators specialize in creating a complete look in styles ranging from contemporary to high fashion to traditional. Rick Pallack features business wear, dress wear, casual and sports wear, everything from suits, sport coats, shirts, ties, sweaters, shoes and complementary accessories. The store also contains an extensive collection of evening wear. Beautiful designs are crafted in the finest quality from all over the world. Items are offered in a range of sizes from 36 short to 52 long. Rick Pallack's philosophy is that a man doesn't have to have a model's body to be well dressed. Pallack advocates appropriate styles for each individual's taste. Prices are considerably lower than in many other men's stores for comparable fine quality and styles. Rick Pallack is known for its great style, service and value.

The store displays all its top quality items in a professional, contemporary, beautiful environment. Rick Pallack wardrobers will coordinate you perfectly from head to toe.

ART GALLERIES

ORLANDO GALLERY
14553 Ventura Boulevard
Sherman Oaks, CA 91403
Tel. (818) 789-6012
Hrs: Tue. - Sat.   10:00 a.m. - 4:00 p.m.

Enter Orlando Gallery and witness the brilliance of the one artist display in the first gallery. Stroll through the second gallery, which houses the permanent African art collection, built over many years by Phil Orlando and co-owner Robert Gino. The third gallery of this warm and homey showplace displays a pageant of paintings, including the work of artists represented by the gallery and the creations of new masters.

Orlando and Gino have built an impressive repertoire of talent into this business, founded in 1958 as a contemporary fine art gallery in the Valley. The primary philosophy of the gallery is to show California's contemporary artists emerging, then mid-career and finally in the mature stage of their career. Orlando Gallery regularly features twenty-five California artists, including realist figurative painters such as Michael Lloyd and Len Poteshman, surrealistic painters, constructionists and sculptors. The gallery also features ceramicists, and many fine expressionists, impressionist figurative painters, and California landscape artists.

Of particular importance is the permanent display of western cultural artifacts from Africa. This impressive display exhibits the unique artistic skills of people from the Ivory Coast, Zaire, Mali, Cameroon and Nigeria, and includes masks, sculptures and ceremonial costumes. Orlando and Gino have been collecting African art for many years and are very knowledgeable about the culture. For a leisurely and educational browse through the world of fine art, visit Orlando Gallery on Ventura Boulevard.

VISUAL ENVIRONMENTS
14510 Ventura Boulevard
Sherman Oaks, CA 91423
Tel. (818) 905-1960
Hrs:　Mon. - Wed.　　　11:00 a.m. - 6:00 p.m.
　　　Friday　　　　　　11:00 a.m. - 11:30 p.m.
　　　Saturday　　　　　2:30 p.m. - 11:30 p.m.
Visa, MasterCard, AMEX, Discover and Visual Environments private card are accepted.

Visual Environments is a *must* for connoisseurs of fine art. Located off the Van Nuys exit on the Ventura Freeway, it is easy to find. You can't miss it, simply locate the Visual Environments sign; an abstract impressionist rendered painting by well known Los Angeles artist, Leal. Enter and find a wealth of twentieth century artistic talent.

A sampling of exhibits includes works by internationally recognized artists such as Yaacov Agam, Mersed Berber, Bruno Bruni and Neil Doty. Marc Chagall, Salvador Dali, Erte, Louis Icart, Mark King, Steve Leal, Joan Miro, Patrick Nagel, Leroy Neiman, Pablo Picasso and Alberto Vargas are also among the artists featured. The gallery publishes the work of Ake Ahlberg, a Swedish contemporary artist who work, in hand drawn lithographs, original drawings and acrylics. Modern surrealist, Jose Puigmarti and internationally acclaimed children's artist, Trinidad Osoria are also featured. The gallery also carries master prints by Rembrandt, Renoir, Manet, Cezanne, Pissaro, Durer, Cassatt, and Morisot. Gallery owner Mark Sawicki enjoys sharing his encyclopedic knowledge of almost every known artist with visiting patrons and purveyors of fine art.

The ambiance is modern and cosmopolitan; definitely Californian. White walls with black exposed beamed ceiling, track lighting and natural oak floors create the perfect backdrop for each piece of art. Impeccable bronze sculptures on white pedestals are symmetrically placed for advantageous viewing. Visual Environments will work with corporate and private collectors to procure the perfect art selection.

BOOKSTORE

DANGEROUS VISIONS, 13563 Ventura Boulevard, Sherman Oaks, CA. Tel. (818) 986-6963. This is a unique book store specializing in the metaphysical and the unusual.

CANDY STORE

SIMONA'S SWEETS
14106 Ventura Boulevard
Sherman Oaks, CA 91423
Tel. (818) 789-7715
Hrs: Tue. - Sat.   10:00 a.m. - 5:00 p.m.
Visa and AMEX are accepted.

Simona was involved in the movie business for many years at the Motion Picture Association, and many of her former associates often come by to sample the delectable sweets. Simona's Sweets is located in the leafy cobblestoned Patio Center. The quaint shop is decorated in pink and grey with lots of mirrors that reflect the trays of inviting sweets.

Long stemmed chocolate chip cookie hearts and roses, homebaked carrot cakes and a luscious variety of Italian cheesecakes are just a few of the appealing sweets. The highlight of the shop, if there is just one, is the Buñuelos. These are a Mexican treat which are coated in cinnamon or lightly dusted with powdered sugar.

A relatively new concept at Simona's Sweets is her High Tea. High Tea consists of sopapillas, buñuelos and tidbits of all of Simona's specialties and a variety of teas. Simona uses her baking ability as an outlet for her creative talents. You will find them as tasteful as they are attractive.

GIFT SHOPS

BODY SCENTS
13826 Ventura Boulevard
Sherman Oaks, CA 91423
Tel. (818) 905-6744
Hrs: Tue. - Fri.   11:00 a.m. - 6:00 p.m.
            Saturday   11:00 a.m. - 5:00 p.m.
Visa, MasterCard and AMEX are accepted.

She walks in mystery, alluring yet elusive, sensuous but not sassy, refined but revealing, and there clings to her a fragrance unforgettable. She has her secrets, of course, and one of them is that she knows Body Scents, the boutique for the fragrance refined.

Body Scents is the dream of two friends, Shirley Turner and Joyce Wilkoff, themselves "incurable" romantics who believe that a woman's perfume, bath soap, lotion, shaving gel and shampoo says as much about her as the clothing she wears, the cosmetics she uses, and the way she wears her hair. They feature over fifty base perfume oils. The customer may select the different fragrances that best suit them and the store blends the oils together to create a unique scent. They also offer a large selection of hat boxes, scented Battenberg lace pillows, delicate romantic cards, crystal and silver perfume bottles, frames and flacons from Florence, and satin pillows and lingerie cases. If you're fond of sachets for your dressing table, drawers and boudoir, you'll find a fine variety here, as well.

If you're one of those who knows that being a woman is being a "total woman," you'll visit this shop today. Dare to be you with a "Best Choice" at Body Scents.

CRUMPS
13616 Ventura Boulevard
Sherman Oaks, CA 91423
Tel. (818)905-9984
Hrs: Mon. - Sat.   10:00 a.m. - 5:30 p.m.
Visa and MasterCard are accepted.

There's a bit of jolly old England in Sherman Oaks. Patterned after the famous Harrods, Crumps is filled with all sorts of English items from teas, to marmalades, to housewares and collectibles.

Stepping into Crumps is like walking into a high class Bond Street store. There is an enormous fireplace at one end and cases and tables piled with a wonderful assortment of silverware, Wedgewood crystal, Port Meirion dinnerware and kitchenware. There are English countryside books, crystal, china and place mats, Royal Doulton, Toby jugs and figurines. Aromatic Norfolk lavenders give the store a homey fragrance. And English perfumes and bath soaps by Bromeley of London make wonderful gifts.

For the sweet tooth there are Cadbury's Chocolates and Biscuits, Scottish shortbread and Terry's of York Chocolates and Toffees. There are teas by Twining, and jams by Fortnum and Mason, as well as heady Indian curries and condiments. Crumps prepares custom gift baskets and offers exquisite gift wrapping service.

Send for a Crumps catalog. Orders are mailed throughout the United States. There is also an exchange service where gifts are delivered to your friends and relatives in the United Kingdom. Telephone orders are accepted for delivery all over the United States. Crumps of Sherman Oaks; they're preserving the best of Britain in the U.S.A.

LOVE N' KISSES
15030 Ventura Boulevard
Sherman Oaks, CA 91403
Tel. (818) 995-1965
Hrs: Mon. - Sat.   9:30 a.m. - 6:00 p.m.
       Sunday   11:00 a.m. - 5:00 p.m.

Marilyn Kove, a former English teacher, began Love N' Kisses in a smaller version than the one customers see today. The original shop was such a glorious success that Marilyn found herself expanding almost immediately. Besides the quality and uniqueness of her merchandise, Marilyn's own natural charisma beams from the creative displays and the generally buoyant atmosphere of her shop.

Love N' Kisses is actually four shops in one. Shoppers can browse through the gift section where they may select from an excellent line of stuffed animals including Avanti plush bears, beautiful gifts for all ages and occasions, then move on to choose helium balloons to tie to the package. Fresh gourmet coffees are features of another area. Custom stationery and invitations are featured along with a lovely selection of boxed stationery and invitations. Party supplies and greeting cards including unusual art cards, contemporary and Hallmark are available. Marilyn employs a professional artist to create original designs in acrylic paint for such items as picture frames, photo albums and mugs. Love N' Kisses also supplies its customers with Perma Plaque lamination to preserve such important personal documents as diplomas and newspaper articles.

Marilyn prides herself on offering her customers courteous, specialized service to suit their individual needs. Shop at Love N' Kisses and try homemade fudge or handmade truffles. Then choose from a wide variety of gifts for all your special occasion needs. A gift basket filled with goodies from Love N' Kisses is always an instant hit.

THE PARTY SHOP
13628 Ventura Boulevard
Sherman Oaks, CA 91423
Tel. (818) 784-8651
Hrs: Mon. - Sat.   9:30 a.m. - 5:30 p.m.
Visa and MasterCard are accepted.

As Lesley Gore once sang, "It's my party and I'll cry if I want to." If Ms. Gore had known about The Party Shop, she'd likely have saved herself the tears. "We wanted a one stop party shop," says Party Shop owner Ron Cole, "so while the store may have started out years ago as just a card store, we're certainly much, much more than that now."

Even the briefest visit will affirm that this is no idle boast. The store, a large, airy room, is packed with an awesome assortment of costumes, masks, hats, wigs, grease paint, glitter, paper plates, napkins, wrapping paper, decorations, balloons, cards, matchbooks, candles, place settings and other holiday paraphernalia.

And if the line impresses you, it's nothing to the service you'll receive from Ron and his assistant, Bill Burns. They believe in having fun and if you're a little uncertain how to coordinate your own celebration, they'll be more than willing to sit down with you, take a look at your budget, the number of guests you've invited, and what it is you want your party to say. They know the stuff of dreams, and of memories as well, and it's that kind of experience that can't help but make any festive occasion unforgettable. So put yourself in the hands of the gala professionals and make The Party Shop your one time party stop.

JEWELRY STORE

L.A. KICKS
14554 Ventura Boulevard
Sherman Oaks, CA 91403
Tel. (818) 990-3350
Hrs: Tue. - Thu.   11:00 a.m. - 9:00 p.m.
        Fri. - Sat.   11:00 a.m. - 10:00 p.m.
        Sunday   12:00 noon - 6:00 p.m.
Visa, MasterCard and AMEX are accepted.

Prior to opening L.A. Kicks with her partner Alison Epstein, Linda Gerston owned a jewelry store for eleven years. The experience was a valuable background when Alison and Linda put their heads together and decided to fulfill a demand for a shop dedicated strictly to accessories. L.A. Kicks is representative of the fun and glitzy side of the Los Angeles area. Stylish lighting accents the pale pink walls and a large bay window jauntily displays pizazz items.

Local artisans supply much of the merchandise at L.A. Kicks. Costume jewelry includes a selection of "Lunch at the Ritz" jewelry. These wildly large earrings are twenty-four karat gold plated or sterling silver, hand painted and decorated with semiprecious and Austrian crystal stones. Each piece represents a unique theme. Materials such as paper, plastics and beads of all colors and designs round out the jewelry display. L.A. Kicks accessory treasures include a wide exhibit of "Cindy Kamin" hats, jackets and hand painted ties. Bags, belts and gloves are part of the imaginative, creative displays. Cut Loose's 100% cotton clothing is also available, as well as a selection of very romantic lingerie.

Alison and Linda sponsor a gift reminder and registration service, and when that final selection has been made, they will be happy to wrap your purchase. L.A. Kicks rents costume jewelry—"the jewelry of your dreams" for the night at a fraction of the cost. They also offer an accommodating shipping service for out of town recipients. Shop L.A. Kicks for an exciting example of local craftsmanship in an upbeat atmosphere.

MAIL SERVICES

**MAIL BOXES OF CALIFORNIA,
SHERMAN OAKS STATION**
4450 Van Nuys Boulevard
Sherman Oaks, CA 91403
Tel.   (818) 986-8522
       (818) 986-8523
       (818) 986-8524
Hrs: Mon. - Fri.   9:30 a.m. - 6:00 p.m.
      Saturday   10:00 a.m. - 6:00 p.m.
Visa, MasterCard and AMEX are accepted.

An independent businessman or woman, especially one just getting started, often doesn't have the facilities and resources to do all that needs to be done. Mail Boxes of California, Sherman Oaks Station, offers businesses the services enjoyed by the big guys.

Conveniently located at the Sherman Oaks Square, they have ample parking facilities. Mail Boxes of California can send a facsimile document anywhere in the world. They also offer telex services, and a notary public is available for your documentation needs. The business owner can effect wire transfers, purchase money orders and save time licking stamps with the station's metered mail service. Mail Boxes of California also offers UPS shipping, custom packaging, bulk rate mailing and overnight mail services. They sport one of the largest mailbox rental facilities in Southern California. Top quality photocopying is also available, with bulk rate copying discounts and a full color copier. For the business owner in need of supplies, the Sherman Oaks Station offers a complete line of business and office supplies, custom letterhead, business cards, rubber stamps and keys. They also carry gift items such as handmade crystal or pewter paperweights, hand tooled desk sets and monogrammed stationery.

Business owners on the go can pick up the day's messages from the station's twenty-four hour message service, and have a gift custom gift wrapped by the station's helpful staff. Whatever service the businessman or woman needs, Mail Boxes of California, Sherman Oaks Station, will serve their needs well.

RESTAURANTS

CAFE 50'S
4609 Van Nuys Boulevard
Sherman Oaks, CA 91403
Tel. (818) 906-1955
Hrs: Sun. - Thu.   7:00 a.m. - 12:00 midnight
           Fri. - Sat.   7:00 a.m. - 1:00 a.m.
Also,

838 Lincoln Boulevard	140 Pier Avenue
Venice, CA 90261	Hermosa Beach, CA 90254
Tel. (213) 399-1955	Tel. (213) 374-1955

If you remember the 1950s, you can recreate that world on a visit to Cafe 50's, a particularly special eatery that brings back the unforgettable flavor of life during those happy days. Rock and roll classics greet you as you enter the glass doors of Cafe 50's. The theme in one room brings back the linoleum counters and Naugahyde upholstery of a roadside diner.

The Poster Room features walls covered with a collage of 50's original posters and magazine covers from *LIFE, TV Guide* and other magazines. You'll see a large section devoted to the politics of the era featuring "Ike" buttons and posters of Ronald Reagan advertising cigarettes. An old television plays reruns of *I Love Lucy* and *Superman*. One room, called Club 55, resembles a high school cafeteria and gymnasium. Along one wall there's a row of lockers and on the upper back wall a scoreboard that reads: "Visitors: 19, Home: 55." Food is typically 1950's, with just a hint of the 1980s. The menu includes the '57 T-Bird, an omelette consisting of avocado, fresh tomato, green onion, spinach and sour cream. Hamburgers are offered nine different ways and include the popular La Bamba burger served with chili and cheddar cheese topped with grilled onions. Wolfman Jack's Midnight Snack is ham, turkey, or roast beef with lettuce and tomato on rye bread.

Blue Plate Specials include the Uptown Meatloaf topped with mushroom sauce and served with mashed potatoes and chicken gravy. Dessert follows the 50's tradition to the letter, with splits, shakes, floats and various cola flavors. The sights, sounds and tastes of Cafe 50's recreate for many the happiest time of their lives.

FIORE D'ITALIA RESTAURANT, 14928 Ventura Boulevard, Sherman Oaks, CA. Tel. (818) 501-9667. You'll enjoy this restaurant with a classic Italian menu in a quiet setting. It was selected for the Excellence Award in 1986.

"FRANTRECOTE"
The French Steak House
15466 Ventura Boulevard
Sherman Oaks, CA 91403
Tel. (818) 783-3007
Hrs: Lunch   Mon. - Fri.   11:00 a.m. - 2:30 p.m.
          Dinner   Tue. - Sun.   5:30 p.m. - 10:30 p.m.
Visa, MasterCard, AMEX, Diners Club and Carte Blanche are accepted.

You may yearn for French cuisine but don't always have the time to wait for a meal in a traditional restaurant. The "Frantrecote" provides a new concept of European eating that offers an authentic French meal served within thirty to forty-five minutes. This does not mean, however, that one necessarily eat in a hurry.

Such a time span is perfect for business people, especially if they have a special client, but only a short time to entertain. Diners will be impressed with the French country style exterior of the restaurant. The interior is a blend of navy blues and peach. The decoration has been inspired by architect's designs of Paris monuments. Soft music invites diners to relax and enjoy the sweet smells making their way out of the kitchen. All lunches and dinners are *prix fixe* including the first beverage, with nominal charges for desserts. The meal begins with a green leaf salad with French champagne dressing and walnuts, followed by L'Entrecôte, a tender New York steak with almost no fat. The dish is presented table side in the European manner— sliced on a large platter, and served with a special family owned secret sauce made with twenty-five ingredients. French traditional *pommes frites* fried in a low cholesterol oil accompany the meal.

White, red and rose wines specifically complement L'Entrecôte. You will be offered a choice of freshly baked or prepared desserts including Profiterol Cream Puffs filled with ice cream or whipped cream and topped with a hot chocolate sauce. Tarte tatin, Paris-Brest and Mont d'Arbois are other examples of what the chef may propose from the dessert list, making a fine end to a quick, yet thoroughly delicious gourmet meal.

HO TOY'S CANTONESE RESTAURANT, 4630 Van Nuys Boulevard, Sherman Oaks, CA. Tel. (818) 783-0460. This is one of the best authentic Cantonese restaurants in the Valley. You'll enjoy the cocktails and exotic Polynesian drinks.

LA FONDUE BOURGUIGNONNE
FRENCH RESTAURANT & BAR
13359 Ventura Boulevard
Between Woodman and Coldwater Canyon
Sherman Oaks, CA 91423
Tel. (818) 501-0181
Hrs: Tue. - Sun.   5:30 p.m. - 10:30 p.m.
Visa, MasterCard, AMEX and Diners Club are accepted.

Owner Robert Chicha once served as maitre'd to one of the greatest Frenchmen of the twentieth century, President Charles De Gaulle. Over the seventeen years he's been attending to the fondue appetites of the Hollywood crowd, La Fondue Bourguignonne, a replica of a Burgundy restaurant, has only validated his own culinary greatness.

Fondue is for sharing, and the rustic decor in which it is served accents the menu itself. The dinners offer a choice of steak, chicken, shrimp, scallops, cheese or wine fondue. And to share the complete fondue experience, order for dessert chocolate fondue with fresh fruits.

If you'd like to dine with the particular and it's important to you to be seen among those who are as distinguished as you are, you can't pass up a chance like this. Whether it's the occasion of your first date, wedding anniversary, birthday or desire to please that special someone in your life, call today for reservations. As Robert Chicha points out, "We go only for the best." So should you. Valet parking is provided.

MARRAKESH RESTAURANT, 13003 Ventura Boulevard, Sherman Oaks, CA. Tel. (818) 788-6354. For something different, visit this restaurant which features authentic Moroccan feasts in an Arabian Nights setting. The dining rooms have traditional low seating, and there's a full bar.

MARY'S LAMB
13624 Ventura Boulevard
Sherman Oaks, CA 91423
Tel. (818) 501-7700
Hrs: Tue. - Fri.   8:00 a.m. - 10:00 p.m.
          Saturday   10:00 a.m. - 10:00 p.m.
          Sunday   9:00 a.m. - 2:30 p.m.
Visa, MasterCard and AMEX are accepted.

Patrons at Mary's Lamb can enjoy the country American atmosphere while sampling the "down home gourmet" recipes which originated as far away as New England and as close as California. Hanging quilts decorate the stenciled walls at Mary's Lamb. The big bay window and stenciled awnings add to the air of intimacy and warmth.

Mary's Lamb started as a catering service and recently expanded to its current restaurant and market. The Mary of Mary's Lamb is an actress, and patrons are sure to find themselves among Mary's fellow professionals as they sample home cooked entrees such as Meat Loaf and Mashed Potatoes, Poached Salmon with Cucumbers and Dill or the heavenly cookies and cakes. A tantalizing selection of main dish salads includes smoked turkey with apples, raisins and walnuts as well as chutney chicken salad and chicken artichoke salad. For an appetizing evening meal, try the grilled swordfish served with fresh salsa or the tri-tip of beef, grilled with port wine and served with whole grain mustard sauce. Selections from the market can be cooked and served to you at table side or taken home to be cooked in your own kitchen.

Mary's Lamb maintains its catering enterprise, specializing in the individual personalized touch for both private and corporate events. Sit back and enjoy the relaxed old world charm and the home cooked meals served at Mary's Lamb.

RIVE GAUCHE CAFE, 14106 Ventura Boulevard, Sherman Oaks, CA. Tel. (818) 881-2216. Rive Gauche Cafe is an intimate French cafe located in the Shady Patio Center, with outside dining and separate lounge.

SHAIN'S CONTINENTAL RESTAURANT AND BAR
14016 Ventura Boulevard
Sherman Oaks, CA 91423
Tel. (818) 986-5510
Hrs: Mon. - Sun.   5:00 p.m. - 11:00 p.m.
Visa, MasterCard, AMEX, Diners Club and Carte Blanche are accepted.

Shain's, well known for pleasing decor and quality food and service, is a landmark on Ventura Boulevard and has been catering to an established clientele for eight years. Resembling Tudor cottage, Shain's is a charming setting for continental cuisine which includes over forty entrees and unusual daily specials.

There is a delightful garden room for dining *al fresco*. You will be quickly seated in a country style room with tables set beautifully with white linen, crystal and silver. Low oak beamed ceilings lend to the cozy feeling and a long oak bar is a natural place for people to sit and enjoy a before or after dinner drink. Care is given to the fine points of dining at Shain's. The service is so gracious you may think you are a guest in someone's home. Sunday Brunch is a special occasion serving many fine delicacies. Try the delicate thin crepes and the Swiss Apple Pancakes. The wine list is extensive and features California, Italian and French wines.

Shain's has become a gathering place for local business people to relax after business hours and a great place for families to visit for Sunday brunch. Banquet facilities are available for parties of all sizes.

TURQUOISE CAFE
15025 Ventura Boulevard
Sherman Oaks, CA 91403
Tel. (818) 995-6575
Hrs: Mon. - Sun.   11:00 a.m. - 11:00 p.m.
Reservations are accepted.
Visa, MasterCard and AMEX are accepted.

Many of America's food traditions are represented at various restaurants in Southern California, including Southwestern and New Mexican.   One restaurant that celebrates these traditions is the Turquoise Cafe in Sherman Oaks. The Turquoise Cafe combines

Southwestern and New Mexican cuisine to create a style few restaurants can match.

You'll easily pick out the Turquoise Cafe by its bright yellow awning and wood fence; inside, you'll see an open kitchen framed in white tile. Cacti complete the Southwestern feel. The menu's emphasis is on fresh seafood and poultry cooked over a mesquite grill. You may choose the Grilled Quail marinated in soy sauce, garlic and ginger, and served with corn relish, tomato salsa, tomatilla salsa and spicy rice. Grilled Salmon is also a favorite. The menu features a variety of unusual salads offered at both lunch and dinner. Diners enjoy the Southwestern Salad of jicama, turkey, blue corn chips, fresh corn and minced lettuce, all served with mustard vinaigrette. Light eaters like the Yellowfin Tuna Salad with slices of papaya and mango on a bed of mixed lettuce with a citrus vinaigrette.

On the more traditional side, the restaurant serves blue corn enchiladas, chimichangas and tostadas. Vanilla Bean Flan and Bunuellos are sweet finishes to your meal. For an interesting cocktail before or after your meal, try one of the house specialty drinks, including the Tropical Fruit Lillet Margarita.

STATIONERY

BURGUNDY GRAY, LTD.
14423 1/2 Ventura Boulevard
Sherman Oaks, CA 91423
Tel. (818) 784-4175
Hrs: Mon. - Fri.   10:00 a.m. - 6:00 p.m.
       Saturday   10:00 a.m. - 5:00 p.m.
       Or by appointment
Visa and MasterCard are accepted. ($15 minimum)
Also,
8809 West Pico Boulevard
Los Angeles, CA 90035
Tel. (213) 859-0050

Anyone who throws a party for a friend or loved one wants their event to be memorable for years to come. Often the way the party looks and feels depends on the kind of atmosphere you create.

Burgundy Gray, Ltd., understands this and wants to take over the worry and headache of creating the best party imaginable to celebrate that special event. Owners Jodi, Bill and Beverly Feinstein will provide you with the finest in party favors, balloon decorations, plates, napkins and anything you'll need to make a special time. Burgundy Gray features custom invitations by Crane, Buening, Jansson and other top names. They'll also do birth announcements with their in-house printing and calligraphy service. But creating a fine party isn't the only thing Burgundy Gray can do for you. Walk into their store with a warm, family atmosphere and select among the fine stationery, picture frames, and other gifts they offer. Burgundy Gray feature such items as personalized lucite bookends, and stunning Val St. Lambert crystal candlesticks for making a perfect romantic evening even more perfect.

Burgundy Gray, Ltd., will serve you right from the beginning; from the moment you enter their shop, you'll know all your party and gift worries are over.

STUDIO CITY

Appropriately named, Studio City was where the old Republic Motion Pictures first started business in California in 1928.

APPAREL

POOR SNOB
12524 Ventura Boulevard
Studio City, CA 91604
Tel. (818) 769-9666
Visa, MasterCard and AMEX are accepted.

His mother was in the fashion business before him, so after owner Robert Shabkie received his business degree from USC, it was only natural that a flair for women's clothing and good business sense should come together at Poor Snob.

The result is an elegant, peach tone boutique in the heart of Studio City where, beneath crystal chandeliers and amidst soft music, Robert outfits the chic of Southern California and beyond. His lines run to casual, sportswear, evening gowns and all manner of accessories.

The Poor Snob, like its name implies, also appeals to the pocketbook conscious who can also receive head to toe outfitting, special after hours appointments and either champagne or orange juice as they wait. So for replicas of the high priced originals, at a price a fraction of the cost, stop by the Poor Snob and let Robert Shabkie, the USC business major with the heritage in women's fashion, be your guide.

SPLASH FOR CHILDREN
12109 Ventura Boulevard
Studio City, CA 91604
Tel. (818) 762-6123
Hrs: Mon. - Sat.   10:00 a.m. - 6:00 p.m.
Visa, MasterCard and AMEX are accepted.

Year round, up to date colors and high fashion styles for the trend setting children of Southern California are offered in abundance at Splash for Children. Making a fashion statement available for kids was the goal of Splash and in the five years since it opened owner Dale Edgecumbe has done just that.

Children's wear in sizes from infant to 8 for boys and girls is featured. Splash also offers 100% cotton clothing, acid washed denims, cute and easy to wear shirt-dresses and sequined or beaded swimsuits for girls, and pull on pants, coordinated shirts and sweaters for boys. Giant teddy bears, peachy faced dolls and crib quilts are among the toys and accessories available for children of all ages.

Although the inventory is constantly changing along with the fashion world you can count on all the latest fashions being at Splash first.

SPLASH FOR WOMEN
12109 Ventura Boulevard
Studio City, CA 91604
Tel. (818) 762-6123
Hrs: Mon. - Sat.   10:00 a.m. - 6:00 p.m.
Visa, MasterCard and AMEX are accepted.

The original intent and purpose of Splash was to give the busy, creative people of Studio City a chance to shop for the most fashion forward look available. From the glass fronted exterior overlooking busy Ventura Boulevard to the well-lit attractively displayed interior, Splash speaks to the contemporary woman.

Because they can find everything from outrageous hand painted, jeweled items to classical outfits, Splash has a large clientele of professional women, many in the film industry. Always avant-garde, this wonderful boutique enables the fashion conscious women the opportunity to keep abreast of the latest and most chic fashions.

Many one of a kind items made especially for Splash can be found on display. Whether you are looking for accessories or entire ensembles you can look to the future at Splash for Women.

WHISPER
12240 1/2 Ventura Boulevard
Studio City, CA 91604
Tel. (818) 762-3658
Hrs: Mon. - Sat.   10:00 a.m. - 6:00 p.m.
Visa, MasterCard and AMEX are accepted.

Explore the possibilities of your fashion spirit, reach into the undiscovered realms of your adventurous personality and blossom into new life with a fashionably integrated, individually stylized new look from the exciting line at Whisper. A combination of classic vintage clothing and up to the moment garments graced with accessories that befit the look will result in an outfit that is uniquely and impressively you.

Proprietor Claire de Ligne has creatively integrated extremely chic, gently worn vintage clothing, hats and jewelry, many of which were owned by well known luminaries, with an outstanding selection of contemporary designs. The woods, creams, pinks and large glass windows tastefully set off the quality merchandise within the lively shop which exhibits a massive display of clothing from the 30s, 40s and 50s, as well as currents for men and women. It is possible to walk into Whisper and discover an haute couture designer original worn only once or twice by, let's say Marilyn Monroe, as well as labels such as Missoni, Kenzo, Ted Lapidus and many others. Another exciting feature offered by Whisper is the distinguished costume rental which has been carefully and astutely put together by Claire over the last decade.

Elegant furs are taken on consignment and Claire will consider the purchase of well cared for vintage items such as clothing, hats and jewelry. If you've always craved Peau de Soie and satin, this is the place to find it. The one of a kind look is the quintessential element at Whisper, a "best bet" and "Best Choice" in LA.

GIFT SHOPS

EMERALD FOREST GIFT & FINE CRAFTS
12638 Ventura Boulevard
Studio City, CA 91604
Tel. (818) 509-8529
Hrs: Mon. - Sat.   10:00 a.m. - 6:00 p.m.
Visa, MasterCard and AMEX are accepted.

The Emerald Forest is a place of enchantment, full of handcrafted jewelry, ceramics, glass, wood, leather, textiles, baskets, stationery, toiletries and Santa Fe and Country French Collections. There is a feeling of wonder and anticipated enjoyment upon entering Emerald Forest. The style of the shop is a combination of Southwestern and Country French.

The treasures found in this forest are delightful and many. Owner Michelle Rack is a jewelry designer and her interest in fine jewelry pieces is evident throughout the shop. There is handcrafted jewelry in sterling, glass, porcelain, fabric earrings, pins and bracelets. Styles of jewelry range from ethnic to contemporary. Beautiful ceramics are everywhere. You will find hand painted Italian bowls, *demitasse* cups and vases by Parrucca. There are Lisa Lindberg contemporary Southwestern style plates, platters and butter dishes. A complete line of Body Shop toiletries such as soaps, bath gels, body lotions and travel gift packs are beautifully displayed. You can choose from a large selection of stationery crafted of handmade paper or choose cards of linen and wild flowers by Papeterie. Children will find a grand selection of plush hand puppets. Baby gifts include pastel leather moccasins and handpainted outfits by Stacy Sterling.

The treasure chest is deep at Emerald Forest. Many wonderful gifts are waiting to be discovered. Draw your map well to this delightful shop; you'll want to return to Emerald Forest many times.

INDIAN ART CENTER OF CALIFORNIA
12666 Ventura Boulevard
Studio City, CA 91604
Tel. (818) 763-3430
Hrs: Mon. - Sat.   10:00 a.m. - 5:30 p.m.

Since 1966, Ed Gooch has been bringing a decades long passion for American Southwest Indian culture to aficionados in the greater Southern California area. The splendor of these civilizations come alive in their spectacular silversmithing: a thousand items of turquoise jewelry, Navajo rugs, pottery and Kachina dolls await your discovery.

His inventory also includes tribal crafts from throughout the United States. Masks, clubs, shields, rattles, drums, pipes, spears, bead work and moccasins are showcased in a spacious environment with large glass windows. His total inventory numbers over 10,000 items and among his regular customers are Indians themselves, who come in to buy the carved stone animals that, according to legend, possess a soul and are, therefore, invaluable in religious and personal growth ceremonies.

It's an opportunity to return to one's roots, to appreciate and understand what it might have been like in the Southwest before Cortez, Coronado and the early white settlers moved into Texas, New Mexico and Arizona. So if you're even remotely interested in Native American history and tradition, you'll stop by. Budget some quality time and let Ed Gooch take you back into the echoes of a distant past.

LION'S LAIR
11360 Ventura Boulevard
Studio City, CA 91604
Tel. (818) 762-1800
Hrs: Mon. - Sat.   10:00 a.m. - 10:00 p.m.
         Sunday   12:00 noon - 6:00 p.m.
Visa and MasterCard are accepted.
Also,
22013 Sherman Way
Canoga Park, CA 91303
Tel. (818) 999-2920

The owner of the gift shop at 11360 Ventura Boulevard was born under the astrological sign of Leo. He promotes his belief that everyone should collect lions by stocking the largest selection of lions most people will ever see. And where else could this collection be housed except in a Lion's Lair?

Lion's Lair is a melange of sight and smell. From the stone lions guarding the entry portals to its unique owner, Lion's Lair is an extraordinary gift shop. The pleasant aroma wafting from over fifty freshly ground gourmet coffees mixes with the tantalizing scent of heady tobaccos. Patrons can choose from a unique selection of pipes from all over the world. Each nook and cranny holds yet a new and unusual delight. Handcrafted meerschaums from Istanbul, Turkey are on display. An exquisite crystal collection features fantasy wizards, dragons and unicorns. Customers can feast their eyes on the brass, silver and pewter objets d'art or run their fingers over the smooth surface of exquisitely hand crafted wooden boxes. Meticulously hand painted glass containers are an enthralling example of craftsmanship from all over the world.

Lions displayed are crafted from every conceivable medium in all sizes and stances. The collection offers something for everyone in prices ranging from a modest five dollars to three thousand. Visit the Lion's Lair and browse through a wealth of fragrant and exotic treasures.

RESTAURANTS

CHEZ NATUREL
11838 Ventura Boulevard
Studio City, CA 91604
Tel: (818) 763-1044
Hrs: Mon. - Sun.   11:00 a.m. - 10:30 p.m.
Visa, MasterCard and AMEX are accepted.

Health food is not just a catch phrase at Chez Naturel. It's a sincere dedication to serving patrons a natural and healthy meal that is also highly appetizing. The unicorn was chosen as the embodiment of Chez Naturel in its representation of purity and the "whimsical and joyous search for goodness."

Chez Naturel uses only ingredients which are certified organic or without chemicals. Dining guests can expect their omelettes to be made from three fertile eggs and they know that the meal and flour for the crepes and corn bread was freshly ground in the kitchen.

Carrot and orange juice are squeezed to order and are offered along with a selection of other fresh fruit and berry drinks including apple, raspberry/apple and pineapple/coconut. Included in a delicious selection of vegetarian entrees is the Mushrooms Royale which are giant fresh mushroom crowns stuffed with blended nuts, cheeses and herbs. The Fiesta de Acapulco is a guacamole taco and enchilada with a vegetarian filling served with salsa, pinto beans and Spanish rice. Chez Naturel also offers an artfully prepared Breast of Chicken, stuffed with a succulent blend of pine nuts, cheeses, herbs and covered with a golden nut sauce. Or perhaps a guest will be more tempted by the Poulet a L'Orange, chicken baked in a special honey/orange sauce. Both dinners are served with the choice of baked potato or herbed brown rice.

Within the spirit of good health and spirit, there is no smoking permitted at the restaurant. Whether dining in the natural setting of Chez Naturel's indoor dining room among the wooden tables and plants or in the fresh air atmosphere of the patio, prepare to enjoy a meal that will delight both your taste buds and your body.

THE ELEGANT TORTILLA
11034 Ventura Boulevard
Studio City, CA 91604
Tel. (818) 509-1527
Hrs: Mon. - Thu.   11:30 a.m. - 10:00 p.m.
          Fri. - Sat.   11:30 a.m. - 11:00 p.m.
          Sunday   5:00 p.m. - 10:00 p.m.
Visa, MasterCard and AMEX are accepted.

If you enjoy a good tortilla but you're leery of the calories and just a bit put off by all the frying involved, The Elegant Tortilla is the place for you.

Owners Roy and Linda Raskin provide a lighter, more modern and more natural Latin fare. They use only the highest quality meats, seafood, vegetables and cooking ingredients, which means no lard shortening or preservatives. In a dusky peach and blue gray/beige setting, diners will enjoy the Peruvian wall hangings and other very subtle art pieces. The Elegant Tortilla is part of the vintage shopping strip through "Tinsel Town" so there is plenty of free parking.

Testimonials mean a great deal in the restaurant business and The Elegant Tortilla has earned one. A leading Southern California hospital recommends the establishment to its cardiac heart patients. So whether it's soft tacos or the Sunrise Tortilla, the Vegetable

Burritos or the Quesadilla Universale, partake freely, and to your health.

> **LA LOGGIA**
> 11814 Ventura Boulevard
> Studio City, CA 91604
> Tel. (818) 985-9222
> Hrs: Mon. - Fri.   11:30 a.m. - 2:30 p.m.
>   5:30 p.m. - 10:30 p.m.
>   Saturday   5:30 p.m. - 11:00 p.m.
>   Sunday   5:00 p.m. - 10:00 p.m.
> Visa, MasterCard, AMEX and Diners Club are accepted.

You can be among the television celebrities who order their cucina Italiana "to go," or you may choose to rub elbows with them and enjoy the constantly changing menu, high quality fare, attentive service and the ambiance of La Loggia. The restaurant is within walking distance from CBS/MTM Studios and a few miles from Universal and the Burbank Studios.

To pique customers' interest and keep them coming back for more, La Loggia offers a menu that changes every three weeks, however, they always feature homemade pasta, very fresh homemade pizza dough, daily specials and a small but well chosen wine list, which includes a good selection of champagnes as well as white and red wines from Italy and California. The contemporary California/Italian decor is crisp, with track lighting, white tablecloths and slanted ceiling. A personal touch is offered by the original abstract modern art oil paintings on exhibit by an artist/customer, Randy Tat, who has named one of his paintings "La Loggia." The hand written, extensive menu items are prepared with the freshest ingredients in an open kitchen, where customers may observe their meals being prepared. The menu is reasonably priced and features Gli Antipasti: Cozze e Vongole, fresh clams, mussels and scallops in a light tomato garlic broth and Radicchi e Capelle Di Fungo. A wide assortment of pastas include Linguine Ai Funghi e Formaggia Di Capra, linguine with wild mushrooms and goat cheese and Bianchi e Neri Alle Capesante, black and white pasta with Bay scallops in a light cream sauce. The pizza selection is unusual and enticing with such titles as Pizza Gamberoni, Pollo and Ratatouille. Many customers choose a combination of antipasti, pizza and pasta for their dining pleasure but an array of entrees are also available: veal, chicken, duck, rabbit, sea bass and snapper are delicately prepared with special seasonings and sauces.

The high quality, attentive service and ambiance of La Loggia makes it a must for Italian food lovers. The owners and waitpersons hail from Spain, Columbia and Italy and offer linguistic variety, which adds to the enjoyment of a meal. Partner Tom Baily, an American, adds his touch of California to the cuisine, too.

TERU SUSHI
11940 Ventura Boulevard
Studio City, CA 91604
Tel.   (818) 763-6201
Hrs: Lunch   Mon. - Fri.   12:00 noon - 2:30 p.m.
        Dinner   Mon. - Thu.   5:30 p.m. - 11:00 p.m.
                       Fri. - Sat.   5:30 p.m. - 11:30 p.m.
                       Sunday   5:30 p.m. - 10:30 p.m.
Visa, MasterCard, AMEX and Diners Club are accepted.

Power? Los Angeles shines with it. Recently rated in the top ten for power lunching among Los Angeles area restaurants, Teru Sushi has developed a fiercely loyal following. For eight years, Teru Sushi has catered to people in the music and television business, and they've come to regard Teru Sushi as an "in" place, as well as a place to enjoy fine Japanese food.

Look for the Japanese style building in the heart of Studio City, and allow an attendant, park your car for you. Take a seat by a waterfall in a traditional Japanese garden, and let your waiter show you the complete Japanese menu. For an appetizer, try the Yakitori, broiled chicken and vegetables on bamboo skewers. Sample the Asari, baby clams steamed to perfection in a hot butter sauce. For an entree, you may try a Teru Sushi special such as Katana Sakana, tender fillet of swordfish in a spicy ginger and mushroom sauce. It's served with vegetables and salad. Dinners include the classic meat teriyakis and tempuras.

If you really want to experience Teru Sushi, come by the sushi bar on a weekend night and feel a different kind of power as it becomes the hottest bar in town. Loud, noisy and filled with rock and roll and glamor, Teru Sushi is the place to watch people and be seen by them.

TARZANA

This Valley community's name came from the creator of the Tarzan character. Edgar Rice Burroughs, who wrote the series of books featuring the swinging jungle man, purchased an estate here in 1917 and rechristened it "Tarzana." By 1931 the post office was using the name for the surrounding business and residential community.

APPAREL

CENTRAL PARK
18735 Ventura Boulevard
Tarzana, CA 91356
Tel. (818) 881-1567
Hrs: Mon - Wed.,Fri.,Sat.   10:00 a.m. - 6:00 p.m.
       Thursday   10:00 a.m. - 8:00 p.m.
       Sunday   10:00 a.m. - 4:00 p.m.
Visa, MasterCard and AMEX are accepted.

Do you love wearing the latest fashions? Do you wish you could take a trip to New York City to purchase the newest clothes as they become available? Or do you simply prefer the more sophisticated fashion designs offered on the East Coast? Now there's a piece of the Big Apple in Tarzana. The same wonderful merchandise found in stores in New York City can be found at Central Park.

You'll be delighted with the wide range of contemporary styles, fabrics and colors you have to choose from. There are gorgeous handknit sweaters, denim dresses, casual wear, Italian knits, elegant coats, dresses, hand painted sweaters and all sorts of exciting outfits distinctively different from the usual clothes carried by West Coast shops. The store's owner, Barbara, has a great talent for matching color and design with the customer's hair and skin tones. If you need help creating the ultimate coordinated ensemble, Barbara is the expert who can help you achieve the look you want.

More than willing to assist you, the sales staff maintains a non-aggressive sales approach, allowing you to be comfortable while browsing. For a delightful and rewarding shopping trip, take a stroll through Central Park and treat yourself to some of the exciting fashion looks from New York.

HONEY TREE BOUTIQUE
18399 Ventura Boulevard
Tarzana, CA 91356
Tel. (818) 881-3597
Hrs: Mon. - Sat.   10:00 a.m. - 5:00 p.m.
Visa and MasterCard are accepted.

Despite an impressive line of European and California designed clothing for children, the Honey Tree Boutique is not just a clothing store for kids (or parents). It couldn't be when owner Lynn Feldman and her manager, Marci Zimmerman, make shopping such an easy task.

They care about children and know that in the fast paced, highly competitive world our kids face today, being attractive, intelligent, even gifted is not enough. If your little boy or girl is going to succeed in school, in the social whirl, in clubs or other cultural activities, they've got to look the part. The term for it is fashion coordination and to that end, Lynn and Marci are nearly fanatic in their desire to match the right line to the right child. Hours and hours are spent researching the European and American fashion worlds and when your child comes in, it's a full consultation he or she will receive.

The majority of their merchandise is made of natural fiber. Lines carried include Tickle Me Fun Sweatsuits, California Sportswear for Girls from Nouvelle and Petit Bateau, a French collection. There are, as well, little knitted cardigans and matching shirts and trousers. You can expect to find a complete assortment of accessories as well. So if you truly care about dressing your youngster—infant to size fourteen—you'll want to drive out to the Tarzana Shopping Center and see for yourself. If caring counts, neither you nor your child will be disappointed.

ART GALLERY

CATCHPENNY ART GALLERY
18555 Ventura Boulevard
Tarzana, CA 91356
Tel. (818) 881-3218
Hrs: Mon. - Sat.   10:00 a.m. - 5:30 p.m.
          Sunday   12:00 noon - 5:00 p.m.
Visa, MasterCard and AMEX are accepted.

Catchpenny Art Gallery offers one of the largest selections in California of important nineteenth and early twentieth century American and European paintings and also represents almost one hundred contemporary traditional and impressionist artists. This unique gallery, which has been in business for over twenty-five years, by now a landmark on Ventura Boulevard, also promotes many younger artists of promising talent. A myriad of subject matter, technique and styles are represented in the showings featured.

The gallery concentrates on fine art done in oils. Historically proven the most appreciated medium, oil paintings are considered more unique and show the greatest value over time. An impressive selection of works by the great academic masters of the nineteenth century such as W.A. Bouguereau, Jules Lefevre, A. Schreyer, Eugene de Blaas and many others are on display in the gallery. The list of major impressionist works that the gallery has sold is long and illustrious; Monet, Renoir, Mary Cassatt and others. The gallery prides itself on being able to offer quality original paintings starting as low as $200.00. The wealth of contemporary artistic talent is vast and includes many artists of international acclaim. Gallery owners Charles Hecht and his son Peter are extremely proud of the works featured and they continually look for new emerging talent among the up and coming artists.

Catchpenny Art Gallery's standard of excellence is well known. Second generation buyers and collectors have come to trust in the quality, authenticity and value behind each work featured. The gallery will also accommodate appraisals, restoration projects and leasing arrangements. Voltaire is known to have said, "Perfection is attained by slow degrees; it requires the hand of time." Catchpenny Art Gallery has acquired that perfection in the area of fine art.

GIFT SHOP

THE STILISH FOX
18625 Ventura Boulevard
Tarzana, CA 91356
Tel. (818) 345-3559
Hrs: Mon. - Sat.   10:00 a.m. - 5:30 p.m.
Visa, MasterCard and AMEX are accepted.

Elaine Stiles and Barbara Fox offered their services for executive and corporate gift selection for a number of years. Their clientele grew and requests became more frequent for year round assistance in gift selection for all occasions. They enthusiastically opened their "toys for big boys" shop overlooking Ventura Boulevard and The Stilish Fox was born.

The Stilish Fox features a versatile and entertaining collection of gifts for men of all interests and professions. The shop is at the same time both spacious and elegantly crammed with items of both practical and amusing applications. Know an executive who has occasional less than congenial board meetings? He needs a blow up Anti-Stress Bag to punch behind locked doors. No electronic addict should be without his very own battery operated Mini-Vac for cleaning hard to reach crevices on stereos, computers and cameras. Do you wish the man in your life knew how to read a wine list? In the generous interest of furthering his self esteem, this gentleman needs the Stilish Fox's hand held wine rater. It's small enough to fit in his hand or jacket pocket and will give him a one to ten rating on 549 worldwide wines. He will be given advise and tips that he can casually toss out to impress his dinner partners. The new wine expert can now look down his nose and mumble in a slightly bored tone all sorts of sage criticisms.

Prowl the multi-leveled Stilish Fox for innovative and unusual gifts. You'll have just as much fun making the selection as he will in unwrapping it.

GOURMET FOOD

SANDY'S GOURMET FOODS, INC.
18663 Ventura Boulevard
Tarzana, CA 91356
Tel. (818) 881-0730
Hrs: Mon. - Thu.   10:00 a.m. - 6:00 p.m.
           Fri. - Sat.   10:00 a.m. - 10:00 p.m.
Visa, MasterCard, and AMEX are accepted.
Also,
23548 Calabas Road
Calabas, CA 91302
Tel. (818) 888-9112

Sandy Gennawey decided early in life to open a business and when she sets a goal, she follows through. Sandy's Gourmet Foods, Inc., already at two locations, offers over forty different kinds of imported coffees and teas, international gourmet foods, deli meats, imported cheeses, chocolates and candies, and gifts for the gourmet.

You can choose from a wide variety of deli sandwiches, daily quiche, fresh gourmet salads, and also items featuring no salt, sugar, or preservatives. Enjoy your selection on the European patio decked with crisp white tables and chairs, and blue floral tablecloths. The store is light, spacious, and airy with lace curtains on the patio's large windows giving glimpses of the wide array of tantalizing foodstuffs and gift ideas ranging from coffees, teas, or candies to custom made gift baskets. Telephone orders are encouraged and Sandy will then ship your order to you. Her special catering for any size party is also available.

Sandy has set her sights on a new location for every year, and her track record in the first year and a half indicates that she will have no trouble meeting this goal. Her growing clientele will be delighted to see this expansion.

LUGGAGE

LAX LUGGAGE
18711 Ventura Boulevard
Tarzana, CA 91356
Tel. (818) 343-4422
Hrs: Mon. - Sat.   10:00 a.m. - 6:00 p.m.
        Sunday   11:00 a.m. - 5:00 p.m.
Visa and MasterCard are accepted.
Also,
2233 South Sepulveda Boulevard
West Los Angeles, CA 90064
Tel. (213) 478-2661

If you spend a lot of years repairing the luggage damaged by those gorillas working in airport terminals, you come to know which luggage is the best on the market. LAX Luggage made a business of repairing luggage for five years before opening their retail outlets.

LAX Luggage carries an enormous inventory of luggage and travel accessories, all offered at discount prices. Tumi fine leather luggage, Lark, cloth luggage by Ventura, the lightweight aluminum line from Halliburton; even the airport apes have a hard time damaging these, and beautiful tapestry luggage from Pegasus. The display area is large and bright, making it easy to distinguish the many styles and brands carried. Racks of leather, electrical, and other stylish as well as functional travel accessories complement the latest in traditional and casual luggage. A full selection of Seiko travel and desk clocks is also featured.

LAX Luggage does personal repairs as well as being the largest authorized airline repair service in Los Angeles. If you need to replace lost luggage or have damaged luggage in need of repair, swing into LAX Luggage, they don't monkey around.

RESTAURANTS

BANGERS
5507 Reseda Boulevard
Tarzana, CA 91356
Tel. (818) 881-8696
Hrs: Lunch   Mon. - Sun.   11:00 a.m. - 3:00 p.m.
         Tea   Mon. - Sun.   2:00 p.m. - 5:00 p.m.
         Dinner   Mon. - Sun.   6:00 p.m. - 11:00 p.m.
         Pub   Mon. - Sun.   11:00 a.m. - 2:00 a.m.
Visa, Mastercard and AMEX are accepted.

If you're looking for a moderately priced, entertaining place to spend the evening, or a quiet place to spend the afternoon, Bangers is the place for you.

You can relax in a smokeless atmosphere with a cozy English tearoom ambiance, sipping and munching a traditional English afternoon tea, which includes a pot of tea such as Tetley, P.G. Tips, Rose or Ty-phoo or coffee; an assortment of tea sandwiches, sausage roll; one scone and two pastries. A la carte items and champagne specialties are also available. After a spot of tea you'll enjoy perusing the provisions and gift shop which carries the Queen's personally selected toiletries for men and women by Floris as well as English soaps and gift baskets. The Tea Room lunch menu is filled with properly made English treats including a favorite Kedgeree, spicy salmon over rice with salad. To savor the flavor of the British Isles you must experience Sunday brunch with your choice of an English breakfast. Offered are banger and bacon, eggs, baked beans, tomato and fried bread; a Welsh or Scottish breakfast; or you can build your own omelette. English pub fare features bangers, fish, chicken and burgers and chips. Also available are savory pies including steak and kidney. If you stop by for dinner bring a hearty appetite with you. The menu features Prime Rib, Yorkshire Pudding, fish, fowl and joints of the day, such as pork, veal and lamb or appetizers and oyster bar menu for lite eating.

Lest we forget, this restaurant is not only known for its many English dishes but for its entertainment. The Pub Room features a dance floor and a band that plays British hits of the 50s, 60s and 70s.

Bangers is the home of the British Exiles. Bangers is also available for private meetings and parties. If you've no room for dessert, wrap up one of the many cream pastries made daily on the premises.

GOURMET GOURMET
19014 Ventura Boulevard
Tarzana, CA 91356
Tel. (818) 344-7111
Hrs: Mon. - Sat.   11:30 a.m. - 9:00 p.m.
          Sunday   5:30 p.m. - 9:30 p.m.
Visa and MasterCard are accepted.

The wonderful aroma of freshly cut spices and cooking food combined with the cozy Country French decor tell you a truly "gourmet" treat is in store for you at Gourmet Gourmet. "Originally, the concept was just gourmet to go," says Chef Joe Donohue. As the dine-in business grew, Donohue expanded the restaurant and began adding a larger in-house menu which eventually included the popular Pritikin style dishes.

Today Gourmet Gourmet offers a complete restaurant menu, a take home menu and full catering service. Overall, the menus are "new American" with tantalizing selections such as meat loaf with smoked bacon and lumpy mashed potatoes, carrot fettuccine with smoked salmon and cream, brie in puff pastry with paté, veal chop with chestnuts and Granny Smith apples, white chocolate and raspberry mousse. Complementing the menu is a small but well chosen wine list featuring predominately California wines. Joe's Pritikin style dishes have attracted the attention of film stars such as Cybill Shepherd, James Coburn and Sally Field because of the dish's small calorie numbers and rich flavors.

Gourmet Gourmet has an open kitchen concept in which the kitchen is located in the dining room. You can see what's cooking as soon as you enter the restaurant. And, what is cooking at Joe Donohue's place is tantalizing, delicious gourmet food at its best.

TONY AND LUIGI
18663 Ventura Boulevard
Wall Street Plaza
Tarzana, CA 91356
Tel. (818) 996-8488
Hrs: Mon. - Thu.   11:30 a.m. - 10:00 p.m.
      Fri. - Sat.   11:30 a.m. - 11:00 p.m.
      Sunday   10:30 a.m. - 10:00 p.m.
Visa, MasterCard and AMEX are accepted.

Tony and Luigi Ristorante provides the diner with authentic Italian fare, and a diverse feast for the eyes as well, by offering two distinctly different dining atmospheres: a cozy wood-paneled "Old World" dining room and a "Contemporary" light and airy dining room. The two rooms are joined by a red and green tiled full-service bar where patrons can watch the chefs at work preparing such delights as Veneto, a Northern Italian combination platter of Scampi, Veal Picatta, Tortellini Romani, eggplant and a vegetable, or other favorites, such as pizzas straight from the woodburning oven and a variety of pasta creations.

At Tony and Luigi's, you will experience personal table side service in the preparation of Fettuccine Al Gusto or Caesar Salad, for example. Brightly colored ceiling banners and an abundance of tile, murals, brass, and neon lighting welcome you to Tony and Luigi's Ristorante. Once seated, you are served with complimentary homemade breadsticks and Tony's homemade sauce. Pepperoncini and a bottle of the featured house wine are also available.

Special services include free valet parking, a pizza take out, free mini-pizzas for children celebrating birthdays, delicious brunches and buffets, and their specialty Northern and Southern Italian festive platters. Tony and Luigi's is sure to entice you to enjoy the great food, value, and service in its authentic atmosphere again and again.

VINNIE'S ITALIAN KITCHEN
5538 Reseda Boulevard
Tarzana, CA 91356
Tel. (818) 705-3800
Hrs: Mon. - Sat.   11:00 a.m. - 10:00 p.m.
         Sunday   4:00 p.m. - 9:00 p.m.
Visa and MasterCard are accepted.

Anyone who loves Italian cooking savors the aroma of garlic and traditional spices issuing from pots and saucepans in the finest Italian restaurants. Your nose will be in seventh heaven once you enter Vinnie's Italian Kitchen, with its mouthwatering selection of Italian food.

The newly remodeled restaurant features a pink and black decor with scenic prints on the walls. On those wonderful Tarzana evenings, diners will enjoy a table under a green awning. This family owned and operated business makes everything to your order and uses only the freshest ingredients available. Neopolitan cuisine is predominant at this restaurant, but other Italian traditions are served also. You'll taste the best of all regional food in dishes using milk fed Provimi eastern veal served a variety of ways, including Veal Piccata, Veal Saltimbocco, Veal Parmigiana and Veal Francese. Vinnie's Italian Kitchen is proud of its fresh seafood including Linguine with fresh clam sauce, Calamari and Pasti, plus Linguine Frutta de Mare. Pizza is a popular choice, made with homemade dough and tomato sauce. Favorite pizza toppings include bell peppers, onion, eggplant, mushrooms, olives, fresh tomato and a variety of meats. Be sure to look for the daily specials such as Veal Chop, Cioppino, and homemade ravioli with four cheeses.

A slice of White Chocolate Macadamia Nut Cheesecake will transform a wonderful meal into an extraordinary dining experience. But if you're on a diet, don't worry, Vinnie's Italian Kitchen can accommodate any need. Vinnie's offers catering and delivery too.

UNIVERSAL CITY

After purchasing an 800 acre ranch in 1912, German immigrant Carl Laemmle built what was to become the first self contained community dedicated to making movies. By the late 1940s, about three quarters of the ranch land had been developed into residential neighborhoods. Today Universal City has developed into a complex that includes thirty-six sound stages, a fifteen story administration and office building, a 286,000 square foot garden terraced office complex, film processing laboratories and two high rise hotels.

The Universal City Tour is a six hour activity that takes visitors through the sets and production facilities by way of a tram. The falsefront streets will create the illusion of being in Europe, New York or a Western town. The variety of demonstrations, shows and activities turn the nation's biggest and busiest motion picture and television studio into a theme park that's enjoyed by four million visitors a year.

UNIVERSAL STUDIOS

Step behind the scenes and come face to face with reality in an industry specializing in illusion. Watch as special effects unfold, and become enlightened as various aspects of the movie making business are explained in detail. Be amused, enthralled and become part of the legendary film making institution that helped put the silver in the "silver screen."

Universal Studios Tour is unquestionably the largest single attraction in the San Fernando Valley. The 400 acre complex is unequalled in number of visitors (over three million tourists a year) and the extent of its displays. TV and sound stages, sets consisting of false front buildings and facades, and glimpses into star's dressing rooms, movie warehouses and labs provide an insight into the how of modern movie and TV program making. The four and one half hour tours have become so popular that one leaves for the back lots every five minutes, seven days a week, from 8:00 a.m. to 6:00 p.m.

The tour begins innocently enough on a "Glamourtrain," a candy striped tram which conveys visitors into the magical world of film, where even reality can become an illusion. Real and perceived adventures await passengers as an understanding of sound stages, props and costuming is provided. The enthusiastic and highly informative guides aboard each tram pass on a wealth of unusual commentary both amusing and interesting.

Carl Laemmle, the founder of Universal Studios, arrived in California in 1912. The New York entrepreneur first operated in the Hollywood area, but moved in 1914 when he purchased a 240 acre chicken ranch on the other side of the Hollywood Hills, in Lankersham Township. What followed was a roller coaster ride for Universal consisting of success and failure that rivaled the plots of many of its own movies.

Universal's tour is filled with flights of fluff and fancy. Although too commercial for serious movie buffs, the guided adventure has proven to be a delight for mom, pop and the kids. During the ride a series of contrived adventures await the unwary traveler. At one point the tram is held captive inside a giant space ship as aliens battle to keep control of the tram and its occupants. After a successful escape, passengers continue to experience a series of scenes reminiscent of Universal's blockbuster movies. Jaws, that scary denizen of the deep,

attacks the tram, a flash flood roars down out of the hills engulfing everything in its path. Stuck on a collapsing bridge, bombarded by an avalanche, even the parting of the Red Sea is not too much to ask for and consequently experience.

Perhaps the most interesting part of the tour comes with a stop at soundstages 30 and 32. In-depth explanations and exhibits provide a factual and fascinating glimpse of the history and hype involved with special effects. Everything from the simple creating and painting of a set to the computer generation of fantastic characters and scenes is explained for the inquiring audience.

Some of the more easily recognizable back lot props include the house from the movie *Psycho*, several of the Chicago street scenes from the movie *The Sting* and the Comedy Screen Test Theater.

The fun and the education don't end with the tram ride. Visitors are treated to a barrage of entertainment upon departing the tram. Constantly changing to reflect the trends and the successes of Universal, these mini movies are acted out live and accompanied by fascinatingly real special effects. Past and current shows have included Conan the Barbarian and his battles with mythical and imaginary dragons, warriors and environmental obstacles.

Throughout the Universal lot a wide assortment of stuntmen, trained animals, monsters, magicians, and actors and actresses roam catching the unwary guest up in the excitement of filmmaking.

The success of the movie industry in general and Universal Studios in particular may ebb and flow over the years. In fact, on more than one occasion the studio found itself facing bankruptcy or business failure only to be rescued time and time again. However, the popularity of the Universal tours has not wavered since 1963, when the first visitors were allowed to drop by the commissary and perhaps catch a glimpse of a favorite star. The tradition continues and the excitement is contagious as visitors to the studio are swept up in the magic of the movies.

The tours are scheduled seven days a week throughout the year with the exception of Thanksgiving and Christmas. As a rule the first tram leaves at 10:00 a.m. on weekdays and 9:30 a.m. on weekends. The last tram usually departs at approximately 3:30 p.m.

RESTAURANTS

FUNG LUM RESTAURANT
222 Universal Terrace Parkway
Universal City, CA 91608
Tel. (818) 763-7888
Hrs: Lunch   Mon. - Sat.   11:30 a.m. - 2:30 p.m.
      Dinner   Mon. - Thu.   5:00 p.m. - 10:00 p.m.
                 Fri. - Sat.   5:00 p.m. - 11:00 p.m.
      Sunday Brunch   11:00 a.m. - 3:00 p.m.
      Sunday Dinner   3:00 p.m. - 10:00 p.m.
Visa, MasterCard, AMEX and Diners Club are accepted.

It's one thing to serve ethnic food to those who have never eaten in its country of origin. It is entirely something else to satisfy the "native" palate and that's what the Pang family has been doing since 1950, when they established their first Chinese restaurant in Shatin, Hong Kong.

The giant golden pagoda overlooking an entire hill adjacent to Universal Studios is considered the most ravishingly arranged

Chinese restaurant in all of Los Angeles. The eleven and a half foot doorway is just the beginning. The Sixty Dragon Dome is a reproduction of the Heaven's Gate Temple in Peking and the remainder of the multi-tiered palace draws its inspiration from those of the T'ang Dynasty.

Over four years in the creation, it seats one thousand in absolute Oriental splendor. The carved wood and embroidered silk motif of the upper level is continued in the lower, where banquet seating for 300 is lit by tasseled wood and brass hanging fixtures reminiscent of the oil lamps which brightened royal estates in ancient Cathay.

Fung Lum is open seven days a week and their Sunday brunch is rated one of the best in Los Angeles. For the discriminating Cantonese palate, it's that huge T'ang Palace on the hill, where venerability and culinary experience make dining there an unforgettable experience.

VICTORIA STATION
3850 Lankershim Boulevard
Universal City, CA 91608
Tel. (818) 760-0714
Hrs: Lunch   Mon. - Sat.   11:30 a.m. - 4:00 p.m.
      Dinner   Mon. - Thu.   5:00 p.m. - 10:00 p.m.
                     Fri. - Sat.   5:00 p.m. - 11:00 p.m.
      Brunch Sunday   10:30 a.m. - 3:30 p.m.

Universal City's Victoria Station restaurant, atop the hill at Universal Studios, for eleven years has been a gathering place for local residents and out of towners visiting the greater Los Angeles area.

Fashioned after the famous Victoria Station in London, guests may dine in one of the authentic English pullman cars or perhaps enjoy themselves in a quiet curtained booth on the grand platform. Although renowned for succulent Prime Ribs of Beef, Victoria Station at Universal Studios also specializes in the freshest of seafood and a variety of specialty entrees.

In addition, guests may dance to the wee hours at Stars, a most unique video nightclub, seven nights a week. Victoria Station is always jumping and full of people so reservations are suggested.

VAN NUYS

Van Nuys first came into being as a farm trade center, then as an administrative center of the Los Angeles City government for the San Fernando Valley, and eventually became the Valley's largest residential community. The General Motors Assembly Plant there is a major regional employer. The community's name comes from I. N. Van Nuys, an early settler.

ATTRACTION

• The **Great Wall of Los Angeles** is a 2,000 foot long mural, stretching from Burbank Boulevard and Oxnard Street along Coldwater Canyon Boulevard, that depicts the history of California's immigrants. Each year, a new "chapter" is added to the lengthy storyboard.

ACCOMMODATION

CARRIAGE INN HOTEL
5525 Sepulveda Boulevard
Van Nuys, CA 91411
Tel.   (818) 787-2300
        (800) 854-2604
Visa, MasterCard, AMEX and Diners Club are accepted.

The Carriage Inn is an island of tranquility in the midst of the hustle and bustle of the San Fernando Valley. The Inn is an excellently situated motor hotel with a friendly atmosphere and attentive service.

Stepping into the Carriage Inn is like stepping into a bit of New England. The rooms are decorated in New England style and feature forest green carpeting, country floral bedspreads, rich, dark wood credenzas which hold color TVs and clock radios. Comfortable dark green velvet Barcalounger reclining chairs offer feet-up relaxation at the end of the day. Coffee service dispensers are in each room.

Computer adaptable, two line telephones are available upon request. There is no charge for Wats line or credit card calls. You can keep up on the daily news with regular newspaper service at your door. A coffee shop and dining room are on the premises.

The Carriage Inn is conveniently located via the largest freeway network in the world to most of the major Los Angeles attractions. Nearby, you can golf at one of three public golf courses. Universal Studios is virtually next door. Balboa Park and Recreational Center is minutes away. Shopping can be done at the famous Sherman Oaks Galleria. Comfortable accommodations, attentive service and a central, accessible location are among the reasons the Carriage Inn has been a continual favorite of San Fernando Valley visitors for more than two decades.

BAR

ROBIN HOOD TAVERN
13640 Burbank Boulevard
Van Nuys, CA 91404
Tel. (818) 997-9660
Hrs: Mon. - Sun.   11:00 a.m. - 2:00 a.m.
      Kitchen   11:00 a.m. - 11:00 p.m.
      Breakfast
      Sat. - Sun.   11:00 a.m. - 2:00 p.m.
      Sunday Roast   2:00 p.m. - 11:00 p.m.
Visa and MasterCard are accepted.

The Robin Hood Tavern draws a regular after work crowd attesting to its success in giving Van Nuys a taste of the English Pub's neighborhood atmosphere. The pub sports a red, white and blue awning in front, a large wooden bar, red velvet curtains and ceiling fans, mirrors embellished with British slogans, comfortable booth seating, and a jukebox, satellite television, and dart boards for entertainment.

The Robin Hood Tavern is a member of the Southern California Darts Association and sponsors nine dart teams, playing Monday, Wednesday and Friday. Of course, no pub would be complete without authentic English bangers and hot mustard, mushy peas, mash, Heinz baked beans, fish and chips, and tasty homemade soups, pies and pasties! Owners Lorraine and Michael Williams also offer an extensive selection of imported draught beers, English cider, friendly service, and solace to fellow Brits who may be a little homesick.

Their homecooked meals, warm camaraderie, and relaxed atmosphere ensure a happy evening down at the pub.

WOODLAND HILLS

An attractive residential community and retail and financial district, Woodland Hills is home to Pierce College, which has the distinction of operating one of the last working farms within the L.A. city limits.   Visitors can take the 1.5 hour tour of the campus and its farm complex.

BAR

PICKWICK'S PUB
21010 Ventura Boulevard
Woodland Hills, CA 91364
Tel: (818) 992-9619
Hrs: Mon. - Sun. 11:00 a.m. - 2:00 a.m.
Credit cards are not accepted.

John McIntosh brought a little bit of England with him when he immigrated to Woodland Hills. Born and raised in Scotland and England, John came to California to escape the British tax system. Opening Pickwick's Pub five years ago, John created the atmosphere and warmth of his homeland's country pub.

The atmosphere and John's accent are not the only things authentically British at Pickwick's Pub. John serves a variety of sandwiches and main courses. For those wishing to get quickly into the British mood of things, try the Ploughman's lunch. It features pork pie served with a Branston pickle or pickled onion and is completed with cheese and a roll. There is also fish and chips or chicken and mushroom pie with chips. Bangers and mash translates to the American as tasty sausage and mashed potatoes. The Pub decor is complete from the long bar to the sawdust on the floor. Evenings at

Pickwick's Pub are lively and fun filled with live music and a choice of fourteen different kinds of draft beer. No self respecting English Pub would be complete without a night devoted to patrons challenging each other in a dart game.

Pickwick's Pub's regulars are a diverse group of loyal customers. Blue jeans and sweatshirts stand beside three piece tailored suits. Whether for a meal or a night of impromptu high spirits, drop by Pickwick's Pub. Don't be surprised if you leave with warmth in your heart and a touch of an accent on your tongue.

BOOKSTORE

BANBURY BOOK SHOP
20929 Ventura Boulevard
Woodland Hills, CA 91364
Tel. (818) 368-1644
Hrs: Mon. - Fri.   10:00 a.m. - 6:00 p.m.
         Saturday   10:00 a.m. - 5:00 p.m.
Visa and MasterCard are accepted.

Jan and Peter O'Donahue opened their cozy bookstore, the Banbury Book Shop, fifteen years ago to satisfy their longing to surround themselves with books and encourage others to "fill their leisure time with the world of words."

Their English-style shop is brimming with well organized hardcover, paperback, and children's books, and the O'Donahues make a special effort to stock the latest releases. In addition to personal attention, they offer special ordering and complimentary giftwrapping for your gift book selection. They invite you to browse at will and are always ready with a helpful suggestion for a gift or a personal choice.

Their excellent selection of children's books will allow you to help "turn on" a child's interest in reading. The Banbury Book Shop promises hours of delight, escape, inspiration, suspense, and excitement, all under the covers of a book jacket.

GIFT SHOP

COUNTRY HABIT
19805 Ventura Boulevard
Woodland Hills, CA 91367
Tel. (818) 347-1141
Hrs.   Mon. - Sat.   10:00 a.m. - 7:00 p.m.
          Sunday   12:00 noon - 5:00 p.m.
          Winter
          Mon. - Sun.   10:00 a.m. - 6:00 p.m.
Visa and MasterCard are accepted.

At the Country Habit you can visit yesterday today. This is not just another country store, but a unique and fascinating showcase of yesterday's warmth, tradition and style.

Owner, Sioux Renfro has a knack as well as a love for shopping and this country style store provides her with an outlet for those talents. In the Country Habit you can find furniture and fixtures to decorate every room in the house, hammered copper cupboards, dried flowers, hutches, quilts and pillows filled with potpourri. Another curio is the Lizzie High dolls. Each comes in an unusual costume and has its own personal story.

Pine Country furniture can be custom made; just another of the personal touches that Sioux and the Country Habit offer to its customers. Custom orders are welcome, gift wrapping is available and the Country Habit will ship anywhere in the United States.

 # RESTAURANTS

ROSATI'S PIZZA
23367 Mulholland Drive
Woodland Hills, CA 91364
Tel. (818) 888-8700
Hrs: Mon. - Thu. 11:00 a.m. - 9:00 p.m.
      Fri. - Sat.   11:00 a.m. - 10:00 p.m.
      Sunday   3:00 p.m. - 9:00 p.m.

There is simply no substitute for experience and Vito Rosati, Jr., owner of Rosati's Pizza, has over two decades of it. His father insisted that he learn the business from the ground up —bus boy, dishwasher, bartender, cook and sauce maker—and now Vito has passed that legacy along to his two young sons.

Rosati's is, then, more than just a pizza parlor. There is homemade Manicotti, Cannelloni or White Veal Saltimbocca. There is Pasta Fagioli, a wholesome Italian soup of beans and macaroni, and Calzones created specifically by Vito himself. The menu also offers a full line of traditional and Sicilian pizzas, all served in an atmosphere of comfortable wooden tables and chairs and aromatic wax candles.

"The smartest people in the world are my customers," says Vito, "they know what they want, how they want it, and about how much it should cost. This is the philosophy of my papa and now of my children, as well." In the highly competitive world of Italian cuisine, it's this kind of devotion which makes all the difference. So if it's more than just pizza you're after, stop by and treat yourself to the Vito Rosati hallmark of excellence in fine dining itself.

SEAFOOD EMPORIUM
19762 Ventura Boulevard
Woodland Hills, CA 91364
Tel. (818) FISH350
Hrs: Market   Mon. - Sat.   9:00 a.m. - 8:00 p.m.
                       Sunday   10:00 a.m. - 8:00 p.m.
       Restaurant   Sun. - Thu.   11:00 a.m. - 9:00 p.m.
                       Fri - Sat.   11:00 a.m. - 10:00 p.m.
Visa and MasterCard are accepted.

Rick Rittner started as a supermarket boxboy and eventually became the owner of one of the largest fresh fish and seafood markets in Southern California. This was in 1963, since then the Seafood Emporium has expanded three times and recently a restaurant was added to take advantage of the fresh seafoods.

Blue and white awnings breeze in the center of Corbin Village. Brick and stone add to the charm of the large open patio eating area. Inside, forty feet of showcases display an unbelievable variety of seafood, fresh crusty sourdough bread and slabs of cheese. Seated in one of the booths, customers can enjoy the finest under $10.00 menu in the area. The excellently prepared dinners have a definite international flavor. Live Maine lobster, Norwegian salmon swordfish from Japan and lemon sole from England are just a few of the succulent seafoods available. For a change of pace there is also a large selection of dishes with more of a land locked appeal.

Many of the Seafood Emporium's customers travel long distances to patronize the restaurant and the market, a fitting testimonial to the quality of the foods and the service.

THE SEASHELL
19723 Ventura Boulevard
Woodland Hills, CA 91364
Tel. (818) 884-6500
Hrs: Lunch   Mon. - Fri.   11:30 a.m. - 2:00 p.m.
       Dinner   Mon. - Thu.   5:30 p.m. - 10:00 p.m.
                      Fri. - Sat.   5:30 p.m. - 10:30 p.m.
                      Sunday   5:00 p.m. - 9:30 p.m.
Visa, MasterCard, AMEX, Diners Club and Carte Blanche are accepted.

The Seashell offers an inviting and warm interior with a fresh feeling and a bright and light decor that achieves a delicate balance between casual and formal. Cantilevered picture windows are framed in greenery and wood paneled walls are highlighted by skylights. The tables are positioned for privacy. Traditional seafood lite meals are served along with some meat specialties.

The Seashell menu focuses on seafood with a special emphasis on the authentic Bouillabaisse. Take your choice of Scampi baked in fresh herbs and garlic, Rex Sole, sauteed with grapes and lemon butter or Lake Superior Whitefish in Dijon mustard sauce. Poached Salmon Fillet in a sorrel sauce and Swordfish Provencal are favorites at The Seashell. There are many daily specials dependent upon market availability. You may find a special of John Dory, fresh Dover Sole or Lobster in season. Constant individual attention is given to each guest at The Seashell and reasonable variations of the menu will receive consideration.

The Seashell has been in existence for fifteen years and owners Christian Desmet and Dieter Wantig credit their longevity to attention to customer needs and consistently high quality cuisine. A banquet room seating twelve to fifty people for private dinners is also available. Valet parking is behind the restaurant.

SAN GABRIEL VALLEY

The San Gabriel Valley enjoys a backdrop of snowcapped mountains and a pale desert sky. It was this setting that lured thousands of home buyers during the 1950s into what was an expanse of citrus groves, vineyards and truck farms dotted with a string of distinctive agricultural communities.

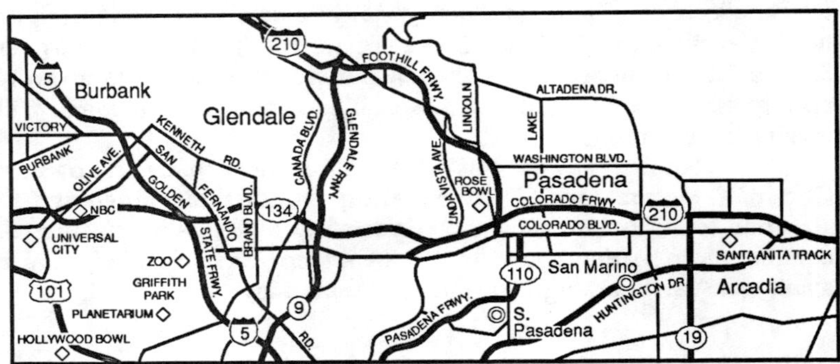

Today the San Gabriel Valley takes a lot of guff for its reputation for being a hot, smoggy and overdeveloped suburb of Los Angeles. Its location directly east of the city allows prevailing coast winds to blow the smog that manages to escape the L.A. Basin into the valley. The neighboring San Fernando Valley is somewhat better protected by the Verdugo Mountains that separate it from the San Gabriel Valley.

The San Gabriel Valley does possess many attractive qualities. By most standards the climate and the surrounding landscape make it a beautiful place to live and work. It has quick access to the nearby mountains of Angeles National Forest, as well as the urban stimulation of downtown Los Angeles. The San Gabriel Valley contains a number of fine museums, lush gardens and parks, as well as excellent restaurants and shopping and Pasadena, which hosts the annual Rose Bowl Parade.

When the San Gabriel Valley was under Spanish ru le, most of the land was owned by the old Mission San Gabriel. During that period the natives, who had been converted to the ways of the mission fathers, tended great herds of sheep, cattle and horses, as well as worked the corn fields and orchards. The region was later divided into a series of ranchos.   Later, a string of self reliant agricultural communities sprouted up on the north slope of the San Gabriel Valley.

Communities such as Pasadena, Arcadia, Sierra Madre, Azusa and Glendora each had characters of their own and tended to attract like minded and socially compatible people. The post World War II building boom turned many of these agricultural communities into large residential tracts. Today development continues, as a new wave of immigrants arrives in the valley.

ATTRACTIONS

• **Descanso Gardens**, located in the community of La Canada, is a lush flowering 165 acres that was once private residences. Formerly belonging to the owner of a Los Angeles newspaper and his wife, the garden contains a vast assortment of camellias. No matter what time of year one visits, there will be plenty in bloom. A Japanese teahouse serves refreshments in the afternoons within the tranquil setting of a formal Japanese garden. For those of vigorous heart, nature tails, as well as picnic facilities and open grassy areas await discovery. Other sections of the garden include an area set aside for native California plants and a native California oak forest. The gardens are located at 1418 Descanso Drive. Take either the Glendale Freeway to Foothill Boulevard, or Freeway 210 to Angeles Crest Highway and on to Foothill Boulevard. Call (818) 790-5414.

• **Mount Wilson**, located on the crest of the San Gabriel Mountains above Pasadena, is known for its fine views of the cityscape below, as well as the heavens above. Visit the Mount Wilson Observatory for a look at the telescope, or hike the nearby **Mount Wilson Skyline Park**. The park offers picnicking facilities and a variety of trails that lead down the southern slope of the mountain. For information, call (818) 577-1122.

• To see where the San Gabriel Valley development began, visit **Mission San Gabriel Archangel**, at 537 West Mission Drive in San Gabriel. The mission, founded in 1771, was the fourth California mission established by Spanish priests. Unique among the missions its the strong Moorish influence on the old building with is ornate facade, vaulted roof, capped buttresses and narrow windows.

- The **Pio Pico State Historic Park**, 6003 South Pioneer Boulevard, Whittier, is the former home of the last Mexican governor of California, Pio Pico. The house has been restored to its 1870 appearance. The grounds contain picnic facilities.
- The **Rancho Santa Ana Botanical Gardens**, 1500 North College Avenue, Claremont, is an eighty-three acre garden. The height of the blooming season lasts from late February to the middle of June.

ROUGHING IT

THE GREAT OUTDOORS IN LOS ANGELES

Hurray for L.A.! Randy Newman sings about it and Kareem Abdul Jabaar doesn't seem to want to retire from it. In spite of the ebb and flow of the movie industry, Hollywood is still the undisputed world's champion when it comes to cranking out that tough thermoplastic we call film. Stars, in every abstract and literal definition of the word, shine in a never ending panorama of sight, sound and an assault on the senses. The magnetic glitter of Hollywood, both past and present, continues to attract more than its share of curiosity seekers, fledgling entrepreneurs and aspiring performers.

A melange of exciting, glamorous and even exotic events, exhibits and natural phenomena await the intrepid L.A. area camper. Before heading into the wilderness, happy Los Angeles campers may want to visit the manmade wonders of this county. A complete list of attractions is too long to even attempt to reproduce, but includes the following:

- **Forest Lawn Memorial Park** in Glendale, is billed as the Disneyland of cemeteries. Within its gates are full sized reproductions of English and Scottish churches, one of which was the sight of the 1940 marriage between Ronald Reagan and Jane Wyman. Superstar evangelist Aimee Semple McPherson's tomb is at Forest Lawn, as are the final resting spots of Jean Hersholt, David O. Selznick, Alan Ladd, Nat King Cole, Errol Flynn, baseball's Casey Stengel and the ashes of Walter Elias Disney.
- **F. Scott Fitzgerald's** apartment in West Hollywood is just up the street from the site of **Schwab's Drugstore**. It was there

Fitzgerald worked on his final book *The Last Tycoon*, spent time with Shiela Graham and died in 1940 at the age of forty-four.

• Downtown Los Angeles at one time boasted of more theaters than any other metropolitan area in the world; over 1500. The theater district, stretching from 3rd to 9th Streets on South Broadway, remains a treasure of American theater history. Names that are still magical light up the night sky: **The Orpheum**, the **Globe Theater**, the **Palace, Roxie Theater** and **United Artists Theater** invoke images of spotlights shooting heavenward, crowds of adoring fans and long sleek limousines depositing their precious cargoes of celluloid gods and goddesses.

• The **Wilshire District** was once home to some of the biggest names in Hollywood, including Mae West and Cecil B. DeMille. Many of the original buildings still stand and attract movie lovers of all ages.

• South of Sunset Boulevard, in Central Hollywood, lies **"The Factory Town,"** the site of many of the giant studios and film processing plants, the virtual heart of the movie industry.

• **"Hollywood by the Sea"** includes an area encompassing Venice, Santa Monica and Malibu. Within the confines of the Santa Monica Mountains is an enormous state park in which several movies were shot, including *How Green Was My Valley* and the original *M*A*S*H*.

• **Venice** has also been a movie making site, but its appeal lies in the manmade attractions of wealthy cigarette manufacturer Abbot Kinney. Kinney attempted to literally recreate the beauty and allure of Venice, Italy complete with canals and colonnaded facades. However, this was in 1905 and little remains of Kinney's "Venice by the Sea."

On the other hand, Venice has metamorphosed almost full circle. From its lowest point in the 1950s, when it was portrayed as the sleazy Texas/Mexican village in Orson Welles' *Touch of Evil*, Venice has been home to the beat culture, and the art culture in the 70s, until it is once again considered as the center of Los Angeles' cultural renaissance, with its restored buildings and impressive murals.

• Finally there is the Boulevard itself; Hollywood at its finest, the glitter and glint, the facade and the "for real," makeup and make believe. The original **Grauman's Chinese Theater**, the **Walk of Fame** with close to 1800 stars now included, the **Max Factor building, Hollywood Wax Museum**, the **Ozzie and Harriet House**, the **Magic Castle** and the **Hollywood Bowl** represent just a few of the seemingly endless array of tourist delights.

Before the "Hollywood dream" became a reality the Los Angeles area consisted of ranches, bean fields and orange and lemon groves. Fortunately, the natural wonders of the area remain intact in spite of the rampant growth that overtook the area as the technicolor world of "tinseltown" flexed its massive muscles. The beaches and mountains, canyons and vistas that ring the Los Angeles Basin, although somewhat urbanized, still offer beautiful, natural communal spots, where one can be surprisingly alone.

The Rim of the World Drive in the San Bernardino Mountains winds through elevations of 5,000 to 7,000 feet. Lake Arrowhead and Big Bear Lake are noted for their natural beauty and picturesque development. Alpine style villages nestle next to ski resorts and marinas. From the mountain ridge south of Big Bear, San Gorgonio's snowy summit beckons to serious hikers and backpackers. San Gorgonio peaks at approximately 11,502 feet and displays an impressive face of solid granite, giving it the nickname of Old Grayback.

The San Gabriel Mountains begin a lazy rise and fall that stretches from the Pacific Coast to the Mojave Desert. Considered the most accessible of the high mountain ranges in the Los Angeles area, the San Gabriels have a virtual network of forest trails, wilderness areas and horse paths. Although these mountains have an excellent highway system, they are best appreciated in a more leisurely manner while on foot or horseback.

Within an hour's drive from parts of Los Angeles, the Angeles Crest Highway and San Antonio Canyon Road both lead to the city's "mountain playground."

Sullivan, Rustic and the infamous Topanga canyons are hidden within the Santa Monica Mountains, an unusual group of mountains in that they run east and west, while most other mountains in the United States run north to south. The Santa Monicas run through the heart of Los Angeles and include the rock formations and distinct gorges of Malibu Creek State Park, Griffith State Park, with its extensive system of hiking and bridle paths, and Will Rogers State Historic Park.

Additionally, the Los Angeles area features a wealth of beautiful and breathtaking natural sights which include the Pacific coastline, the Los Angeles National Forest, Vista del Mar, Paradise Cove, Lake Shore State Park, Puddingstone Lake, Bedrock Mountain, Cienga Canyon and many, many other superb wilderness locations.

In spite of some very obvious differences, there are many similarities between visiting the great outdoors and shopping Rodeo Drive. The first is hiking and foot care. No matter the environment, special attention must be paid to the feet, since hiking the Burnt Peak Canyon trail head to the back country and getting a peek at Greta Garbo's house on Chevy Chase Street both require extensive standing and hiking, under less than ideal conditions.

A universal tip is to wear some type of foot pad (preferably sponge rubber) inside a comfortable, broken-in shoe. Most shoes, boots or sandals purchased immediately before departing on a vacation will invariably rub something, somewhere, the wrong way. Serious hiking, such as a day spent at Disneyland or Magic Mountain keeping up with the children, can make for an uncomfortable day's end for the feet and their owner unless proper precautions are taken.

Wearing the proper clothing will also enhance any excursion, whether you are viewing Frank Lloyd Wright's fantastic Ennis-Brown house on Glendower Avenue or hiking the Pacific Crest National Scenic Trail in the Los Angeles National Forest. This doesn't necessarily mean pulling out the designer labels for that stroll through *Rodeo de las Aguas* (Beverly Hills), or throwing on a sequined mini skirt, Gucci boots and Revo sunglasses for a jaunt along Hollywood Boulevard. Serious sightseers, as well as campers and hikers, should know that dressing in layers allows for a modicum of climate control.

A tourist's day in L.A. usually starts out early in the morning when it can be cold, or at least cool. By mid-afternoon that coolness will have turned to warmth, and by late afternoon temperatures may have moved upward as much as thirty degrees. Dressing in layers seems much wiser than having goose bumps by dressing too lightly for chilly mornings or walking around soaked with perspiration in the late afternoon. With today's miracle fabrics it is not difficult to dress in light clothing that is easily removed and stored or carried as needed.

Whether you are exploring the frozen tundra or the frozen yogurt shop at Hollywood and Vine, having and understanding the proper maps will reduce your stress level, as well as the time involved getting around in a strange environment. For sightseers, a myriad of maps are available either in the L.A. area, from travel bureaus in your hometown or the American Automobile Association, if you are a member.

Those dedicated to more rustic endeavors can send ahead for maps from the Department of Agriculture's Forest Service. These maps detail streams, lakes, trails and accessible roads, and are available by contacting the USDA Forest Service, Office of Information Pacific Southwest Region, 630 Sansome Street, San Francisco, CA 94111. The Forest Service is an excellent source of information concerning peak seasons, restrictions as they apply and campsite fees for the state and national parks.

What follows is a partial listing of RV sites in the L.A. area. Most of the locations offer standard amenities including rest rooms, showers, sewer hookups and laundry facilities. Many of these locations also feature a more extensive list of accommodations. This may include, but is not limited to, swimming pools, cable TV, a grocery store and boat, horse or bicycle rentals. For specific details as to space availability, fees and amenities, travelers are encouraged to phone ahead.

- **Shoreline RV Park.** Tel. (800) 822-CAMP. Seventy RV spaces, fireplaces, groceries and laundry facilities. Go south on State Route 7 to the intersection of Shoreline Drive and Pine Avenue. Open all year, the site is thirty minutes from Disneyland, Knott's Berry Farm and Universal Studio.

• **Dockweiler Beach RV Park.** Tel. (800) 822-CAMP. 160 spaces, piped water and flush toilets. Twelve miles south of Santa Monica on Vista del Mar. Fishing and swimming are available at the nearby beach.

• **Malibu Beach RV Park.** Tel. (213) 456-6052. 125 RV sites and forty tent spaces, cable TV, showers, playground and sanitary dump station. Four miles north of Malibu on State Route 1. Open all year and situated on a bluff with a spectacular view of the Pacific.

• **Travel Village.** Tel. (805) 255-4222. 231 RV spaces and 195 campsites, electrical and sewer connections, swimming pools, propane gas and laundry facilities. Five miles northwest of Valencia at 17946 Henry Mayo Road.

• **Castaic Lake RV Park.** Tel (805) 257-334. 103 RV spaces and fifty tent sites, health spa, arcade, heated pool and piped water. Drive to Castaic off I-5 to Ridge Route Road. 1150 foot elevation, located within an hour of all major Los Angeles attractions.

• **East Shore RV Park.** Tel. (714) 599-8355. 426 RV spaces and twenty-five tent sites, piped water, showers, propane gas and groceries. Five miles northwest of Pomona, via I-10, to 120 East Via Verde. Situated on Puddingstone Lake, offering a resort environment. Swimming, fishing, waterskiing, golf and more are available.

The following locations are strictly tent sites and are located on government land. Amenities are sparse to non-existent, in some cases even water is not available. Reservations are not necessary and there is a wide range of fees, with many sites being free. Few are open all year long and finding the locations can often times prove frustrating. Information on any of these sites and others in the area can be obtained by telephoning **Angeles National Forest Headquarters** at (818) 574-1613.

• **Atmore Meadows.** Six tent sites, no water available, elevation 4300 feet. Located at the trail head to the back country and Cienga Canyon.

• **Sawmill Meadows.** Ten tent sites, no water, elevation 5200 feet. Located on the Pacific Crest Trail near the Burnt Peak Canyon Trailhead.

- **Lower Shake**. Five tent sites, no water, groceries and laundry nearby. Near Lake Hughes just off County Road N-2.
- **Prospect**. Twenty-two tent sites, piped water, fireplaces and vault toilets. On Lake Hughes Road near Elizabeth Lake Canyon Creek.
- **Hollow Tree**. Five tent sites, no water, fireplaces, grocery store nearby. Fourteen miles northeast of Saugus on Bouquet Canyon Road.
- **Lupine**. Eleven tent sites, piped water, vault toilets, fireplaces. Eighteen miles northwest of Wrightwood.

From the glitter of thousands of neon lights to the glimmer of a million night's stars, Los Angeles County area has few peers. Miles of trails, paths, sidewalks and roads can lead to a diverse and thoroughly enjoyable "magical mystery tour."

ARCADIA

Arcadia lies along Interstate 210 east of Pasadena. The city was developed in the late 1880s by Herman A. Unruh of the San Gabriel Valley Railway. The town's name is a reference to the district in Greece often depicted in pastoral poetry for its rural beauty and simplicity.

ATTRACTIONS

- The **Los Angeles State and County Arboretum**, at 310 Baldwin Ave, is so lush and green that it was once used to film Tarzan movies. One can almost hear his jungle call among the one hundred foot tall palm trees surrounding an idyllic lagoon. You can easily spend a day among the beautifully landscaped public gardens inhabited by wandering peacocks. Also on the grounds is a restored adobe, first built in 1839. Alongside the adobe you'll find a reconstructed **Native American village** of reed huts. The nearby **Queen Anne Cottage,** built in 1881, is furnished in the styles of its day, right down to the bouquets of fresh flowers in every room. The coach barn contains displays of old tools. The park was originally the private residence of the publisher of a Los Angeles newspaper.

 # RESTAURANT

CHEZ SATEAU
850 South Baldwin Avenue
Arcadia, CA 91006
Tel. (818) 446-8806
Hrs: Lunch
      Tue. - Sun.   11:30 a.m. - 2:30 p.m.
      Dinner
      Tue. - Sun.   5:30 p.m. - 10:30 p.m.
      Sunday Brunch   10:30 a.m. - 2:30 p.m.
All major credit cards are accepted.

Owner and chef Ryo Satyo, whose background includes Maxim's of Paris, L'oustau du Beau, and the Connaught Savoy of London established Chez Sateau because he wanted free reign for his own culinary creativity. The results over the last six years have astounded diners from throughout Southern California.

The restaurant is located in a large brick and beige stucco building softened by flowers and creeping vines in planters. Large double wooden doors invite guests into a spacious, pastel, turn of the century ambiance replete with fluted, frosted glass wall scenes, period pictures, and a dark wood paneled bar area with small cocktail tables and subdued lighting. Befitting a master European chef, the menu ranges from rack of lamb to fillet of salmon and includes appetizers such as Crab Royale, Escargot, and Mosaic of Smoked Salmon. The desserts are baked on the premise and offerings include crepe suzettes, cherries jubilee, apple tarts and Baked Alaska. The Sunday Champagne Brunch is already becoming legendary and features unlimited champagne, eight appetizers, ten entrees and dessert. The prices are amazing for this kind of haute cuisine and, as one customer recently remarked, "It's like buying a Picasso at bargain rates."

This restaurant has been rated three stars by the Restaurant Writers Association and Ryo Satyo has been named by them "Chef of the Year." Los Angeles Mayor Tom Bradley gave him the key to the city as a result of the week long culinary celebration he created for a number of distinguished dignitaries. Even for Southern California, a capital of fine dining, it simply does not come any better than this.

CANOGA PARK

Once known as Owensmouth, Canoga Park was one of several communities developed around 1911 after water became available from the Owens Valley. Its present name is probably borrowed from Canoga, New York, which was a Native American term meaning "place of the floating oil." Among the aerospace firms located in Canoga Park is Rocketdyne, a manufacturer of liquid fuel rocket engines.

 ## FURNITURE STORE

FROCH'S WOODCRAFT SHOPS, INC.
6659 Topanga Canyon Boulevard
Canoga Park, CA 91303
Tel.   (818) 883-4730
        (800) 228-4877
Hrs: Mon. - Sat.   9:00 a.m. - 6:00 p.m.
       Friday   9:00 a.m. - 5:00 p.m.
Visa, MasterCard and AMEX are accepted.
Also,
7945 Van Nuys Boulevard
Panorama City, CA 91402
Tel. (818) 787-3682

How many times have you searched the closet for a special outfit but couldn't find it? You promised yourself you'd get organized some day. Froch's Woodcraft Shop offers you the perfect opportunity to organize with an extensive collection of solid wood closet organizing systems.

Closets aren't the only places you can improve with Abe Froch's designs. Froch has created organizing designs in unfinished hardwood for all the rooms of your home, even the garage. Kitchens are a specialty at Froch's. Froch, with a staff of forty dedicated craftsmen, have put together a variety of base, pantry, and upper cabinets that provide extraordinary design features. Froch's contemporary styles use every square inch of space. Pull-out trays allow you to reach over-sized pots and pans without strain, and handy spice racks fit conveniently inside cabinet doors. A book tray which fastens to the underside of any cabinet eliminates the need for awkward cookbook holders; it simply folds up underneath the cabinet. Buyers rave about the innovative rotating corner, which turns dead corner space into usable, accessible storage. Froch's stands for nothing less than top quality; particle board is never used.

Old world craftsmanship expresses itself at Froch's when each artisan proudly signs his name on the back of the finished piece. Whether you install these organizing systems yourself, or have them installed, you'll know you have the best of the best.

RESTAURANTS

EPICURE INN
7625 Topanga Canyon Boulevard
Conoga Park, CA 91304
Tel. (818) 888-3300
Hrs: Lunch   Mon. - Fri.   11:30 a.m. - 2:00 p.m.
      Dinner   Monday   5:30 p.m. - 9:00 p.m.
                 Tue. - Sat.   5:30 p.m. - 10:00 p.m.
Visa, MasterCard, AMEX and Diners Club are accepted.

Enjoy an unforgettable adventure in fine dining at Epicure Inn. The ambiance within the English Tudor styled restaurant, with its charm and reminiscence of the "old country," is like stepping back in time. Exquisite antique and brass fixtures are appointed throughout the dining salon and high back wooden booths ensure a quiet intimate repast.

Epicureans will delight in discovering the rich and varied culinary creations by European trained chef and entrepreneur, Manfred Fuehr. Leading the list of savory entrees is Veal Garvazzi, scallopini of veal laden with shrimp in a delectable sauce served with buttered fettuccine; and Carpet Bagger, a filet mignon stuffed with oysters, broiled to your preference and coated with butter. Dare to be adventurous with Duckling a la Jubilee, half a duckling roasted to perfection and served with a special black cherry sauce. Another culinary delight is Beef Wellington, a filet of beef topped with liver pate placed on a duxelle of mushroom and enveloped in puff pastry. Entrees are served with two fresh vegetables and choice of rice, potato or pasta. Weekly specials include Wiener Schnitzel, Sauerbraten, Crabmeat Florentine and Rouladen of Beef. A full bar is featured as well as an extensive wine list.

"Eat, drink and be merry" at Epicure Inn. Join in the "Sing-Along" featured every Friday night in the cocktail lounge, and feel free to ask well-known entertainer and pianist, Irene to entertain you with your favorite.

McGUIRE'S STEAK HOUSE
8232 De Soto Avenue
Canoga Park, CA 91304
Tel. (818) 341-5510
Hrs: Buffet Lunch
       Mon. - Fri.   11:30 a.m. - 2:00 p.m.
       Dinner
       Mon. - Sat.   5:00 p.m. - 10:00 p.m.
       Sunday   4:30 p.m. - 9:00 p.m.

For a good meal you can sink your teeth into and a relaxed atmosphere, check out McGuire's Steak House. Family owned and run, these folks know how to cook a steak so good you'll swoon with pleasure when you taste it. With forty years of experience in the restaurant business behind them, the McGuires know how to put the right combination of atmosphere, service and darn good food together.

McGuire's features thick juicy steaks of the best quality beef, Australian lobster tails with hot butter, fresh fish to tickle your fancy and prime rib that will literally melt in your mouth. They offer a large full service salad bar with all the fixings. They also maintain a well stocked cocktail bar. The restaurant offers buffet luncheons as well as the salad bar for the lighter eater. There is live entertainment on Friday and Saturday evenings and dancing if you have a mind to.

McGuire's is located in the heart of Canoga Park, just minutes from the big hotels. So don your comfortable clothes and join the relaxed atmosphere of McGuire's Steak House, where you'll find quality food and prompt friendly service.

GLENDALE

Located between the San Fernando and San Gabriel valleys, Glendale is a residential community of frame bungalows with a downtown area currently under development. The skyline has already changed with the addition of several new highrise office buildings. Within the community are a variety of shopping opportunities ranging from fashionable boutiques to major department stores. Many of the 157,000 people who live here like to browse through the shops and dine in the restaurants along Brand Boulevard or at the Galleria, which features six department stores and 280 mall shops. Cultural activities within the community include the nationally known Glendale Symphony Orchestra and several theater groups.

Before 1910 Glendale was a drowsy little hamlet, but a combination of factors including cheap land and power, convenient transportation and an open shop labor policy, contributed to the city's rise as the third largest in Los Angeles.

ATTRACTIONS

• Foremost among the attractions is the **Forest Lawn Memorial Park** with its displays of gleaming statuary and stained glass, and quaint reproductions of three European churches. The remains of scores of famous people including Jean Harlow, Carole Lombard, Clark Gable, Will Rogers, Gracie Allen, two of the Marx brothers and one of the Three Stooges rest at Forest Lawn.

APPAREL

PURE SWEAT
22268 Glendale Galleria
Glendale, CA 91210
Tel. (818) 240-9736
Hrs: Mon. - Fri.   10:00 a.m. - 9:00 p.m.
       Saturday   9:00 a.m. - 6:00 p.m.
       Sunday   11:00 a.m. - 5:00 p.m.
Visa, MasterCard, AMEX and Discover are accepted.
Also,
3819 East Foothill Boulevard
Hastings Ranch Center
Pasadena, CA 91107
Tel. (818) 351-8047

Pure Sweat is a store where you can find your favorite classic style sweats from heavy weights to their exclusive lightweights.

Display cases running from floor to ceiling are filled with a rainbow of colors and fabrics that cannot be found anywhere else, created just for Pure Sweat and shipped direct from the mills.

If you want durability, comfort and style, Pure Sweat is the store for you.

Starting just a few years ago in Santa Monica, Pure Sweat has grown to thirty-nine stores including locations in Huntington Beach, Sherman Oaks and Hastings Ranch Center in Pasadena.

CANDY STORE

MON TRESOR, 3153 Glendale Boulevard, Glendale, CA Tel. (213) 662-8925. This shop was selected as importer of the finest chocolates for 1985-86 by the National Association of Specialty Foods. You'll enjoy their Belgian and domestic chocolates.

DELICATESSEN

TIP TOP MEATS AND DELI
1215 North Central Avenue
Glendale, CA 91202
Tel. (818) 246-8377
Hrs: Mon. - Sat. 9:00 a.m. - 7:00 p.m.
         Sunday   9:00 a.m. - 6:00 p.m.
Visa, MasterCard, Diners Club and Discover are accepted.

"Our Cleanliness and Quality is a way of Life" is the slogan for Elizabeth and Steven Suli's Tip Top Meats and Deli. The Sulis have built their reputation on their meticulously clean shop and their expertly prepared cuts of meats, poultry and fish.

The cases in the neatly laid out red brick shop display a cornucopia of delicious meats and deli items. Breakfast items range from fresh fruit and muffins to lox, bagels and cream cheese, to an assorted Danish tray with butter and jam. The lunch trays are outstanding in quality and quantity. On the assorted sandwich trays you'll find tender roast beef, meat loaf, Burgundy ham, steak sandwiches, breast of turkey, imported cheeses, lean peppered beef, chicken salad, corned beef, tuna salad and much more. Seafood and main course meals include such deluxe items as the jumbo shrimp and lobster tray and a wide assortment of red meat and chicken entrees. Tip Top's roasts are the finest cuts available. Any meat you order will be cooked free of charge and the beautiful fresh fruit trays offered at Tip Top make unusual centerpieces and add a special touch to any meal.

Tip Top presents the very best selection in catering. The trays are attractive, plentiful and delicious. Tip Top Meats and Deli takes pride in going beyond the ordinary.

MARKET

FISH KING, 722 North Glendale Avenue, Glendale, CA. Tel. (818) 244-2161. When in the mood for delicacies of the deep, visit this excellent seafood market.

PASADENA

Pasadena is one Southern California community that does not have an identity problem. Millions of people who have never been to California are familiar with the street on which the Tournament of Roses Parade marches every New Year's Day. Pasadena has also been able to retain its sense of community and heritage in its Spanish style architecture, historic buildings and well known institutions.

Though the Tournament of Roses Parade and the accompanying football game are the events non-residents think of first when Pasadena comes to mind, the city is also known as the home of the Jet Propulsion Laboratory, the California Institute of Technology, the Norton Simon Museum and the Pasadena Playhouse.

The city's central business district lies between Pasadena Avenue, Corson Street, Mentor Avenue and California Boulevard. Both single story structures as well as multistory office buildings and elevated freeways can be found there. East Pasadena, which lies along Foothill Boulevard, is home to a variety of high-tech and light manufacturing companies. The Northwest section of town contains a mixture of retail and service outlets along with manufacturers.

Among the shopping areas are Old Pasadena, where the community's original business district is enjoying major restoration efforts on turn of the century buildings. This designated historic district, bounded by Pasadena Avenue, Walnut Street, Arroyo Parkway and Green Street, has attracted a variety of unusual shops, galleries, antique dealers and restaurants. Another favorite shopping haunt is the Cal-Fair Plaza at the corner of California Boulevard and Fair Oaks Avenue. Cal-Fair Plaza's developers have restored old buildings and erected new ones to form a plaza containing a variety of specialty shops and restaurants. Other shopping opportunities include Colorado Boulevard, Hastings Ranch, Hen's Teeth Square,

Orangewood Shopping Center, Pasadena Antique Center, Plaza Pasadena and South Lake Avenue.

The breadth of cultural events in Pasadena is quite impressive. The city boasts a number of sites that cultural events and performances a regularly held at. At the Ambassador Auditorium, the 1,200 seat hall frequently hosts world class performers such as Vladimir Horowitz, Marcel Marceau, Luciano Pavarotti and the Berlin Philharmonic Orchestra. The Beckman Auditorium on the campus of the California Institute of Technology hosts an annual lecture series as well as a variety of musical and dramatic events.

The venerable Pasadena Civic Auditorium, which was built in 1931, is not only a historic landmark but a venue for many prestigious events, including the Emmy Awards Ceremony, The Los Angeles Philharmonic Orchestra and the American Ballet Theatre. The Pasadena Playhouse offers live theater featuring revivals of favorites as well as premieres of new works. The theater's audiences have enjoyed performances by Dustin Hoffman, Robert Preston, Gene Hackman, and William Holden, to name a few.

The community of Pasadena began in 1873 with the utopian vision of a group from Indiana seeking the warmth of the Southern California climate. The "Indiana Colony," as it was called, soon succumbed to financial misfortune, but the settlers were quick to reorganize as the San Gabriel Orange Grove Association. In 1875 the members went to great lengths to find a euphonious name, preferably in some Native American language. They settled for Pasadena, the Chippewa term for "crown of the valley."

Pasadena's famous parade had its start in 1890. The Valley Hunt Club sponsored the event patterned after a European festival which was designed to celebrate the city's natural beauty and sunny climate during a time when most of the nation lay under a blanket of snow. Today the event has grown so complex that planning is an on-going year round effort by the Tournament of Roses Association. Participants typically spend $50,000 or more on floats that, according to the rules, must be completely covered with flowers or some other natural material. Visitors sometimes camp out along prime viewing locations on the street the night before the parade. For those planning ahead, tickets can be ordered for grandstand seating.

For further information about the community, contact the **Pasadena Chamber of Commerce**, 199 South Robles Avenue, # 210, Pasadena, CA 91101. Tel. (818) 795-3355.

ATTRACTIONS

• The folks at the **Jet Propulsion Laboratory** boldly go where no man has gone before, electronically that is. There, unmanned Voyager, Viking and Mariner spacecraft have brought the world spectacular pictures of the remote reaches of our solar system. This research and development center is operated by the California Institute of Technology for the National Aeronautics and Space Administration (NASA). Scientists there also conduct research in aviation, biomedicine, energy and other areas to determine how new technologies might lead to solutions for earthly problems. The lab is located at 4800 Oak Grove Avenue. For information on tours and other programs call (818) 354-2337.

• At the **Kidspace Museum,** 390 South El Molino Avenue, children can view and touch exhibit items to learn about the wonders of the world around them. A friendly robot tells visitors they can be whatever they want to be, and the participatory exhibits go further to support that notion. For information call (818) 449-9144.

• One of the world's greatest collections of paintings, tapestries, sculpture and prints are housed within the walls of the **Norton Simon Museum of Art.** The exhibits include everything from European paintings of the Middle Ages through twentieth century works. The museum holds an extensive collection of Picasso graphics. The Degas gallery contains many of the artist's famous paintings of ballet dancers. The museum is located at 411 Colorado Boulevard. For information call (818) 449-6840.

• The **Pacific Asia Museum** is the only archive specializing in Asian and Pacific art in Southern California. The museum is housed in a 1920s era building authentically reproducing the style of a Chinese imperial palace with a courtyard garden, green roof tiles and bronze dragons. Multi-media shows featuring special effects of music and aromas are shown regularly. For information call (818) 449-2742.

• The **Pasadena Historical Society and Museum** at 470 West Walnut Street, contains an array of priceless antique furnishings and memorabilia of early Pasadena. Also housed in the same turn of the century building, that once served as the Finnish Consulate, is the **Finnish Folk Art Museum,** the only museum of its kind outside of Finland. For information call (818) 449-1660.

• If you're not in town New Year's Day, you can still see a part of the Tournament of Roses at the **Rose Bowl.** The expanded 1922 vintage stadium contains the **Rose Bowl Hall of Fame** featuring an exhibit of mementos of past celebrations. For information, call (818) 793-7193.

• The opulent Italian Renaissance style mansion at 391 South Orange Grove Avenue was once the home of chewing gum tycoon William Wrigley Jr. The **Wrigley Mansion,** as it is called, now houses the Pasadena Tournament of Roses Association. The 4.5 acres of grounds are open to the public every day except New Year's. Free tours of the house are offered Wednesday afternoons February through September. For information, call (818) 449-4100.

ACCOMMODATION

PASADENA HILTON
150 South Los Robles
Pasadena, CA 91101
Tel.   (818) 577-1000
           (800) Hilton's toll free reservations.
Visa, MasterCard, AMEX and all other major credit cards are accepted.

If you have ever longed for the elegance of the finest European hotels with their rich woods, lush plants and distinctive ambiance, all within minutes of Los Angeles, then there is a treat in store for you. It is the Pasadena Hilton. A refreshing draft of effervescent elegance, the Pasadena Hilton is located just eight minutes from downtown Los Angeles. It provides a luxurious haven from which to plan excursions to any of the countless attractions nearby.

For your convenience the hotel offers a variety of fine foods, wines and liquors. Two excellent restaurants are available within the hotel. Skylights, a gourmet penthouse restaurant, offers continental cuisine in an elegant relaxed atmosphere with an unrivaled view of the city. The Cafe Madagascar offers a unique array, from snacks to full meals. There is both a piano bar and penthouse lounge. The hotel features 250 luxurious guest rooms with private balconies, and one entire floor is devoted to non-smoking patrons.

The Pasadena Hilton has so ably served the discerning sojourner that such notables as Bob Hope, Betty Ford and President Reagan have elected to make it their temporary home. The Pasadena Hilton's warm personalized service assures a most comfortable and enjoyable stay.

APPAREL

CLOTHES HEAVEN
110 East Union
Pasadena, CA 91103
Tel. (818) 440-0929
Hrs: Tue. - Sat. 11:00 a.m. - 5:00 p.m. or closing
Visa, MasterCard, AMEX and Discover are accepted.

High quality, high fashion, gently worn designer women's wear is available at the aptly named Clothes Heaven, "where good clothes go when they're passed on." The racks are filled with such luminous labels as Perry Ellis, Calvin Klein, Oscar de la Renta, Channel, Albert Nipon, Adolfo, Anne Klein; the list goes on but the prices don't.

Located in Old Town, the intimate, inviting little shop with hand painted tile entry decorated with fresh flowers is overseen by personable proprietor, Larayne Brannon, who has earned a solid reputation in the art of apparel selection as well as for her talent in helping clients to choose their best styles and colors. And there is a fabulous selection indeed! At resale prices up to seventy and eighty percent off retail, some of the incredible items that have appeared on the racks are the likes of an Evan Picone skirt for $16 ($60 retail); a like new St. Tropez silk print two piece dress for $39 ($160); a leather jacket for $49 ($160); and a Basile wool suit for $189 ($800). There is always a terrific selection of new Anne Klein and Calvin Klein at Clothes

Heaven (Larayne has excellent contacts!) and you'll find only natural fiber fabrics in the most current styles. Some of the lines are procured from couture representatives, some have been used for commercials, others are from such far reaching and diverse areas as New York, Arizona and La Jolla. All are in superb condition, hardly worn, and often, never worn. Many are ahead of season designer samples. In addition, there is an abundance of silks, fine shoes and jewelry.

Buying resale is "like borrowing from a friend. We've all done it." At Clothes Heaven, for little more than you'd spend when borrowing, you'll *never* have to give it back!

MALE I.D. SPORTSWEAR
12 West Colorado Boulevard
Old Town Pasadena, CA 91105
Tel: (818) 405-0222
Hrs: Sun. - Mon. 11:00 a.m. - 8:00 p.m.
      Tue. - Thu. 10:00 a.m. - 10:00 p.m.
      Fri. - Sat. 10:00 a.m. - 11:00 p.m.
Visa, MasterCard and AMEX are accepted.

The Pasadena retailer's roots are at the intersection of Fair Oaks Avenue and Colorado Boulevard, the city's first business district which grew from orange orchards a century ago. Today it's the location of Male I.D. Sportswear, Pasadena's prime retailer in progressive men's fashions.

Male I.D. carries the hottest lines from many of today's leading designers: WilliWear, Zylos, Glen Williams, I.D. #____, Tom Taylor and Tony Lambert Collection, among others. Lines include the latest looks in suits, shirts, trousers, sweaters, activewear and men's accessories. The Male I.D. focus is on clean, upbeat, timeless styling, not the latest trends or fads. Owners Cathy Fujimi and Lance Vasquez know that when people invest in fashionable clothing they expect a look to endure beyond the next season. Male I.D. offers more than great clothing. Cathy, Lance and the staff have one goal always in mind: help each customer create a fashion statement he enjoys and is comfortable making. Your needs are discussed before any combinations are recommended. Customers leave Male I.D. with a coordinated wardrobe and an individualized look. Basic alterations are done at no charge.

Pasadena's fashion headquarters is located in the historic Dodsworth Building restoration project, in the heart of Old Pasadena. One of the largest commercial historic districts in the United States,

Old Pasadena features a unique mix of restaurants and theaters, art galleries, clothing stores and unusual retail outlets. Check out Male I.D. and you'll know why Southern California is shopping in Old Pasadena.

MODE ARETE
150 Colorado Boulevard
Old Town Pasadena, CA 91105
Tel. (818) 792-2474
Hrs: Tue. - Sat.   11:00 a.m. - 7:00 p.m.
Visa, MasterCard and AMEX are accepted.
Also,
8707 Santa Monica Boulevard
Los Angeles, CA 91105

"Certain lines for certain times" is the theme of this fashion forward exclusive apparel shop located in the beautiful Old Town Plaza of Pasadena. Owners Robin Tarrant and JoAnn Magidon specialize in fashion accessories and interesting articles of clothing.

Art in cloth may be a better way to describe many of the beautiful pieces shown by Robin and JoAnn. Artists from throughout the United States display their work in Mode Arete. Exclusive accessory lines shown here are carried by the Rodeo Drive shops. Once you have chosen your special piece, Robin and JoAnn will gift wrap it for you in such a way as to make the wrapping a work of art in itself. Your purchase will be shipped anywhere in the U.S. for you. Mode Arete offers you complimentary valet parking.

Enjoy a stroll through the beautiful Old Town Plaza to Mode Arete where you will find a palate of delightful clothing and accessories for women.

PURE SWEAT
Hastings Ranch Center
3819 East Foothill Boulevard
Pasadena, CA 9110
Tel.   (818) 351-8047
Hrs: Mon. - Fri.   10:00 a.m. - 9:00 p.m.
         Saturday   9:00 a.m. - 6:00 p.m.
         Sunday   11:00 a.m. - 5:00 p.m.
Visa, MasterCard, AMEX and Discover are accepted.

You've probably noticed many of those people breaking out in a glowing sweat while on an early morning jog not only feel great, they look great. Maybe they just like what they do, or maybe they stopped in at Pure Sweat in the Hastings Ranch Center.

You won't find just the ordinary gray flannel sweatsuit at Pure Sweat. Quality conscious craftsmen create most of the items out of a 50/50 fleece blend, known for it's washability, durability and color fastness. You'll look fast on the running track in one of Pure Sweat's light sweatsuits, as you speed by in one of the multitude of colors Pure Sweat offers. Stop in at Pure Sweat, and you'll see a complete range of drawstring pants, tank tops, shorts, crew neck tops and muscle shirts in a wide range of sizes. Buy your official college sweatshirt from Pure Sweat, and maybe you'll run into one of Pure Sweat's fashionable customers, such as Linda Evans or Burt Reynolds. Let the friendly staff help you select from all kinds of reasonably priced clothing for the man or woman with a workout in mind.

Breaking out in a sweat is not only good for your health, it's fashionable. So feel your best while you're on that morning run, and drop by Pure Sweat, "America's No. 1 Sweat Shop," so you'll look your best, too.

BAKERIES

AUX DELICES
16 West Colorado Boulevard
Old Town Pasadena, CA 91105
Tel. (818) 796-1630
Hrs: Monday   8:00 a.m. - 2:00 p.m.
      Tue. - Thu.   8:00 a.m. - 10:00 p.m.
      Fri. - Sat.   8:00 a.m. - 11:00 p.m.
      Sunday   9:00 a.m. - 9:00 p.m.

Riz Sarmiento's childhood dreams did not include standing in a hot kitchen all day. In fact, she spent a number of years as a scientist. Now the only formulas Riz mixes are in the kitchen of Aux Delices where she and her two chefs, Patrick Amor and Ralph Brust, take pride in turning out the best French pastries in Old Town Pasadena.

Aux Delices is reminiscent of a cafe `a la Paris. The rose toned tiles are accented by the sophisticated black tables and chairs set out for the patrons. Off grey walls provide a perfect foil for the Art Deco prints adorning the interior walls. The atmosphere is a mood setter for the delectable aromas that tease your nostrils. Patrons choose from an assortment of delicacies all made from natural ingredients with absolutely no preservatives added. Orange mousse, strawberry Napoleons, chocolate eclairs, raspberry concorde, mousse cheesecake and fruit tarts are tantalizingly displayed in a glass case.

Aux Delices also serves sandwiches, soups and a selection of fresh salads which can be enjoyed in the dining area, or Riz and her friendly sales staff will be happy to pack your selection into a special lunch picnic basket. Whatever your preference, a private picnic lunch for two or a lingering break over a cup of gourmet blended coffee and a French pastry, enrich your morning with a stop at Aux Delices.

NOREN'S HILLCREST SWEDISH BAKERY
1384 East Washington Boulevard
Pasadena, CA 91104
Tel. (818) 794-5411
Hrs: Mon. - Sat.   7:00 a.m. - 6:00 p.m.
Visa and MasterCard are accepted.

If you remember the day of the neighborhood bakery where you could indulge yourself in the tantalizing aromas of freshly baked bread, rolls and cakes, then you're certain to enjoy a visit to Noren's Hillcrest Swedish Bakery.

A true neighborhood bakery in the same location for over fifty-two years, Noren's offers a full range of exquisite baked goods. The delicious aromas greet customers even before they walk through the door. Inside, find a neat, clean establishment with many appealing displays of freshly baked breads, pastries and cakes. Owner John Ellis offers a wide variety of sumptuous items such as squaw bread, four types of Swedish limpa (plain, orange, fruit and anise), cinnamon, whole wheat, and honey bran bread. Nearly every type of pie one could imagine can be found at Noren's, all freshly made with quality ingredients. All the goodies are made from scratch with plenty of farm fresh eggs and real butter. John is especially proud of his cake decorating service, offering over 1250 artistic creations for every occasion. An extremely talented baker, he delights in short notice cake decorating and has "baked, decorated and boxed 197 cakes, all in one day." John also does catering of all kinds from full sit down dinners to wedding receptions and party platters.

So, when you have a little hunger pang and can't quite decide what you want, stop at Noren's Hillcrest Swedish Bakery. You'll probably make a number of tasty decisions.

COFFEE

THE COFFEE BEAN & TEA LEAF
The Commons
146 South Lake Avenue, Suite 107
Pasadena, CA 91101
Tel.   (818) 440-9744
        (800) TEA LEAF
Hrs: Mon. - Sat.   9:30 a.m. - 5:30 p.m.
Visa and MasterCard are accepted.

The Coffee Bean & Tea Leaf has fifteen retail stores; a testimony to its quality, excellence and popularity. Glass fronted counters display the myriad varieties of coffees and create a rich contrast to the warmth of solid oak walls and counters. Customers can relax and enjoy a "cuppa" at the coffee bar while perusing the selections reflected in the polished copper topped ceiling.

Only the finest quality coffee beans are selected to be marketed at The Coffee Bean & Tea Leaf. Small batches of these beans are roasted daily. Twenty blends are available and include Costa Rican, a sharp aromatic coffee with a strong smokey taste; House Blend, which consists of a 100 year old gourmet blend recipe; and New Guinea, popularly coined as Echo Coffee; "you taste it once when you sip it and again when you swallow." Coffees are imported from around the world and are ground to your specification. Only the finest and most pure "chested" (first and second flushed leaves) teas are available at the shop and customers will enjoy the newest line of products, including hot chocolate. Flavors include Dutch, Hazel Nut, Almond and English Toffee. A luxury office coffee service permits you to have the same sublime selection when you're away from home.

The Coffee Bean & Tea Leaf manufactures two distinct coffee makers which will make the best coffee in the world; Our Keeper and the Classic 100 Coffee Maker. Other accessories include mini-grinders, honey, the Jena Tea Set, tea taster sets and more. If having a cup of coffee or tea means more to you than just a habit, you'll not want to pass up a visit to The Coffee Bean & Tea Leaf. "Happy brewing."

DELICATESSEN

THE KITCHEN FOR EXPLORING FOODS
1434 West Colorado Boulevard
Pasadena, CA 91105
Tel. (818) 793-7218
Hrs: Tue. - Fri.   12:00 noon - 6:00 p.m.
           Saturday   10:30 a.m. - 6:00 p.m.
Credit cards are not accepted.

Peggy Dark, creator of The Kitchen For Exploring Foods, is a shining light in the world of catering and take out food. A superb presentation of intriguing eclectic cuisine is her specialty and she succeeds admirably with the brightness of her own personal flair and the assistance of a multi-talented staff.

Although the largest part of her business is catering, Peggy emphasizes the gourmet food take out aspect. A copious glass refrigerator in the front of The Kitchen For Exploring Foods displays the day's specials. Dishes often take on an ethnic flavor according to the holidays or time of year. If it is Cinco de Mayo, Mexican food is featured. The intricate and unusual menu can range from a celery root salad to Balsamic Vinegar Baked Onions to Poached Chicken Breasts On Angel Hair Pasta. Peggy likes to offer something a bit unusual with each meal, so she often accompanies her main dish with eggplant rolls, Swiss chard packages or asparagus bundles. Meals are always served with emphasis on color and flair.

Peggy has successfully pieced together a network of friends who are involved with the everyday workings of the business. Chef Mary Don presides over the kitchen, the attractive open kitchen design of Peggy's shop was designed by Nan Crocker and aspiring actors, actresses and models make up a smart, personable staff. She shares her cooking secrets through regularly scheduled fall and spring cooking classes. Peggy Dark's Kitchen for Exploring Foods takes you on a unique cuisine adventure.

ENTERTAINMENT

THE PASADENA PLAYHOUSE
39 South El Molino
Pasadena, CA 91101
Tel.   (818) 356-PLAY Box office
        (818) 792-8672   Administration
Hrs: Box Office
        Mon. - Sun.   10:00 a.m. - 6:00 p.m.
        Administration
        Mon. - Fri.   10:00 a.m. - 5:00 p.m.
Visa and MasterCard are accepted.

Once again the curtain of excellence rises at the Pasadena Playhouse. Reopened in 1986 after four decades of brilliance and two decades of darkness, the beautifully restored State Theatre of California has again positioned itself to regain a leadership role in the ranks of major American regional theaters.

Under the sensitive leadership of Susan Dietz and Stephen Rothman, the Playhouse is offering a diverse and delicious selection of theater. The Playhouse serves as a greenhouse in which to sprout the seeds of new and innovative plays. The block busting play *Mail* found fertile ground at the Playhouse and is the latest sign that the Pasadena Playhouse is capable of fulfilling its historic role as one of the nation's great theaters. The 1988 bill of plays has proven to further secure the Playhouse's pre-eminence. The season begins with an American premiere *Breaking the Silence* by Stephan Poliakoff, considered by *The London Times* to be "one of the best plays of 1984." Next, a West Coast premiere, *Death of a Buick* by John Bunzel, a play shot through with insanely funny dark currents reminiscent of Joe Orton. Next in the Mainstage season will be Garson Kanin's American comedy *Born Yesterday*, and the season's grand finale: a musical repertory, *Jaques Brel is Alive and Well and Living in Paris* and *Harry Chapin: Lies and Legends*. Concurrently in the Balcony Theatre they will be presenting an Australian comedy-thriller *Down An Alley Filled with Cats* by Warwick Moss.

To receive a list of dates of the current plays, write or call the theatre at (818) 356-PLAY. The Pasadena Playhouse is an alive and vital part of this country's theatre tradition. A ticket to The Pasadena Playhouse is a ticket to superb entertainment and a front row view of history in the making.

FLORIST

JACOB MAARSE
655 East Green Street
Pasadena, CA 91101
Tel. (818) 449-0246
Hrs: Mon. - Sat.   9:00 a.m. - 6:00 p.m.
Visa, MasterCard, AMEX and Diners Club are accepted.

The City of Roses combined with Jacob Maarse Florist make the perfect arrangement! Jacob Maarse's roots in the floral business go back to the middle of the nineteenth century, when the famous Dutch Aalsmeer Flower Market owed much of its creation to Jacob's grandparents. Lured to the West Coast as a young man, Jacob settled into floral work in Pasadena, and gives much credit to the area for his success.

Located in a vintage 1928 automobile sales building, Jacob's floral business is one of the world's most unusual flower shops. The enormous building holds a beehive of activity, and the shop itself is a collage of fragrance, textures, sounds, color and movement. Lavishly filled containers of fresh flowers are everywhere. A wealth of party entertainment accessories share the space with dried flowers. Gift wrapping and note cards coordinate in color and image with the flowers, and splashing water from the shop's tumbling fountain refreshes the fragrant air. There is a constant jingling of telephones as friendly salespeople answer the many orders coming in by phone.

Jacob Maarse Florist is a total custom business. The creative staff is highly responsive to the needs of the customer and it is not uncommon for one of them to pay a visit to the customer's house in order to adequately evaluate the environment in which the flowers will be set. The combination of beautiful flowers, years of floral design skills and the love of the business has made Jacob Maarse Florist a delight for all who experience it.

GIFT SHOPS

CHEZ MONCHE
925 Boston Court
Pasadena, CA 91106
Tel. (818) 793-4760
Hrs: Mon. - Sat.   10:00 a.m. - 5:30 p.m.
         Thanksgiving to Christmas
         Mon. - Sun.   10:00 a.m. - 5:30 p.m.
Visa, MasterCard and AMEX are accepted.

Few stores can claim to specialize in the "art of giving," but Chez Monche does, and deservedly so. Any visitor to this store in Pasadena who comes away without a wonderful gift for some friend or member of the family just hasn't seen all the items Chez Monche offers.

Chez Monche is more than just another boutique. The store is in a beautiful old home that dates back to 1905. Store owner Diane Manchee purchased the building several years ago. The restoration was so impressive that interior designers come from all over Southern California to view the result. In 1985, the house took the *Pasadena Beautiful Award*. The wide variety of merchandise is also beautiful and much of it is tailored to one or more holidays. You'll find items specific to Easter, Thanksgiving, Valentine's Day and other holidays. Christmas is an especially glorious time at Chez Monche, with its vast collection of ornaments and gift items. Shoppers find a mix of old and new collectibles, plus antiques and home accessories. Every piece is hand chosen and often handmade for the store's customers. Ideas include handpainted basketry, wooden boxes, pillows and ornaments. Look for the line of original watercolors and oil paintings. The store is famous statewide for its imaginative gift wrapping.

One of the most interesting features of this store is the romantic Italian fountain filled with carp. It's found in the Solarium, and many visitors come to the store just to see and experience this unique room. Within such an atmosphere, shopping for that perfect gift becomes a perfect art.

ESPRIT DE CUISINE
143 West California Boulevard
Pasadena, CA 91105
Tel: (818) 793-8855
Hrs: Mon. - Sat.   10:00 a.m. - 6:00 p.m.
         Sunday   12:00 noon - 5:00 p.m.
Visa, MasterCard and AMEX are accepted.

"Create a Gift - Combine a Gift" is the slogan at Esprit de Cuisine. Owner Lynne Carl is really into the spirit of helping others. Not only does she sponsor a shop which is a haven to all cooks, amateur and expert alike, but she also goes that extra mile to offer specialized, individual help to her clients.

Advice for special use kitchenware is free for the asking. Conferencing over a tricky recipe is a common occurrence at Esprit de Cuisine. Lynne offers a unique gift service where clients are encouraged to bring in their own baskets or gift items. Lynne will help combine these beginnings with other items from the store to create a "one of a kind" gift. Selections in the store run through a wide array of kitchen items that includes the modern, the antique and the hard to find. Shoppers can browse among the Fitz & Floyd hand painted porcelain, Calphalon or Copan copper cookware. Esprit de Cuisine also carries mini and giant muffin pans, tart pans, molds, bowls and a large selection of wooden utensils. And no kitchen supply shop would be complete without gourmet coffee and teas, sugar free dessert toppings, a selection of dip mixes and cookbooks that will keep your creative talents busy for months.

Lynne will gladly ship an order anywhere in the United States. Gift wrapping is complimentary, of course. When shopping for kitchenware as a gift or personal purchase, shop Esprit de Cuisine for that extra individualized flair.

EXTRAS
163 West Colorado Boulevard
Pasadena, CA 91101
Tel. (818) 795-1555
Hrs: Mon. - Fri.   10:00 a.m. - 8:00 p.m.
     Saturday   10:00 a.m. - 7:00 p.m.
     Sunday   11:00 a.m. - 5:00 p.m.
Visa, MasterCard and AMEX are accepted.

As open and spacious as a Southwestern sky, are the show rooms of this newly opened studio. As varied as the flowers on the desert, are the items for sale. Owner Jay Dunton believes Extras is a studio where the "onlooker can see eclecticism at work."

Decorative accessories and gifts have been collected from all over the world. All are light and bright in texture and color, each with an emphasis on hand crafting. Buyers will find antique oversized, bleached wood furnishings, handmade trunks and armoires, oversized sofas and armchairs in the fashion of Santa Fe. If things small and elegant attract the shopper, Extras offers silver jewelry of the Southwestern style, beautiful in colors of turquoise, purple and peach. No matter what the item found in Extras showroom, it will reflect spaciousness, color and quality.

Extras is a mecca for the colorful and the unusual—a gallery of home furnishings and gifts in the Southwestern tradition.

THE FRIEND SHIP
350 South Lake Avenue
Pasadena, CA 91101
Tel. (818) 796-1596
Hrs: Mon. - Fri.   10:00 a.m. - 6:00 p.m.
     Saturday   10:00 a.m. - 5:00 p.m.
Visa, MasterCard and Discover are accepted.

The Friend Ship is an uncommon needlework shop. You won't find the average, the usual or the mundane, what you will find instead is the handmade beauty of needlework.

An ancient and honored craft, needlework has a long, rich history. From the famous Bordeaux Tapestry depicting the Battle of Hastings in 1066 to its use in contemporary modern art, needlework has been an important source of beauty and culture for hundreds of years. Owners Karen and Jim Smith feature works in both needlepoint and counted cross stitch. The walls of their shop are lined with dozens of handpainted canvasses. There are colorful pillows decorated with designs of all types. Charts, graphs and kits for counted cross stitch and needlepoint are to be found throughout the shop as well as colorful displays of the fibers used in all types of needlework. Karen and Jim offer everything in needlework supplies, from needle and thread to framing and finishing materials. Custom work is also available. Their shop is neat and attractive, with many displays readily visible through large glass windows.

From novice to old hand, everything you need for the fine art of needlework can be found at The Friend Ship.

SUMMERHOUSE ANTIQUES AND GIFTS
380 South Lake Avenue, Suite 11
Pasadena, CA 91101
Tel. (818) 793-5643
Hrs: Mon. - Sat. 10:00 a.m. - 5:30 p.m.
Visa, MasterCard and AMEX are accepted.

When you're looking for a distinctive gift, that something special for a special person in your life, then you need look no further than Summerhouse Antiques and Gifts.

Located in the Burlington Arcade, a delightful reproduction of a late 1800s English arcade, the Summerhouse offers unique items from antique shops in Europe and England. Owner Nina Wysocki specializes in silver items of all kinds. Her shop features a large collection of English silver in both silver plate and sterling as well as a variety of American works, principally from New England. From the graceful crystal to the one of a kind bridal and bay shower items, Nina also offers some specialty items from France and Germany as well as English and French pine furniture. Summerhouse is a delightfully quaint shop filled with antiques and gifts for every occasion.

Nina Wysocki's love of things old and beautiful is expressed in every corner of her shop. Drop in to Summerhouse Antiques and Gifts, you'll receive personal service and you're sure to find that special gift.

ICE SKATING

PASADENA ICE SKATING CENTER
300 East Green Street
Pasadena, CA 91101
Tel. (818) 578-0800

Hrs:		
	Mon. - Tue.	12:00 noon - 5:00 p.m.
	Wednesday	7:30 p.m. - 9:30 p.m.
	Thursday	12:00 noon - 5:00 p.m.
		7:30 p.m. - 9:30 p.m.
	Friday	12:00 noon - 5:00 p.m.
		7:45 p.m. - 10:30 p.m.
	Saturday	1:00 p.m. - 4:00 p.m.
		7:45 p.m. - 10:30 p.m.
	Sunday	1:00 p.m. - 4:00 p.m.

Credit cards are not accepted.

Ice skating in Southern California? Where else, thanks to the Pasadena Ice Skating Center. Originally created to give young hockey players a place to practice and play, the Ice Skating Center has since expanded both its facility and its services.

In addition to an ice skating school the Center provides instruction for various city park and recreation classes and school field trips. Providing classes at all skill levels, starting at the age of two, the rink is also the home of Christopher Bowman, currently the number two ranked men's skater in the country.

Originally a ballroom, the Center also has a complete boot and blade shop. An occasional celebrity, such as Dorothy Hammell, Scott Hamilton and Olympic champions Tai and Randy can be seen at the rink. In addition, hockey games, ice shows and broomball, an exciting game played without skates, make the Pasadena Ice Skating Center the premier facility in L.A. County.

INTERIOR DESIGN

FAIROAKS DESIGN GROUP
18 South Fair Oaks
Pasadena, CA 91105
Tel. (818) 440-9979
Hrs: Mon. - Sat.   9:00 a.m. - 7:00 p.m.

The French call it *trompe l'oeil* and it means, literally, trick of the eye. It's an artistic way of altering a stationary environment so that it seems larger or smaller, cooler or warmer, plush or more spartan. It's also the Fairoaks Design Group's stock in trade.

They're a band of interior designers who decided that it wasn't just enough to color coordinate, to match furniture styles or creatively manipulate screens and room dividers. True artists, they have always tried to pull from their clients that essential vision locked inside the imagination. They know that environment is all, whether it be that first nursery, the new den, that office you've been dreaming of for years or an entire living mode. It must be you or it is not itself.

They've got over a decade of experience behind them, much of it gleaned from the art centers of Europe, and it happens to be a personal passion with them as well. If you believe that the most pleasure, maximum efficiency and peak contentment come from your vision, you'll be meeting with the Fairoaks Design Group soon.

MAPS

PASADENA MAP COMPANY
985 East Colorado Boulevard
Pasadena, CA 91106
Tel. (818) 795-6437
Hrs: Mon. - Fri.   9:00 a.m. - 6:00 p.m.
         Saturday   10:00 a.m. - 3:00 p.m.
Visa and MasterCard are accepted.

You'll never again have an excuse for being lost, not if you visit Carol and Gary Kroah's shop. The Pasadena Map Company has a map for just about every locale and every need. Originally begun about fifty years ago by a surveyor who bought and stocked topographical maps, the Kroahs took over the shop seven years ago and take a great deal of pride in the versatility of their business.

Maps abound in glass cases, topographical maps create a tapistry on the walls, prints and guide books fill stands and counters. And you won't have to settle for a one sided view. As well as the standard map, clients can select from relief maps, aeronautical charts, navigational charts, United States and European rail maps as well as European city maps. Clients wishing to sneak a look into the past can study the historic map selections which include American maps, city plans or the historic prints showing the world at different time periods.

The Pasadena Map Company offers the largest inventory of globes in Southern California in every conceivable size. Carol and Gary also offer the service of framing and mounting all types of maps and other art work. They have even found themselves, upon occasion, renting out props for commercials. The shop offers a mail order catalog and ships throughout the United States. Visit the Pasadena Map Company for a fascinatingly fresh concept of the word *map*.

MUSIC

OLD TOWN MUSIC COMPANY
32 East Colorado Boulevard
Pasadena, CA 91105
Tel. (818) 793-4730
Hrs: Mon. - Fri. 10:00 a.m. - 5:30 p.m.
      Saturday   10:00 a.m. - 4:00 p.m.
Visa and MasterCard are accepted.

Tick, tock the metronome talks. Violins play. Customers delve deep into ream upon ream of sheet music. Bursts of joy are heard as a long sought after tome of music is found. Old Town Music Company once again lives up to its reputation of having the most extensive sheet music collection in Southern California.

Specializing in music from Brahms to Broadway, Old Town Music offers chamber music, opera, vocal selections, piano works, instrumental works of all kinds, and music education materials. Exquisite violins line the walls. On hand is a highly experienced staff prepared to assist a musical newcomer or a seasoned performer. Music instruction is available for violin, piano, clarinet, flute, guitar, bassoon and saxophone. Suzuki teaching materials and classical sheet music are featured. Old Town Music is an authorized dealer for Yamaha products. Instrument rentals are available.

Walking into Old Town Music Company is like entering a music conservatory replete with helpful, knowledgeable staff waiting to assist you with any musical need.

RESTAURANTS

BECKHAM PLACE, 77 West Walnut, Pasadena, CA. Tel. (818) 796-3399. With a friendly atmosphere and English country decor, this restaurant boasts three cuts of the best prime rib available, spinach souffle and creamed corn—all at reasonable prices.

BIRDIES CAFE & MUFFINERY
17 South Raymond Avenue
Old Town Pasadena, CA 91105
Tel. (818) 449-5884
Hrs: Sun. - Thu.   7:30 a.m. - 9:00 p.m.
          Fri. - Sat.   7:30 a.m. - 10:00 p.m.
Visa, MasterCard and AMEX are accepted.

Filled with old world charm, Birdies Cafe & Muffinery has customers coming back again and again to sample the unique atmosphere as well the sumptuous delicacies. Situated in the heart of Old Town Pasadena, this eatery exudes an airy yet quaint attraction. Numerous plants are displayed against the wood accents of the dining area and bricked patio.

True to the name of the eatery, each entree is named for a member of our feathered population. Besides the unique selection of aromatic, freshly baked muffins for which Birdies is famed, morning guests can choose from a breakfast menu that includes such titillating entrees as the Mockingbird. The Mockingbird features eggs scrambled with loads of mushrooms, fresh spinach, Spanish onions and ground beef. The Osprey is an ambrosial way to start the day with Norwegian Smoked Salmon, bagel and cream cheese, sweet red onions, sliced tomato and capers. Luncheon diners can deviate from the usual with an Albatross, a sandwich of albacore tuna on rye, or a Wood Duck sandwich of duck sausage served with sauteed sweet peppers, onions and melted Jack cheese on open faced sourdough and served hot. For the innovative, try the Bald Eagle, an entree of pan fried trout, or the nectarious Sand Piper Prawns. Birdies also has a wide selection of salads including tantalizing pasta salads from every corner of the world.

A more versatile selection of dishes would be difficult to find anywhere. Dine at Birdies Cafe & Muffinery for a gratifying venture into the unusual.

BONA CORSO'S
655 North Lake Avenue
Pasadena, CA 91101
Tel. (818) 795-6816
Hrs: Mon. - Thu. 11:00 a.m. - 11:00 p.m.
      Fri. - Sat.   11:00 a.m. - 12:00 p.m.
      Sunday   3:30 p.m. - 11:00 p.m.
Visa and MasterCard are accepted.

There is nothing like good Italian cooking with its seemly infinite combinations of pasta, garlic, basil and tomatoes, but finding a good Italian restaurant can be difficult, unless you've discovered Bona Corso's.

Bona Corso's offers one of the most complete Italian menus you're likely to find anywhere in the country. Owner and chef S. Bonaccorso and his sons and co-owners Nelson and James have assembled a full range of veal and chicken dishes such as Veal Cutlet Parmigiana, pan fried, lightly breaded and seasoned veal covered with melted mozzarella; or Chicken Picatta, boneless breast of chicken sauteed with mushrooms and onions in a wine and lemon butter sauce. For an appetizer you might try his Sauteed Artichoke Hearts, pan fried with Romano cheese and wine. The food is nothing short of perfect and the atmosphere, delightful. Inside Bona Corso's you'll find one large room, softly lit, divided by comfortable booths and decorated with live plants, wood paneling and china dishes. On the street side of the room there is a small atrium with tables dressed with fresh flowers where you can enjoy one of chef Bonaccorso's many pasta dishes such as Baked Lasagna, a mixture of Ricotta cheese, beef and meat sauce topped with mozzarella cheese. For pizza lovers, Bona Corso's offers over twenty-five different toppings.

The moment you walk into this pleasant restaurant and catch the tantalizing aroma of fresh garlic and basil, you'll know you've found a little slice of Rome or Sicily in downtown Pasadena.

CAFE SIXTY NORTH
60 North Raymond Avenue
Pasadena, CA 91103
Tel. (818) 793-9000
Hrs: Mon. - Thu.   7:00 a.m. - 9:00 p.m.
        Friday   7:00 a.m. - 10:00 p.m.
        Saturday   8:00 a.m. - 10:00 p.m.
        Sunday   8:00 a.m. - 2:00 p.m.
Credit cards are not accepted.

Here is a restaurant whose specialties are as wide and varied as hearty European country style cuisine. Served in a place which conveys the atmosphere of a restaurant of the left bank, or the feeling of an open cafe in the Mediterranean, the total sense is one of relaxation and enjoyment.

In the large, airy main dining room with its European style wooden chairs and tables you can select from such specialties as Moussaka, Pasta a la Grec, grilled meats and seafoods, and Beef Bourgignon. If you prefer, you can choose from the same menu while enjoying the air in the patio, overlooking Old Town Pasadena and the railroad, claimed to be the only people and train watching dining patio in the city. There is an excellent breakfast menu featuring omelettes in a toasted croissant, continental breakfasts and delicacies such as Belgian Waffles and Eggs Benedict. Lunches feature a long list of hot and cold sandwiches, soups and specialties.

Everything Cafe Sixty North serves is made on the spot, including the bread, croissants and the flaky, tender triangles stuffed with cheese, spinach, or beef. The desserts are out of this world, among them the Chocolate Fantasy Cake which won top honors from the Chocolate Lovers of America.

CAMERON'S SEAFOOD MARKET & RESTAURANT

1478 East Colorado Boulevard
Pasadena, CA 91107
Tel.   (818) 743-FISH
Hrs: Mon. - Thu.   11:00 a.m. - 9:30 p.m.
        Fri. - Sat.   11:00 a.m. - 10:00 p.m.
        Sunday   12:00 noon - 9:30 p.m.
Visa, MasterCard, AMEX, Diners Club and Carte Blanche
are accepted.

When a fish market is part of the restaurant, or vice versa, you can depend on fresh food, but that's just one of the things that Cameron's can be proud of. Behind the market you'll find a pleasant but unpretentious place in which to enjoy some of the best eating in Pasadena, whether you take it all at a table or start things off at the Oyster Bar where tempting beginnings are served.

One side of the restaurant is dedicated to the preparation of varied items ranging from delicious Manhattan or New England clam chowder, Dungeness crab, fresh grilled shark and sea bass, all served with a piping hot loaf of sourdough bread. This is a large and noisy place, serving big portions of food for lusty appetites. It's a fun kind of place to eat, truly of the sea, rather than simply having nautical decor. There's a large bar area where you can sit in one of the big leather chairs or in the charming wicker room and sun lounge and enjoy one of Cameron's special drinks.

Save room for a slice of the famous New York cheesecake, or an astonishing creation called Chocolate Suicide, but allow plenty of time to eat it.

THE CHRONICLE, PASADENA

897 Granite Drive
Pasadena, CA 91101
Tel. (818) 792-1179
Hrs: Lunch   Mon. - Sat.   11:30 a.m. - 2:30 p.m.
        Dinner   Sun. - Thu.   5:00 p.m. - 10:00 p.m.
                     Fri. - Sat.   5:00 p.m. - 11:00 p.m.
Visa, MasterCard, AMEX, Discover and Diners Club are
accepted.

The excellence of The Chronicle has not gone unnoticed. As you   enter the Chronicle's inviting entrance you will see a wall of awards meriting The Chronicle's fine wine and cuisine. Service is of the utmost priority at The Chronicle. You will receive a warm reception and be offered a comfortable dining space in an exquisite dining hall. The interior design comes from the popular old San Francisco style bar and grill. The walls exhibit prints and memorabilia of Pasadena's rise as the "Crown City" during the turn of the century.

The Chronicle features tableside food preparation and a knowledgeable wine steward to assist with wine selections. Tableside specialties include Tiny Lobster Tails sauteed with garlic, shallot, fresh lemon and white wine, or Chateaubriand with a bouquet of fresh vegetables. The Chronicle is also well known for its selection of deliciously prepared fresh seafoods. Proprietor, Lud Renick is the wine expert and oversees one of the world's great wine lists. You may choose from more than 1,400 separate wine selections! California and French wines are featured. Lunch at The Chronicle finds a menu with varied cold kitchen choices as well as delicious hot dishes. Half Broiled Chicken, Fillet of Sand Dabs Sauteed Meuniere with mushrooms or Calamari Sauteed Capucine are excellent luncheon selections.

The Chronicle is a Pasadena tradition in fine wining and dining. Award winning cuisine, unique tableside preparation and impeccable service make this a "Best Choice" in Pasadena.

CROCODILE CAFE, 140 South Lake Avenue, Pasadena, CA. Tel. (818) 449-9900. This trendy restaurant features pizza, pork with black beans, homemade spicy sausage, polenta and chicken with molé sauce.

DINO'S ITALIAN INN
2055 East Colorado Boulevard
Pasadena, CA 91107
Tel. (818) 449-8823
Hrs: Mon. - Sun.   from 4:30 p.m.
Visa, MasterCard and AMEX are accepted.

The *California Restaurant Writers Association* has awarded Dino's Italian Inn their Two Star Award every year since 1978, and it is a well deserved honor which not only considers the quality of the food, but the style, surroundings, price and service.

This is a traditional Italian restaurant, an intimate atmosphere, fresh tablecloths, gleaming silverware, flowers and sparkling crystal, and a menu featuring a large selection. Seafoods are one specialty, with dishes such as Scampi al la Dino, and cioppino. Fresh pastas underlie all the great recipes such as baked halibut with dill sauce or the manicotti stuffed with ricotta. If you'd like to watch one of your favorite foods being prepared, place your order in the Saute and Oyster Bar. If a bit of relaxation is in order before dinner, Dino's offers a wide choice of wines and beers. If you're inclined to meatless dishes, you won't have to settle for a basket of the fresh baked bread, although one could almost make a meal from it. You'll find a meatless menu that Dino's is justly proud of.

All of the sauces and dressings are made in Dino's kitchen, and the selection of desert crepes and Italian pastries will make your espresso or cappuccino taste that much better. You'll not soon forget your evening here.

GREEN STREET
146 South Shopper's Lane
Pasadena, CA 91101
Tel. (818) 577-7170
Hrs: Mon. - Thu.   6:30 a.m. - 9:00 p.m.
           Fri. - Sat.   6:30 a.m. - 10:00 p.m.
           Sunday   8:00 a.m. - 9:00 p.m.
Visa, MasterCard, AMEX and Diners Club are accepted.

If you're looking for good food and a quiet atmosphere, you can't do any better than Green Street. Located on a quiet side street in the midst of the financial district, Green Street is known for its tremendous variety.

A six page menu offers over 175 items to choose from. There are fifteen different sandwiches including the Stephen's Sandwich, a grilled chicken sandwich with avocado, sauteed mushrooms and lots of sour cream served with your choice of bread and cheese, and Big John's Meat Loaf, sliced meat loaf grilled with Parmesan cheese and onions and served on your choice of bread. If you're in the mood for a salad, they have sixteen varieties to choose from including the signature of the restaurant, the very popular Dianne Salad, fresh lettuce tossed with chicken, crisp noodles, toasted almonds, sesame seeds and served with Dianne dressing. The list goes on and on, including thirteen varieties of hamburgers, seventeen types of omelettes and fourteen different desserts. They even serve twenty-six different types of beer from nine different countries as well as twenty-one wines from around the world. There are complete menus for breakfast, brunch, lunch and dinner. There is even a special test kitchen selection where you can try new dishes being considered for their permanent menu.

Green Street is a restaurant "where expectations are exceeded"; a place where it can be truly said, "They have something for everyone."

KONDITORI PATIO RESTAURANT AND BAKERY
230 South Lake Avenue
Pasadena, CA 91101
Tel.   (818) 792-8044
        (818) 792-6600
Hrs: Mon. - Sat.   7:30 a.m. - 5:00 p.m.
        Sunday   8:00 a.m. - 4:00 p.m.

Konditori is a German word translated to mean a place serving very fine pastry or food. The Konditori Patio Restaurant and Bakery, opened twenty-six years ago in Pasadena, has lived up to its name. The open air patio is a favorite gathering spot for breakfast and lunch patrons. In fact, it was voted by the Pasadena Weekly readers as "The Best Breakfast in Town."

The Konditori serves a variety of European and American food in a patio atmosphere of umbrellas, plants and comfortable seating. All food and entrees served at the Konditori are freshly made on the premises. This includes the delicious homemade pastries such as strawberry tarts, Napoleons and Budapest meringue. Or you may prefer a fluffy breakfast omelette. If you can't decide upon an omelette listed on the menu, combine your own choice of ingredients and build your own. The Swedish pancakes, of course, are unbeatable. The Scandinavian style sandwiches, served cold, range from the traditional Danish ham to the exotic Shrimp and King Crab. For a break from ordinary luncheon fare, try Konditori's Swedish Meatballs, served en Casserole with German fried potatoes and lingonberries. Biff Med Lok is also a tantalizing lunch for the hungry. It features a New York Steak smothered with grilled onions and complemented by German fried potatoes.

Homemade breads are a specialty of the house, as anyone who has sampled the popular Swedish Rye Bread will tell you. Dine at Konditori Patio Restaurant and Bakery for quality served at extremely reasonable prices.

LA COURONNE, 142 South Lake Avenue, Pasadena, CA. Tel. (818) 793-3151. This beautiful restaurant features French cuisine with an excellent wine list. You'll find extraordinary dining and fair prices.

MALDONADOS, 1202 East Green Street, Pasadena, CA. Tel. (818) 796-1126. The performances at this opera-cabaret restaurant include Lizue opera and musical comedy, with Bill Maldonado at the piano.

THE MARIANNE, 45 South Meutor Avenue, Pasadena, CA. Tel. (818) 792-2535. This restaurant with fresh flowers and private booths available, features an excellent selection of French dishes.

MERIDA
20 East Colorado Boulevard
Pasadena, CA 91105
Tel. (818) 792-7371
Hrs: Mon. - Sun.   9:00 a.m. - 10:00 p.m.
Visa, MasterCard, AMEX, Diners Club and Carte Blanche are accepted.
Reservations are requested for parties of eight or more.

It's straight from South of the Border, replete with strolling minstrel guitarist Louis del Angel and it's been an Old Town Pasadena tradition for over five years.

Specializing in food from Latin America, Merida does not offer your usual Mexican fare, but instead draws from a variety of Hispanic influences. Consider the Conchinita Pibil, reputedly the most popular dish on the Yucatan Peninsula, and which consists of Adobado pork wrapped in banana leaves, and served with red onions, rice, beans and tortillas. The Chile Colorado is a tender beef chunk stew, cooking in mild red chile sauce and served with rice, beans and tortillas.

Merida is high ceilinged, spacious and accented by purple carpeting, black chairs and tables, a large skylight, and table cloths under glass. The walls themselves are festooned with Latin American artifacts guaranteed to keep the diner more than occupied while his meal is being prepared. So if it's something different you're looking for in Mexican food, drive over to Old Town Pasadena.

MEZBAAN
80 North Fair Oaks
Pasadena, CA 91103
Tel. (818) 405-9060
Hrs: Lunch   Mon. - Fri.   11:30 a.m. - 2:30 p.m.
     Dinner   Mon. - Thu.   5:30 p.m. - 9:30 p.m.
                 Fri. - Sun.   5:30 p.m. - 10:00 p.m.
Visa, MasterCard, AMEX and Diners Club are accepted.

Through the doors of Mezbaan lie mystic India, the land of ancient civilizations, holy men and dining fit for a raja. The authentic dishes, Mughal architecture, soft Indian music and stone color paintings of native royalty at play contribute to the exotic ambiance.

Mr. Sheikh, Syed and Puthawala, the owners, purchased the restaurant last year, and now offer authentic Northern Indian cuisine and friendly service. Begin your meal with a fine wine or beer, and choose one of Mezbaan's tantalizing appetizers. Try the Vegetable Samosa, deep fried patties stuffed with spicy potatoes and green beans, or Vegetable Pakoras, fresh assorted vegetable fritters. Entrees include a large selection of chicken, beef, lamb, seafood and vegetable curry dishes. The house specialty at Mezbaan is Tandoori cuisine, in which meats are pre-treated with yogurt and special spices, then cooked in their own juices in a buried clay oven. The outcome is an outstanding taste sensation, served sizzling hot on a bed of onions and fresh lemon with mint chutney. Tandoori Specialties include juicy and mildly spicy Tandoori Shrimp, tender Chicken or Lamb Tikka, and Seekh Kabab, minced meat with onion, herbs and spices molded on the skewers.

For after dinner refreshment, enjoy mildly spicy Indian tea, Lassi Punjabi or Mango Lassi, a delicious drink made with yogurt and mango. Don't forget dessert; the selection at Mezbaan includes Kheer Khas, rice pudding garnished with nuts; Kulfi, Indian ice cream flavored with cardamom and pistachio, and Gajar Halwa, a sweet carrot treat. For take-out or catering needs, or for a unique, authentic Indian meal, Mezbaan offers you good food and a warm welcome.

MIJARES
145 Palmetto Drive
Pasadena, CA 91105
Tel.   (818) 792-2763
        (818) 792-2778
Hrs: Mon. - Thu.   11:00 a.m. - 9:00 p.m.
        Fri. - Sat.   11:00 a.m. - 10:00 p.m.
        Sunday   10:00 a.m. - 9:00 p.m.
Visa, MasterCard, AMEX and Diners Club are accepted.
Also,
1806 East Washington
Pasadena, CA 91105
Tel. (818) 794-6674

Strong Mexican households always have a vital sense of tradition and sometimes this translates into a restaurant that prides itself on its service. Mijares, a restaurant featuring classic Mexican food, treats its diners as if they were part of the family that owns it.

Mijares has a tradition that goes back six decades, to the time when Jesucita Mijares, a young Mexican mother with three little ones, started making tortillas in her Southern California home. Her fame quickly spread, and she started supplying local restaurants and stores. The young widow remarried, and the couple started a restaurant. Though the restaurant has changed over the years, diners will appreciate the tradition behind the Mexican cuisine, which features the chef's special: a medley of shellfish, crab, chicken breasts sauteed lightly with bell pepper and a dash of picante salsa. Try the Baja Special, featuring scallops and shrimp sauteed lightly with bacon, onions and mushrooms together with corn tortillas. One item that certainly doesn't taste like its name is Mijares' Fabulous Garbage Burrito, a flour tortilla filled with a mixture of ground beef, cheese, olives, onions, guacamole and shredded lettuce topped with a special sauce and melted cheese.

After dinner, stop by the bar which sports a painted tile and wood counter, and taste the perfect margarita, fashioned by mixologist George Palma. Palma and the staff at Mijares want to treat you to traditions that will make you part of their family.

MIYAKO, 139 South Los Robles, Pasadena, CA. Tel. (818) 795-7005. Sukiyaki, Batayaki and Shabu Shabu are the specials which are prepared at your table. Superb vegetable, seafood and meat Tempura are also featured.

OAK TREE INN
1315 Fair Oaks Avenue South
Pasadena, CA 91030
Tel.   (213) 682-2882
Hrs: Mon. - Sun.   11:30 a.m. - 10:00 p.m.
Visa and MasterCard are accepted.

The Oak Tree Inn is not a run of the mill Chinese restaurant. It is a tribute to the imagination and youthful outlook of the owners, Warren and Amy Wang. She, an interior decorator, and he an entrepreneur and restaurateur, combined their talents to bring together this unusual restaurant with its eclectic atmosphere and outstanding selection of fine foods.

It's easy to focus on the building, its furnishings and decor at the expense of describing the food, but it provides such unusual and enjoyable surroundings it must be done. The outside is a combination of white Greco-modern with classical columns surrounded by gardens. The inside is a hi-tech atmosphere painted in gray, white and Wedgwood blue with accents of dusky rose and black lacquer. Light pours through large windows which face the outside gardens, through the skylights and glass brick, illuminating this elegant and stylish scene. Don't let the design and architecture fool you into believing the fare is not oriental. It is, and it is outstanding. Lunches and dinners are treats for those who appreciate authentic, beautifully prepared Chinese dishes. What to choose can be a problem: the Moo Shu Shrimp? The Sweet and Sour Pork? The Peking style crisp fish, or the Oak Tree Beef? It's all tempting, and it's all delicious.

This is a family style restaurant, both from the owner's end and for the clientele. The pride in setting and gardens is equaled by pride in the food.

PARKWAY GRILL, 510 South Arroyo Parkway, Pasadena, CA. Tel. (818) 795-1001. Parkway Grill has an exciting Southwestern menu ranging from black bean soup with smoked pork and lime cream to gourmet pizza. Oven roasted crispy duck is glazed with molasses and crushed black pepper and served with shoestring yams.

PIE 'N BURGER
913 East California
Pasadena, CA 91106
Tel. (818) 795-1123
Hrs: Mon. - Fri.   6:00 a.m. - 10:00 p.m.
         Saturday   7:00 a.m. - 10:00 p.m.
         Sunday   7:00 a.m. - 8:00 p.m.

Since 1964, the folks at Pie 'N Burger have been giving a whole new meaning to the term "lunch counter" and it's not just because they also serve breakfast and dinner.

When you walk into the place, you are seated at a rambling counter facing the food preparation area and can then watch your meal prepared from scratch. You'll also be able to eavesdrop on conversations of some of those who have been calling Pie 'N Burger home for the last two decades. The food, of course, is great, and they put as much care into their burgers as they do into their pies and other dishes. Their chili is also made from scratch. If you like omelettes, they've got ham, ham and cheese, cheese and Swiss cheese, all served with homemade toast and hash browns. In addition to your Prime Beef Hamburger, there is also Baked Ham, Grilled Cheese, Swiss on Rye, Roast Beef, Grilled Tuna or Patty Melt, all served with potato salad. But make sure you save room for the *piece de résistence*, a piece of homemade pie; seventeen varieties including fresh strawberry, peach or ollallie berry, in season.

If you feel you warrant a break today or you simply want to see how much ecstasy your taste buds can handle, make it on down to Pie 'N Burger, a two decade tradition and a feast for the palate.

RESTAURANT SHIRO
1505 Mission Street
South Pasadena, CA 91030
Tel. (818) 799-4774
Hrs: Tue. - Sun.   6:00 p.m. - 10:00 p.m.
Visa and MasterCard are accepted.

Foodies looking for something different on the gourmet scene probably already know about Restaurant Shiro in South Pasadena. It combines French and Asian cooking into something uniquely Californian.

Visitors to the humble restaurant placed between a photography studio and equally low profile stores won't be blown away by the restaurant's simply painted and sparsely decorated eating area. The decor hints at chef and owner Hideo Yamashiro's Japanese background, though his cooking is more French. Hideo brings with him wonderful credentials, having been associated with Ma Maison, Les Anges, and most recently, with Pasadena's Cafe Jacoulet. Hideo wants to present his own style especially for the health conscious. With this in mind, much of his menu focuses on seafood, such as an appetizer of warm oysters dusted with curry and pan fried in hot olive oil. You may wish to sample an entree of Mexican shrimps with garlic butter, Japanese chili and Italian parsley. Another entree specialty is Pacific swordfish charbroiled with horseradish sauce.

For dessert, try an apple tart or a piece of Chocolate Mousse Cake. The restaurant also offers beer and wine, or espresso and cappuccino. Gourmets will find Restaurant Shiro a fine mixture of traditional and modern, in a setting that won't overwhelm.

STONEY POINT, 1460 Colorado Boulevard, Pasadena, CA. Tel. (818) 792-6115. Open for lunch and dinner, the Stoney Point's continental style food is different everyday. Specially prepared, each dish reflects what the chef is excited about that day.

WOLFE BURGERS, 46 North Lake Avenue, Pasadena, CA. Tel. (818) 792-7292. This restaurant is known for honest hamburgers with the necessary accouterments. Also, enjoy their magnificent "woofles," Belgian waffles.

POMONA

Pomona lies along the Los Angeles-San Bernardino County line south and east of the city of Los Angeles. The name "Pomona" is taken from the Roman goddess of orchards and gardens and was adopted in 1875 as a result of a city naming contest won by Solomon Gates, a local nurseryman.

ACCOMMODATION

SHILO INN AND RESTAURANT
3200 Temple Street
Pomona, CA 91768
Tel.   (714) 598-0073
        (800) 222-2244
Hrs: Restaurant Sun. - Thu.   6:00 a.m. - 10:00 p.m.
                    Fri.- Sat.   6:00 a.m. - 11:00 p.m.
        Lounge open until 2:00 a.m.

Everything you need for a delightful short or long stay is at the Shilo Inn and Restaurant. It is conveniently located near the Los Angeles County Fairground, Cal Poly and Disneyland. The 162 room inn offers full service conference facilities, a fine restaurant and lounge, a large outdoor pool with spa, exercise rooms, and a steam and sauna room. Other Shilo extras include satellite TV, guest laundry, airport shuttle and such options as handicapped assistance rooms and non-smoking units.

The elegant restaurant specializes in American cuisine. The breakfast and lunch menus are varied and imaginative and there is a "light" menu available for all three meals. The dinner menu offers a good selection of appetizers, seafood, steak and chicken. There are specialties such as rack of lamb, roast pork tenderloin and a great selection of salads. On Sundays you can enjoy a sumptuous champagne brunch.

Shilo Inns, an Oregon based company with locations in most Western states, has built a reputation for "Affordable Excellence." Try it for yourself and see just how they have earned their fine reputation.

ROSEMEAD

This community along the Pomona Freeway, and near the Whittier Narrows Recreation Area, received its name in the 1870s from a famous horse farm there.

ATTRACTIONS

• The **Whittier Narrows Dam Recreation Area** is a 1,092 acre facility where you can do everything from water skiing to quiet nature walks. The large lake is popular for boating and fishing. Around the lake are hiking and equestrian trails, sports fields, playground and picnic facilities. The nearby **Whittier Narrows Nature Center**, along the San Gabriel River, is 270 acres of wildlife sanctuary protecting more than 150 species of plants and animals. Within the sanctuary are four small lakes which attract hundreds of migratory birds. Visitors can stroll along miles of self-guided nature trails. Take the Pomona Freeway to the Rosemead exit.

RESTAURANT

DI PILLA'S ITALIAN RESTAURANT
9013 East Valley Boulevard
Rosemead, CA 91770
Tel. (818) 286-0275
Hrs: Monday   11:00 a.m. - 2:00 p.m.
       Tue. - Thu.   11:00 a.m. - 9:30 p.m.
       Friday   11:00 a.m. - 10:30 p.m.
       Saturday   4:00 p.m. - 10:30 p.m.
       Sunday   4:00 p.m.- 9:30 p.m.
Visa and MasterCard are accepted.

Restaurants that make you feel like a part of the family are among the best, and Di Pilla's Italian Restaurant stands out as a warm and loving establishment. From the friendly smiles of the table servers to the loving care put into the food preparation, this restaurant meets all qualifications for a "Best Choice."

Every item is made with only the choicest ingredients. Pasta is homemade on the premises as well as the pizza dough and the sauces. The menu features all the classic delicacies of Italian cuisine, including appetizers such as homemade minestrone soup and antipasto. Di Pilla's attracts a loyal lunch crowd that chooses, among other items, sandwiches such as the Hot Roast Beef, the Meatball or the Sausage Sandwich. You'll find Di Pilla's truly shines at dinner, especially after tasting the Lasagna. It's baked in a special sauce and topped with a thick slice of melted mozzarella cheese. Other delicious pasta specialties include Cannelloni, Manicotti and the Manicotti Special, which is stuffed with meat and ricotta cheese. Chicken Cacciatore and Linguine with Fresh Clams are favorites, as well as Veal Parmigiana and Veal Milanese. This dish contains fresh lean veal, breaded and fried and served with lemon wedges, a side of spaghetti and meat sauce. The wine list offers the best in domestic and imported beverages to complement any meal.

As in any loving family, children aren't forgotten. The small ones can choose their meal from the restaurant's children's menu, which features some of the house specialties. Once you've dined at Di Pilla's Italian Restaurant, you'll say to yourself "Absolutely wonderful."

SAN GABRIEL

Now a residential suburb and tourist center, the city of San Gabriel was founded in 1771 as a mission by a small band of monks and Spanish soldiers under the orders of Father Junipero Serra.

NURSERY

SUNNYSLOPE GARDENS
8638 Huntington Drive
San Gabriel, CA 91775
Tel. (818) 287-4071
Hrs: Mon. - Sat.   8:00 a.m. - 5:00 p.m.
        Sunday   9:00 a.m. - 4:30 p.m.
Credit cards are not accepted.

Fifteen to thirty new species are added to the already 1,200 varieties of chrysanthemums at Sunnyslope Gardens each year. Marketed to hobbyists throughout the world, Sunnyslope Gardens has been in business for over fifty-five years. Carnations and other live and cut flowers are available as well as a large selection of fancy *koi*, a rare Japanese carp.

Sunnyslope Gardens sits on fourteen acres, but unless you are familiar with the nursery and its owner Phil Ishizu, you will not be initially impressed. However, as you become familiar with chrysanthemums, some blossoms ranging from one half inch to more than seventeen inches across, you begin to get a feel for the expertise and creativity involved in producing these flowers. Phil's father began the business over fifty-five years ago. He is also the first person outside Great Britain to receive a silver medal from the Royal Chrysanthemum Society.

You are more than welcome to stop by and ask Phil questions, shop, or just browse in the colorful, aromatic atmosphere.

SAN MARINO

San Marino is a tiny community of stately homes and beautifully landscaped neighborhoods. Some 14,000, mostly affluent people, make their home in the 3.75 square miles within the city limits. The community has had a long tradition of controlling commercial development. Consequently, the town has no industry, no multiple family residences, no door to door salespeople and no theater. There are no churches, but then there aren't any bars either. City officials readily admit that its hard to find anything open after dark. Although the city has a few restaurants, don't bother asking for a cocktail before your meal.

ATTRACTIONS

• The world famous **Hunting Library** is a combination library, art gallery and botanical gardens. Its art gallery, focusing on British and French eighteenth and nineteenth century art, includes the familiar *Blue Boy* by Gainsborough. The library contains a superlative collection of rare books and manuscripts including a Gutenburg Bible. The Botanical Gardens include Shakespearian, rose, Japanese, palm, camellia and desert gardens. The building and 200 acre grounds were once the home of railroad tycoon Henry E. Huntington. The Huntington Library is often associated with neighboring Pasadena. A few years ago a proud San Marino resident threatened to sue the L.A. County Board of Supervisors if it did not stop financing tourism advertising that mistakenly placed the Huntington in Pasadena.

• The **California Historical Society** maintains a variety of historic exhibits including the first water powered grist mill of the region. **El Molino Viejo,** as it is known, is located at 1120 Old Mill Road. For information call (818) 449-5450.

FLORIST

MILO BIXBY, INC.
2640 Mission
San Marino, CA 91108
Tel. (818) 799-7143
Hrs: Mon. - Sat.   9:00 a.m. - 6:00 p.m.
Visa, Mastercard and AMEX are accepted.
Also,
545 South Figueroa
Los Angeles, CA 90071
Tel: (213) 622-8184

"I am constantly thinking about flowers, grown or cut. I think of myself as an artist. Like a painter, I endeavor to reproduce what I see in nature. When arranging flowers, I try to imitate the way they grow, the textures and colors of their natural surroundings. I believe each flower should be treated as a precious jewel."

Milo Bixby is a florist and his creations have captured the hearts of royalty. They're still talking about that particularly small, delicate nosegay that Queen Elizabeth liked so well she adamantly refused to relinquish it to her lady in waiting, as is the custom. Instead, she wore it, and proudly, herself. He was also florist to the late Princess Grace of Monaco and in Tinsel Town, they definitely know his work.

His shops complement his wares, with a terra cotta colored plaster motif accented by dark blues and greens. These, in turn, give way to the riot of color that is perpetual spring at Milo Bixby, Inc. The most comfortable way to experience it all is to browse leisurely through the thousand treasures that await you. And when you finally make your selection, remember that your taste ranks with the crowned heads of Europe. It's Milo Bixby, then, florist to the Queen.

OUT OF AREA ATTRACTIONS

Though Los Angeles County offers everything a visitor could possibly want, from camping, fishing and hiking to art on the beach to mad shopping sprees, fabulous eateries, chic hotels, big business and show biz; there are, believe it or not, many exciting places to visit in the area surrounding L.A.

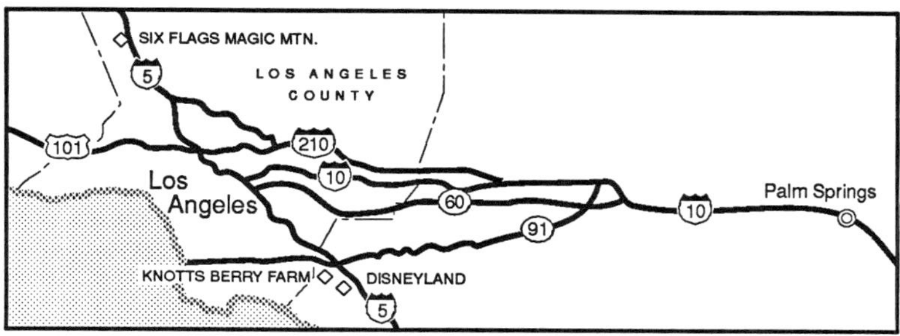

Perhaps you want to spend a day or two recovering from a sedentary and thoroughly satisfying day catching rays on the beaches in Santa Monica, by rocking on the roller coasters at Knott's Berry Farm. Maybe you want to take in the rarified air of the desert in Palm Springs or feel a cosmic confrontation with Mickey Mouse is in order. L.A. is a perfect base camp for all of your sojourns into the wilds and civilization outside of Los Angeles County.

DISNEYLAND

Well over 200 million dollars worth of excitement has been compacted into a little over 200 acres at an amusement park by the name of Disneyland. Located at 1313 Harbor Boulevard in Anaheim, Disneyland is the brainchild of Walter (Walt) Elias Disney. The park opened in 1955 and caters to the child in all of its ten million annual visitors. Fairy tale attractions, lavish reconstructions of periods in American history and electronic, aeronautical and industrial exhibits vie for the attention of American and international visitors alike.

Walking down the Main Street in Disneyland is a lot like walking backwards into the history of almost any American city, with one major difference: this Main Street leads to all of the seven fantasy lands which have helped Walt Disney's amusement park become a household word. A haunted mansion, animated, historical and fantasy figures, riverboats, submarines and fireworks displays, every evening, are sure to keep each family member engrossed for the entire day.

Tomorrowland is perhaps the most difficult of the seven distinctly different sections to keep current. Constant changes in the fields of science, medicine and technology in general, inspire matching changes in the displays and entertainment. Offering a glimpse into the future, as well as a mirror of the present, Tomorrowland is perhaps best known for Space Mountain, a fast paced shot through a collage representational of the galaxy and consisting of the wonders of modern technology.

Frontierland portrays life in the United States as it once was. Affectionately referred to as the good ol' days, this rugged period, when the pioneer west was carving out a place for itself, is realistically depicted by the rides, exhibits and period costumes. The paddle wheel *Mark Twain*, the three master *Columbia* and a ride known as Big Thunder Mountain are the main attractions.

Adventureland is sure to raise the blood pressure of the hardiest constitution. Jungles, almost too realistically alive, provide a total environment. Sound, sight and even smell combine to bring out the Tarzan and Jane in all of us. A massive tree with three separate treehouses recreates the adventures of the Swiss Family Robinson. An additional attraction is the Enchanted Tiki Room. Designed to inspire thoughts of the South Pacific, mechanical birds and flowers will enchant the entire family.

Bear Country is a delightful romp with Swingin' Teddi Barra and his entourage of bear buddies. This grizzled group will bring a smile to even the most sourpuss as eighteen lovable bears present a country and western revue. Canoes are also available which allow visitors to paddle along imaginary rivers. The Country Bear Jamboree is a musical extravaganza guaranteed to liven up any afternoon or evening.

Fantasyland lives up to its name. Snow White and her seven dwarfs, Pinocchio, the puppet come to life and Jiminy Cricket, and a host of related Disney creations are on hand to entertain. Peter Pan, Tinkerbell, Alice in Wonderland and the Mad Hatter are just some of the familiar storybook characters. Constantly being updated and altered the Daring Journey is a new ride in the Pinocchio section. Beneath the famous peak of the Matterhorn fog, icy caves and an Abominable Snowman await.

New Orleans Square offers the downhome flavor of the bayou country. The spicy Creole cooking and the genuine Cajun hospitality do the state of Louisiana justice. The Blue Bayou Restaurant and the jazzy French Quarter provide intriguing after dark entertainment. The Haunted Mansion combines animation and mechanization for an eerie and often silly romp with spooks and skeletons. The Pirates of the Caribbean ride recreates the flavor of life on the high seas under the skull and crossbones flag.

Main Street 1890, in Home Town, U.S.A. features the animated show **Great Moments with Mr. Lincoln.** The precise, drill team Disneyland Band adds a colorful array of sight and sound to the entrance of the park. The Disneyland railroad Park Tour departs from Main Street and the roads to all of the attractions also head out from this nostalgic setting. Ice cream parlor, silent movie house and Town Square add a realistic touch to this historical flight of fantasy.

An excellent tip to enjoying as much of the park as possible, is to pace oneself. There are enjoyable attractions throughout the park that offer visitors the opportunity to sit for a while. In between extensive amounts of time on your feet it is advisable to schedule "rest stops." The **America Sings** revue, **Adventure Through Inner Space**, and **Peoplemover**, a transportation mode, are some of the special exhibits and shows that provide a respite for weary fun seekers, as well as entertainment for all.

The **Disneyland Hotel** is an adventure in and of itself. Currently the largest hotel in the county, it is connected to the park by a monorail that eventually arrives in Tomorrowland. A sixty acre resort, the hotel offers fourteen theme restaurants and shops, a marina, various pools and a multitude of courts at Tennisland. Outdoors, on the marina, a floating barge contains delightful entertainment ranging from a waterfront bazaar to waterfalls, a palm laden beach and multi-colored *koi*. The hotel is also an excellent place to view the almost nightly display of fireworks.

To reach the park at 1313 South Harbor Boulevard some preplanning is necessary. State Highway 91 and Interstate 5 freeways have southbound Harbor Boulevard ramps leading directly to the park. Visitors arriving on State 22 and 861-405 can reach Disneyland by taking the north Harbor Boulevard ramp. When approaching the park on the Orange Freeway, State 57 the adventure begins by taking Katella Avenue west.

For exact and timely information about Disneyland, call (714) 999-4565. The scheduled hours are Monday through Friday 10:00 a.m. to 6:00 p.m.; Saturday 9:00 a.m. to midnight; Sunday 9:00 a.m. to 7:00

p.m.; except during the summer. From June 19 to September Disneyland is open from 9:00 a.m. to midnight during the week and 9:00 a.m. to 1:00 a.m. on the weekends.

KNOTT'S BERRY FARM

Picture if you can a small roadside stand. It's 1920 and Walter Knott is riding his tractor through neatly plowed rows, in a field across the narrow dirt road that would eventually become State Route 39. Raising a crop of hybrid berries created by Rudolph Boysen (boysenberries), Walter and his wife Cordelia began to market their berry products. In addition to Cordelia's delicious pies, jams and jellies the Knotts began to serve chicken dinners somewhere in the mid 1930s.

After building a restaurant and as the line outside grew, Walter began to provide attractions to help fill in the time spent waiting. For more than half a century Walter and Cordelia Knott oversaw the operation and growth of Knott's Berry Farm. From the 1848 replica of a gold rush town built by Walter himself, to the opening of the replica of Philadelphia's Independence Hall in 1966, to the six acre, $10 million Camp Snoopy opened in 1983, children and adults alike have flocked to this Buena Park attraction.

The number three amusement attraction in the country, behind Disneyland and Disneyworld, the 150 acre park now boasts of an annual attendance in excess of five million visitors. Part of the attraction is that the entire park is designed for family enjoyment. Steamboats, sternwheelers, rollercoasters and even mule powered carousels make for a day every member of the family will remember.

Ghost Town is one of the oldest and most visited amusements at Knott's. An authentic reproduction, visiting prospectors can ride the Denver & Rio Grande railroad, a narrow scale, smoke belching, steam powered train. Be prepared for the gun-totin' bandits who "hold up" the train on a regular basis.

Fiesta Village is a brightly colored array of sights and sounds from south of the border. The Cantina features food with a distinctly Mexican flavor and yet it is gringo enough to please the entire family. The Montezooma's Revenge ride is not for the squeamish and should perhaps be ridden before dinner. Mexican artists and artisans display their wares, as well as their techniques in the many quaint shops.

The **Roaring 20s** section of the park is a delightful journey to an era of bootleggers and Bonnie & Clyde. Model T Fords and gangland bumper cars provide fast paced excitement with period decor and costumes.

Knott's Airfield features some of the more exciting rides in the park. Among these are the Corkscrew and the Parachute Sky Jump. Guaranteed a thrill a minute, these rides are complemented by the accompanying exhibits and less thrilling entertainment such as the Soapbox Racers.

Knott's Lagoon relives the regal splendor of the romantic south. The impressive *Codelia K*, a side wheeler steamboat is reminiscent of the days when adventuresome souls plied the country's rivers.

Camp Snoopy is one of the newer attractions and one youngsters will long remember. A sky high playground built into the tree tops, it is accessed by swaying suspension bridges and overlooks a fantasy adventure. Included in the six acre attraction are tall trees, waterfalls, streams and the serenity of a large lake. Snoopy himself is on hand to greet all of the guests.

Additional treats within the confines of the park include, the Old Wooden Mill and funhouse, the vaudeville show in the Calico Saloon, the 180 degree omnivision theater and the Good Time Theater. The theater seats over 2,100, is air conditioned and features top name entertainment the year round. All in all over 165 rides and an almost unimaginable array of exhibits, shops and decorative treats await the Farm's visitors.

There are a couple of tips applicable to visiting Knott's Berry Farm. No matter how charming the park becomes, it still seems to be overshadowed by its neighbor, the number one amusement park in the country, Disneyland. To best appreciate Knott's Berry Farm, if you are also planning to visit Disneyland, stop at Knott's first. Once at the park, it is advisable to go straight to the more popular rides first, before long lines begin and warmer temperatures set in.

Over the sixty plus years the park has been entertaining visitors to the Southern California area many things have radically changed to enhance the enjoyment of all its visitors. One thing however, has stood the test of time. Knott's Berry Farm still serves one of the best chicken dinners in the area. In fact, the many and diverse menus featured throughout the park will tempt the taste buds and titillate the tummy.

Knott's Berry Farm is located in Buena Park, California along La Palma and Beach Boulevard. The park is open Sunday through Friday 9:00 a.m. to midnight; and Saturday from 9:00 a.m. to 1:00 a.m. during the summer. The winter months see the park shorten its hours to 10:00 a.m. to 9:00 p.m. during the weekend and 10:00 a.m. to 6:00 p.m. on weekdays. Parking is free and further information can be gained by calling (714) 827-1776.

PALM SPRINGS

Situated in the desert at the base of a 10,000 foot mountain east of the Los Angeles metropolis is Palm Springs. It is a city of sparkling swimming pools, palm lined boulevards and lush golf courses. In this playground for the leisure class you'll find sophisticated shopping areas, exquisite restaurants and a vibrant nightlife.

Palm Springs is one of a string of desert communities that include Rancho Mirage, Cathedral City, La Quinta, Palm Desert and Indio. Palms Springs is by far the best known, and offers the most for the visitor.

Palm Springs is a delight in the winter, when you can laze by the swimming pool and bask in eighty-degree temperatures. Just a short tram ride away, you can cavort in snow up on Mount San Jacinto. More than thirty-five miles of bicycle paths wind through the city. Visitors can pick up a map at from the Department of Leisure Services at City Hall and rent a bike at a local bicycle shop.

To reach Palm Springs from Los Angeles take Interstate 10 to Highway 111.

ATTRACTIONS

•	The **Palm Springs Aerial Tramway** offers spectacular views as it heads up the mountain to Mount San Jacinto State Park. The ride takes about eighteen minutes. At the park a restaurant, snack bar, snow equipment rental and observation decks overlooking the valley are available. For the stout of heart, a six mile hike to the top of the mountain is in order. The lower tramway station is located 3.5 miles from Highway 111. For information call (714) 325-1391.

•	The **Palm Springs Desert Museum**, 101 Museum Drive, Palm Springs, is a 75,000 square foot building housing displays devoted to the arts, natural history and performing arts of the region. Exhibits include a diorama of desert life that demonstrates how such creatures as coyotes, bobcats and roadrunners eke out a living in the desert environment. For information call (714) 325-7186.

ACCOMMODATION

SHILO INN PALM SPRINGS RESORT
1875 North Palm Canyon drive
Palm Springs, CA 92262
Tel:　(619) 320-7676
　　　(800) 222-2244 US

Are you planning a trip to Palm Springs? Is it going to be an overnight stop, or an extended stay? Well, you'll be happy to know that the luxurious and affordable Shilo Inn Palm Springs Resort can satisyfy all of your accommodation needs during your visit, either short or long term.

Relax and enjoy the atmosphere of this resort, surrounded by a beautiful, private courtyard with a gazebo and spectacular mountain vistas. Relish the two outdoor pools, one for adults and one for families, work out in the exercise room and simmer down in the spa or steam and sauna rooms. You'll have your own private patio, in room refrigerator and such options as kitchen units and handicapped assistance rooms. Other Shilo Inn extras include a complimentary Continental breakfast, free airport shuttle, remote control satellite TV, free fruit and guest laundry.

For meals, Shilo Inn is in the vicinity of several fine restaurants, such as the Elegant Billy Reed's Restaurant, just across the street. Local features include art galleries, golf courses, boutiques and an aerial tramway ride into the mountains. Business and conference facilities are available, accommodating as many as sixty people. This beautiful inn also has group rates and weekend senior citizens discounts. Ahhh, this is truly a "Best Choice" in Palm Springs. The Shilo Inn, an invitation for affordable excellence.

SIX FLAGS MAGIC MOUNTAIN

Coming down into Los Angeles County off I-5, just before Valencia, you will find Six Flags Magic Mountain, an exciting entertainment complex with over 100 rides, shows and attractions. Open daily throughout the summer months and on Saturday, Sunday and holidays, Magic Mountain offers exciting rides such as the Shock Wave, the Roaring Rapids, looping roller coasters and a 384 foot Sky Tower.

The TDK Showcase Ampitheater features name entertainment. Live music, restaurants and an animal farm with a petting zoo will complete a full day at Magic Mountain. For information call (805) 255-4100.

INDEX

Index

Index

Index